Practical API Design

Confessions of a Java Framework Architect

Jaroslav Tulach

■ ■ ■

Apress®

Practical API Design: Confessions of a Java Framework Architect

ISBN 978-1-4302-0973-7 [*Originally published as a hardcover first edition on July 29, 2008.*]

ISBN 978-1-4302-4317-5

ISBN 978-1-4302-4318-2 (eBook)

President and Publisher: Paul Manning
Lead Editor: Clay Andres
Editorial Board: Steve Anglin, Mark Beckner, Ewan Buckingham, Gary Cornell, Morgan Ertel, Jonathan Gennick, Jonathan Hassell, Robert Hutchinson, Michelle Lowman, James Markham, Matthew Moodie, Jeff Olson, Jeffrey Pepper, Douglas Pundick, Ben Renow-Clarke, Dominic Shakeshaft, Gwenan Spearing, Matt Wade, Tom Welsh
Coordinating Editor: Kylie Johnston
Copy Editor: Susannah Davidson Pfalzer
Compositor: Gina Rexrode
Indexer: BIM Indexing & Proofreading Services
Artist: Kinetic Publishing Services, LLC
Cover Designer: Anna Ishchenko

Distributed to the book trade worldwide by Springer Science+Business Media New York, 233 Spring Street, 6th Floor, New York, NY 10013. Phone 1-800-SPRINGER, fax (201) 348-4505, e-mail orders-ny@springer-sbm.com, or visit www.springeronline.com.

For information on translations, please e-mail rights@apress.com, or visit www.apress.com.

Apress and friends of ED books may be purchased in bulk for academic, corporate, or promotional use. eBook versions and licenses are also available for most titles. For more information, reference our Special Bulk Sales–eBook Licensing web page at www.apress.com/bulk-sales.

Any source code or other supplementary materials referenced by the author in this text is available to readers at www.apress.com. For detailed information about how to locate your book's source code, go to www.apress.com/source-code/.

Contents at a Glance

Contents

PART 1 Theory and Justification

PART 2   Practical Design

PART 3 Daily Life

About the Author

JAROSLAV TULACH is the founder and initial architect of NetBeans, which was later acquired by Sun. As creator of the technology behind NetBeans, he is still with the project to find ways to improve the design skills among all the programmers who contribute to the success of the NetBeans open source project.

Acknowledgments

This book could not have been written without the generous help of Geertjan and Patrick, the best editors I've ever met. Thank you and everyone else very much, guys. Visit `http://thanks.apidesign.org` to learn details.

Prologue: Yet Another Design Book?

"There are more than enough design books in the programming world already," you might think. In fact, there are so many that it makes sense to ask why I would write—and especially why you would read—yet another one. Particularly, there is the famous *Design Patterns: Elements of Reusable Object-Oriented Software*,[1] about design patterns in object-oriented systems, written by the so-called "Gang of Four," which is a must read for every developer making use of any object-oriented language. In addition, there are many specialized books describing design patterns, all of them useful when writing specific types of applications. Moreover, there is the unofficial Java programmer's bible, *Effective Java*.[2] In light of these facts, is there really a need for yet another design book?

I believe the need exists. I've been designing NetBeans APIs—that is, application programming interfaces—since 1997. I've passed through almost all the possible stages a person designing a framework or a shared library can pass. In the early days, I slowly gained a feel for the Java language while trying to apply coding styles that I knew worked well in other languages. Later, I became fluent in Java. At that point, applying various known patterns to my code written in Java seemed so simple, although after a while I realized that things are not always as easy as they seem. I realized that traditional patterns are not appropriate for an object-oriented application framework such as NetBeans, and that you need a completely different set of skills.

The oldest NetBeans APIs were designed in 1997. Some of them are still in use and working adequately even after ten years of service, although to be honest, these are not exactly the same APIs as they once were. Over the years, we needed to accommodate new requirements, extend library functionality, and fix beginners' mistakes. Despite that, the API clients that compiled their code then are still able to execute their code, even with today's latest versions of those libraries. This is possible because we always tried, as far as reasonably possible, to maintain backward compatibility. As a result, the programs written against our decade-old libraries are likely to work even in their current versions. This preservation of investment—that is, our decision to let our libraries evolve in a backward-compatible way—is something not seen in common design books, at least not in the ones I've read so far. It's not that all NetBeans APIs were evolved without problems, but I've come to believe that the NetBeans team has now mastered this skill to a high degree, and also that this skill is widely needed among other groups of programmers. That is why a large part of this book talks about retaining backward compatibility and about special API design patterns that produce code suitable for maintaining in a backward-compatible way.

---

1. Erich Gamma, Richard Helm, Ralph Johnson, and John Vlissides, *Design Patterns: Elements of Reusable Object-Oriented Software* (Upper Saddle River, NJ: Addison-Wesley, 1995).
2. Joshua Bloch, *Effective Java* (Upper Saddle River, NJ: Prentice Hall, 2001).

The other challenge we faced when working on the NetBeans project was scalability of teamwork. In those early days, back in 1997, I wrote the APIs on my own. The other NetBeans engineers "just" wrote the code; that is, they provided user interfaces and implementations for various parts of the NetBeans IDE, while continually making use of the APIs that I provided. Unsurprisingly, this created a bottleneck. I came to realize that the number of people working on various NetBeans IDE features had grown to a capacity where one "architect" was unable to handle the demand for APIs. Over time, change was urgently needed. We needed a majority of the NetBeans development team to be able to design their own APIs. At the same time, we also wanted to maintain a certain level of consistency between the APIs created by different people. This turned into the biggest problem, not because developers didn't want to be consistent, but because I wasn't able to explain to them what I meant by consistency. Maybe you know the feeling of knowing how to do something, without knowing how to explain it coherently. That was my situation: I thought I knew how to design APIs, but it took many months before I managed to formulate the most important constraints that I wanted others to follow.

A LATE NIGHT API TALK

I've been interested in API design and API publishing for a long time. I've given various presentations inside Sun Microsystems and for NetBeans partners on this topic. However, my first public talk that related to this topic took place during JavaOne 2005 in San Francisco. My friend Tim Boudreau and I had submitted a proposal entitled "How to Write an API That Will Stand the Test of Time." It was scheduled to start at 10.30 p.m., probably because the abstract didn't contain buzzwords such as "Ajax" and "Web 2.0." That time of night is not ideal for a presentation, as we had to compete with parties, free beer, and other late-night distractions. We were pessimistic and expected one or two friends to show up to console us. Our mood got even worse when we arrived at the venue and saw that right next door a JDBC driver presentation was going to be held. The corridor was filled with people. Our assumption was that everyone there was interested in the database stuff. However, to our surprise, most of the people there were waiting for our talk instead! Our room filled quickly. All the seats were taken. People started sitting on the floor or standing up against the walls; they even had to keep the doors open, and several had to listen from outside in the hallway. In the end, it was the most exciting presentation I've ever been involved in.

Since then, I've known the need for information relating to API design is real. The memory of that presentation encouraged me whenever I began losing motivation while writing this book. It helped to remind me that the rules for proper API design that we had discovered needed to be documented. These rules, though based on the knowledge spread across common design books, are highlighted and expanded upon in this book, because designing APIs has its own specific demands.

API Design Is Different

The reason why the existing design books are not enough lies in the fact that designing a framework or a shared library is a more complicated task than designing an in-house system. Building a closed system, such as a web application running on your own server with access to a private database, feels like building a house. Some houses are small, some are big, sometimes they're skyscrapers. However, in all cases, a house has one owner at a time and the owner is in charge of making changes. If necessary, the owner can change the roof, replace windows with new ones, build new walls inside rooms, pull down existing ones, and so on.

Of course, certain changes are easier to make than others. Replacing a roof is likely to cause no great harm to the floors. Changing windows for different ones of the same size is unlikely to influence other parts of the house. However, trying to replace windows for larger ones might not be that simple; doubling the size of an elevator is normally an almost impossible task. Except in rare situations, nobody is seriously going to experiment with inserting a new first floor while moving the existing first floor and the floors above it upwards. Doing so would cause so many problems that the benefits are unlikely to outweigh the costs. On the other hand, all this seems technologically possible. If the owner has the need, it can be done.

In-house software systems seem to exhibit similar behavior. There is typically a single owner and the owner normally has full control. If there is a need to upload a new version of some part of the system, it can be done. If you need to change the database schema, it can be done as well. Clearly, certain changes can be more complicated than others. A change to a database schema is likely to have a much bigger impact than a change to a one-line bug fix that prevents a `NullPointerException` somewhere. Still, any change is conceivably possible. The owner has full control, and if there is a real need for a major upgrade of the system, the owner can even shut the system down for a while. In addition, there are a lot of design principles to help us manage changes to in-house systems. There are books about design patterns that help developers structure their code. There are methodologies for designing systems and for testing their correctness. There are books describing how to organize and lead people's work. At the end of the day, maintaining an in-house system appears to be a pretty well-understood and documented process.

However, writing APIs is different. As an analogy, consider the universe. Though not as straightforward as the "house" analogy, this train of thought will prove useful. Let's start with recalling the "known" universe. I explicitly call it "known," as no human knows the whole of it—that is, all the existing stars, galaxies, other objects, and to provide an immaterial example, all the physical laws. Humans can only see just a small fraction of the universe, so far anyway. Our horizon defines all that is seen of the universe. In other words, what is before the horizon is the "known" universe. It contains numerous objects and effects, but our expectation and experience tells us that there are other stars and galaxies behind the horizon, and that these are thus far unknown to mankind. This experience is based on the fact that from time to time people manage to shift the horizon further and discover new objects or new rules, through building better equipment or by recognizing and understanding new laws of nature.

The universe is not constant; it's always changing. However, it doesn't change completely arbitrarily. Some rules guide what happens with planets, stars, and other objects. For example, if someone shifts the horizon and discovers a new star, it's no surprise that the star is going to be there tomorrow, and the day after tomorrow, and the day after that. Indeed, it can move, it can rotate, and it can even explode. However, the laws of nature guide all this. Nobody seems to be releasing Universe Milestone X every other week, where a star would appear, disappear, or move randomly. If the world behaved like that, it would clash with our understanding of the universe as we perceive it today. We simply know that *once a star is discovered, it is going to be with us forever.* We even believe that it stays there when nobody is watching. Well, obviously. The star can be observed by someone on earth, someone from another place in the solar system, potentially by some other creature in the universe, or by nobody at all. However, the star itself doesn't know if it's being observed, and the only thing it can do is to follow the laws of nature, and therefore, *once discovered, stay with us forever.*

Good APIs are similar. Once a shared library introduces a new function in some version, it's like discovering a new star. Anyone who gets the new version can see the function and can use it. They can, but don't have to, which depends on the programmer's horizon. It's possible to add functionality that is almost invisible for most API users. However, you cannot rely on that. My experience tells me that API users are really creative. Sometimes the API user's horizon is farther than that of the API designer. If there is a way to misuse something, users are likely to do so. As a result, it's likely that neither the function itself nor its author know if it's being used and how often. There might be many users in the world, or there might be none, but unless you want to break the laws of good API design—that is, break backward compatibility—you have to assume someone is observing, and therefore, the function has to be kept and maintained. "APIs are like stars; once introduced, they stay with us forever."

There is yet another analogy between the universe and API design. It involves the way we improve our understanding of the universe and the way we evolve our libraries. Ancient Greeks could identify and observe the movements of the planets, all the way to Saturn and Jupiter, and thus define the planets of their "known" universe. However, although they tried to explain the reasons behind the planetary movements, they weren't successful according to our current standards. Laws causing the planets to move were still beyond the horizon. This continued during the Renaissance, when Nicolaus Copernicus proposed the heliocentric system and Johannes Kepler discovered his three laws describing the trajectories and speed of planets on their path around the sun. This discovery enriched the known universe by providing a very precise explanation of "what." However, nobody knew "why"! It took until 1687, when Isaac Newton provided an explanation of Kepler's laws, and introduced the notion of a physical force. This not only explained why Kepler's laws held true, but also started a magnificent expansion of the known universe, because physics could explain nearly everything happening between objects of the known universe, thanks to Newton's laws.

All seemed well until the end of the 19th century, where various measurements showed that there are behaviors, especially of objects with great velocities, unexplained by the use of Newton's laws. The accumulating evidence that something was not quite right helped Albert Einstein to discover his theory of relativity, which provided an enhanced understanding of the universe, including objects moving with very high velocities. In fact, Einstein's theory is an extension of Newton's: when objects move reasonably slowly, both theories yield the same result.

What does this physical and historical excursion have to do with API design? Let's suppose, for the next few paragraphs, that some god communicates with people through an API library. The library gives mankind an interface to the "known" universe. Ancient Greeks would be using version 0.1 of the library, which would only enumerate the planets and their names. It's clearly not a very rich API, but for some users and for some time, it may be enough. For example, it's enough to let us look at the planets and name them. Regardless of the state of an existing library, there are always going to be a few people suggesting improvements. Similarly, the universe 0.1 library was found insufficient because Kepler really wanted to understand the rules for the motion of planets. Therefore, the imaginary god of this paragraph gave him an update called universe 1.0. This version of the library could provide the space coordinates for each planet at a specified time, while the original functionality provided by the Greeks would stay the same and would continue to work.

However, users are never satisfied, and the physicists weren't either. That is why our imaginary god had to help Newton release a new major version called universe 2.0. Not only did this version provide information about the actual force of gravity between the sun and each planet, but also a handy set of subroutines to calculate forces, acceleration, and speed of the objects in space, not just limited to planets. Needless to say, all the functionality of the previous versions, provided by the Greeks and then by Kepler, would continue to work as in the previous versions.

Up to this point, all the additions were straightforward. The imaginary god of the previous paragraph simply added new features. But what to do at the points in history where physicists claim that all the laws of the universe are known and physics itself is seen as having nothing left to explain? Let's tease mankind! The imaginary god invents the Michelson experiment, which leads Einstein to formulate his theory of relativity. The latest version of the universe library now really faces the problem of no longer being easily backward compatible, because the new idea introduced into it is that everything the previous physicists did, including Newton, was slightly wrong! However, even such a radical change is manageable in backward-compatible mode. Only very high velocities are in danger of incorrect results. These velocities are much higher than Newton and his predecessors could measure, and therefore, although there was an incompatibility, nobody was able to prove an inconsistency in the previously performed measurements, or to prove that the behavior of the universe library had changed.

The moral of this absurd physics fable lies in the observation that our understanding of the universe is continually evolving. This is also the case with the API of our libraries. Although optimists might disagree, I am afraid that mankind will never understand the whole universe. Yet, my guess is that we'll continue to learn more about it. Although some developers might think differently, I am sure that the APIs of almost all our libraries in active use will never be final. They'll always evolve. We must be ready for that. We must be prepared to modify our understanding of the universe and we must be ready to enhance and improve our library APIs.

Different from building a house or an in-house software system, this requires developers to think about the future while coding the current version of their API. As far as I can tell, this is not a common approach taken with API design so far. Also, the current books and their suggestions don't help much with this kind of thinking. Their design patterns are mostly used to describe a single version. People who use them only think in the context of the current version. They often only minimally need to refer to older versions or only marginally think about what will happen in future releases. Still, these skills are needed when writing shared libraries and frameworks. We need to stop designing a house, and learn how to design a universe. We need to learn that "once an API star is discovered, it is going to stay with us forever."

Who Should Read This Book?

If you are holding this book while standing in a bookstore and deciding whether to buy it or not, you might be wondering if this book is for you. I cannot answer that question because I don't know you. However, I can explain why I needed this book myself and why I decided to write it. When I was designing the NetBeans APIs, I was learning on the fly. In the beginning, I was guided by instinct, and I thought that writing APIs was some kind of art. Well, that might be true, because you need to be creative. However, it's not just an artistic discipline. Over time, I started to identify a structure behind all the work I had done and I formulated measurable standards that turn an ordinary API into a *good* API.

This book describes the standards the NetBeans team adheres to when measuring the quality of our APIs. It also explains why we adhere to them. It took us several years of trial and error to get where we are now. Since reinventing the wheel is not the most productive expenditure of your time, I recommend this book to every API architect who prefers a bit more engineering design over a purely artistic one. In the beginning of NetBeans, I was the only person who wrote the APIs. At that time, we even believed that "a good API cannot be designed by committee." One designer is able to maintain consistency without any formal rules. However, one designer simply doesn't scale. We discovered this in the context of NetBeans, too. So, my task was to find a way to let a broader set of people design our APIs, while maintaining overall consistency. At that time I started to write this book, to describe the theory behind API design, the motivation that leads us to write APIs, and the rules that we must adhere to when evaluating whether an API is good or not. Then I passed my approach to the developers working on NetBeans, I let them write APIs, and then I monitored and mentored them at the beginning and end of their design task. As far as I can tell, this has worked out well enough. Given that they've evolved for ten years and we've learned on the fly, our APIs are relatively consistent and satisfy most of our requirements. If you are in a position where you need to monitor the design of APIs, you may find this book's suggestions useful too.

When I was defining the meaning of the term "API" for myself, I found that it is in fact very broad. You don't need to write a framework or a shared library to write an API. Even if you just write a single class that is consumed by your colleague in the next office, you are in fact writing an API. Why? Because the developer who has to use your class isn't going to be very happy if you delete or rename methods it used to have, or if you change the behavior of the methods in your class. Exactly the same problems arise when writing an API for a shared library. You probably have more than one user of your class, and requiring all of them to do a rewrite when you change the class can turn into a nightmare of inefficiency. That nightmare should be completely unnecessary. Treat your class as an API and you'll have many fewer headaches. Moreover, it's not hard to think about it in that way. It means you need to design your class more carefully, evolve it in a compatible way, and apply other good API design practices. From this point of view, nearly every developer is or should be in the API design business.

An essential part of an API is the way it works. Testing plays an important role in describing how things work. It's nearly impossible to write a good API without properly testing it. Several chapters of this book outline testing patterns; that is, ways to test externally visible aspects of a library so that they hold true over multiple releases. I'll mention various kinds of tests, including signatures, unit tests, and compatibility kits. So, this book has value for people who need to check API compatibility too.

Last but not least, having a library that is in wide use can be a good asset for the person who creates it. Increasing this asset means satisfying your existing users, while attracting new ones to join and use it as well. Only with a sufficiently rich user base can you really monetize the work dedicated to creating and maintaining a library. This book discusses this too, and therefore can also be of interest to people examining software development from a more business-oriented perspective.

Is This Book Useful Only for Java?

NetBeans is an integrated development environment (IDE) and framework written in Java, and as most of my API design knowledge is based on working on the NetBeans project, it's correct to ask whether this book can be useful beyond Java development. My answer to this question is *yes*. In this book I discuss generic guidelines for good API design. These guidelines and principles are applicable to any API in any programming language. Discussions in this book include reasons why you would create an API at all, the rules and motivation for writing and structuring good API documentation, and the principles of backward compatibility. Such principles can be applied to a wide variety of languages, including C, FORTRAN, Perl, Python, and Haskell.

Of course, when it comes to more detailed descriptions, I cannot avoid mentioning features specific to the Java-like languages. First of all, Java is an object-oriented language. Designing an API for object-oriented languages has its own concerns due to all the support for inheritance, virtual methods, and encapsulation. So, some of the principles discussed in this book are more applicable to specific kinds of object-oriented languages, such as C++, Python, or Java, than to the "old but good" non-object-oriented languages, such as C or FORTRAN.

Also, Java belongs to the camp of newer languages that use a garbage collector. In fact, the widespread industry acceptance of Java has proven that it's possible and beneficial to use a garbage collector in production applications. In the pre-Java age, the industry preferred classical memory management, provided by common languages such as C, C++, and so on, where the developer explicitly controls allocation and deallocation. Languages with garbage collectors existing at that time, such as Smalltalk or Ada, were generally seen as being experimental or at least adventurous to use by most of the software industry. Java has changed this completely. Currently, the majority of software engineers no longer laugh at the notion of a high-performance programming language with an automatic memory management system, and programmers are no longer afraid to use one. However, an automatic memory management system has implications on the API you produce. For example, in contrast to C, Java requires only `malloc`-like constructs to allocate new objects, but there is no need for paired deallocation APIs. You get those for free. That means certain approaches in this book are more applicable to languages with a garbage collector—in other words, the newer languages that use the memory approach popularized by Java.

Java has also popularized the use of the virtual machine and dynamic compilation. During static compilation, Java source code is transferred to many class files. These are then distributed and linked together, but only during program execution. Moreover, these class files are in a format that is independent of the actual processor architecture on which the final application is executed.

This is achieved by a runtime environment that not only links individual class files together, but also converts their instructions into those for a real processor. During Java's early days, this was yet another area where Java deviated. Everyone knew that a well-performing program could not be interpreted by a virtual machine, that it needed to be written in FORTRAN and directly compiled to use the most optimized features of the assembly language on the operating system that runs it. Some, myself included, admitted that it was possible to write in C or C++ and produce fast programs as well, but again, the approach taken by Java was seen by many as unlikely to succeed.

However, time has shown that languages based on virtual machines have certain advantages. For example, all numeric types have the same length, regardless of the platform the program runs on, which greatly simplifies the need to understand the underlying architecture. Also, Java programs don't crash with a segmentation fault when something goes wrong. The virtual machine guarantees that memory won't become corrupted by improper C pointer arithmetic, and that variables will always have the correct type. Still, performance problems persisted in early Java implementations. However, over time even the interpreters sped up and were replaced with just-in-time compilers that produced code that was fast enough to attract additional new languages to try this "virtual" path too. As a result, currently the term "virtual machine" is accepted and has widespread use. Virtual machines are covered in this book, to some extent, although I spend more time concentrating on the format of class files, since that is the *lingua franca* of the virtual machine.

It's important to understand the format of class files to correctly grasp what a Java language construct means to the virtual machine itself. It's handy to speak its language and see the class file using the virtual machine's eyes. Though other programming languages, such as C, have their abstract binary interfaces (ABI) models, the one used by Java is special in at least two respects. First, it's naturally object-oriented. Second, it allows late linkage; that is, it contains far more information than a plain C object file would. As a result, the knowledge gained from studying the virtual machine is less applicable to the old but good non-object-oriented languages, although it can be useful for other modern languages that have a virtual machine mimicking Java's.

Java is also one of the first progenitors of associating documentation for APIs with the actual code. Java has popularized commenting of code for public use through the Javadoc. This makes the actual behavior of the APIs and their documentation much closer, allowing it more simply to stay up to date. Even though every other language allows commenting, the Javadoc actually produces browsable documentation from those comments and forms the basic skeleton that gives consistency to every API documentation in Java. On the other hand, this is no longer Java specific. This has proven so useful that almost every language created after Java includes a concept similar to the Javadoc. For other, already existing languages, additional tools retrofitting this association of code and documentation are being created. That is why, when analyzing the usefulness of the Javadoc and the pros and cons of its format for simplifying the understanding of an API's users, this book will make conclusions applicable to almost any programming language.

Java 5 has changed the Java language to provide support for generics. While this book doesn't want to be an ultimate source of information about this language construct, it cannot ignore it. Generics form an important new phenomenon in API design. Why new? Because traditionally object-oriented languages encouraged reuse by inheritance. The second most common form of code reuse—reuse by composition—was possible, but only as a second-class citizen. One of the most important reasons for this was that inheritance was built as a language construct, while composition could only be coded by hand and it was difficult to type correctly. At the same time, a stream of languages was produced that preferred reuse by composition and made inheritance a second-class citizen, especially in the cases of modern functional languages such as Haskell. Some people feel that both approaches have their benefits and spend a lot of time trying to marry object-oriented languages with polymorphically typed functional languages.

Generics in Java are the result of this kind of marriage. Some criticize them for being too complex, though my own research in 1997 implied that this could hardly be done in a better way. I like what the language team managed to achieve, as now inheritance and composition are more or less on par. That is why I'll talk about generics in this book as well. Doing so will bring parts of this book closer to languages such as Haskell.

There is another reason why this book can be applicable to other languages: it accepts Java as it is. It doesn't try to invent a new language more suitable to handle the API design problem. No, throughout the book we work with Java as we know it. All principles and recommendations are about specific coding styles, not about adding new keywords, pre- or post-conditions, or invariant checks. This is needed in software engineering, as often the language is a given, and the goal—for example, to produce a library for general usage—needs to be achieved within that constraint. This is not really surprising. Learning new APIs might require a bit of work, but it's nothing compared to learning a new language.

Since the language to be used is almost always a given, API design principles have to be expressed in that language. If it's possible to write a good API in C, there should be no reason not to write a good API in Java. That is why plain Java is good enough for this book. In short, this book has general parts applicable to any programming language. Other parts talk more about object-oriented concepts, and whenever we need to dive deeper, we demonstrate the case in Java.

Learning to Write APIs

Without a doubt, there are people who develop APIs correctly; otherwise there would not be as many great and useful software products out there as there currently are. However, sometimes it seems that the design principles, the *main rules* of API design, are acquired subconsciously. Designers tend to follow rules without actually knowing or understanding the original motivation leading to the choices they make. As a result, the subconscious knowledge of good API design is built by trial and error, which obviously takes time. Moreover, the result of this process is typically a loose collection of tips on how to do things "right." Though this is a useful step forward, such a collection often suffers from two problems. First, tips of this nature are often tightly tied to a particular operational area. For example, they might work fine for one project or for a dedicated group of people, but the usefulness to other teams or the applicability to other projects is not guaranteed at all.

Second, in these cases it's difficult to transfer knowledge to people with a different way of thinking. If your experience shows that Java classes are preferable to Java interfaces, while this experience is gained from working on a specific problem, the experience becomes difficult to transfer to a different scenario. You can try to convince others that this is the correct approach, but in the end, without an appropriate explanation of the related reasons, you can only hope for adoption on the basis of faith. Faith can only create believers and rejectors, which is not the intention of knowledge transfer.

SUBCONSCIOUS NETBEANS API DESIGN

It's fair to admit that the members of the NetBeans project went through such a period too. We went through many different experiences doing API design where we somehow "felt" what worked and what didn't. However, this knowledge wasn't built from the bottom up. That is, it wasn't built using serious reasoning, or an understanding of the reasons for such design decisions. It was more a feeling, and the reasons that created such feelings lay undiscovered in our subconscious. This formed a problem when trying to transfer knowledge to other people, because they simply lacked our experience and had no reason to trust us. This forced us to think much more deeply about the reasons and the actual experiences that helped us formulate the measurables of good API design. This book is a result of such thinking. We believe that our experiences exposed us to information that helped us to uncover the hidden logic behind the assumptions we'd been making. We turned this logic into something conscious, something that we have become aware of, and something we can reasonably explain to everyone who wants to listen.

The foremost questions that deserve an answer are, "Why create an API?" and, in fact, "What is an API?" This book discusses these questions in detail.

Our experience shows that even without reading, understanding, or even agreeing with everything we advise here, it's useful for everyone participating in the development of software products to understand our basic motivations and terms. This will lead to an increased awareness and understanding of the problem and bring its complexity out into the open. When all members of a development team can see the "API design" with their own eyes, communication is simplified and decisions need no explanation, because they become part of the shared knowledge base. In turn, this improves cooperation between members of a development team, as well as between the team and its distributed partners, which leads to better quality software.

That is why this book is intended for everyone. It explains the basic motivations to anyone who wants to listen, it provides examples and tricks useful for developers, it describes the aspects of good architecture for those who design them, and it provides measurable principles for assessing API quality.

If you are still asking yourself whether you should read the book or not, here is a much shorter answer: "Yes, you should read this book!"

Is This Book Really a Notebook?

When I began thinking about the right style for this book, I examined a wide range of approaches available between two extremes. On one extreme, I could write a strict scientific description of the motivations, reasons, and processes required when practicing API design. This would produce a set of suggestions and rules applicable to any project. Of course, this is a specific goal of this book. It has to be generally applicable and not simply a description of what we did on the NetBeans project during the past ten years. On the other extreme, I strongly believe that advice without proper explanation is useless. I really dislike following the "what" while not being able to understand the "why." I always want to understand the context, evaluate various solutions by myself, and then choose the one that appears to be the best under the circumstances. That is why I also want to share with you the context that motivated us to accept our design rules. The best way to provide this context is to describe the real problems the NetBeans project faced at the time. As a result, this book is very close to a notebook.

Also, the lab journal format pretty much follows the process of creation of this book. It was not written in one go; its topics have been added over several years. Whenever we needed to solve a problem that looked general enough, I added a new topic to the book's table of contents, thought about the solution, and then later wrote it down. This was the most effective way of recording our rules, and indeed as a result, the final product resembles a lab journal: a lab journal where a note is not written per day, but per problem!

To get the best of both approaches, each topic analyzed in this book contains a note describing the real situation that the NetBeans project had to solve. The problem is then converted into a general recommendation applicable to any framework or shared library project. This resembles the "thought path" we used: first there was a problem, then we analyzed it and came up with rules to overcome it. As well, this gives the reader a chance to verify our "thought path" and check that the advice is really applicable in other situations and that our generalization is really correct. In all cases you can start with morphing the state described in the "note" into your own project, and then applying the same thought steps and checking whether they really result in our advice.

The world of API design is beautiful, and so far, mostly unexplored. Yet its knowledge is needed. The software systems being built today are becoming extremely large and we need to apply the best engineering practices to build them properly and make them reliable. API design is one such practice. Let this book be your guide for 21st century software development! Let our NetBeans API design adventures be your learning samples, and let the general advice extrapolated from them help you to eliminate similar mistakes. It's my hope that this book will help you pass through your API design phases smoothly and without reinventing the rules that we discovered on our journey, starting all the way back in 1997.

PART 1

■ ■ ■

Theory and Justification

The process of inventing, designing, and writing application programming interfaces (APIs) can either be seen as an artistic or as a scientific pursuit. Depending on your point of view, the API architect is an artist trying to change worlds or an engineer building bridges between them. Most people I know would rather be artists, because artists are associated with creativity, spontaneity, and beauty. However, a purely artistic approach has one significant problem: emotions are not transferable. They are extremely subjective. Explaining them to others is fraught with complexity. Although it is possible to create work that generates an emotion, ensuring that two people respond identically is beyond the capabilities, and probably also the goals, of art. As a result, an architect writing an API, just like an artist producing a painting, risks the possibility that the work will be misunderstood. In that case, developers using it will create a feeling very different from the architect's intentions.

This might not be all bad. However, problems arise when the API architect decides, or is forced, to develop an API in a group. Immediately, various attributes of an API are at risk. For example, one of the most important attributes of an API is consistency, which avoids unpleasantly surprising the API users. For an API to be consistent, there needs to be significant coordination between members of the designing group. Coordination is difficult to achieve when each member approaches the work as an individual artist. There needs to be a shared vision. There needs to be a vocabulary that the group can use to describe the vision. And there needs to be a methodology that can be used to create a result that fulfills the vision. As soon as this is recognized, the API architect probably begins praying for the API design process to become an engineering discipline, rather than an artistic one.

Anyone who has ever tried to organize the work of 20 artists, and compared it to the work of 20 engineers, can easily understand why.

DESIGN BY COMMITTEE

I designed and wrote most of NetBeans' APIs from its earliest days. At the time, we strongly believed that *a good API cannot be designed by committee*. That is why the goal for the other developers was mainly to use the designed API, write implementations of their features against it, and potentially comment on and improve what already existed. But gradually some of the other developers started to create their own APIs too.

I monitored such attempts closely. I commented on them, occasionally telling the others to do something differently or to remove pieces that looked odd to me. I sometimes even rewrote them myself and insisted that they use my version. However, I found myself in an increasingly uncomfortable position. Although I knew how I wanted the APIs to look, I was unable to explain my vision properly. Nor could I explain why they should consider my advice useful, because my colleagues did not always want to listen and follow my advice. I could use my right to veto their work, but that did not solve the problem either. I felt that something was wrong. However, I was unable to explain what or why. We lacked a shared set of terms, which limited our communication. This situation was inevitable because the APIs had been designed by means of a purely artistic approach.

I found proof of this a year later. One of the APIs developed further and, as NetBeans is an open source project, it attracted an external developer. At first, the external contributor worked on bug fixes. Next, he started his own subproject and designed its API. The original owner of the API came to me and asked me whether I could help him find reasons why the subproject's API was turning out badly: he did not like the newly created API and wanted to prevent it from being integrated into his project. However, he was not able to formulate what was wrong with it. At most, he managed to say that it did not adhere to his *original vision*. That was absolute déjà vu for me. I used to tell him that his work did not fit into the NetBeans API's vision—or at least my own interpretation of it!

Although it took me a while, after a few years of designing APIs and working with others to design APIs that I liked, I came to realize that API design can be approached as an engineering discipline. Although it's not obvious at first, this discipline does have a lot of objective attributes. As a consequence, it's possible to turn the *API design* process into something that engineers can understand—a kind of science.

Every real discipline needs a theory behind it: a theory that defines the world that forms the subject of its domain. Such a world needs to be sharp and clearly defined. The less sharp it is, the less rigorous the science is, and the more it becomes an art. This chapter defines the world of API design. It identifies the various objects you have to deal with in API design. It analyzes situations that you have to face during the process of designing an API. Moreover, it begins to build a common vocabulary that people knowing the same theory can use to better identify the objects of the API world and their relations. Based on these fundamentals, we can later build in more complicated and less obvious conclusions about the subject of API design theory.

It's hard to write good APIs that can be consumed by a wide audience of users, especially an international one. Everyone has their own style of understanding and their own way of viewing problems. Satisfying all of them is hard. Satisfying all of them at once is usually impossible. Moreover, if your API is targeted to an international audience, it needs to deal with various cultural differences. That's why writing good, widely approachable APIs is hard.

Writing a book for an international audience is hard as well. Again, the matter of personal and cultural preferences influences the way people want to read. Some would like to understand the background first. Others would like to jump to examples directly to find out if the whole thing is useful to them or not. Satisfying both these camps at once seems impossible. Ultimately, as Edsger W. Dijkstra wonderfully describes in his text, "On the fact that the Atlantic Ocean has two sides,"[1] some people believe that a theoretical approach is difficult and boring and that, by extension, practical examples are much more interesting. They are probably right, at least in their cultural context. On the other hand, another group of people would rather spend time building a common vocabulary and increase their understanding of the world being explored step by step. This is difficult without a thorough introduction. Without it, terms can have dual meanings, often leading to confusion. Obviously, it is hard to satisfy both camps at once. However, I will do my best to make everybody happy.

A STABLE API

One of the basic terms in the world that our discipline wants to explore is *stable API*. I had been using this term quite a lot when talking to various people in the NetBeans project, without expecting any problem. All along, it seemed to me to be a word with a clear and obvious meaning.

Then I listened to an explanation of the term by one of my colleagues. He said that the *API is stable if and only if it will never undergo change*! Although a stable API is likely to have some kind of "stability," it will still need to change sometimes.

I face this kind of misinterpretation all the time, where a term from the basic API vocabulary has different meanings for different people. Of course, this ruins the whole conversation. If people think they understand each other, when in fact they do not, then it is better not to talk at all. The images that crystallize while talking are completely divergent, and as such are absolutely useless for communication.

That's why I believe it's good to spend some time defining basic terms.

---

1. Edsger Dijkstra, "On the fact that the Atlantic Ocean has two sides" (1976), http://www.cs.utexas.edu/~EWD/transcriptions/EWD06xx/EWD611.html.

To avoid confusion about terms, this part is dedicated to vocabulary building and analysis of the general aspects of API design. It builds a vocabulary of basic terms, describes the motivations of the whole API design effort, and outlines the main goals of the design process. If this isn't your preferred style of learning and if you believe you don't need this elementary material, feel free to jump directly to Part 2, which contains many more code samples, tips, tricks, and various hacks. Don't be surprised if the purpose of some of them seems strange. That might be a sign that you're missing the background material discussed in this part. Also, if you're eager to acquire more practical advice on tools, compilers, and so on, feel free to start reading Part 3. However, again, keep the previous warning in mind: if the advice given doesn't make sense, that might be due to a missing piece of understanding relating to the API design theory behind it.

Without further ado, let's dive into the theory. First we'll go over the basics, which will help us all to get up to speed. To get us in the mood for proper API design, let's start with the most basic questions that address the why, what, and how.

CHAPTER 1

The Art of Building Modern Software

The history of software development is short. It has been less than one hundred years since people wrote and managed to execute the first computer program. Although brief, this history is reminiscent of the history of any other intellectual invention. The most interesting parallel I've heard so far is the comparison of the history of computer science with the way people tried to understand the real world. One result of this comparison also yields an explanation of why a good application programming interface (API) is needed. Let's walk down that road now.

Rationalism, Empiricism, and Cluelessness

The renaissance of modern science seemed to create two major, yet extreme, philosophical approaches. Rationalism treated reason to be the primary source of information and postulated that using just a pure thought, it is possible to understand and describe the real world. The set of philosophers supporting this idea includes the progenitors of modern science Rene Descartes (1596–1650) and Gottfried Wilhelm Leibniz (1646–1716), as well as Benedict Spinoza (1632–1677), the creator of pantheism.

The initial impulse for this kind of understanding came from Galileo Galilei's law of falling objects, which postulates that two objects regardless of their weight always fall with the same acceleration. This goes completely against natural expectations, as anyone who has tried to drop a brick and a piece of paper knows that they are unlikely to reach the ground at the same time. The brilliance of Galileo and other modern scientists was that he attributed that to mutual cooperation of various natural laws, where the law of free fall was just one of them. How did Galileo discover his law? He did a mental experiment. He imagined two solid balls of the same size and weight being dropped. Indeed, they would reach the ground at the same time. Then he imagined the same experiment but with one solid ball and one ball cut in the middle into two parts, but with both parts being closely attached to each other. The result of this experiment ends up exactly the same as the first one—both objects fall synchronously. Now what happens if we slowly start to separate the two pieces of the ball? We can even keep them connected with a small wire to still form one body. Indeed, regardless of the two halves of the ball being a centimeter, meter, or even further apart, this object would continue to fall with the same speed as the full solid ball. And last but not least, the same result would be obtained even if we remove the wire! This result is completely against natural experience.

Experience says that a piece of paper falls more slowly than stone. This pure mental experiment explains that weight does not affect acceleration of falling objects.

UNCONSCIOUS MATH AND PHYSICS

You'll find, while reading the book, that I am obsessed with physics parables. Yes, I am, because, after reading Petr Vopěnka's book[2] about the importance of unconsciousness in the success of modern mathematics and physics, I just cannot get his philosophical explanations from my mind. From time to time I reuse some of his observations, however only in a very condensed form, as his book has more than 800 pages and carefully builds proper understanding of all the terms. That is not the case for this book. Deep explanation of all his concepts is beyond its capacity and purpose. As such, please excuse occasional simplifications.

People say that Galileo discovered his famous law by throwing stones from the leaning tower of Pisa. Maybe he really tried that, but it was the mental experiment that could explain the behavior without doubts. It was the first time that just plain thought could prove observation and experience wrong. Although in reality lighter objects fall more slowly than heavier ones, which is what we know from our experience, we now know that other laws interfering with gravity cause differences in falling speed. This was the experiment that showed the power of pure reason and that gave Leibniz and Descartes their impetus to favor reason over experience. It was the catalyst for the whole philosophical movement of rationalism. Indeed, this approach believes that the subject of research is and has to be reasonable. Indeed, if discoverable by reason, it needs to have a reasonable origin.

On the other side of the English Channel there was empiricism. Nearly at the same time, great British minds such as David Hume (1711–1776), John Locke (1632–1704), and George Berkeley (1685–1753) insisted that the primary source of understanding is experience. Without seeing, hearing, or feeling the world, the mind has no chances to "think it up." To understand means to experience—or, in a more scientific way, to do experiments. Even here we can trace the roots of Galileo, the first scientist who propagated scientific experiments as a source for verification that an idea or a hypothesis is valid. From the empiricist point of view, the world does not need to be reasonable. It might not be fully known, it might even not exist at all, and in fact doesn't matter. It isn't necessary to understand it all if the perception of the senses makes sense.

From today's point of view those two extreme ways to perceive the world are not in fact that far away. At least current science understands the value of an experiment to verify its theories. Also, Descartes understood the need for an experiment in science as well. So for us it shouldn't be a big problem to merge two opposing views into one. And yes, these days it's quite easy to do so. For most of our lives we don't care much about the philosophical aspects of our surroundings, we care more about the results. Life is supposed to be entertaining, not boring, and reasonable. However, things we use daily "just" need to work—we usually don't care *how* they work. For example, we're completely clueless about cars and mobile phones. We feel it's reasonable to use them, we just have no clue how they do what they do. We live in total cluelessness.

---

2. Petr Vopěnka, *Úhelný kámen evropské vzdelanosti a moci* (Prague: Práh, 1999).

RATIONAL APPROACH TO CLUELESSNESS

Writing APIs and books for an international audience is hard. Personal preferences and also cultural differences influence the way we approach problems that we face. Rationalists prefer to talk about theory—about the internal connections behind real objects—and only later they create real examples mapping the theory to the real world. Empiricists, on the other hand, would like to gain as much practical experience as possible, and only later, if ever, make judgments about the relation between objects of the world.

This book explains API design from the viewpoint of selective cluelessness. It sees APIs as a perfect tool to help us maximize cluelessness, while getting reliable results. It is essential to get a correct feeling for what cluelessness really is. However, we'll build our understanding of that term from a rationalist's point of view—we start with theory and not examples. This might not be the preferred approach for everyone; however, I cannot satisfy both camps at once. Anyway, do not despair—as soon as the theory is over, and we have a common vocabulary for the science of API design, there will be more than enough practical applications.

Cluelessness is a way of life for a majority of us. It is the result of the merging of rationalism and empiricism that applies these days. It is everywhere around us. It is present even in the way we program and do software engineering.

Evolution of Software So Far

In the 1940s and early '50s, programming was hard. People had to learn machine code to speak the computer's language, know the sizes and number of registers, and in worse cases even handle the screwdriver and connected wires that physically carried the signal between individual computing units. The ratio between the work needed to think up an algorithm and the slavery to turn it into an executable program was harshly tilted toward the boring, mechanical jobs.

FORTRAN was like heaven-sent simplification. Just like an empiricist, it allowed programmers to perceive the world of computation of mathematical formulas with just limited senses. Programmers no longer needed to understand assembly language or worry about the technical internals of computers. They could completely forget about these details and concentrate much more on the important thing—on converting a mathematical formula into algorithmic steps to compute it. FORTRAN simplified the software development process while only minimally limiting the things people could compute: a huge win for empiricism.

However, programming still was not an easy discipline and the appetite for simplicity continued to grow. New languages such as COBOL came up with visions such as "approachable by novice programmers" and "language readable by management," and simplified certain tasks associated with programming even more. Today nobody is seriously considering writing a new system in COBOL. However, in those days COBOL significantly reduced the amount of knowledge needed to access and manipulate a database compared to what was needed with plain assembler or even FORTRAN. Empiricism was on the rise.

However, not everyone liked this. There are and always have been people who believe in reason—who think that the world and things in it should be reasonable. Those people can be found all around us, even among programmers. In the '50s, rationalists such as John McCarthy invented the LISP language based on the mathematical model of lambda calculus, which as such had a strong theoretical back end. As mathematics is almost always a rationalistic discipline, this back end was backed up by pure reasoning. It's rumored that during the design of LISP there was a period when "mathematical neatness became more important than anything else." What a sign of rationalism! The language need not be useful, it might not even be implementable, but it has to be pure and clean and reasonable.

Some say there have been two schools of computer science—European and American. Although the Americans are usually more pragmatic (of course, as pragmatism was invented there), the Europeans often search for the great vision. You can observe this in computer engineering design as well. There are various examples where great European minds prefer rationalism over functionality. Edsger W. Dijkstra—the inventor of message-based computing and the semaphore synchronization pattern—wrote in *Selected Writings on Computing: A Personal Perspective* that "programming emerged as a tough engineering discipline with a strong mathematical flavor."[3] If it was, then we would all go with the way of rationalism. However, when I look around and see how people program all those accounting programs, hospital patient databases, and so on, I have a feeling that there is just as little math in that as in cooking. Indeed, good algorithms may require mathematical background. However, as another influential European mind, Niklaus Wirth—the inventor of Pascal, Oberon, and other systems—noted: "Simple, elegant solutions are more effective, but they are harder to find and require more time." Of course, he was right. In an era when time to market is one of the most valued measures of success, there is no time to invest in what could be a never-ending search for pure and clean solutions.

It looks like it's time to confirm that the rationalist approach has no space in today's software engineering world, especially because we are running out of programmers who worship at the church of rationalism. Or, as Figure 1-1 illustrates, we are running out of programmers almost completely. This is not new, as another quote from Dijkstra illustrates: "Good programming is probably beyond the intellectual capabilities of today's average programmer." True. However, the hunger for new programs is increasing. What can be done about that?

Figure 1-1. *Will code HTML for food*

---

3.   Edsger Dijkstra, *Selected Writings on Computing: A Personal Perspective* (New York: Springer-Verlag, 1982).

Following the analogy of understanding our world, where rationalism or empiricism are not of nearly any importance to regular human beings, the obvious advice is to get clueless. The situation with programming is similar. The world, or at least our society, doesn't need every human to be a philosopher to work. It's organized in a way that there is room for the less educated—that is, the more clueless of us—and still things seem to work. Similarly, software engineering doesn't need every programmer to be a highly educated scientist. If we want to deliver as much software as we do now or even more, we need a system where programmers can be clueless and still produce reliable systems.

Indeed, the aforementioned cluelessness is not complete unawareness of programming. Obviously, just randomly typing characters on the keyboard is unlikely to produce a compilable program. Knowing how to code is indeed a prerequisite for a programmer (just like the ability to watch, absorb, and discuss TV ads is a necessary skill among certain human societies). The point of software engineering cluelessness is to enable the programmers to know less and still achieve good results. It cannot be generally said which bits of knowledge are necessary and which are not. However, the goal is to find such coding practices that allow developers to know less than everything—that is, to select the pieces of knowledge they need. I'll call this *selective cluelessness*.

Gigantic Building Blocks

An average system built in the first decade of the 21st century is like a massive pile of dirt with no—or just a little—elegance behind it. The primary motivation is always to get things done with as little effort as possible. As such, engineering teams tend to reuse existing software frameworks even when they are more heavyweight than needed.

PUTTING A WEB PAGE ON THE WEB

Recently I needed to put a dynamic web page on my server. I had two choices: either open a socket on some port, read streams from incoming connections, and write something in a reply; or assemble the system from existing technologies. I tried both.

The "write from scratch" approach worked fine. I read the specification for HTTP, parsed the incoming header, and wrote out the output. That was a relatively small piece of code and worked well after a little bit of debugging. However, then I needed an additional feature—the ability to secure the page, handle POST requests, and so on. I could read the RFC documents and implement these as well. However, this turned out to be more work than I wanted to spend on it.

That is why I tried the "assembling" approach. I took the Tomcat web server, wrote one servlet, tuned a few properties in the config files, and voilà! Everything worked—with just one drawback. Instead of 50KB of code, I suddenly had over 1MB!

Systems these days are composed of huge building blocks. Nobody writes the whole stack of technologies alone. Instead, you are more likely to install a reliable and cheap operating system. Then on top of that, place a commonly used web server and add a database server. With this multimegabyte installation, you're ready to solve the basic problems—such as generating an HTML page. At that point this is an easy task. However, nobody can claim that the whole system is simple. In fact it's quite complex, and no single person on the planet could understand it all. This is a perfect example of cluelessness: the programmer who creates the HTML page gets the job done while having just a minimal understanding of the whole system.

This whole approach brings to me the image of coding with a bulldozer—if a database is needed, let's use raw power and put a database server into the system. Or if we need a more reliable runtime, let's install Java and an application server. Regardless of how heavyweight these frameworks are, you can always find a big enough bulldozer to move them on top of the pile of dirt—that is, the application. If the application starts to consume too much memory, from the rationalism point of view you might consider optimizing it. However, when you have a bulldozer, all the problems look the same and you just buy another few gigabytes of memory. If the system continues to be sluggish, you might invest in clustering or some form of virtualization—and the pile of bits of the application just grows and grows and almost never gets smaller.

The question is whether using the bulldozer coding approach is that bad. In fact, it's likely more productive than trying to search for Wirth's "simple, elegant solutions" that are more effective, but too time-consuming to find. If you look around the Web, you can see pretty good applications and servers (likely) written using some sort of bulldozer-like approach. Amazon, Yahoo!, and so on are gigantic sites, which work well and without major problems. That seems to indicate that the bulldozer style is a viable way of designing and coding modern software systems. The incredible computing power we all have tilts the balance heavily toward brute-force computing. It really works!

Beauty, Truth, and Elegance

I'm pretty sure many of you found the previous glorification of cluelessness irritating. How can a pile of dirt massaged with a heavy crawler tractor replace elegance? How can such applications be correct when they're so ugly? This cannot work! Well, it can; we just need to look more closely at the preoccupation many of us have.

The roots of our sciences are still beneath us and they influence the way we think all the time. They were lain down by the ancient Greeks many centuries ago and still form the way we treat the relationship between truth and beauty. From the Greek philosophers' point of view, the most valuable scientific knowledge was clear—with its meaning not hidden by any associated misinterpretations—and sharp; that is, not fuzzy. Unsurprisingly, the most highly regarded science was geometry. The main reason was that it wasn't a science about the real world, but rather the geometric one—that is, the one where a line between two points is straight, where a sphere is absolutely round, and so on. This level of perfection was unmatchable by any other science, especially those concerned with the study of the real world. A spherical stone might look like a geometric sphere when seen from a distance. However, the closer you get, the more it is obvious that its spherical shape was just an illusion of perception. So the science of rocks is less sharp and cannot be as clear as pure geometry. It needs to take into account mistakes made in the formation of its objects.

A significant difference between the Greeks' geometric world and the real world was its stability. Although the objects in the real world are ever changing—for example, today's stones can be smashed to pieces or carved out into sculptures tomorrow—objects of the geometric world are absolutely stable. For example, a circle around a square is always going to be the same, and a right angle will always be 90 degrees. As a result, thoughts and reasoning about geometry—about its objects and their relations—will have eternal validity. A truth in geometry, unlike a truth about the real world, will last forever. That is why the Greeks saw geometry as a science about absolute truths.

Objects in the geometric world vary by their complexity. For example, to define a circle you need its center and radius. To define an ellipse, you need two radii instead of one. That means the circle is easier to define than the ellipse. Similarly, defining a square is simpler than defining a rectangle. Given geometry's preference for clarity, it follows that the circle and the square are more "pure" or more beautiful than the ellipse and rectangle. As soon as Greek philosophers realized this, the geometric world became not just a place of truth, but also a place of beauty. Since then truth and beauty have been seen as mates, not only in geometry, but in art and elsewhere. Greek sculptures are so geometric, created with so much attention paid to various ratios between their parts (for example, a head is supposed to be 1/8 of the whole body, there is the golden ratio, and so on) that they engaged the geometric truth, beauty, and elegance.

The classic Greek style and Greek ideas of proportion, beauty, and harmony became ubiquitous in both art and science during the Renaissance. Indeed, the arts of that time, as the name suggests, built upon the Greek aesthetic heritage. However, the influence extended significantly beyond the field of arts. It entered philosophy as well as the new science about the real world just being born: physics. Galileo and others brought geometry into the real world. They took the ideal and perfect geometric world and put it behind the real one. They started to look through the real world as through a glass pane, seeing not only the real world, but also the geometric one behind it. For example, they started to see objects of the real world as mass points, their movements as trajectories, their rotation as movements on a circle. This all drew geometry closer and closer to the real world. The geometric world became the world behind the real one. And together with geometry, truth and beauty entered the real world.

The enormous success of Renaissance physics, which was mastered by Isaac Newton's physical laws and its previous marriage with geometry, makes physics look like the most perfect science. Not only did it describe the real world, but also it did so with the same elegance as geometry. Planets move on elliptical trajectories; objects thrown from a tower fall following laws of the real world, which science knows and understands. Based on this knowledge, it is possible to predict the future. Physics knows the world, knows how it behaves, knows the truth behind its laws. As a result, the world is no longer a dark and obscure place, but instead it is fully beautiful. Once again, those who know Newton's physics can confirm that truth and beauty are engaged again, this time not just in the geometric world, but in reality.

Newtonian physics is the final masterpiece of the Renaissance; it is the finished version of Renaissance physics. It is elegant, correct, and beautiful. It describes the world as built around Euclid's geometric space, and in fact it is the best and most finite form of rationalism. Such a world is discoverable by the pure mind without using experience. However, since then physics has changed. Einstein helped us recognize that space is not like that of Euclid, but rather that it is curved. Quantum theory disqualifies geometry (for which size is no issue) from being the model of the real world. Things just get too complicated, and modern physics isn't related to Greek geometry at all. Science can still be useful and predict various truths, but as a side effect of moving away from geometry, the world seems to be a less and less suitable place for beauty.

On the other hand, most adults (including software engineers) know just as much about physics as was discovered by Newton. Many of us have heard about the theory of relativity. However, not many of us can explain it. That is why the illusion of the world being well organized and beautiful is still with us, and it even seems to be supported by the sharpest of natural sciences—Newton's physics. That is why we seem to be convinced and expect that other parts of the world will be beautiful as well. Indeed, every science tries to be as pure as geometry and physics. Only if it merges truth with beauty is it generally accepted as good science. Perhaps beauty is simply more naturally recognizable and memorable, as opposed to chaotic theories with no structure.

ENIGMA MOVIE

Recently I had a chance to see the movie *Enigma*, a romance on top of a security encryption story from World War II. The main mathematician was asked whether he liked math. His answer: "I like numbers, because in numbers the truth and beauty emerge. You find out, you are walking in the right direction when everything becomes nicer. And then the numbers get you closer to the secret matter of all things." I can hardly imagine better glorification of the Greeks' ideal of truth, beauty, and elegance. How deeply inside of most of us the feeling that these three belong together has to be, when a sentence like this appears in a romantic movie for nonscientists.

Computer science and software engineering are no exception in their preference for beauty and truth. However, you should keep in mind that the primary goal of making software is to get a reliable release out the door. In the rush of the final stages of the release cycle, beauty is indeed one of the last things engineers think about. We prefer to fix or, more accurately, work around critical bugs and then release the product. In fact, simplicity and elegance is not the goal at all. There is no place for it, although the feeling that it is needed is still there. Now that we are aware of this, we can respond by offering cluelessness as the software development methodology for now and the future.

More Cluelessness!

We've seen that simplicity and elegance are not the goal of today's successfully deployed software systems. Just like in philosophy, rationalism is too academic for everyday understanding of the real world. The most promising development style seems to be a pragmatic use of the "bulldozer" approach: reuse components that are already available, compose applications from big chunks of premade libraries, glue them together, and make sure it works, even without fully understanding *how*. Although many would reject this point of view, it is the de facto style, mostly unconsciously, behind today's biggest software projects. The question to ask is whether we can make this clueless approach work even better, now that we have become fully conscious of it.

The thing to admire about the bulldozer style is that it can produce good results even as the participants, mostly programmers, don't understand most of the system. This might be frightening at first. On the other hand, we do this all the time. You don't want to understand the design of a car to drive it. You don't need to understand chemistry to clean teeth. In a similar way, you don't need to understand Windows' code to write a simple Win32 application. You can become pretty efficient in programming for Windows just by having a working knowledge of the APIs (in this case the Win32 API) and knowing where to find the appropriate documentation. This is true for almost all systems. To code for Linux, Java, and the Web, you can learn just a tip of an iceberg and that is enough to get most of the coding done. The reason for this is the abstraction that wraps around every library or framework. This abstraction—the API—hides all the complexities. This brings us to the main theme of this book.

The more selectively clueless you are, the more reliable the system is. Throughout this book, we'll explore various ways to help people not understand everything yet still use your library at once at its certain revision, in a way that will continue to work in subsequent releases.

THE ORIGIN OF CLUELESSNESS

My first encounter with the term "cluelessness" dates to October 2006 when I heard a presentation at the OOPSLA conference in Portland, Oregon. Martin Rinard, an invited speaker at that conference, had a controversial, yet inspiring talk called "Minimizing Understanding in the Construction and Maintenance of Software Systems."

He provided the observation that the human brain is finite and can handle only a limited amount of data. If the goal is to build larger and larger applications, we need to learn how to do it while knowing just limited amounts of them. His talk outlined three directions to explore:

- Program verification

- System engineering

- Living with errors

In his presentation he then continued to explore how to make a program acceptable while having some errors in it. Indeed, it was a horrible vision for those who love truth, beauty, and elegance; however, an acceptable compromise for those who try to produce real software systems.

Although I liked Mr. Rinard's introduction very much and I agree with his conclusions with respect to errors, this book will now concentrate on system engineering and, to an extent, program verification. However, learning how to reach as much cluelessness as possible, while still producing reliable systems, will still be a tempting and desirable goal.

The term *cluelessness* is not meant to be offensive. It is here to distinguish between different types of understanding. There can be shallow understanding, where we understand any subject just as much as necessary to use it, and deep understanding, where we understand the principle behind things. In everyday life we usually need only shallow understanding. If we need to use a television, we don't need a deep understanding of how televisions actually work. If we need to figure out the right location, we don't need to understand the elaborate system of satellites flying around the Earth. Their function as well as the importance of their mutual positions is beyond our horizon; for us it is enough to recognize the latitude and longitude on the display of our GPS. Of course, there are situations when someone needs to understand more. For example, people who repair GPS devices, cars, or TVs need to have a much wider horizon. Still, even those people need only shallow understanding. They don't need to know about every little detail. It's certainly possible to learn almost everything about TVs and cars, and if we needed to, we could do so. However, such deep understanding isn't usually necessary, and that's why most of us stick with shallow knowledge in our day-to-day actions.

In a similar sense, cluelessness in software development means that we can rely only on shallow understanding, at least most of the time. The term "selective cluelessness" is here as a reminder that we actively choose what is and what is not important for us to know about deeply. That's why *selective cluelessness*—for the rest of the book called usually only *cluelessness*—is a thoroughly positive term.

■ ■ ■

CHAPTER 2

The Motivation to Create an API

Designing an API is neither easy nor cheap. Trying to create an API is definitely more work than releasing a product without any API at all. Still, in the context of "cluelessness," the main message of this book is that with a proper API, you can design better systems while minimizing your own understanding of them. Properly designing and using the APIs of individual components of the system can improve the system engineering methodologies used to design them. Improving your system engineering skills is a way to maximize the benefits of cluelessness.

Distributed Development

The cluelessness model is based on using big building blocks collected from software projects all over the world. By reusing as much as possible, and not writing everything entirely in-house, product teams can concentrate on the most important differentiator: the actual logic of their application. They no longer need to spend time creating and writing the infrastructure; instead, they can reuse frameworks and other useful libraries produced by others. Nobody writes an SQL database server in-house anymore. People reuse database servers provided by established commercial vendors or emerging open source alternatives. Bothering with an implementation of an SQL database server for private use would be seen as an ineffective waste of resources. The same is happening in many other areas of software technology. Web and application servers, languages and their libraries, integrated development environments (IDEs), and rich client application frameworks are all becoming well-established building blocks. Just like prepackaged dinners or prefabricated blocks of apartments, they can just be taken off the shelf, assembled, and then polished as needed. This approach greatly shortens the development time necessary for producing a software system.

When assembling the whole application, you need to glue together individual building blocks. These blocks need to talk to each other somehow. Usually they do so by means of well-defined APIs. Each component's API is an initial step toward increasing your cluelessness. It isn't necessary to understand and know all the internals of each component; it's usually enough to read the component's documentation and use its API to include it successfully in your own application. The API minimizes the need to understand every detail of a component serving as a building block.

ABSTRACTIONS LEAK!

An API can be seen as an abstraction over the functionality and internal implementation of each component. Usually it's enough to understand just the abstraction, but in some cases the internals of a component "leak out" through an API. As an example, let's look at a filesystem abstraction. A common filesystem is a set of files and directories organized in a tree-like hierarchical structure. Knowing a resource, you can ask either for its content, or for a list of subresources. The content is represented as a stream. This is a well-known abstraction used in almost all operating systems available today. It helps isolate common application programmers from the internals of dealing with the actual storage and type of a filesystem. To read a file, it is not important to know whether it comes from a hard drive, CD-ROM, flash disk, or network. The abstractions are always the same.

However, sometimes the actual implementation behind these abstractions leaks out. For example, when dealing with flash drives, the disk can disappear while reading its content, as the end user unplugs it. Or, in the case of a network, you can observe big latencies if the network is slow or of poor quality. In these situations, you need to understand not only the abstraction, but also, at least partially, the implementation behind it.

On the other hand, this is quite acceptable from the viewpoint of selective cluelessness. The common API is just a basic abstraction and serves its function when you don't care about latency or crashes when trying to read files from removed disks. If you care, then there are more advanced ways to detect and adapt to such situations. Therefore, the filesystem API helps us to be clueless, but it does not prevent us from increasing our knowledge when necessary. This should be true for any functioning API.

A typical application doesn't consist of one or a few libraries. The applications developed today make use of many open source libraries available all around the world. The set of open source offerings starts with a Unix-like kernel, base C libraries, and command-line utilities. It continues with web servers and web browsers, to Java utilities such as Ant, Tomcat, JUnit, JavaCC, and many more. In fact, each of these libraries has its own API, and as a result, everyone writing such software is in the API design business, whether they are cognizant of the fact or not.

This kind of assembly approach is a common model of operations for *Linux distributions*. The software is written by various people, then simply taken, packaged, and glued together. Usually the distribution vendors write the central management utilities and provide some quality assurance to make sure all the selected components work well together. This seems to work well for most vendors and users, and it helps lower the cost of creating a distribution. As evidence of the success of this model, let's note that Mac OS X is a FreeBSD Unix distribution with a bunch of add-ons from Apple.

Distributed development has its own specifics. The most obvious is that the source code for the whole application is no longer under the developer's complete control. It is spread around the world. Building software in this way is unquestionably different from building an application entirely from source code within your in-house source repository.

You need to be aware that in this model you don't fully control the whole product's schedule. Not only the source code, but also the developers, are spread around the world and are working on their own schedule, which you cannot fully control. However, the situation is not as unusual or dangerous as it sounds: anyone who has tried to schedule a project with a team of more than 50 people knows that the idea that you ever have "full control" is at best a comforting illusion. You always have to be ready to drop a feature or release an older version. The same model works with distributed development. The basic right everyone has is the freedom to use newer or older versions of a library.

In fact, open source is not the only driving force behind the growing need for good APIs. Commercial vendors also produce a lot of shared libraries and frameworks. Many of them either implement existing standards, such as SQL, or provide their own APIs. However, the open source movement with its liberal licensing schemes has become the primary source of components to use as reusable building blocks. The open source solutions are well known by end users who can use them without any fee. However, because there are no licensing restrictions, they are also important for developers. It's easy to take an existing component and use it as part of your own application. It's almost always just a matter of time before someone does it. This means that every open source component sooner or later is going to need an API. These components are developed by a range of developers, from university students starting their own projects, to long-time developers playing with their own toy projects, to developers working for and being paid by companies that see the open source style of development as a business opportunity. These people have different skills and different working styles. Regardless, it's important to create good APIs, because APIs are the first step to clueless usage of their libraries. The more libraries and frameworks we have, the better. However, it's almost essential for the success of clueless reuse to let the APIs closely reflect the internal spirit of such libraries. That's why API design is important, and that's one of the main motivations for this book.

Modularizing Applications

Modular applications are comprised of individual components developed by highly distributed teams. These components often provide an API, but they also require certain APIs or other features in their execution environment to be able to function properly. For example, a Tomcat server requires an implementation of the Java runtime. Similarly, the standard C++ templates library needs `libc` so that it can call `printf`. When the number of components becomes extensive, one of the most important challenges is to be able to see the whole picture. Only then are you able to "understand" the whole system, so that all its mutual component interactions are satisfied. We saw in the previous section that component APIs allow us to selectively choose what is important—ignore the internals in most cases and just concentrate on the APIs. However, if hundreds or thousands of components are in the system, even this is still too large an amount of information to be handled cluelessly. That's why we'll now look at possible ways to improve your ability to assemble a working system from these components, while minimizing your understanding of them.

The first and foremost lesson to learn is that you need names for your components. These names have to be unique, have to identify the component in the system, and should be descriptive. `kernel` is a good name for the Linux kernel; `libc` is a fine name for the basic C library; `org.netbeans.api.projects` is a perfect name for a NetBeans component describing how to work with projects. Generally, all existing components have a name, so it seems natural to expect that they need to have one. However, when you look at this aspect more closely, you can see that these names are more important for humans than for machines. If they were meant just for automatic processing, then you could simply use some hexadecimal form, such as 0xFE970A3C429B7D930E. The fact that components usually share human names is proof that they're targeted primarily at people. Names are useful to customers and end users who use them to discover the functionality they should pull from the provider. They are also useful to providers and their assemblers who use these components to build their applications.

When you know how to name the individual components that you operate, it's time to look at the required environment for each component. No component can live in a vacuum. It will inevitably require services from its surroundings. Once again, it's possible to fully understand the actual needs of each component, most accurately by inspecting its internal implementation—or, even better, by observing what it needs from its environment during its execution. However, this is far from the selective cluelessness mode of operation, because it would imply that the assembler knows nearly every detail of each library, before using them as building blocks for newly created applications. If this was necessary, then it would be a massive showstopper to the acceptance of a library. In fact, most users of a library have little clue what is going on inside of it. That's how it should be. They should have just a minimal understanding and still be able to get their job done. That can be achieved by properly writing and describing individual components. If each component carries the information about its required environment in such a way that it can be automatically processed, then the assembler can be as clueless as possible, because the necessary environment can be inferred without human interaction with compilers, linkers, or assembly time tools.

Each component in a modular system carries information about all the other components it requires. The author of the component needs to specify this set of information only once, or in certain cases the packaging tools may infer it automatically. For example, `rpmbuild`, the system used by Linux distributions such as Fedora, Mandriva, and SUSE to create individual packages of their distributions, automatically inspects each native dynamic library to discover which other libraries it is using and automatically adjusts dependencies on the packages that provide these libraries. Regardless whether this is done automatically or manually, this is done just once. It can be done by the developer who produces the individual component: the one who knows its internals, understands its required environment, and can correctly specify its dependencies. This is yet another example of selective cluelessness: one engineer thinks hard and spends time on specifying the component dependencies. Then all the users of such components—those assemblers of final applications or other developers who just want to depend on the component's presence—can just cluelessly specify a dependency on the component's name and let the automatic system handle the rest.

THE CLASSPATH ASSEMBLY NIGHTMARE

The days when every Java application was written on top of plain Java are gone forever. The set of useful open source libraries for Java is huge and growing daily. As a result, nearly every Java application written these days depends on an already written and packaged JAR, such as Apache Commons, HttpClient, JUnit, Swing widgets, and one or more of many others. Indeed, to start such an application, you need to set up its classpath correctly. It's easy to include all the directly used libraries, but each of them often has its own additional dependencies that need to be satisfied as well, together with dependencies of these dependencies, and so on, which can turn into quite a dark nightmare.

Recently I had the opportunity to include FreeMarker, a nice templating engine, in the NetBeans sources as a library. Including the `freemarker.jar` was easy, but when I tried to verify that all its classes could be linked successfully, I was unpleasantly surprised. The JAR had additional references to many other projects, including Apache Ant, Jython, JDOM, log4j, and Apache Commons Logging. Were all these projects the required environment for FreeMarker? Or could FreeMarker run without these libraries? If the latter, what kind of functionality could trigger these classes or in fact crash execution? I didn't know, and in fact I didn't want to know. I wished I could be clueless; however, I could not. I needed to inspect the sources and verify that these classes were not used during our regular usage of FreeMarker. I prayed for FreeMarker to use some modular system to specify its needed dependencies, such as the one used by the NetBeans Runtime Container.

The technological answer to the challenges of distributed development is modularization of applications. A modular application—in contrast to one monolithic chunk of tightly coupled code in which every unit may directly interfere with any other—is composed of smaller, separated chunks of code. These are well isolated and uniquely identified, expose well-defined interfaces for others to use, and carefully describe the environment (such as the need for other components or units to function correctly) that they need to function correctly. It is believed, and also revealed by the Linux distribution vendors, that separate teams can then develop those chunks with their own life cycle and their own schedule. One central authority (the distributor) can then assemble the results, and this style of work helps to minimize risks related to schedule and team separation. Also, it allows operation in clueless mode: if developers producing their units manage to describe their dependencies correctly, the people assembling them need to have little to no knowledge about the component's internals and still successfully compose the final application.

However, a new challenge is on the rise. Components are evolving. They aren't static; they change. Due to bug fixes, enhancements, and new features, an API potentially changes on a continual basis, and as a result it isn't enough to use just a name to identify it uniquely. To make sure that those independent components work together, you need to identify which API the component is actually supposed to offer.

For example, if a class written in Java references the String.contains(String) method, then it can run on Java 5, as that version of Java provides this method on the String class. However, it can also run on Java 6, as the same method is available in that version of Java as well. Due to the compatibility policy of the Java team, it also remains available in the latest builds of Java 7. On the other hand, such a class cannot run on older versions of Java, as those did not provide that method. Therefore, the class cannot be correctly linked in those Java versions.

In fact, when you need to capture the exact requirements of a class or of an application, you must enumerate all the methods that it calls, and all the classes and fields it references. Of course, such a description of dependencies would be too verbose, unreadable, and sometimes even larger than the actual source code itself. Just imagine a class saying, "I need a version of Java that provides java.lang.String with a constructor and length and indexOf methods, and my class also depends on java.io.Serializable, which it implements," and so on. Indeed, such a detailed specification of the actual version of some component goes directly against the cluelessness approach that I want to emphasize. Even though a machine could verify these constraints automatically, for humans these are too hard to use. Humans prefer simple schemes; for example, using natural numbers to number each revision of a component. That way you would simply be able to say, "Give me Java 5 and my library will be fine."

However, simply using numbers can also lead to complications. Imagine that you want to assemble your application from component A (which defines a dependency on Java 5), and component B (which defines a dependency on Java 6), as visualized in Figure 2-1. In this case, there can be just one Java running both A and B, so the question is which one to use. To solve this problem, most API development models work with the concept of compatibility. Usually this means that if some API is introduced in version N, it will be there in subsequent versions N+1, N+2, N+3, and so on. This solves the example in the figure, and means that the assembled application should run on Java 6: component B needs it explicitly, and component A requires just Java 5, but will also work in Java 6 due to the compatibility between these two versions. Indeed, this greatly simplifies the lives of the people assembling the final application. They can be pretty clueless when composing. Everything needs just one "little" prerequisite: to maintain backward compatibility. This is not a small task at all. It's pretty complex, not something that can be done cluelessly, and therefore something that will be the center of our attention throughout this book. This is part of the "selective cluelessness" that we need to concentrate on: to maximize our cluelessness when assembling big applications from components created by distributed teams, we need those teams to develop the individual components and their APIs carefully, and moreover to do that in a compatible way.

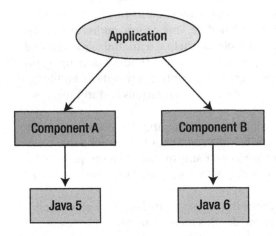

Figure 2-1. *An application that needs two different versions of a component at once*

Nonlinear Versioning

The most frequently used software numbering system isn't based on natural numbers. Instead, people use a dot-separated decimal system. This is needed to accommodate nonlinearities in software development, where there is no single direction of development, but many branches representing bug-fix releases, and bug-fix releases of bug-fix releases, and so on. As Figure 2-2 shows, a version such as 1.1.1—which you'd expect to contain less functionality than version 2—can in fact be released later than version 2.

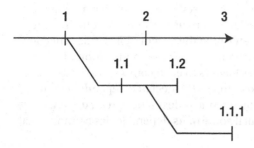

Figure 2-2. *Version numbering forms a tree.*

Each piece of a modular application has a version number, usually a set of natural numbers separated by dots, such as 1.34.8. When a new version is released, it should have a new and larger version number (according to lexicographic order), such as 1.34.10, 1.35.1, or 2.0.

You can express dependencies on other components of the modular system by specifying the identification name of such a component and the minimal needed version. You can request the presence of an Extensible Markup Language (XML) parser, installed database driver, text editor, or web browser, all of these providing a specific version of their interfaces. For example, a piece of functionality could require xmlparser >= 3.0 or webbrowser >= 1.5, and so on. This assumes full compatibility: that is, it is expected that the assembled system will work fine even with newer versions of its modular units.

Trying to encode the whole history of a library's changes into a single version number seems a bit silly. Nevertheless, it is reasonably practical and, most importantly, it allows you to reach limitless levels of cluelessness, while giving the individual developers of each library a chance to encapsulate sets of changes into easily recognizable numbered versions.

Using a dependency scheme can work only if certain rules are followed. First, if a new version is released, all contracts that worked in the previous version will work in the new one as well. Of course, this is easier to say than do—otherwise nobody would need a quality assurance department. Rule number two is that as soon as a set of external dependencies changes, you need to communicate that. Therefore, if a piece of a modular system starts to rely on new functionality, such as an HTML editor, it needs to add a new dependency htmleditor >= 1.0. Also, if you start to use new features of a web browser introduced in version 1.7, you need to update the dependency to require webbrowser >= 1.7.

Some versions of components can contain bugs that need workarounds. For this reason, a secondary version—an *implementation version*—is usually associated with a component. In contrast to the specification version, this is usually a string, such as Build20050611, and can only be tested for equality. This is usually better for working around bugs because the fact that a bug is present in (specification) version 3.1 doesn't mean it will also be in version 3.2. That's why, for reasons of bug fixing or special treatment of certain versions, associating an implementation version with a library can be useful.

The system of versions and dependencies needs a manager to ensure that all requirements of every piece in the system are satisfied. Such managers can check when installing each piece that everything in the system will remain consistent. This is how Debian or RPM packages work in Linux distributions where the dpkg and rpm commands are used for installation and uninstallation of software packages. However, you can also use such dependencies to handle certain runtime aspects during execution.

For example, any NetBeans-based application is composed of modules that are loaded at runtime. The NetBeans module system uses the declared dependencies not just to find out what components need to be present, but also to determine the parent `ClassLoaders` needed for each module, thus isolating the selection of components from the composition of their classpath. This system also provides individual class loaders to each component, ensuring classpath isolation of independent modules. It also enforces the declared dependencies of each component: a module cannot call code in a foreign one unless it declares a dependency on that foreign module, and it won't be loaded at all if some of its dependencies cannot be satisfied.

It's All About Communication

At this point, the contours of our ideal application should be clear. They are based on the concept of cluelessness, trying to take it to the limit for those who do the final assembly of an application. As a result, our ideal application is based on a modular architecture. It expects that each module is written by different groups of people spread around the world. It accepts contributors operating on their own schedules and doing their work for their own interests to fulfill their own goals. Such a setup clearly reveals the main problem.

Most modules don't exist in isolation. They rely on an environment provided by other modules. Only a limited set of functionality can be written in a vacuum without using APIs someone else provides. In fact, most modular components need services offered by others. This means that the developer writing such modules needs to discover and understand how to use an API provided by a foreign module. As the other module is also written by a programmer, we're facing a potential communication problem.

APIS ARE NOT FOR MACHINES

It took me a long time to realize that the primary target of an API is not the computer, but a human: the developer. My original expectation was the opposite. In fact, when you think about compiled programs, their primary and in fact only desired consumer is the computer. Programs are written and then compiled to be executed. As a result, it's reasonable to expect that a programmer is supposed to communicate with the computer.

However, this isn't true in the case of APIs. APIs are verbose, documented, and, in fact, very different from what a computer needs. When I realized this, I found that it isn't enough to use the common coding practices I learned while being taught to program in school. Designing APIs is different. I hadn't been taught to do it and I have a feeling that other programmers haven't been taught to do it either.

The producers of shared libraries and various frameworks need to contact their users. They need to talk to developers who can potentially use their libraries. There are many ways to communicate. For example, they can exchange e-mails and participate in conference calls, but this requires face-to-face or ear-to-ear interaction. However, the most commonly used communication channel is the API itself and its documentation. It is the document that users of the API find and study most of the time. If the development of a modular application is to be successful and effective, a clear and easily understood, well-documented, and as far as possible, self-documented API is needed. This is what will facilitate the work of individual developers, regardless of where they are physically.

Such an API has to be based on shared knowledge and has to be easily understood by its potential users. If it is to be reliable, it must prevent its own misuses and has to be ready for evolution: few if any APIs are perfect in their first incarnation. Much of what we need to discuss here is how to avoid mistakes that will limit the possibility of improving an API in the future.

The important condition here is *separation*. With separation comes the need for rules for designing and maintaining an API. If there was no separation and the whole product was tightly coupled, built once and forgotten, there would be no need for bothering with an API. But because real-world products are developed in a modular manner, with componentized architecture and teams that don't necessarily know about one another, operating according to independent schedules and building their projects independently, there is a need for a *stable contract* that can be used for such communication.

NOT ALL PROJECTS NEED API-LIKE QUALITY

Some time ago I talked to my cousin about our work, the projects we work on, and the way we organize them. I introduced him to the concept of cluelessness and the proposition that more selective cluelessness can help us create more reliable software systems. We agreed on that point for the most part, though he presented a slightly different point of view.

Sometimes, especially when delivering end-user functionality, it doesn't seem necessary to strive for an API-like quality of code. The user of the system is "only" human, and humans are often more tolerant of slight errors than automated systems. Moreover, it's unlikely the system will ever change after its deployment. It serves for a few years and then, if necessary, can be replaced with one that is completely rewritten, or actually assembled, from scratch.

This is different from writing modular units with APIs. These are here to stay like stars in the sky and cannot be easily thrown away and replaced with new ones. However, this means that not all projects need to adhere to the principles outlined in this book. These principles are mostly good for reusable components that play essential roles in the system. The leaves of functionality, on the outer reaches of the system, can be made to work without worrying about the future, which is an example of the "write once and then throw it away" software methodology.

However, these functional leaves are usually built around a central component that is the heart of the whole system. Such a component is the subject of this book, and is developed according to the best practices of API design. In fact, even my cousin had to admit that he had a core library in his system that needs to be treated properly, as it is likely to be in use for many years to come.

Empirical Programming

Few people approach a new API from a rational perspective. Nobody studies an API and tries to understand every idea that's hidden within it. Quite the opposite: these days people want to get their job done quickly, without understanding everything that is possible. There's no need to think about the API that much if it does what you need it to do.

The empiricist philosophers mentioned in Chapter 1 would be proud. Instead of considering, studying, and using reason to understand, developers often just try to call one method from an API, and if that works, they're happy. If not, they call something else and see what happens. Among NetBeans developers, this has become known as *empirical programming*: perform an experiment using the API, and if that doesn't work, try something else. Experience comes first; understanding may follow—but sometimes it need not.

This affects the structure of APIs. The API needs to be self documenting: in other words, usable without any documentation. It has to lead the user of its elements naturally through the tasks that need to be solved. Solutions should be easily discoverable while typing, and although an IDE offers various hints, they should be on topic, and should not distract the user from the right path. Only in this way can experiments using an API empirically succeed.

RETURN VALUE CANNOT BE NULL

I have to admit that I also prefer the empirical programming style to a deep understanding of the APIs that I use, especially with respect to return values of method calls.

The Java language `null` value is special. Any variable of any object type can be assigned to `null`. When dereferencing it, you get a `NullPointerException`. In a well-behaved program, it's desirable to eliminate these exceptions. You can do this either by always checking `obj != null` before calling methods, or by accessing fields on `obj`. However, this clutters the source code and makes it hard to read.

This has led some groups of programmers to treat `null` as an exceptional value, and when designing libraries they avoid its usage as much as possible. This often leads to comments in the Javadoc saying, "This method never returns `null`." The NetBeans project decided that this is in fact the default: unless a method declares in its documentation that `null` is accepted as a parameter or can be returned from a method as its result, then the method won't accept it or it will never return it.

However, regardless of such promises made in documentation, it's still possible to find a lot of checks for the returned values not being `null`. Such checks cannot be `false`—but no one knows for sure, especially if you don't read the documentation.

This is a kind of defensive empirical programming, which I also use from time to time. It's better to be safe than sorry. It's easier to check for `null` and silently exit than to get a `NullPointerException` when a program is already released and distributed to thousands of users.

Sometimes it helps to create illustrative code samples that can be copied and easily modified for the purposes of a first-time evaluator of an API. If they cover the most frequent usages of the API, they increase the chance that the initial encounter with the API will be pleasant. After that, coding can become more complicated, and potentially it might become necessary to read some documentation. That is acceptable. If someone invests his own time in experimenting with the API and successfully gets the job done, then the attitude toward the API is already positive. And in a positive mood it might seem more useful to spend some time reading documentation and discovering more hidden features the API provides, because it has already proved its usefulness.

The empirical programming style is with us, and each API should be ready for this type of user. The more the API method names, class names, or grouping of methods support the creation of the right code, the greater is the likelihood that the empirical first-time user succeeds in using it and decides to learn more about it.

The First Version Is Always Easy

If you want to convince other programmers to use your API, then you first need to obtain their trust. You need to gain their confidence in your ability to produce and maintain a stable API for more than one release. Regardless of how hard it is to use the API, the fateful moment comes when a new version of the component is released and all the client code that depended on it suddenly needs to be rewritten. Consider how many vendors would write applications for Microsoft Windows if such applications wouldn't work when the end user installed a new version of the operating system. Therefore, API design is about trust: by following the best practices I describe, you can maximize the probability that you will be able to avoid backward-incompatible changes, and thus earn and maintain that trust.

Compatibility breaks may sometimes be inevitable: we live in the real world, which is often imperfect. However, avoid compatibility breaks where possible. Users of a component might accept such a break, given a notice of deprecation, suitable advance warning to set expectations, and good documentation of how to migrate existing code that uses the deprecated component. However, if such a rewrite is needed with every release, clients are likely to abandon an API in favor of another project that won't have such painful migration problems. Compatibility breaks incur a significant cost to the user of a component: they are in effect a punishment for having used the component in the first place. They are a breach of trust.

Some people say that if you try hard, you can achieve a perfect API in its first version. They might be right, but you have to work extremely hard to achieve that goal. In spite of your best efforts, the requirements that the API was created to satisfy are likely to evolve over time. If requirements change, the best-case scenario is that the API will be merely insufficient. The worst case is that it becomes completely useless. In any case, it's much wiser to make the API ready for a world where requirements change and allow it to change as well without breaking existing clients. Therefore, a lot of what I will discuss relates to API future-proofing.

THIS IS NOT AN EXCUSE!

The fact that the first version will almost never be perfect is not supposed to be an excuse for intentionally designing it poorly the first time around! It's always much easier to design the first version than to make changes to it. That's why you should try to make the first version as perfect as possible, without forgetting that what seems perfect from today's standpoint might be poor from tomorrow's perspective. The time for change will come.

Producing the first version of an API is always easy. The challenge is in producing the later releases. Making changes and adding new possibilities to an API without compromising the way it used to work is a delicate art where you have to envision all possible usages of the older API and ensure that its contracts are still satisfied in newer versions.

Evolution is inevitable, and creating an API that is capable of evolving compatibly is necessary for API clients. We must maximize the probability that the component is reliable, and at the same time preserve the author's ability to fix bugs and address new requirements. Colloquially, you want to avoid "painting yourself into a corner." An API designed to be ready for evolution won't require work on the part of clients when an upgrade is made.

LIKE FREE SPEECH

There are other important aspects of good API design besides the ability to evolve. An API has to be documented. It also has to be understandable and easy to use. However, of all these, the ability to evolve is paramount. If you can evolve an API, you can always fix the problems that the API had in its initial version.

This is much like human rights. Of all the human rights, the most important is the right to free speech. If you have the right to speak, you can talk about the other missing rights and ask to be given them. If something else is missing, you can fight for it and potentially get it.

If an API is ready for evolution—even if it is ugly, undocumented, and hard to use—you can release a new version and update the API to fix these problems. That's why I see evolution as one of the most important aspects to consider when architecting a library and its interfaces.

Because developers don't appreciate unnecessary work—especially work imposed by an inconsiderate library vendor—creating APIs that are poised to be evolved compatibly is critically important for anyone writing libraries that other software components will use.

CHAPTER 3

■ ■ ■

Determining What Makes a Good API

Among people writing libraries in Java, there is a common misconception that APIs are comprised of nothing more than classes and methods, and the Javadoc used to annotate them. Indeed, the Javadoc serves as an important index of API visibility, but "API" is a far broader term than this view would indicate and includes many other types of interfaces.

Once again, let's remind ourselves why we're interested in the development of APIs: we want to cluelessly assemble our applications from large building blocks, such as shared libraries, frameworks, premade application skeletons, as well as combinations of these. We believe that if people designing these blocks do their job well—that is, write their APIs properly—then assembly will be a simple operation and we won't need to waste our time debugging, reading source code, patching it, and generally trying to understand what others did. In short, we'll be able to operate in "clueless mode."

WORKING WITH THE SOURCE CODE

This is the first chapter that contains various code samples, so it makes sense to mention how to work with them. All the code snippets in this book are taken from real projects. You can download them and play with them. Just visit `http://source.apidesign.org` and follow its instructions.

An API seen from this point of view is much richer than the Javadoc-bounded idea of "API" that might originally have appeared in your mind. To make the understanding of the term more concrete, this chapter enumerates a few sample API types.

Method and Field Signatures

The most obvious and least controversial example of an API is a set of classes, their methods, and their fields. Probably everyone producing a library in Java will package it into a JAR file containing classes. These classes and their members then become the library's API.

Of course, not all signatures are part of an API. If you use nonpublic classes, or private or package private fields and methods, common sense suggests that these elements aren't part of the contract that other programmers should use. Often it's possible to access such elements by using reflection or other low-level techniques, but these are commonly and correctly considered to be hacks: if reflection is needed for communication between a system's components, it indicates that something is wrong or that the available API is insufficient. You can expect that such hacks will break across versions, as no API contract specifies that they should work at all.

However, it's not true that reflection cannot be used to form valid and useful APIs. Even in the basic Java platform, you can find examples where reflection is successfully used to simplify coding and sometimes even to define new coding patterns. For example, in the JavaBeans specification, the user of the bean gets a list of methods and fields that are available at design time and can be modified through the use of reflection. In other places, it's common to require a public constructor for a class to exist, because some code will use `Class.newInstance` to get an instance of a class without knowing its name statically. Therefore, using reflection can be helpful, but you must do so with care; in particular, you must document clearly for those coding against such APIs that tricks of this kind are in use.

Files and Their Content

A bit less obvious, but important nonetheless, is the set of files the application reads or writes, as well as their format.

As an example, let's consider how communication between a telnet application and the Kerberos authentication subsystem can be achieved. These two components are unlikely to have been developed by the same people, as the skill set for writing encryption is somewhat different from that required for handling socket communication. An API can enable these components to work together.

The telnet application reads its configuration files from a shared system location, such as `/etc/telnet.rc`, as well as via user personal preferences from `$HOME/.telnetrc`. Kerberos relies on this, and at install time modifies the content of the shared file with instructions for telnet to call the authentication subsystem. The telnet application then uses this information to load appropriate libraries and authenticate the user's login password.

SANDWICH-BASED FILE CONFIGURATION

Unlike Unix applications, some Java applications can exist without touching the disk at all. On the other hand, the NetBeans Platform, and especially its configuration, is built around files. However, it doesn't deal directly with files on disk. Instead, it's based on the concept of virtual files.

The configuration area of any NetBeans Platform–based application is similar to the content of Unix's `/etc` directory. Every utility (in Unix) or a module (in the case of the NetBeans Platform) has one or more dedicated locations that it reads to acquire configuration parameters. For example, the system that builds the NetBeans Platform's menu and toolbar as shown in Figure 3-1 reads its data from the `/Menu` or `/Toolbars` directories. In fact, locations of this kind form an important API, because other modules need to know them to register their own configuration files there. Their names cannot change arbitrarily, as that would mean that currently existing registrations would no longer be recognized. Their content needs to be stable as well, for the same reason.

Figure 3-1. *The NetBeans menu and toolbar are built from the content of file directories.*

This is comparable to Unix's /etc configuration area. However, there is one significant difference. Most of the files in the NetBeans configuration directory are just virtual; that is, they are taken from many XML filesystems. Just like a giant sandwich, the configuration is composed from various layers. Each component (a NetBeans module) is capable of providing an XML filesystem layer with many file registrations, such as this one:

```
<filesystem>
<folder name="Menu">
  <file name="Open.instance"/>
</folder>
</filesystem>
```

The system then merges all these layers together into one filesystem. This works similarly to unionfs in modern Linux distributions. This big, merged filesystem is then used to provide the actual configuration data for a running NetBeans system. All this feels like a big sandwich composed of individual component layers.

I am fairly proud of this invention of mine, which I created in 2000, because it eliminates many small configuration files on disk, replacing them with virtual files read directly from each module. Moreover, it provides a significant advantage: the provided files are always consistent with the list of installed modules, which might not be true if they are copied to disk when a component is installed and removed when it's uninstalled.

The importance of this "file-based API" is obvious. If the location of the shared file that telnet reads changes, for example, to /etc/telnet5.rc, any modifications made by Kerberos in the original location will be useless, as nobody will read the modifications. Also, if the format of the file changes, Kerberos might perform syntactically incorrect changes during installation. In turn, this might cause the changes to fail and can prevent the whole file from being read successfully, preventing the telnet client from being run.

Environment Variables and Command-Line Options

Environment variables and command-line interfaces are not often important in the context of libraries. However, as demonstrated by the presence of the section "ENVIRONMENT" in the Unix man pages, these "interfaces" are extremely important in certain environments. In the Unix world, it's common to write an application in a shell by means of chained invocations of small tools.

To execute these tools, a lot of information is taken from environment variables. For example, the search path for executed programs is stored in the variable PATH. By changing it you can change the meaning of the executed programs. For example, one of the basic tricks to hack a computer is to redefine the meaning of the su utility. Simply sit at someone's unlocked computer, write a shell script to mail you the password, name it **su**, and change the PATH so it first finds your version rather than executing the standard one located at /bin/su. Providing different values for the environment variables a program reads can significantly influence the program's behavior. The point here is that files and environment variables are no less an API than class names and method signatures. This applies to software libraries in a modular application, as well as to Unix command-line utilities. Output and ad hoc strings that are accessible from foreign code are part of a component's API.

ENVIRONMENT VARIABLES IN JAVA APPLICATIONS

For a long time (from Java 1.1 to Java 5), the Java APIs lacked a way to read environment variables. This was probably due to the feeling that these variables aren't available on all operating systems and that code relying on them wouldn't be portable. However, it's sometimes hard to write real applications without the use of these variables. For example, the NetBeans IDE CVS and Subversion support plug-ins needed to invoke command-line tools to perform version-control operations. These tools provide an environment API to control their behavior on Windows and Unix systems. It was necessary to invoke these with the appropriate environment variables from inside the NetBeans IDE. Often, it was also necessary to propagate certain global user variables to them. For this reason, we needed to read the current environment variables from inside the Java application, and we did this with a special launcher script. However, now we can remove these old tricks, because Java 5 provides a standard API to read environment variables.

Java has a partial replacement for environment variables: system properties. Any method in Java can use System.getProperty, with a string name, to read a value associated with the property. This is similar to Unix environment variables: system properties can be passed to the Java Virtual Machine when it starts. It's also possible to change property values while the Java Virtual Machine is running.

Often, we use these *property-based APIs* in NetBeans for changing the default behavior of certain parts of the system, which we want to make possible but we don't want to advertise too much. This enables fine-tuning, such as slightly different behavior during drag and drop, the disabling of certain hacks involving access to the clipboard, and the changing of behavior to be more suitable for running tests. This kind of API isn't needed while using the NetBeans IDE or writing modules for the NetBeans Platform; it's mainly aimed at people and companies building various customized applications based on the NetBeans Platform. Although not as prominent as classes and methods in the Javadoc API, we do document this API properly and we do our best to ensure this API won't break in future releases. It's a real API to us, and it serves everyone well for certain purposes.

Of course, Unix utilities don't react only to environment variables. Another important API used is the list of arguments passed at the time of invocation. For example, in the previous case the su utility knows who to log in, because it's invoked with that argument. Obviously, changing the way arguments are interpreted, the order in which they can be provided, or abandoning support for some that used to be supported might completely break an application that invokes a new version of a utility with old-style arguments. Therefore, input parameters, and any documented variables that can affect the operation of the system, are also APIs.

Text Messages As APIs

The use of pipes makes Unix unique compared to its predecessors and many of its successors. Tool utilities aren't controlled just by environment variables and parameters provided on the command line. You can also send any text input to a utility and get a result in return. Chaining such utilities into an application is a common practice on any Unix system and constitutes one of the most powerful and well-understood coding patterns for any Unix system user. As a result, anything a program reads or prints can be seen as—and often is—an API. So, it has to undergo careful review, as I'll describe in the next section.

The text you print and the text you read can become an important API. I've already mentioned the case of configuration files and input and output streams sent to and from a program, but that isn't all. Java assigns to every object the ability to convert itself into a string, using the toString method. The default implementation that prints just class names and hexadecimal object hash codes isn't terribly useful. For debugging purposes, Java objects often override toString methods to return more meaningful information. This can become a problem, as sometimes the value acquires too much meaning and foreign components come to rely on it. Any unintentional API such as this can compromise the promise of distributed development: the main motivation for having an API in the first place.

MISUSE OF TOSTRING

A misuse of the toString method happened to NetBeans with FileObject.toString(). FileObject is a NetBeans wrapper around java.io.File that allows you to plug *virtual filesystems* such as FTP, HTTP, XML filesystems, and so on, into the NetBeans Platform. The toString method originally returned a concatenation of two strings that by chance exactly matched the local file name. As a result, you could do **new** File(fileObject.*toString*()) and access the right local file. However, this was just an accidental effect. It didn't work for files controlled by CVS or other version control systems, or for members of JAR files. However, developers testing their code on their own local disk, where such code would appear to work, would end up using this trick in production modules. Of course, it broke as soon as any other virtual filesystem was used.

We decided to fix the problem. We tried to return a URL from *toString*() and told people to use the *getPath*() method, which they should have been using anyway. However, a few weeks later, we found our colleagues had started to rely on toString returning URLs! Thankfully, we discovered this pretty quickly, before the release, and could change the toString method to return a value that had no meaning. Now a string with a prefix, then a URL, and then hexadecimal System.*identityHashCode*() is the value of toString. This seems to have achieved our goal and clearly communicated that this method wasn't useful. As a result, our colleagues are using *getPath*(), which is the actual API those developers should have been using to get a relative path from the root of the virtual filesystem in the first place. However, this is not a happy ending. Although the Javadoc of *getPath*() warns that this is just a relative path, it was accidentally also the actual path on the disk in the case of file objects representing local files. Quite a few people started to rely on **new** File(to.*getPath*()) really existing, and as a result we broke their code when we wanted to change the relative root. Déjà vu?

In a similar case, we discovered that providing discoverable string names to graphical user interface (GUI) components in an API caused abuse whereby innocent changes to that GUI component unexpectedly broke clients. It's clear that any available information from a component in a modular system can and will be abused. So, it's important to be clear in specifying what is and what is not part of the API contract.

Beware of situations where there is no alternative to parsing text messages! If the information isn't available in other ways, people will parse any textual output generated by your code. For example, this happened to the JDK's Exception.*printStackTrace*(OutputStream). Until JDK 1.4, there was no other way to understand the origin of an exception than to parse this output. Indeed, we did it in the NetBeans IDE, as did many others in their own applications. As a result, the originally informal format of the stack trace became an API and could not be changed without breaking client code. If you are serious about your API, you want to avoid such situations.

In Java 1.4 this misuse of the API was understood and fixed. The Exception class acquired the new getStackTrace() method that returned the same information in a more structured format. This was supposed to completely remove the need for parsing the textual output, and likely it did, for new applications. However, nothing changed for those that were written prior to Java 1.4. Those applications continue to rely on parsing the textual format and don't acknowledge the new methods at all. As a result, it's still necessary to keep the textual format untouched! This is a result of APIs being like stars: once someone discovers them, they need to stay and behave well forever.

Protocols

Protocols are related to textual and file-based APIs. They are the formats of messages sent over a network, and as such they are of especially great importance. Whenever you open a socket, either for reading or for writing, you immediately enter an API transaction. It's not just an ordinary transaction, but one that is potentially even more dangerous than the common usage of APIs through local interfaces.

The first issue is that, except where externally provided, there is no access control. In Java you can use public, private, protected, or package private to guard access, but an open socket offers no such choice. Everyone able to access your computer and a given port can now open the connection, start to talk to you, and become dependent upon you. What's good about this kind of API is that unless you distribute your application to other parties that run the server independently, you can count and analyze access frequency and communication, as it all happens on "your" server. This can help you analyze possible misuses of your socket. You know what others do when using it, you can analyze their requests, and you can make sure your responses are sane. You can adjust your responses over time, but you still have to ensure that you can deal with any connection, as there is no way to restrict those who can connect to your port. Your port, which is now your API, is open for everyone.

The other issue amplified by the use of network protocols is the widespread proliferation of various clients and protocol versions that are used to talk to your application. I once read an interesting article about the development of Subversion, the version control system, regarding the challenges developers faced during their program's evolution and the protocols it uses.[1] In fact, Subversion's developers need to fight on various fronts, because they have a wide range of APIs. As a command-line tool, Subversion is dominated by arguments and environment variables. As a version control system, Subversion needs to store and understand metadata about locally checked-out files. Last but not least, developers also need the client to connect to their server with some protocol and make updates and checkouts over the wire. This would be simple if there was just one version of the Subversion system. However, as with any other software, the

---

1. Garrett Rooney, "Preserving Backward Compatibility" (2005), http://www.onlamp.com/pub/a/onlamp/2005/02/17/backwardscompatibility.html.

system evolves. There is a need to fix existing bugs, and there is a constant need to add new features. As a result, the local checkout might be done with one version of the tool from a few weeks ago, while the operations might be performed later with a newer version. Those versions need to understand their data or at least identify whether it can operate on them or not. Identification is the most important part: once Subversion is sure that a different version produced the data, you can refuse to operate on them and ask the user to update the tool. This is an acceptable way to solve a mismatch of versions. However, this only works locally.

The mismatch might happen in local operations, but it's certain to happen in server communication. The version of the Subversion system on the server is almost guaranteed to be different from that used on local computers that access the server. Why? Because there are usually innumerable client computers, each running its own distribution with a different revision of the Subversion client. The server might try the same trick and ask the clients to upgrade to some specified version, but this won't work. First of all, it might not be easy to get the new version of a Subversion client for each system. However, even if it were, the problem wouldn't be solved. There are many Subversion projects, each running their own server, each guaranteed to use a slightly different version of the system. If each of the servers required a specific version of the client, you would need to have svn1, svn1.0.1, svn1.1, svn1.2.3, and so on installed on the client system and always remember which one to use to connect to each Subversion server. Such a proliferation of various incompatible versions of the same tool would create a horrible user experience and would likely lead people to another version control system that would do a better job at keeping backward compatibility of its protocols.

The reason why protocol-like APIs need to evolve in a backward compatible way is because they multiply the problem of the independent life cycle of each participant. Once a protocol is defined, its usages start to live on their own. There can be various client programs that speak to the protocol. Those programs have multiple versions, and these versions are upgraded completely arbitrarily on various computers all around the world. As a result, it's almost certain that two programs speaking to each other use different versions and that they need a slightly different version of the protocol. Still, despite that, they do need to communicate.

LOCALLY RESTRICTED SERVER

Although applications based on the NetBeans Platform, including the NetBeans IDE, are mostly desktop-based, I had the opportunity to "enjoy" a protocol-based API and its evolution problems. NetBeans applications are singletons. For example, usually there is only one instance of the application per user. If the user invokes the same application for the second time, it shouldn't do anything itself, just tell the previously running instance to move its window to the front and finish itself. As a result, no second instance should be started. This is achieved using a lock file combined with a socket server. On startup, each NetBeans-based application allocates a random local port, writes its number into a lock file, and listens to it. Whenever another instance is started, it checks for the existence of the lock file. If the lock file is found, it reads the number of the port and attempts to connect to the port to determine if the previous instance of the application is still alive. If so, then these two processes exchange command-line arguments, perform some computations, and send each other input and output streams, after which the second instance exits. This is useful if you want to pass additional arguments to the already running application, such as --open filename.

The communication protocol is quite simple and proprietary. When I coded it, I had no need for it to be extensible or bulletproof. I used it just for communication between two instances of the same application.

I thought that I had full control over it and that I could safely add new features to it, if I correctly changed the sender as well as receiver side of the communication channel.

After a few NetBeans releases, I found that I had been naive. I received bug reports that, after a lot of investigation, showed that for some reason people were trying to connect to an already running NetBeans IDE 5.5 via NetBeans IDE 6.0. Because these versions use slightly different versions of the protocol, this doesn't work.

Since then I've learned that the initial sentence of each protocol should be dedicated to a proper handshake—even if the protocol is used just for local, private communication.

Breaking the protocol is like switching from Subversion to another version control system, which is painful to say the least. That is why it's important that the protocol be capable of some kind of handshake. The handshake should be the first activity it performs when communication is established. It should introduce the version of each of the peers in the communication, allowing them to choose a common language to understand. The other requirement is to have a common language for all the possible mixtures of versions of the clients. The language might not allow complicated tasks to be expressed, just as "basic English" is enough for common situations, such as Subversion checkout, status, and diff.

The protocol is likely to evolve as new features need new expressions in the protocol language. However, there should never be a need for the end users of a Subversion tool, or users of Subversion libraries, to deal with the protocol changes themselves. It shouldn't matter whether you need svn1, svn1.0.1, svn1.1, svn1.2.3, or some other version. The decision of which protocol to use should be hidden inside a single Subversion binary or library. Internally, it can even contain independent copies of svn1, svn1.0.1, svn1.1, and svn1.2.3 code bases to talk different dialects of the same protocol, but for common usages this shouldn't be exposed to the clients for the sake of API usage simplicity.

Behavior

APIs exist to shield us from a component's internals. They exist to allow us to be clueless yet still able to build our applications using the black-box building blocks. Does that mean that an API's definition stops at the surface? It would be nice if this were true. However, it usually isn't: regardless of how good the abstractions provided by the APIs are, the underlying implementation often leaks out and thereby also becomes part of the API.

I've met a lot of people who thought that an API ends at the signature of a class or method. Whatever happens behind it is "implementation," and these details don't belong to the API at all. I am guilty of thinking in this way as well. When the NetBeans QA department asked whether we were backward compatible, I claimed that because we didn't change the public signatures of our APIs, we were backward compatible. However, I was wrong. The main goal of producing components is to simplify building modular systems. Compatibility means that you can replace a piece of the system with its newer version and the system will continue to work as it used to. The observation that "things will work" is the most important constraint of compatibility. This is influenced by the internal implementations of methods deep below the signature level.

If a method claims to return a non-null value in one version, then changing it to return null is in fact an incompatible change, because this change can be observed from the outside and negatively influences the component's users. If a method of an interface is said to be called in the Java AWT Event Dispatch thread, then changing the component to call this method from any thread can break an existing implementation of the interface. It might no longer be possible to create visual components, interact with the user, show dialogs, and so on. Many other behavioral aspects of an API are relevant here, such as program flow, call order, and the locks that are unwittingly being relied upon.

These examples show that although the *behavior* of an API is much harder to grasp, it's a very important—if not the most important—part of the API contract. Only if the behavior of a component remains unchanged can its users cluelessly replace versions of the component in their final application. Only then can they trust that the functionality will not be compromised by upgrading to a newer version. That is why this book will treat *behavior of components* as an API.

I18N Support and L10N Messages

Not all APIs are designed for everyone. If I am only a Linux C developer, I don't need to care about the internal APIs between the Linux kernel. They're too low level, far beyond my cluelessness level. It would be completely distracting for a C developer to be overwhelmed by all these details. I want these to be completely beyond my own programming horizon. On the other hand, people do care about these APIs, and for them they form proper and interesting APIs.

It's normal for different APIs to be targeted at different groups. One of the most extreme cases is internationalization support, used by localization groups to translate individual modules into different languages. Internationalization in Java is usually handled using ResourceBundle. Instead of hard-coding textual messages in the code itself, you define a key and then ask the ResourceBundle for the actual text for the given key. The mappings between keys and messages are placed in Bundle.properties, Bundle_en.properties, Bundle_ja.properties, and so on, and then read from the bundle associated with the current user's language during program execution.

Developers usually provide just a Bundle.properties with the default language, which is usually English. Someone other than the author of the code then develops and distributes the localizations to other languages. These translations are often independent efforts, with different schedules, done by groups of people located all around the world, potentially far away from the original code developer.

From the viewpoint of a regular API user, such as the developer coding against a library, the Bundle keys are low-level implementation details. Using them is just like using reflection to access private classes, methods, or fields that are not exposed publicly in the API itself. Relying on them is against good habits and common sense. It makes no sense to document these in Javadoc, or to bother regular API users with them. This kind of API is completely beyond the horizon of these groups of users.

SOLARIS WITH A JAPANESE LOCALE

NetBeans uses a slight extension of the `ResourceBundle` class and most of the time this works well. However, sometimes we need to go beyond this contract and define some extensions. This is usually asking for trouble.

Recently, I defined a semi-online contract, where part of the NetBeans user interface (UI) is read from a web site. From a common address I read an HTML page, parsed it, partially displayed it, and partially used it to create UI buttons, labels, and so on. I managed to make this work easily on my Linux installation. However, when the translation group started their work, I immediately received several error reports.

As the localizers often use Solaris and translate mostly to Japanese, we receive most bug reports from this combination. It's not much fun to try to reproduce them: booting up Solaris; starting a Japanese login session; and then trying to find out how to invoke a terminal, NetBeans, or a browser is a topic for a separate story. However, the reason we had so many problems with this combination is that, in contrast to most of our Linux installations, most Japanese systems don't use UTF-8 encoding, but euc_ja. Conversions from and to various encodings often reveal inconsistencies in the application.

It's best to test your application under the most stressful conditions. In the case of NetBeans and localization-related APIs, we know that the most complicated combination, revealing the most errors, is Solaris in a Japanese locale.

For the localization groups, the bundle keys form an important API, and perhaps the most significant API. To simplify distributed development between programmers and localizers, it's better to follow the rules of good API evolution, such as limiting the removal or renaming of existing keys, because these are in fact incompatible changes.

Wide Definition of APIs

As is probably clear by now, the definition of an API stretches far beyond a simple set of classes and methods, or functions and signatures. The API, in the sense useful for the clueless assembly of big system components, ranges from simple text messages to complex and hard-to-grasp behaviors of the components themselves. Just imagine what a mess you can cause by arbitrarily changing database or XML schemas or by redefining the meaning of WDDL, REST, or IDL services. These all fall into the API category and deserve to be designed with evolution in mind.

How to Check the Quality of an API

As previously mentioned, people tend to associate correctness with elegance. In a similar way, when it comes to discussing the properties of a good API, many will say that a good API should be beautiful. Indeed, being beautiful is an advantage. A good impression is always created in the first encounter and if something is nice and we like it, it has a much greater chance of being accepted. That is why it's acceptable to strive to design beautiful APIs, but beauty cannot be the only measure of a good API.

The definition and measurement of beauty is subjective. No two persons can agree on beauty; everyone has their own preferences. Applied to API design, this means that each API is original and that each requires different skills from its users. This might prevent widespread usage of APIs. Beauty belongs to the world of art, while software engineering is, well, engineering. The primary goal of engineering is to produce working systems. The fact that deep in our minds we have the old Greek heritage, the feeling that if something is correct, it also has to be beautiful, should not distract us from the main goal: designing APIs that are easy to use, widely adopted, and productive. An engineering approach needs an objective way to measure the quality of its products. We need to formulate this for each API to measure the extent that a given objective is satisfied.

In the following sections, we'll study the various aspects visible to an API's user, and analyze their importance and ways to conform to them. Given the fact that the expected reader of this book is an engineer, and engineers are taught to measure everything, all the measuring we are about to do will be some compensation for the sad necessity of rejecting beauty as unquantifiable and therefore as a poor criterion of quality.

Comprehensibility

Those who have to use an API must be able to understand it. This is a vague statement, but also the most important. I have already mentioned that an API is about communication between the programmer who writes the API and the programmer who writes an implementation against that API. As in spoken language, if these two cannot communicate, then something is wrong with the way we are using our communication channel—that is, the API.

The most similar activity to writing an API is writing a book: one writer and a lot of readers. The readers know something of the writer, but the writer knows little or nothing about the readers. Guessing their skills and knowledge correctly is part of the delicate art of making an API that is easy to understand.

Everyone's view of the world is defined by the horizon. Items that are closer to us are seen clearly; those that lie nearer the horizon become less and less distinct. What is beyond the horizon is not known at all, vanishing into nothingness. Concepts provided by a good API have to lie inside the user's horizon, otherwise they won't be understood. The API designer needs to understand what is common knowledge across the target audience and use this knowledge when designing the API. From time to time it's acceptable to go past the horizon, and expand it by introducing a new concept. However, this has to be built in incrementally, step by step, as going past the horizon is always associated with the danger of getting lost in unexplored territory.

When coding in Java, it's safe to expect that people know concepts used in most of the java.* libraries. Iterators, enumerations, I/O streams, JavaBeans, listeners, and visual components are objects that nearly any Java programmer has encountered. Use of familiar terminology, classes, and terms reduces the learning curve, which in turn places fewer cognitive demands on an API's user.

When coding constructs are unfamiliar, there is a simple solution based on the observation that most users of an API first search for existing applications that do something similar to their task, copy the application, and modify it to suit their needs. That is why it doesn't matter how exceptional an API might be. Having many examples of how to use it increases the likelihood that developers can find something close to their needs. This also greatly increases the probability that they will come to understand the API. The more novel the concepts an API uses, the greater the benefit of extensive examples.

Consistency

Another important aspect of an API that can be easily checked is whether it's consistent. If the users of an API have to invest time to learn a concept, it's important that the concept be applied consistently across the entire API. For example, if there is a way to register, say, factories for objects, then all types of factories should use that one registration mechanism. This reduces the number of caveats and special cases a user of the API needs to track.

Similarly, it's preferable to allow the same threading model to be used across the whole API or class, rather than documenting that certain methods must be called only from a certain thread.

From the point of view of the lifetime of an API, it's important to follow the same style of development or at least clearly communicate the evolutionary style of an API. It's inconvenient to find that certain parts of an API have evolved in a different way than others.

As an example, let's mention the case of the `org.w3c.dom` interfaces. They became part of the JDK in version 1.3, and although there was a warning about them being "public domain," nobody said that those interfaces could not be implemented by clients as any other interfaces in standard Java APIs can be. Implementing `java.lang.Runnable` is supposed to be safe. For example, nobody will ever add a new method into `java.lang.Runnable`, because so many clients implement that interface. However, the addition of new methods to `org.w3c.dom` did happen in newer versions of the JDK. This is problematic because those who had implemented the interface could not rely on the implementation to compile anymore. Despite the fact that most applications are fine, compatibility of certain pieces is gone, and the way developers are informed of this is that they can no longer compile code that was perfectly legitimate in earlier versions. This type of evolution, unless clearly communicated at the outset, is the worst kind of betrayal of trust.

Discoverability

Even the most beautiful API is useless if those who are supposed to use it cannot find it or easily understand how to use it.

Few situations are worse than finding a project that claims to provide an API to help solve your problem, which then sends you to the Javadoc of 5 packages and 30 classes, without entry points or guidance. An example of this is the Javadoc for `java.awt.Image`. It's a class that represents graphical images that can be painted on screen or saved in standard image formats. It's an abstract class, but of course what most users want is to load an image from disk. It contains this cryptic instruction: "The image must be obtained in a platform-specific manner." A clever reader of the Javadoc might notice the subclass `BufferedImage` and look there. Empty images of this class can be constructed, but throughout the documentation of these image classes, there is not a hint as to how you might either obtain an instance of one loaded with an image from disk, or draw an image on the screen, or save one. This is a perfect example of meeting the requirements of reference documentation while providing no help to the user trying to find an entry point to do something useful with the features being documented.

In most cases, the set of classes is not what interests most API users. They are interested in getting their job done. For these purposes it's more important to see examples of API usage, enabling the selection of the idiom that is closest to what you want to do. This partially explains the success of open source projects, as usually you can just copy existing sources to get started. In fact, the source can serve as documentation and provide initial guidance. Consider the history of HTML itself: in the early days of the Web, most budding web designers copied examples of code they saw in their browsers. The World Wide Web might be the ultimate open source project itself.

Regardless of what type of API you provide, it's important to create a single place that can serve as a starting point and can send people in the directions that solve their problems. As people don't think in terms of classes, it's important to organize this entry point in an optimal manner, based on the actual or at least expected goals and tasks.

Simple Tasks Should Be Easy

Sometimes an API supports multiple target audiences. For example, Java's JNDI allows people to discover an object by its name and also to plug in their own name resolvers. These two actions are created for two completely different groups of API users.

JNDI is just an example, but in fact this happens to many APIs: different audiences will consume it. The first and most basic mistake is putting items of interest to different parties into one API. This hurts discoverability, as people interested in just one aspect of the API will be distracted by the parts of the API that are designed for a completely different audience.

The common approach to take is to split an API into two or more parts: one targeted for callers, the other ideally in a separate package or namespace, for providers plugging into the API to provide its services or extensions. A good approach taken by JNDI was the creation of separate interfaces for those distinct audiences, splitting them into completely different packages. Callers into the API just use javax.naming and javax.naming.event, while the implementors are more interested in javax.naming.spi, and so forth.

This sort of separation is even more important than documenting the API in that it provides automatic scoping: the different audiences for the API can easily focus their study and concern on the area that's of interest to them, without having to ask the question, "Is this something I need to care about?" for each class they see in the documentation index.

Doing this sort of split incorrectly—or worse, optimizing for the wrong audience, which is typically smaller—can seriously diminish the API's usefulness. For example, the JavaMail API contains an enormous number of concepts and classes. It requires quite a bit of work on the developer's part simply to send mail or to get a list of messages from a mail server, with a great deal of boilerplate code required. On the other hand, the entire API is optimized to make it extremely easy to write providers that implement new protocols. The problem with this is that *there are vastly more applications that will want to send and receive mail than there are wire protocols for mail-like messages.* Although perhaps not provable, it's certainly probable that this misoptimization is single-handedly responsible for the relative rarity of Java-based mail applications.

Preservation of Investment

It's important for anyone designing an API to treat partners fairly—in other words, to treat the API's users well. Users of an API beget more uses of that API, and vice versa. The more people who write applications in Java, the more other Java applications are likely to be written in the future. The more developers use the JUnit library, for example, the more important the library and the development style it represents become. To become a user of a library, you need to understand it and to be convinced that it saves work. But above all, for the users of an API to be truly comfortable with it, they must believe that their work won't break or vanish when a new version of the library is released. Coding to a library is an *investment* of time, study, effort, and money. The first and foremost responsibility of the API designer is to preserve the investment of those who use it.

The users of the API are its jewels. Their work has a right to be respected and admired. The better the user experience, the better they will speak of the API, the better they will feel using it, and the better it will be promoted and evangelized. This will all lead to a happier API-using community. That is why it's important to preserve participant investment and always to try to evolve API contracts in a compatible—or at least predictable—way. Each new version of a library should ensure that existing client modules continue to execute in a reasonable way, or failing that, that it's easy to update existing sources to compile and use the contracts of the new release. The expectation of a need for updates must be set well in advance of any possible incompatibility.

There are two modes of using a library. In less flexible environments or in more distributed ones, an end user might have an application binary installed that uses the old version of the library. To satisfy everyone, when a new version of the library is updated, the application needs to continue to work without problems. If this is achieved, we can claim that the investment made by the author of the application is well preserved.

Less strict setups have the flexibility to get source code, fix it, and recompile it. This is common in the open source world and manifested in Linux distributions, for example. In these setups, it might not be necessary to have absolute compatibility of binaries; it just has to be easy to recompile a new version. If that state is achieved and expectations are set correctly, the goal of preserving investments has also been mostly reached.

On the other side of these kinds of preservations is the well-intended desire to make the API of a library "nicer": renaming methods to be more self-explanatory, restructuring API patterns to be more understandable, and so on. These activities are welcome before the first release. However, after the first release, they cannot outweigh the problems related to the burden of breaking existing API client code. Only those who don't value their users have this attitude.

CHAPTER 4

■ ■ ■

Ever-Changing Targets

Many people think about the design and development of software systems, including APIs, as something that is complete at the release date. This is rarely the case. Few nontrivial pieces of software are ever "finished." Usually the initial release is just the first step in the life cycle of a software system. Hopefully, many subsequent releases will follow. This applies also to APIs. The definition of a good API is not one that simply looks fine at the initial release, but one that has survived several years and is still in good shape.

The First Version Is Never Perfect

I already discussed in the section "The First Version Is Always Easy" in Chapter 2 that creating the first version is easy. I also mentioned that the first version is unlikely to be perfect. These two observations indicate that nearly every API needs to evolve over time. The requirements for the API will change as time goes by, and those that might have been valid in the past might no longer be applicable. Also, in every program there is at least one bug. Bugs need to be fixed from time to time, which leads to another commonly held belief: fixing a bug usually introduces two new ones. These common observations are true for any software system and APIs are no exception.

Now is the right time to give up and admit that "the first version is never perfect." Regardless of how much you try, the released version will contain bugs and users will attempt to use it for valid tasks that are beyond the scope of your design. Short of owning a crystal ball, you can't do much about this except accept it as a fact of life.

This observation need not lead to pessimism. The fact that the API needs to evolve isn't a sign of anything bad, but simply a recognition of reality. If you design for evolution, preferably in the first version, evolution should be possible without causing problems for API users. Every API writer needs to have an evolution plan; that is, to know on a strategic level what will happen to the API in future releases. There are two possible approaches to such a plan. One extreme suggests giving up and rewriting everything from scratch, and the other prefers to try to fix reported problems and enhance the existing API while not changing behavior for existing clients.

The incremental improvements approach can, in ideal cases, deliver bug fixes and potentially also performance enhancements and a nicer look and feel, without any work on the side of the API clients. Clients can still rely on the old API and also work with the newer and better versions. This would be a winning strategy, except that every bug fix is likely to introduce two new ones. Every new release can introduce problems for existing API clients, which is why achieving this level of cooperation can be difficult.

Giving up and writing another API to perform the same task avoids the problem of incompatibility. The old API can stay the same, so no potential problems occur for its clients, and the new API can offer new and better possibilities. The only problem here is that old clients will stick with the old API unless they rewrite their code and upgrade to a new version of the API. Therefore, the drawbacks are also nontrivial.

The complete rewrite has the advantage of avoiding small incompatibilities, but has the disadvantage of locking your customers into a release that will never benefit from the improvements that a newer release would give. The improvements are important, but compatibility is more so. Balancing between these two extremes is the delicate art of making an API useful.

Backward Compatibility

The ability of newer versions of an API to work with clients written and/or compiled against older versions is called *backward compatibility*. Being "backward compatible" is a mantra for nearly every API writer, as that increases the trust of the actual and potential users. However, there are multiple levels of backward compatibility, and achieving different levels is of differing importance and also complexity.

Source Compatibility

The first aspect you face with respect to compatibility is the ability to compile. If I write my program against, say, Java 1.3, will it compile on Java 1.4? If every possible program would do so, then the Java versions 1.3 and 1.4 could be called *source compatible*. However, source compatibility is hard to achieve. This is mostly caused by all the *syntactic sugar* that the language adds on top of the execution format: the class file. For example (and we faced this exact case in the NetBeans IDE), say someone wrote the following class against JDK 1.3:

```java
public class WrappingIOException extends IOException {
  private IOException cause;
  public WrappingIOException(IOException cause) {
    this.cause = cause;
  }
  public IOException getCause() {
    return cause;
  }
}
```

This would compile in Java 1.3, but would fail in Java 1.4, as the compiler would think that the code is trying to override a method that was introduced in Java 1.4. However, that method returns Throwable, so cannot be overridden by a method returning IOException. The Java 1.4 language rules forbid overriding a method by using the same name and also arguments, but a different return type, so compilation would fail. Surprisingly, in version 1.5 this would be okay, as the Java language evolved and accommodated changing the return type to be more specific as a valid step of evolution.

Adding new methods into classes that can be subclassed endangers source compatibility, but that's not the only point I want to make here. Adding new classes into existing packages might also cause problems. Imagine the following code written in Java 1.1:

```
import java.awt.*;
import java.util.*;

/** Could be compiled on JDK 1.2, before java.util.List was created */
public class VList extends List {
    Vector v;
}
```

This compiled without a problem in Java 1.1, but as soon as Java 1.2 appeared, the code snippet became invalid. Java 1.2 introduced new collection classes, among them java.util. List. As a result, the class name List became ambiguous in the preceding code snippet, as it can mean java.awt.List (as during the Java 1.1 compilation) as well as java.util.List. In short, adding new classes into existing packages isn't source compatible.

You can see that adding new methods to classes can cause source incompatibility and that adding new classes can also cause incompatibility. Removing methods or classes is incompatible, so what can you do? Never make any changes at all? Give up on source compatibility? Faced with this dilemma, giving up on source compatibility is probably the better choice.

Of course, trying hard to make sources compilable with a new version if they could be compiled with previous version of an API is a reasonable goal, but as has been shown, it's difficult and can be broken by syntactic language additions such as wildcard imports. That's why it doesn't make sense to try too much to ensure absolute source compatibility in Java. The language isn't designed to extensively support source compatibility. It has different goals, and if someone is recompiling from source anyway, it isn't that hard to fix mistakes. For example, replacing wildcard imports with explicit ones is relatively easy.

Binary Compatibility

You can achieve binary compatibility if any program compiled with a previous version of a library can be linked with newer versions of the API without recompilation. This is a useful goal, as it supports two scenarios. First, you can write an application and then compile it with one version of the library, while letting people use it with any other version. This greatly simplifies maintenance, packaging, and distribution of an application. Second, it allows a user who only has the binary, built against the older version of the library, to migrate to the new library version without waiting for someone to recompile the application. Both these scenarios are desirable and useful as they increase the flexibility of configuration and give module writers and users more freedom. To achieve this level of interoperability, you should understand at least a bit of the binary format to which the sources are compiled. In the case of Java, this means understanding the format of the class file and the way it is loaded into the Java Virtual Machine (JVM). The next paragraphs give an overview and highlight some of the differences between source and binary compatibility.

The .class file format is close to—but not the same as—the original source code. The first difference to note is that the problem with wildcard imports experienced by source compatibility is gone, because all names in a class file are fully qualified. Also, the name of a field or method contains not just the name expressed in the source, but is also annotated with the actual type of the method or the field. For a method, this means the types of all arguments and, more surprisingly, also the return type. Consequently, it's possible to have two methods with the same name and arguments, with different return types in the class file, although this isn't possible in the Java source:

```java
/** This is not Java code, but it is fine inside the bytecode */
public abstract class DoubleReturnType {
 public abstract String getName(int x);
 public abstract StringBuffer getName(int x);
}
```

The preceding source isn't valid in Java and would be rejected by any Java compiler version I know. On the other hand, even though the preceding code won't compile in Java, it's perfectly valid if encoded into the class file. That is one of the most significant differences between the Java language and its binary format.

MANGLING THE CLASS FILE CONTENT

It's fine to advise creating a class file that contains two versions of the same method, with each version having a different return type. However, the question is how to write the Java code that will actually compile to such bytecode.

The answer to this is to use a little bit of bytecode patching. For example, you can perform an operation directly on the content or the structure of the class file. This is a bit more complicated than changing the source code of a Java file, as .class is another binary format. However, its content is well documented and relatively easy to understand. Moreover, various tools help you analyze and modify bytecode with higher-level libraries, such as jasm, BCEL, classfile, and many others.

At one time, the NetBeans project needed to fix a backward compatibility problem. We needed two getIcon methods: one returning javax.swing.Icon and one javax.swing.ImageIcon. It turned out that the simplest way to do so was to name these methods differently and then do a search and replace on the resulting class file. That's why we compiled the following, which is a valid Java source:

```java
public static ImageIcon getIcon() { return null; }
public static Icon g3tIcon() { return null; }
```

We then replaced g3tIcon in the bytecode with getIcon. Simple and effective. Two methods with the same parameters and names and differing only in return type were created:

```xml
<!-- This is the target that does the whole trick - e.g. it compiles
     the Java source and then replaces tokens
     inside of the .class file
-->
<target name="-build-and-rename">
    <mkdir dir="build/apimerge/classes"/>
    <javac
        srcdir="src-apimerge" destdir="build/apimerge/classes"
        source="1.4" target="1.4" classpath="${cp}"
    />

    <!-- this is the replace. As the replace is done textually,
```

```
    we need to use some reasonable encoding that treats all
    byte values as characters. E.g. it is not possible to
    use UTF-8 as it does not like the standard Java header
    0xCAFEBABE. Western Europe encoding is fine
-->
<replace
    dir="build/apimerge/classes" casesensitive="true"
    encoding="iso-8859-1" summary="true"
>
    <include name="**/*.class"/>
    <replacetoken>g3tIcon</replacetoken>
    <replacevalue>getIcon</replacevalue>
</replace>
</target>
```

You should also be aware that access to a field encodes the name of the class the field is defined in. The virtual machine searches for the field only in the specified class, while the search for a method also checks all possible superclasses. Consequently, it's better to expose a method instead of a field, as that gives you a bit more freedom for what you can do in the future.

When dealing with an object-oriented language, you must have an idea of what it means to declare a method and what it means to override it. Though in modern virtual machines such as HotSpot the implementation is different, the old "virtual methods table" description illustrates the concept well enough for our purposes. When you define a class with a set of nonfinal methods, you actually create a table. The table maps the names of methods, along with a description of the types of arguments and return value, to the actual piece of code that is to be executed when the method is invoked. If you create a subclass, then it creates the same table; it just fills it with different pointers to new pieces of code that are to be invoked when a given method is called. The calling code then always checks the table, finds out the right method from the signature, and invokes the actual piece of code registered in the table. Simple, yet powerful. In this way, the actual execution of a program is dynamic, as the actual piece of code that gets executed depends on the object, class, and its "virtual methods table." It's useful to keep this picture in mind, as it can explain a lot about inheritance behavior in object-oriented languages.

Table 4-1 demonstrates what will happen if certain base methods defined by java. lang.Object are called. For example, the "toString" row says that when you have an object of type Object and you call the toString method on it, it might actually end up in a method definition provided by String, if the actual type of the object is String. This kind of table is associated with every defined class. Whenever a virtual method—which in Java is any method not marked as final—is called on some class, you can see that as a lookup in the appropriate table. The correct table is deduced from the runtime type of the object on which the code makes the call. This is not magic. However, it's useful to remind ourselves of the core technologies behind object-oriented programming. For example, it's good to be reminded that the sole purpose of overridable methods is to replace a table mapping method name with actual code snippets.

Table 4-1. *Sample Virtual Method Table for Basic Java Classes*

Method	Object	String	Number	Integer
"equals"	Object.equals	String.equals	Object.equals	Integer.equals
"toString"	Object.toString	String.toString	Object.toString	Integer.toString
"finalize"	Object.finalize	Object.finalize	Object.finalize	Object.finalize

Binary compatibility in Java has its own gotchas. For example, you might think that if a program compiles against two versions of a library, then the resulting bytecode will be the same. Well, sometimes it might be; however, often it won't. The gotcha lies in the *overloaded methods* concept. Here, two methods are overloaded if they have the same name, but differ in their parameters. For example, `java.util.Arrays` has many `toString` methods, each accepting different array types, such as **byte**[ ], **short**[ ], and Object[ ]. These methods are therefore overloaded. When called, the compiler chooses the best one depending on the type of the parameter that is passed for method invocation. If multiple methods can be applied, the compiler selects the "closest" one, according to rules defined in the Java Language Specification.

INCOMPATIBLE ADDITIONS TO STRINGBUFFER

For several years the NetBeans project has supported the two latest versions of Java. This has the advantage that our users aren't forced to upgrade to the latest Java version. However, it also has the drawback that we're restricted to using features and APIs introduced in the previous release of the Java language and run-times.

When Java 1.4 appeared, we were tempted to use some of its new libraries. We could have used reflection to invoke the newly added methods and classes that weren't present in version 1.3. However, that wasn't comfortable to use. Type control from the compiler is missing and you always need to catch a lot of exceptions when working with reflection. That's why we decided to modify our build scripts to ignore source files ending with *14.java when compiling on Java 1.3, and compile them only when building on Java 1.4. That way we could stuff all the Java 1.4–only calls into those classes and still compile on both versions of Java. To demonstrate the idea, see the `conditionaluseofapi` sample project (available in the downloadable code), where a facade is defined:

```java
interface AddString {
    public void addString(String msg);
    public String getMessage();
}
```

Now we have two different implementations and we need to select the right one, depending on whether we're running on an older or newer version of Java:

```java
AddString add;

try {
    Class onlyOn15 = Class.forName("java.lang.StringBuilder");
    Class codeOn15 = Class.forName(
        "conditionaluseofapi.StringBuilderAdd15"
    );
```

```
    add = (AddString)codeOn15.newInstance();
} catch (ClassNotFoundException ex) {
    add = new StringBufferAdd();
}
```

As a result, if we compile on the latest Java version, we have all the classes we need and we can use all its features. Meanwhile, when compiling with older versions, we get fewer classes, but their execution is guaranteed to work on those versions. We considered this quite a safe solution. Indeed, we were afraid of the accidental usage of APIs that are only available in the newer version of Java. That's why we ran parallel compilations on both the supported versions. The parallel compilations guaranteed that no newer introduced API was used unconditionally, and the production build ran on both versions of Java, or so we thought.

To our surprise, we received a NoSuchMethodError from time to time. After some investigation we found that this was caused by the following:

```
StringBuffer sb = new StringBuffer();
StringBuffer another = new StringBuffer();
sb.append(another);
```

In fact, the problem was that Java 1.4 introduced the new StringBuffer append(StringBuffer sb) method, which wasn't present in the 1.3 version. However, since Java's earliest days, there used to be a StringBuffer append(Object obj) generic method. As a result, the preceding code compiled fine on both JDKs, although they compiled to a completely different method call!

As can be seen, the trick with double compilation didn't work as expected. Code compiled on Java 1.4 couldn't be run on 1.3. However, our desire to use 1.4 features was strong, so we improved our production build. Instead of compiling with 1.4 only, we compiled twice: first with Java 1.3, which ignored all **/ *14.java classes, but correctly resolved all methods to the Java 1.3 API. Then we ran the compilation with JDK 1.4 again, which left the previously compiled classes untouched, but just added those **/*14.javas that were missing from the previous compilation.

Overloaded methods aren't the only unexpected surprise you can run into when thinking about binary compatibility. For some reason, the bytecode format treats strings and primitive values such as integers in a special way. If you define a public static final string or integer constant in an API class, its value is not just referenced, as is usual in case of Object or other types, but instead it's copied to the class that references it. This means that changing a value of such a primitive constant in a new version of an API doesn't change the value that already compiled clients of such an API see. You can use this for some odd tricks, such as this one with versioning, used by the JBuilder APIs:

```
public abstract class API {
    public static final int VERSION = 1;

    protected API() {
        System.err.println("Initializing version " + VERSION);
        init(API.VERSION);
        System.err.println("Properly initialized: " + this);
    }
```

```java
    protected abstract void init(int version) throws IllegalStateException;
  }
public class Impl extends API {
    protected void init(int version) throws IllegalStateException {
        if (version != API.VERSION) {
          throw new IllegalStateException("Wrong API version error!");
        }
    }
  }
}
```

Look at the preceding code snippet. Why is the strange check inside the init method? The passed-in value is VERSION, and then we verify this value to VERSION again. Indeed 1 == 1! These have to be equal. Well, yes, they have to be if the API and Impl classes are compiled simultaneously. But imagine that the Impl class is already written. For example, say someone has already written an extension module for JBuilder, and then tries to run it in a new version of the API without recompilation:

```java
public static final int VERSION = 2;
```

Here the check in the Impl.init methods fails. The check actually compares 2 != 1, because the Impl class remembers the value of API.VERSION from the time of its compilation when it was 1. Surprising, yet true. So, just remember that changing values of primitive constants is not compatible!

The bytecode format is similar to the Java source. This is both good and bad. It's good, because it is easy to understand. It's bad, because it can easily be misleading. However, when writing APIs, the binary format is the final judge deciding whether an application will link to a library that it uses. This is why it's important to understand what bytecode the Java code of your library translates to. When in doubt, disassemble your class and check its actual state. And be prepared for surprises!

Functional Compatibility—the Amoeba Effect

The fact that a new version of a library can replace previous ones, and still successfully link with the rest of the application, is not all that's needed for achieving the cluelessness goal. Remember what I mean by cluelessness: the ability to assemble applications from modular pieces, while knowing just as little about the individual pieces as possible. If we have binary compatibility, the system is guaranteed to link, but linking doesn't guarantee that the system actually works. Binary compatibility is just the initial prerequisite for this more important kind of compatibility.

The goal of clueless assembly and upgrading of a component-based system is to enable distributed development. Independent groups of programmers must be able to compile their applications at various times and against different versions of libraries, and still allow workable combinations of the resulting binaries to be deployed to their end users. For that purpose, it isn't enough to make things link together. Of course, linking is a necessary condition, but the next additional level is to make the pieces work in such a way that they do what they are supposed to do. This can be called *functional compatibility*.

It's simple to define functional compatibility. As discussed previously, a new version of a library is source compatible with a previous version if any code that can be compiled against the previous version can also be compiled with the new version. It is binary compatible if every application that could be linked, can still be linked. A library is functionally compatible if a program executed against the new version always produces the same results as against the previous one. This is a simple definition, but with terrifying implications.

Imagine that you know how your library should behave and that there is an excellent specification, perfect documentation, and other good descriptions of the expected behavior. Of course, this is just a fantasy. There is never something like excellent documentation. In reality, documentation is always out of date and usually describes just a piece of the whole real estate. But let's suppose that someone did the ideal analysis and knows exactly how the application is supposed to look. For example, it could look like Figure 4-1.

Figure 4-1. *What we think our application looks like*

However, as a known truth of software development, you have to remind yourself that in every application there is at least one bug. But what does that mean? A bug is a violation of expected behavior. So in fact, even though people might believe that the application's behavior matches Figure 4-1, the actual functionality will be different in some way from the expected state. In certain respects, the code doesn't fully implement the expectations, and in others, it does more than was expected. The situation can be visualized better in Figure 4-2.

Figure 4-2. *How it really looks*

The problems are hidden in the deltas! Imagine that the picture describes the expected and actual behavior of a library. There is a clear specification and an implementation that sometimes doesn't do what it should. Sometimes it does more. Programmers who code against that library are unlikely to read the specification. In practice, almost nobody actually reads the specification unless they are completely stuck. Until then, they use the "try and see" approach. For example, they write some code, try it, and if it works they're done. But, of course, they observe the behavior of the implementation and not the specification. In this way they might end up relying on behavior that is either unspecified or contradicts the specification. Obviously, both these situations are dangerous for the smooth coexistence of future versions of the library and applications that are using it. When you release the new version of the library, with a few bug fixes and maybe also a few new features, the actual behavior shifts, as in Figure 4-3.

Figure 4-3. *Look of the application in the next version*

Again, implementation diverges from expectation. Moreover, it diverges in a different way than the previous version. Such a shift is likely to happen with each new version. The actual behavior of the library will change its shape like an amoeba changes its shape. As a result, certain usages of the library might no longer work, and the main goal of creating a compatible API is compromised. The API no longer supports communication between distributed teams, with distributed release schedules, allowing various versions to work together.

PROMISING THE UNKNOWN

My NetBeans experience tells me that people more easily accept source and binary compatibility than functional compatibility. There might be multiple reasons for this, but I'll mention the one I feel is the main cause.

When exposing an API that can influence source or binary compatibility, you have to perform some action. For example, to create a class, you make it public and add a public method. Although some people object that not all their public classes are part of the API, it's relatively easy to convince them that they are. In the case of functional compatibility, you don't need to expose anything. The behavior just "happens."

As the amoeba model shows, the actual behavior always differs from our expectations. Misbehavior is always present, though not because of any conscious actions. Unfortunately, consumers of the API have no way of distinguishing intended behavior from coincidence. The main problem arises when external developers write code against the original version of the library and start to rely on a functionality that is beyond the specification but works, and can therefore be used successfully to get the job done. In the next version of the library, this might stop working and the *functional compatibility* comes to an abrupt end. Who is to blame?

Any good shopkeeper knows that blaming customers is not a winning strategy. Similarly, if the user of an API uses it incorrectly and that usage fails in the next version of the API, the blame is likely to fall on the owner of the API, especially if the API is supposed to be successfully and widely used.

Accepting this is difficult. Nobody likes to sign blank checks with the promise that every behavior of the current version is part of the API. Nor do you want to swear an oath that every misbehavior falls under the contract of functional compatibility. Doing so feels unnatural. However, if the art of building huge systems using cluelessness is to become widely accepted, this is simply the attitude you have to adopt.

API designers need to become responsible for the entire amoeba, not just the parts they envisioned as part of the specification.

It's tough to be responsible for your own actions. So, a primary goal for the API designer is to minimize the amoeba effect by bringing the behavior of the API as close to the specification as possible. This isn't an easy task. It requires a clear understanding of what an API is supposed to do, having good techniques to express that in the actual programming language, and anticipating how users of the API will use it (and how they will abuse it). The next sections outline the steps to achieve this and show you how to minimize the amoeba effect.

The Importance of Being Use Case Oriented

Be aware that if an API is widely used, it is unlikely that you will be able to know all its clients. For example, the writers of the Linux kernel cannot know all the motivations, goals, and ideas of everyone around the world trying to use `ioctl` calls to get something from the kernel. The only option they have is to anticipate and work with a vision of the user tasks when designing the kernel interfaces. Also, people who develop Java and its core libraries are unlikely to know all its users and the ways they use them. Still, these API writers, as well as any other API writer wishing to make successful and widely adopted APIs, need to attain a vision of the API user to understand what should be done with the API libraries, why, and how to do it.

Because you cannot speak to unknown clients, there are only two solutions: either find your users and do a usability study, or be *use case oriented*. Work with use cases—that is, visions of the API user's action—and then optimize specifically for these. Getting responses from users via a usability study is good and can verify that your expectations about the use cases are correct. Anyway, the starting point for any design should be an analysis of *the why, the what, and the how.*

ERRORLESS API WITHOUT REAL USERS

I've heard some people express a concern that it is hard to imagine a perfect API, or at least an API without errors, designed artificially by a designer without interactions and comments gathered from real users. It's true that the ultimate measure of success of any API is the satisfaction of its users. Users are usually satisfied when they can do what they need to and do it easily.

This is just like any other chicken and egg problem. You won't have users without an API, and to create a good API, you need to listen to their comments and include them in the API design. You might think that this situation has no satisfactory solution. However, we need a solution, because we face this situation all the time. In fact, whenever you design any kind of system, you need to deliver the first version. This version cannot be based on comments of real users, as there are none yet. What can be done about that? You need to imagine your users—you need to think up and estimate what they are likely to do. You need to imagine their use cases.

Indeed, these use cases are only artificial. They might be far from the reality and differ quite a lot from the real requirements that you receive as soon as those real users of your API appear. From this point of view, the first version can never be perfect. However, it can still be errorless. An error in the API design is not because some API is incomplete. That is common— new requirements are being gathered all over the lifetime of any system—but the API cannot be extended in subsequent revisions to accommodate them. You can achieve this even without breaking the code written by early users of the first versions of the API, as you'll learn throughout this book.

A use case is a description of the intended usage of the API, showing the problem that a potential user can have, without concrete solutions. Getting a set of potential problems as close as possible to the actual list of problems that people are likely to have is an excellent initial step to creating a genuinely useful solution, which in our case is the API. Let's look at an example of a use case from the NetBeans database explorer API provided as part of NetBeans, showing how to register JDBC drivers:

> *An external module can register JDBC drivers. A typical example is a module that provides integration with a database server. In this case, the module contains the JDBC driver for that database server and uses the Database Explorer API to add it to the Database Explorer. Another client of this API could be a module providing integration with a J2EE application server. Sometimes a J2EE application server bundles a database server for improving the out-of-the-box experience. When the server is registered in the IDE, the JDBC drivers for the bundled database server are added to the Database Explorer.*

Based on a use case such as this, you should start to think about ways of allowing this to happen in the API. Let's call such a description of the actual steps that need to be done in the API a *scenario*. A scenario is in fact an answer to the question stated by the use case. The use case asks, "How do I do this?" and the scenario answers, "Well, you need to do this and that, and then you are done." As an example, let's see the answer to the use case for registering the JDBC driver:

> *The drivers are registered by making calls on JDBCDriverManager or by registering an XML file which describes the driver in the module layer. The XML file is described by the JDBC Driver DTD. An example of a registration file describing the JDBC driver for PostgreSQL follows:*

```
<!DOCTYPE driver PUBLIC
    '-//NetBeans//DTD JDBC Driver 1.0//EN'
   'http://www.netbeans.org/dtds/jdbc-driver-1_0.dtd'
>
```

```
<driver>
<name value='postgresql-7'/>
 <display-name value='PostgreSQL (v7.0 and later)'/>
 <class value='org.postgresql.Driver'/>
 <urls>
   <url value='file:/folder1/folder2/drivers/pg74.1jdbc3.jar'/>
 </urls>
</driver>
```

This file should be registered in the Databases/JDBCDrivers folder of the module layer. To address a bundled JAR inside the IDE the nbinst protocol can be used in the URLs: nbinst:/modules/ext/bundled-driver.jar.

The scenario links the abstract use case with its actual realization in the API. It describes which classes or interfaces you need to implement and where and how to put the declarative files to register them. Also, it provides links to deeper, more detailed APIs: the Javadoc of JDBCDriverManager and the Document Type Definition (DTD) for JDBC Driver. The idea behind this is that users of the API can quickly discover if they are interested in the use case, just by reading its abstract introduction. If so, you can get a basic idea of what needs to be done from the example described in the scenario. If that is not enough, the user knows where the ultimate source of documentation is found: in the Javadoc, DTDs, or sometimes also in the sources themselves.

The NetBeans documentation is structured in such a top-down way, and we believe that this organization helps our users to better navigate and find the information they need. However, we use the "use case," "scenario," and "Javadoc" separation for our internal purposes as well, because it helps us to evaluate whether the API is good.

The amoeba model shown earlier talks about the "differences" between the specification and actual implementation as the source of the most important problems in the maintenance of the APIs. That is why it's reasonable to fight hard to make the differences as small as possible. However, to let this happen you need at least an adequate specification; otherwise there is nothing to measure the difference against.

Once upon a time, during the development of the NetBeans APIs, the only up-to-date specification we had was in the head of the programmer writing the code and the Javadoc. There was no way to check whether the result of the work was good or not. We couldn't establish whether it satisfied what it should. We didn't know if it overreached its aims. In other words, we couldn't tell if the actual shape of the amoeba matched expectations. The only person capable of making such measurements was the actual author of the specification. However, the author was usually too emotionally attached to the implementation to do it independently. Of course, if the author was a good designer, everything would be done right. If you have skilled persons of this kind, then you should trust them. However, remember that "the first version is never perfect." On top of that, if your guru moves away from your project, everyone else, regardless how skilled, will just inherit an unmaintainable mess. A library without enough documentation, missing high-level views, might be a work of genius in every way. However, it is potentially very fragile: any small effort to change its behavior will either do nothing or will push the whole amoeba completely out of shape. The new shape might mean that everything that used to work now fails.

Certainly, people work this way and are able to produce nice results. However, this is a better model for artists than engineers. And, like it or not, sustainable software engineering requires a different, more quantifiable precision than art typically does. When the NetBeans team finally realized this and began insisting more consistently on "use cases," "scenarios," and "Javadoc" separation, we didn't need to work long to see the results. Our APIs now start with higher-level views and they can be evaluated by more reviewers in addition to the writer of the API. Now that we have better, more thoughtful, and more thorough documentation, our APIs are also more maintainable. All this is because to a far greater extent, we now understand the motivations behind our libraries.

API Reviews

NetBeans went through various levels of API development. Originally, the APIs were developed by one dedicated architect. Then we discovered that I was becoming a bottleneck, slowing the progress of the whole team. We switched the style and had a group of people with a benevolent dictator. Now the whole team develops APIs. Though each of these states has unbeatable support in software development theory, none is ideal.

It used to be thought that design cannot be done by committee—that it needs one architect to decide things. Although that can simplify things, it only does so to a certain degree. It definitely cannot scale. However, even before the scalability limits, the pressure on the lead architect is hard. His responsibility is to do the design, maintain the APIs, or at least properly communicate how the APIs should be, and this takes time and has its limits.

As the one who played that role for NetBeans in the first few years, I can confirm that it did not scale. As the team grew, it was harder and harder to satisfy all its requirements. The solution was to select the most skilled people and let them design the APIs they needed themselves. However, this caused a shortfall in consistency, as everyone ended up doing the API in their own personal style. This was not good for API quality.

The NetBeans team has recognized that the API exists primarily for communication with users. Also, we recognize that each good design must have general motivation. That's why our current situation is a dedicated and open one, consisting of a group of people wanting to perform reviews, together with a lot of API writers. In fact, given the range of objects that can be considered to be part of an API, every developer is also, in fact, an API writer.

Whenever there is a need to change an API, anyone can submit a request for a change. Others then review it before integration, to make sure it has all the necessary attributes of being a good API. For example, we check to make sure that the "Rules for Successful API Design" are satisfied:

- *Use case–driven API design*: The motivation is stated on an abstract general level mapping the general design decisions against actual scenarios and the final realization of the API, for example via Javadoc.

- *Consistent API design*: The APIs produced by individual developers must match the general "good practices" shared by the whole team. An interface that is predictable serves better than one that is locally optimal but inconsistent across the whole set.

- *Simple and clean API design*: Simple and common tasks should be easy. If the use case–driven design is used, you can check whether naturally important use cases are satisfied by easy-to-implement scenarios.

- *Less is more*: Only the required functionality, as described in use cases, should be exposed. This prevents the deltas between the amoeba model's expectations and reality.

- *Evolution ready*: The library must be maintainable in the future. When new require-ments appear or the original maintainer leaves, the future of an API shouldn't become compromised.

A focused, small team can check these aspects of API design. The good news is that the team doesn't need to be expert in the area the API covers. As the questions are topic-neutral and more concerned with the general aspects of the API, anyone can measure them. So, Net-Beans currently does design by committee, but we can still achieve consistency and scalability through our large team. Lead reviewers can never stop to explain why and what to do, but the tasks are distributed and the API design is open to everyone. Join us at http://openide.netbeans.org/tutorial/reviews.

Life Cycle of an API

I've already mentioned a few times that the process of making APIs is about *communication*. There are people who consume the APIs and people who write them, and either side can initi-ate communication.

Possibly, people write code and then others discover its worth and want to plug into it. In this case, the API starts in a *spontaneous way*. Someone develops a feature; someone else finds it useful and starts to use it. Later they find out about each other, share their experiences, and likely find that the feature's original design isn't generic enough or that it was never intended to be treated as an API. To evolve it toward being an API, they discuss changes to improve the feature. After a few iterations it can become a useful and stable contract.

CONTRIBUTE, DO NOT HACK!

Common will to cooperate is a prerequisite of this style of API development and contributes to each devel-oper's success. At a minimum, new API users wishing to contribute should pass along information to the original developer on their particular use of some API functionality. Without this, the status of the API is unlikely to change. Its usage will continue to be more of a hack than a proper usage of the API.

On the other hand, the API's provider needs to be ready for such requests and should know how to answer. It's useless to say, for example, "Do not use this, it is not an API!" without giving an alternative. Instead, both sides should find a way to cooperate and maintain the API together. A common concern is that such main-tenance is costly. However, as discussed in the section "Minimizing Maintenance Cost" in Chapter 14, this need not be the case.

On the other hand, some API designers do want to reach their readers without actually being asked to write or provide an API. This kind of API development looks more like being created *by design, by vision*. In this scenario, there is a known or at least expected need for a contract between two components in the system. The requirements are collected, the prob-lem area investigated, the use cases understood, and then someone designs and writes the API. Now others can use it in the real world. Now they can comment, file bugs, and advise enhancements. All these comments help the API to evolve into a state where it is a useful and stable contract.

LONG-TERM INVESTMENT

APIs are needed. Without them, it is not possible to assemble applications cluelessly. However, you need to be aware that just creating an API might not automatically lead to its widespread use.

For instance, we had a need for a command-line API in NetBeans. At the least, we wanted it to support --open file name arguments sent to the NetBeans executable for opening the file in the editor. Due to NetBeans' modular nature, this cannot be coded in one place inside a single component. The module that knows about the command line is supposed to know nothing about files. The module that understands files was not able to access the command-line parameters. For several releases we had a private, undocumented API for connecting these two modules and handling the file open request appropriately. However, for the NetBeans IDE 6.0, I prepared a rewrite that created an official API that everyone could use.

No other module in NetBeans 6.0 IDE currently uses the command-line parsing API. Does that mean it was pointless to create the API? I don't think so. Now that it is properly documented, I can already see questions on mailing lists about its usage. That means people are starting to discover it and are considering its usage. Its existence increases the viability of the NetBeans Platform and might attract new developers. However, it will take time before it will be widely adopted. The APIs created for public use—that is without a requestor who would use them immediately—are generally a long-term investment.

Despite these cases starting differently, they share the same attributes: both need time for feedback and evaluation before the API can be said to work. Not every effort ends its life as a stable API: sometimes the chosen way might lead nowhere. In such cases, it is better to abandon the work. Sometimes it might be found that the sides of the contract don't need a *real quality* conversation. In that case, they can just chat. If their negotiations don't work during the next release, they are close enough to each other to find a new way to talk to each other easily.

All this is possible. However, as the problem lies in the communication between developers, it's important to express yourself clearly. If you create an API and it is not yet fully "baked," there should be a clear warning saying, "Hey, this is not ready yet; try it, but be careful." On the other side of the spectrum is the proud announcement, "Here is the most brilliant API that I've ever created! Use it! I guarantee you full support for your whole lifetime!" This can win the hearts of your API users, but the most important thing is to be clear and explicit about the state of your API.

For example, the Linux kernel and its external interfaces use the dot followed by an even number to label stable versions, and the dot followed by an odd number to mark development versions. So 2.0, 2.2, 2.4, and 2.6 are stable releases, while 2.1, 2.3, and 2.5 are used to denote those under development. This clearly establishes an expectation, and users select the release that suits their taste: either living dangerously on the edge of the new technology or having a stable release, but without some of the new features and improvements.

A transparent way of communicating with users of your library about a lack of stability is to mark your release as 0.x. It is commonly understood that something that has not reached version 1.0 is still under development and that it will probably change. Whatever style you choose, the most important thing is to make sure that users of the API understand it and its implications.

Here is a small attempt at explaining the NetBeans API's stability rules. One of the complications that NetBeans—and probably also any other bigger project—has to face is that our APIs are not one big piece, but more like a set of relatively independent sets of APIs, each in a different state of evolution. Although some of our APIs would still like to fall into the 0.*x* category, other APIs are already grown up and we have no fear of committing them to the highest levels of stability.

To communicate clearly what stage an API is in, whether it is still evolving or whether it is stable and ready to use, the NetBeans team decided to use a system of stability classifications for APIs. The aim is to give API authors a way to express their intention with a particular library, and give the users of the API the information needed to decide if they want to rely on a particular API or wait till it becomes more mature. To do that, NetBeans annotates each of its APIs using one of the following categories:

- *Private* is a category for features that are accessible but are not intended for use outside of their modules and libraries. What kind of features belong to the *private* category? I have discussed what an API can consist of: environment properties, files that a code reads, and so on. In many cases code and even API libraries read properties and files that aren't intended for public communication. An example can be properties that turn on logging, or files used as caches. The content of these external factors can influence the behavior of the libraries, but it is unreliable to depend on them. They might work in an existing version, but they are subject to change in each release; depending on them is risky and should be avoided. API review before change is not necessary, but is recommended as a way to ensure that the feature is properly hidden and documented as private, and also as a way to ensure that there is no better way to achieve similar behavior.

- The *friend* API is designed to be used by other parts of the system, but only by a restricted subset. This is often needed, as it is unlikely in a large system that a component could work on its own, without dependencies on any other part. NetBeans requires a "signing agreement" between the producer and consumer of an API, such that they agree on the contract and agree that it can be changed incompatibly. Such a "written agreement" can mean anything that the involved parties agree to. In NetBeans, we have a way to enforce this by allowing each module to specify a list of "friend" modules that can access its API, enforced during runtime. This encourages a conscious decision to make an API available to just a limited set of "testers." Doing so makes sense only if there is a close personal relationship between the producers and users of the API, because often the sources and binary compatibility might be compromised if the API is changed in such a way as to require recompilation. That is why NetBeans encourages this kind of API relationship just for *modules produced by the same team* and *built at the same time*. Because the list of clients of the API is known and they agree to adapt to changes, a friend contract can change in every release.

- *Under development* denotes an incomplete contract expected to become a stable API. This category is the NetBeans version of Linux 2.3.*x*, 2.5.*x* annotations for unstable development releases or the 0.*x* releases of many libraries. Such an API is available to any client. However, incompatible changes might appear between releases, though they should be rare. Reasons for incompatible changes should be justified, such as unsolvable performance problems or a completely wrong design. In no way should we polish the look with "cosmetics" but improve nothing else. Users of the API are advised to subscribe to a proper mailing list, where all changes should be announced via proper API review before the actual change is integrated. The Javadocs for APIs with this stability level should be published daily for every build of the development version.

- The *stable* category is used for interfaces that have reached production quality and are ready for public usage. Clients can rely on such APIs without fearing incompatibility when a new version is released. This is similar to the stable kernel versions (2.4.*x*, 2.6.*x*) or libraries that announce they are 1.0 and later versions. Once such an API is released in a product, it should be maintained compatibly until it is deprecated and properly "end of lifed." Stable contracts should preserve the investment of their clients, and their evolution should be guided from this point of view. All changes have to be announced and discussed via a proper API review before they become part of the code base. The Javadocs for stable APIs are published daily for the development version and they are also published for each release of the NetBeans IDE.

- *Official* APIs are *stable* and are also packaged into one of NetBeans' official namespaces: `org.netbeans.api`, `org.netbeans.spi`, or `org.openide`. By packaging a contract into this package and making it part of a release, we notify others that the contract is stable with all the related consequences. The goal is to give users a simple way to recognize what is a stable contract and what is not. By seeing a class in one of the official package namespaces, you can be sure that it represents a stable contract.

- *Third-party* interfaces are provided by other parties that don't follow the NetBeans rules and thus are hard to classify. Try not to expose such interfaces as part of your own contracts, as discussed in the section "Beware of Using Other APIs" in Chapter 10.

- *Standard* is similar to the *third party* classification. Also, someone outside NetBeans provided it; however, that person is expected to evolve the interface in a compatible way, such as is the case with Java Community Process and their specification requests. The standard is not expected to change frequently or incompatibly.

- *Deprecated* is the final category. After some time, nearly every API, regardless of what state it is in, becomes obsolete. Usually newer, better support for the same task has been developed, replacing the old API. In such cases, mark the old API *deprecated*. A previously stable API that changed its stability to *deprecated* should be supported for a reasonable amount of time, such as the span of a release, to communicate to users that they should migrate from it to the new replacement. After that time, the API can be removed from the product, while trying to preserve it for old clients by making it available in alternative ways, such as in an available but not turned on library, or in a library that can be downloaded if need be from the online NetBeans module registry.

At the beginning of this chapter I discussed two different models of API development. Developing an API *spontaneously* means, in light of the preceding API categories, to introduce a *private* or *friend* API. When someone else discovers it and finds it useful, it evolves into a *stable* contract. On the other hand, an API developed by design is more likely to begin its life with an *under development* status and after a bit of work, preferably at the time of first release, change to *stable* status with all the promises and guarantees associated with that.

Incremental Improvements

I've mentioned many times that the first version will not be perfect. In fact, no version will ever be perfect. At any point, something will no longer be accurate or will no longer match the previous scenarios. There are two extreme styles of responding to change: either by incremental evolution or by enacting a small big bang.

An incremental change is, for example, the addition of a new method or class, a new element into an XML DTD, or a new property that influences the functionality of the library. A new API then appears, although the previously available API continues to work.

On the other hand, a *big bang* usually describes an action that completely revamps the existing API and creates a new version. Obviously, clients using the previous version are unlikely to switch easily to the new version. They need to decide which version to use. A single component in the system can only work with one version; it is impossible to work with both versions at once. To use the new version, you have to do a painful and big rewrite.

However, seen from an optimist's perspective, it is "just" a rewrite of a single module. A much more complicated situation might evolve when the two versions—before big bang and after big bang—cannot coexist. Then all the components in the system might either use the old or the new, but no mixture is allowed. This magnifies the migration problem, as all existing users of the API need to migrate to the new version at the same time. This huge reorganization project needs to be well coordinated. This is challenging, but possible. However, clearly it goes completely against the spirit of distributed development.

The problem with an incremental improvement is that it is a fallacy to believe that the clients of the previous version of the API will continue to work because the changes are "just minor." Every change is potentially dangerous, as it can introduce one or more incompatibilities. Every incompatibility, even one that seems minor, can have severe effects on the ability of clients of the API to cooperate with the API. In terms of the amoeba model, you need to start with as close a match between the specification and the reality as possible. Only then can you reliably promise that the "minor" incremental changes will cause no harm.

The big bang is realistic with respect to backward compatibility, and clearly states that the users of the library, when migrating to a new version, need to spend time on adapting their code to the new API. At least this is an honest position. However, it is problematic on several levels. First of all, it is easy to switch to a new version of the library if you don't need to do anything differently. However, if you have to invest time to rewrite an implementation completely, the reason to switch has to be genuinely compelling. If there are no compelling reasons to switch, users will simply stay with the older version. Remember that the toughest problem of every project is scheduling the required set of features. Nobody is interested in spending time upgrading to a new version of a library if there are more important things to do.

This type of attitude toward API clients doesn't create the most cooperative environment. However, there are even worse levels of noncooperation. It is the *all or nothing switch*. Sometimes it is acceptable to perform a big bang if the clients can migrate one by one to a new version. However, the all or nothing attitude makes this impossible and says, "Either everyone stays and uses the older version or everyone immediately starts to use the new version." Such a statement is difficult to enforce among distributed groups doing distributed development, as described at the beginning of this book. Making frequent big bang changes, and also requiring frequent all or nothing switches, is the best way to inform API clients that they need to find alternatives.

An example of an incremental update would be the evolution of the JDK libraries. Packages, classes, and methods are added in a newer version, but in a style that more or less guarantees that the previous clients of the APIs will continue to work in the newer version. As a result, you can run on newer versions of the JDK while still having code compiled against older versions of the libraries. This is a win-win situation.

An example of the big bang style of evolution can also be identified in the JDK. The language features in Java 5 force clients to make an important decision: either don't use generics and run on the runtime of Java 1.4, or use them and also switch the runtime. The speed of adoption of the new Java 5 language features proves that this is a tough decision to make. Often it is delayed because there are more important things to do than to switch to a "nicer language," especially if the application already works.

An example of the all or nothing dilemma is the switch from the Linux 2.4 to 2.6 kernel. These two kernels are not fully compatible, so applications need to be adapted to work with them. Moreover, it is impossible to run both versions of the kernel at the same time. That would let you use the 2.6 version with newer applications while older ones continue with the 2.4 version. All applications in one distribution had to be adopted during one release, which was not an easy task. Fortunately, the kernel layer is not that big, and incremental, phase-by-phase adoption was possible. At least some distributions managed to make almost all applications ready to run on both versions of the kernel at once.

THE ENTROPY OF SOFTWARE

One other important aspect is associated with big bang changes, which is the momentum of software development. My NetBeans colleague Tim Boudreau calls it the *entropy of software*, and invented the "funny faces model" that describes it. In contrast to the amoeba model, which sees the situation from a global, objective point of view, this model describes how the state of a software project looks from the point of view of its maintainers.

The first version of every software project is nice. It starts from scratch, building everything from zero. As there is nothing in "zero," there are no inherited problems either. The first version always builds in a bug-free state. Of course, the developers doing the coding do their best. That means that looking with their own eyes, the result is perfect: beautiful, well designed, and organized, just like Figure 4-4. The application is split into modules organized into a nice star-like structure: the one in the middle provides all the APIs, while the others use it for mutual communication. The design, dependencies, and everything else are so nice and clean!

Figure 4-4. *The first version is always nice.*

As soon as the first version is released, bugs start to be discovered and reported. They need to be fixed. Immediately a much more difficult starting position is created for the second version. The second version builds on something that is known to be buggy. Moreover, as is usual in most software projects, there is not enough time to do things properly. As a result, the changes to the system are no longer as nice and clean as in the case of the older version. As shown in Figure 4-5, people introduce shortcuts, use libraries other than the official API, and so on.

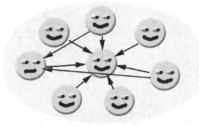

Figure 4-5. *Happiness does not last long.*

This increase of entropy continues in subsequent releases (see Figure 4-6). Code becomes harder to maintain. Developers maintaining it complain all the time, especially if they inherit the code and the original creator has vanished.

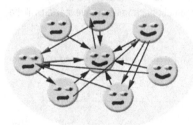

Figure 4-6. *Entropy increases.*

At some point, the project reaches a stage where developers just say, "Please don't touch it!" (as shown in Figure 4-7). The code is so messy that any change causes a regression somewhere else. The problem might get so huge that it becomes apparent even to management that something is wrong, and they might approve the development of a complete big bang rewrite.

Figure 4-7. *Oops, do not touch this!*

More than likely, the new version will take more time than originally promised. It might not even have all the features of the previous one. However, it is nice and clean (as shown in Figure 4-8)! That's obvious, because you started it from scratch. There is no reason for it to contain design flaws. It is as beautiful as the first version we used to have. And, now, we are finally where we wanted to be . . .

Figure 4-8. *A rewrite is always nice.*

Unless . . . what if we're not? In fact, the same entropy that undid our first version is likely to apply to our rewrite as well, as shown in Figure 4-9. Once again, the code will become messy, will need to be maintained, hacks will be introduced, and slowly the first version's decline will be repeated. As a result, the big bang change that was supposed to improve everything forever doesn't deliver on this promise at all. Although it was a lot of pain to implement and finish the major rewrite, we are almost back to where we started. All the pain of the switch was useless.

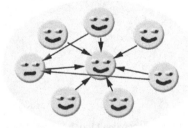

Figure 4-9. *Entropy strikes back.*

The common problem with big bang changes is that we often expect to get better results, although we end up doing things afterward in the same way as before. There is no reason why this should work. If you need a better result, you need to change the way you develop. Maybe you need to change your coding style. Possibly, the problem lies in your design and testing practices. Only if you change the way you work can you expect better results. Only then can the big bang rewrite be successful. However, if you can change your working style, you can also likely improve your software project, even without undergoing a major rewrite. True, you can hardly make it slick and elegant unless you're working on the first version. However, as discussed in the section "Beauty, Truth, and Elegance" in Chapter 1, beauty is not the most important quality of software engineering. More than that, we need the reliability of its components and the responsibility of its designers. Only then can we increase our cluelessness when assembling our applications.

HOW MANY PEOPLE HAVE TO DIE?

I grew up in the former communist bloc as a "young pioneer." This was an organization for youth, similar to the Hitlerjugend in Nazi Germany. I look at that period of my life with ironic bitterness, especially when I see that the illusions common to us back then are still common today.

One of the most profound illusions was the vision of "making the world a better place." Though the goal is laudable, the road taken is often unsound. Communism, as well as Nazism, started with identifying those responsible for the poor state of the world and claiming that all the evil in the world would disappear if we got rid of those people. Communism identified those who owned factories, farms, banks; Nazism identified Jews, among others. These categories were then scheduled for elimination—either physical or at least professional. The world was then supposed to be better. Needless to say, even 40 years later, in the case of Communism, the world is no better than before.

As a result, I always have to ask, "How many people have to die?" whenever I hear someone proposing to make the world a better place. If the answer is greater than zero, the idea is invalidated. If implemented, there will be victims, but the world will not improve at the end of it all. Making something better doesn't happen just by killing someone. It requires hard work, and likely hard work by ourselves, not others. In my opinion, the only thing that has verifiably made the world a better place is hard work, such as Churchill's promise of "blood, sweat, and tears" that helped England win the war.

This is the underlying reason why I don't like big bang changes in API design. They always pretend to save the world. However, most of all they hurt people. All the users of an API are immediately punished for using the API. Only then, usually much later, while the project continues slipping, can you see the benefits that might make the world a better place. Sometimes they do—however, only if library developers also change their attitude and start to develop the API more responsibly. If not, the arrival of a better world is delayed. At least, until the next big bang . . .

In conclusion, get ready for incremental changes! They will be needed and they are typically the least harmful, especially when compared to big bang rewrites. If they are not possible because the API is in terrible shape, justifying a big bang change can only be predicated on a fundamental change in the style of development. This book mostly talks about proper API design practices for incremental modification. If we touch on the topic of big bang changes, we mostly stress the coexistence of multiple different "big" versions together. Only this style can guarantee that the API becomes better, while minimizing the suffering of the API's clients.

PART 2

■ ■ ■

Practical Design

We've dealt with enough theory for the moment. It's time to jump straight into the real world! Without further ado, let's enter the world of practical design.

The previous part discussed the motivation and goals of API design. Some readers might have been bored because they didn't learn anything new or controversial. Nonetheless, the general introduction to API design theory was needed, because many misunderstandings can arise when people apply different meanings to the same terms.

The theoretical sections might not have been perfect. However, they at least sought to outline the goals of API design and to provide a rational approach to measuring an API's quality. Now the time has come to apply the theory to some practical examples. We'll discuss how our theoretical basis can be reflected in Java.

YOU NEED REAL SOURCES!

The code examples in this book are real. They are views of parts of the sources that actually exist. You can compile, modify, execute, and debug them. In selecting samples, I've tried to find the right balance between cohesiveness and readability. It should be possible to read and understand the code snippets within this book without needing to access the sources themselves. However, nothing can replace the real experience. Whenever you see an interesting example, you can download the sources at http://source.apidesign.org. This is the book's dedicated page with instructions for accessing and playing with its related code.

This part of the book will likely be less agreeable than the previous part. That's not a problem because, after all, I intend for it to be a bit controversial. However, be sure to take the following suggestions with a grain of salt. Some of them might seem strange and some might seem too complicated. Therefore, use your own judgment and apply them appropriately to your real-life scenarios. All the suggestions here are taken from the experiences of the NetBeans project, from 1997 to the present, so they aren't completely random. Though these might not always have been the best solutions, they all solved our actual problems to a greater or lesser extent.

I've mentioned several times that APIs are about communication. Because communication is usually more successful when people share the same language, it helps if API designers use commonly understood constructs. As the basic design terminology is usually built around design patterns, it's natural to use them as a starting point. Design patterns are well known; several books have been written on the subject. They're widespread and commonly taught in programming courses. So, they're well suited as a basic communication vocabulary between API designers.

A design pattern is a "recurring solution to a software design problem." It should consist of a *common name*, a *description of the problem*, and a *solution and its consequences*. Having all this connected in our heads allows us just to pronounce a name and make the same—or at least a similar—bell ring in every listener's head. Giving a simple name to complex data structures simplifies communication. For example, by calling something a "singleton," you can easily express a lot of different facts, such as the relation between the class, its instance, and its life cycle. You can set up initial expectations. All that just with a single word! That's why a design pattern simplifies the description of the library or API architecture.

Traditional design patterns are mostly targeted to in-house system development. However, that doesn't mean they have no value in the worlds of APIs and distributed software development. Quite the opposite. The API designers need to know them by heart. However, as explained in the Prologue, it's slightly more complicated to design a universe than to build a house. As a result, we need an enhanced version of the design patterns. We need patterns that help us design a "universe."

As a consequence, let's bring *API design patterns* into the picture. These are still design patterns in the sense that they help to simplify the description of an API's architecture. However, they have one additional attribute: an emphasis on evolution. In addition to the pattern's name, problem description, and solution, there is also an "evolution plan": a plan that describes what should happen after the API's first release. I've already mentioned several times that the "first version is never perfect." As such, we need a plan to describe how the solution can be changed and improved while still preserving compatibility for users of the previous versions of the API.

Almost every API will need improvements. As a result, the emphasis on API evolution is extremely important. Having the chance to fix a less than perfect API is a sign of a good and suitable pattern for API design. Knowing the right patterns that support this is your ticket to successful software development in the 21st century. In that light, let's begin our practical API design journey.

CHAPTER 5

■ ■ ■

Do Not Expose More Than You Want

There are many attributes of good API design, and this book will discuss many of them. But let's start with the most trivial advice. This advice is widely known, explained in every good design book, yet so important that it deserves to be repeated all the time: the less you expose, the better.

Some API designers just love helping others and believe they're doing so by putting a lot of helper methods and utility classes in their API. They make every class public. A lot of their classes have members that are either public or protected. These designers believe that one day someone might find their exposed functionality useful. Though there's nothing to be said against altruism, these designers often cause more problems than they solve. Always remember that it's much easier to add a new class or method to an API than to remove it. Furthermore, the more you put into an API, the more you have to maintain in a compatible way. The more that's visible, the less flexibility you have in changing the internals of the implementation. Exposing more than is needed can, in fact, prevent future improvements in the API.

Fundamental dilemmas involve deciding whether something should or shouldn't be part of an API. The answer to that, at least according to the NetBeans project "methodology," is to construct *use cases*. A valid use case is the justification for a class or a method in an API. If there's no use case for a given method or class, or if the use case is slightly suspicious, then it's better to leave that element out of the API. One way of doing so is to make it package private. When a user of the API complains and requests the element to be visible, you can still make it visible. However, don't do so sooner than requested and not without a convincing use case!

THE LESS SKILL, THE MORE VERBOSE THE API

My experience shows that the less skilled an API designer is, the more elements the API exposes. In many cases, this can be attributed to a lack of understanding of use cases. Lack of understanding results in making an existing method or class public whenever some functionality from a library is needed. This style of evolution, where there is no strategy at all, will almost certainly lead to a set of isolated API elements that are randomly glued together. An absence of use cases indicates a lack of strategy and leads to a cluttered result.

Less experienced designers, lacking the wisdom that comes with maintaining an API over several years, often don't realize that everything they leave in an API can get misused. Every method and class exposed by an API will be misused—in other words, used in a different way than intended by its author. Almost every API designer I know has observed this to be true. And almost every API designer has come to the same conclusion: the longer you spend designing an API, the less you are willing to expose.

So, the first piece of advice is to remove everything that can be removed prior to the first release of an API. Realistically, not everything will be removed as a result of this advice. Behind every altruistic will to share there has to be some hidden need—something that drives and motivates the API's design. The API designers feel the need for their work and they are eager to share it. I know that feeling; I've felt it many times. It feels good; however, you need to keep in mind that publishing an API is just first the step. By publishing it, you promise to do much more in the future. You promise to develop the API compatibly, to maintain it properly, and much, much more. In fact, by taking the first step you set a direction and promise that every other step will follow that direction. There's nothing wrong about taking such a step if the API designers feel there's a need to create the API. On the other hand, we need to learn how to prevent promising "directions" when we're just "walking." The simplest and most effective solution is to hide the fact that we're taking steps from our end users.

A Method Is Better Than a Field

The first technique we'll look at for hiding the API is the practice of hiding fields. It's better to use methods—typically getters and setters—to access fields than to expose them directly. This is true because, first, a call to a method can do a lot of additional things, while accessing a field can only read or write the value. When you use getters, you can do lazy initialization, synchronize the access, or compose the value using a computational algorithm. Setters, on the other hand, allow checks for correctness of the assigned value or notify listeners when the change takes place.

The other reason to prefer methods over fields can be found in the JVM specification. You're permitted to move a method from a class to one of its superclasses and still maintain binary compatibility. So, a method initially introduced as `Dimension javax.swing.JComponent.`*`getPreferredSize`*`(Dimension d)` can be deleted in a new version and moved to `Dimension java.awt.Component.`*`getPreferredSize`*`(Dimension d)`, as the `JComponent` is a subclass of `Component`. A change like this really happened in JDK 1.2, and this could be done only because the field was encapsulated by a method. An operation like this isn't allowed for fields. Once a field is defined in a class, it has to stay there forever to maintain binary compatibility, which is another reason to keep fields private.

IT IS NOT SLOWER!

Once I heard a .NET architect confess his need to sacrifice encapsulation for performance. He said that .NET has a data structure with a few fields that were accessed so often that wrapping them with getters and setters caused a significant performance impact on the speed of the application. Well, maybe .NET needs to do that. Bear in mind that Java doesn't need such tricks at all.

In the autumn of 1998, I visited a Sun Microsystems conference in Berlin, where JavaSoft's boss said something like, "Yes, interpreted code can be faster than code that is compiled." At that time I wasn't working for Sun yet, and I also knew how terribly slow Java was. So I laughed, along with the majority of the audience. However, since then I've spent time thinking about those words. In the meantime, the JVM saw significant improvements when Sun released its HotSpot virtual machine. HotSpot first interprets bytecode provided by class files and then monitors the application to find critical pieces of its code and its setup. After some time, it compiles the parts of the application that are executed most frequently. But unlike with static compilation, which precedes linkage, the HotSpot compiler already knows the result of a linkage because the classes are already loaded. So, the HotSpot compiler can optimize the compiled code for the current setup and not for the general scenario as a regular compiler has to do.

As a result, the HotSpot compiler can, for example, inline virtual methods. Anyone who has tried to simulate virtual methods in C knows that this requires at least one access to memory and one indirect jump. The HotSpot compiler can do much better. As it knows the linkage information, it can find out that some virtual method isn't overridden at all, or that, for example, two other classes override it twice. Then it can replace the regular call directly with the method's body. Alternatively, if there is more than one, but less than many, it can replace the memory indirection with a simple switch. This is a lot faster than the plain virtual methods table that static compilation or a programmer trying to simulate this in C has to use.

Though it's true that interpreted code is unlikely to be faster than code that Is complled, If we correct the statement I had heard in Berlin a bit, we can justifiably say, "Dynamically compiled code can be faster than code that is statically compiled," which was likely the point of the talk to begin with. We can, with the help of the HotSpot compiler, see that this statement has turned out to be true.

Remember that the HotSpot virtual machine is capable of inlining method calls, including virtual method calls if the method is being called too often. As a result, frequently used getters and setters have no performance impact, as HotSpot eliminates them. Thus, there is no need to sacrifice API encapsulation for performance in Java.

Never expose fields in an API, except for `public static final` primitive or string constants, `enum` values, or immutable object references. Instead, always use methods to access your fields. If you follow this advice, the next version of the API can alter method content, provide validations and verifications, overload methods to do other wild things, move methods to superclasses, and change the synchronization model.

A Factory Is Better Than a Constructor

You facilitate an API's future evolution when you expose a factory method rather than a constructor. Once a constructor is available in an API, it guarantees not only that an instance assignable to a given class will be created, but also that the instance will be of the *exact class*, because no subclasses are allowed. In addition, a *new instance* will be created every time.

If a factory method is provided instead, you have more flexibility. A factory method is usually a static method that takes the same arguments as the constructor and returns an instance of the same class in which the constructor is defined. The first advantage of factory methods is that you don't need to return the exact class. You can instead return a subclass, which lets you use polymorphism and possibly clean up the code. Second, you can cache instances. Although in the case of a constructor a new instance is created every time, a factory method can cache previously instantiated objects and reuse them to save memory. Third, you can synchronize better when invoking a factory method, unlike with a plain constructor where this is more limited. That's because a factory method can be synchronized as a whole, including potential code before the object creation, the code that creates the instances, as well as the rest of the code that runs after the object is created. This isn't possible in a constructor at all.

We recently found yet another benefit of factory methods as we were rewriting the NetBeans APIs to use generics: factory methods let you "think up" the parameterized type for the returned object, and constructors don't. For example, we've had the following class in the NetBeans APIs for ages:

```java
public final class Template extends Object {
    private final Class type;

    public Template(Class type) { this.type = type; }
    public Class getType() { return type; }


    public Template() { this(Object.class); }
}
```

When we migrated the NetBeans sources to JDK 1.5, it was natural to parameterize the Template class with a type parameter identifying the internal class object. This worked fine . . .

```java
public final class Template<T> extends Object {
    private final Class<T> type;

    public Template(Class<T> type) { this.type = type; }
    public Class<T> getType() { return type; }

    // now what!?
    public Template() { this(Object.class); }
}
```

. . . up until the last constructor. It's supposed to create an instance of Template<Object>, but this cannot be expressed in Java 1.5. The language isn't flexible enough to express this kind of situation. This might be seen as our design mistake. However, when we initially designed this class, we had more pressing things to solve than verifying that it would easily fit into the Java 1.5 generic type system that had not yet been designed. Later, it was too late. The only chance we had was to deprecate the constructor, use an unchecked cast, and tell people to use the other one, with a class parameter. On the other hand, if we had followed the advice of this book—using a factory method instead of exposing the constructor—our situation would have been much better. There would be a create() factory method, and it would be much easier to generify such a method, as the following code is syntactically correct:

```
public final class Template<T> extends Object {
    private final Class<T> type;

    public Template(Class<T> type) { this.type = type; }
    public Class<T> getType() { return type; }

    @Deprecated
    @SuppressWarnings("unchecked")
    public Template() { this((Class<T>)Object.class); }

    public static Template<Object> create() {
        return new Template<Object>(Object.class);
    }
}
```

This example demonstrates that there is much more flexibility when typing methods. That's because methods—including factory methods—aren't constrained by the type of the enclosing class, while constructors are. This is another reason to prefer factory methods over constructors.

Make Everything Final

Often, people don't design with subclassing in mind, but allow it regardless. Unintended and dangerous consequences follow from this, as the number of ways in which the API can be used increases significantly. Take a simple method in a subclassable class such as this:

```
public class Hello {
    public void hello() { System.out.println ("Hello"); }
}
```

This method can cause problems, because external code can call it:

```
public static void sayHello() {
    Hello hello = new Hello();
    hello.hello();
}
```

Meanwhile, you can also override it to do something else:

```
private static class MyHello extends Hello {
    @Override
    public void hello() { System.out.println ("Hi"); }
}
```

It can also be overridden with a call to super:

```
private static class SuperHello extends Hello {
    @Override
    public void hello() {
```

```
        super.hello();
        System.out.println("Hello once again");
    }
}
```

More than likely, a far wider range of choices is presented here than was originally intended. However, the solution is simple: simply make the Hello class final!

When writing an API without wanting to let users subclass its classes, it's better to disallow this behavior. If you don't explicitly disallow it, you can be sure that some of your API users will subclass your API. As the Hello example shows, you'll then need to support at least three different ways of using the methods that your classes expose. For the sake of future evolution, it's better to disallow subclassing. In relation to this, also see Chapter 8.

Again, the simplest solution is to make your class final. Other approaches include nonpublic constructors, which you should use anyway (as explained in the section "A Factory Is Better Than a Constructor"), or making all—or at least most—of your methods final or private.

Of course, this only works for classes. If you decide to use interfaces, you cannot forbid foreign implementations on the level of the virtual machine. You can only ask people in the Javadoc not to do it. The Javadoc isn't a bad channel for communication, but if subclassing isn't prohibited people will always ignore the Javadoc advice and implement the interface anyway. Consequently, unless there are performance implications, it's preferable to prevent the subclassability on the virtual machine level by using final classes.

Do Not Put Setters Where They Do Not Belong

One lesson we learned the hard way after years of NetBeans API development is, "Don't put setter methods in the true API." By "true API," we mean the interfaces that must be implemented to provide something. If setter methods are needed at all—and usually they aren't—they belong only in the convenience base classes.

Let's look at javax.swing.Action as an example that violates this rule. The setEnabled(**boolean**) method doesn't belong in the Action interface. Probably it shouldn't exist at all, but if so, it should be a protected method in AbstractAction, which is a support class to simplify implementation of the Action interface. The boolean isEnabled() method is the API! It's the method that everyone should call. But who is supposed to call setEnabled(**boolean**)? At most only the creator of the action; this is an implementation detail for everyone else. If your action happens to have a global enablement state that a listener normally manipulates by turning it on or off programmatically, setEnabled(**boolean**) is a handy protected final method to have in a base class such as AbstractAction. However, Action.setEnabled is wrong for the following reasons:

- It implies that unknown external clients should call this method. They certainly should not.

- It makes no sense for context-sensitive actions, though the Action API generally is lacking in this area. We tried hard to find some reasonable way to use Swing's actions in this area and we can certainly report a success. However, it's clear that the original Action class design was done by people who didn't have to think about modular design at all.

- It makes no sense to have a `setEnabled` method for an action that is always enabled. Those actions just want to return `true` from `isEnabled` regardless of anything that happens around them.

- It makes no sense to have an action whose enablement is computed in `isEnabled` on demand. If you want to compute the state of your actions just when you are asked to do it, then a setter isn't the right method to use. If you need to implement a "pull" strategy, then you want to provide the result, but not pretend you know anything about the global state of the action. Instead, you want the system to query you for the right state again when the value of `isEnabled` is needed.

This advice isn't meant to discredit every setter in an API. Sometimes they're useful. Sometimes, as in the case of Spring's dependency injections, they're essential. However, often they're redundant. Similar examples of too many setters can be found in other places and they're usually the result of a desire to make the API rich with functionality, which is in fact counterproductive. Maintenance becomes increasingly cumbersome. In addition, as shown in the Action example, the semantics of such an API are hard to grasp. The advice here is simple: beware of unneeded setters in an API.

Allow Access Only from Friend Code

When trying to prevent exposing too much in an API, another useful technique is to give access to certain functionality only to "friend" code. Functionality that falls within this category could include the ability to instantiate a class or to call a certain method.

By default, Java restricts the friends of a class to those classes that are in the same package. If you want to share functionality just among classes in the same package, use the package private modifier in the definition of a constructor, field, or method. These will then remain accessible only to their "friends."

NO MORE "DO NOT CALL THIS METHOD!" METHODS

You're likely to have come across APIs with methods marked in the Javadoc with sentences like, "Do not call me, I am part of the implementation" or "Only for internal use." I've seen such methods so many times that I consider this one of the worst API design antipatterns. Not only do these methods make an API less professional, they distract the reader of the API with unnecessary implementation details that are easy to avoid.

Methods of this kind usually imply that parts of the implementation residing in separate packages need privileged—that is, friend—access to functionality provided by the API package. This is exactly the case for which the *friend accessor* pattern was invented.

Some claim that the friend accessor pattern is too complicated and that they don't want complicated code in their API. Nothing is further from the truth! It's true that the friend accessor pattern in Java is slightly complex to code. However, that remains just an implementation detail, invisible to the external API user. It achieves the cluelessness goal, giving users of your API fewer methods to worry about and a greater opportunity of being cluelessly successful in using your API.

Therefore, please don't include "I am an implementation detail" methods in your APIs!

It might sometimes be useful to extend a set of friends to a wider range of classes. For example, you might want to define two packages, one for the pure API and the other for the implementation. If you take this approach, the following trick might be useful. Imagine there is an Item class, as follows:

```java
public final class Item {
    private int value;
    private ChangeListener listener;

    static {
        Accessor.setDefault(new AccessorImpl());
    }

    /** Only friends can create instances. */
    Item() {
    }

    /** Anyone can change value of the item.
     */
    public void setValue(int newValue) {
        value = newValue;
        ChangeListener l = listener;
        if (l != null) {
            l.stateChanged(new ChangeEvent(this));
        }
    }

    /** Anyone can get the value of the item.
     */
    public int getValue() {
        return value;
    }

    /** Only friends can listen to changes.
     */
    void addChangeListener(ChangeListener l) {
        assert listener == null;
        listener = l;
    }

}
```

This class is part of the API, but cannot be instantiated or listened to outside the friend classes that are in the API package and other packages. In this scenario, you can define an Accessor in the non-API package:

```java
public abstract class Accessor {
    private static volatile Accessor DEFAULT;
    public static Accessor getDefault() {
```

```
        Accessor a = DEFAULT;
        if (a != null) {
            return a;
        }

        try {
            Class.forName(
                Item.class.getName(), true, Item.class.getClassLoader()
            );
        } catch (Exception ex) {
            ex.printStackTrace();
        }

        return DEFAULT;
    }

    public static void setDefault(Accessor accessor) {
        if (DEFAULT != null) {
            throw new IllegalStateException();
        }
        DEFAULT = accessor;
    }

    public Accessor() {
    }

    protected abstract Item newItem();
    protected abstract void addChangeListener(Item item, ChangeListener l);
}
```

This Accessor has abstract methods to access all the "friend" functionality of the Item class, with a static field to get the accessor's instance. The main trick is to implement the Accessor with a nonpublic class in the API package:

```
final class AccessorImpl extends Accessor {
    protected Item newItem() {
        return new Item();
    }

    protected void addChangeListener(Item item, ChangeListener l) {
        item.addChangeListener(l);
    }
}
```

You register the Accessor as the default instance the first time someone touches api.Item. Do this by adding a static initializer to the Item class:

```
static {
    Accessor.setDefault(new AccessorImpl());
}
```

Now the friend code can use the accessor to invoke the hidden functionality from the impl package:

```
Item item = Accessor.getDefault().newItem();
assertNotNull("Some item is really created", item);


Accessor.getDefault().addChangeListener(item, this);
```

SECURE CODE WITH RUNTIME CONTAINERS

A runtime container, such as the one in the NetBeans Platform, can secure your code even further. You can forbid access to the impl package on the class-loading level, by specifying OpenIDE-Modules-Public-Packages: api.**. The Accessor methods need not be protected, as only the module that defines the impl.Accessor can access that class. Access from other modules would then be disallowed on the class-loading level.

Future versions of Java might provide an additional access modifier to allow mutual access among multiple packages compiled together. However, why wait? The new access modifier will likely require changes in the virtual machine, which will likely prevent the code using it from running on older versions of Java, including Java 6. The accessor pattern replaces a special language construct with an intrinsic arrangement of classes, which makes it work on any version of the JVM while achieving almost the same result. I explicitly say "almost," as one thing cannot be directly mapped to this pattern: the new access modifier allows code in a friend package to extend classes in the API package, which others might not even see. However, this kind of limitation is easy to eliminate: instead of using subclasses, use delegation, as suggested in the section "Delegation and Composition" in Chapter 10.

From time to time I refer to this kind of API design pattern as a *teleinterface*, as illustrated in Figure 5-1. Similar to a spaceship in any good sci-fi book, traveling in hyperspace from one open gateway to another, it is invisible and unobservable when outside regular space. The teleinterface pattern allows two distinct parties to communicate so that no one else can observe the interaction, but it's known to exist.

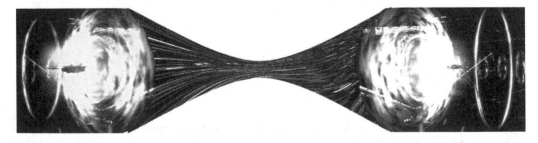

Figure 5-1. *Teleinterface*

The friend accessor is an example of such an API design pattern. Two sides need to communicate with each other, while no external piece of code is able to monitor the interaction. It's carried out in "hyperspace." This is a powerful design metapattern, and this book will introduce several kinds of teleinterfaces.

Give the Creator of an Object More Rights

Not every user of an object should have access to all its functionality. "Some code is more equal than other code." This is an old object-oriented truth embedded in the roots of many object-oriented languages. As a result, C++, Java, and similar languages contain access modifiers that define who should access what. Java offers `public`, `protected`, `package private`, and `private`, which respectively grant access to everyone, to subclasses and code in the same package, only to code in the same package, and only to code in the same class. This is a fine-grained set of controls. Some developers, such as those who come from the Smalltalk world where everything is public, might even complain that this is too complicated and unnecessary. On the other hand, even this set of access modifiers might be seen as limiting. For example, the section "Allow Access Only from Friend Code" shows that there's often a need to give more access rights to "friend packages." This section talks about yet another common case in which one piece of code needs more privileges than another piece of code.

No one with a basic knowledge of Unix—or any other nonpersonal computer system targeted for use by multiple users—should be surprised that certain operations can be performed only by a restricted set of individuals known as system administrators. It's fine to query a database or to publish your own web pages under the $HOME/public_html folder. Typically, everyone is allowed to do that. However, the right to configure the caching policy of your Apache web server, to modify the database, or (imagine how daring!) to touch and change its schema, is usually given only to a selected subset of people. Before performing these kinds of operations, those individuals need to prove to the system that they have the right to perform the operation in question—that is, that they have the appropriate identity. Everyone can try to lay claim to having the appropriate identity. However, without being party to a secret, the false claim is unlikely to succeed. Typical authentication is based on secret name-and-password pairs with roles assigned to each name.

The world of object-oriented systems is similar. Objects travel between various parts of a system, and to ensure certain invariants and the basic consistency of their internal states, it isn't wise to let every piece of code in the system modify and configure each object. In fact, as mentioned before, access modifiers are your best friend. If you don't want something to be visible to external code, don't make that functionality public or protected. However, this turns your code into the "administrator," with everyone else being regular users. This might work in in-house systems. However, when designing APIs this isn't enough, because you don't want your API to be an "administrator." Instead, you want your API to be a library that serves administrators as well as regular users. Let's look at ways you can achieve this.

First of all, let's see what doesn't work. A common attempt at separating the rights of a creator from the API is to create an API interface or class together with a support class that extends it. The support class then provides additional controls, specifically for the creator. All the other methods in the API are then supposed to use the base interface class, while the implementors use the support class to easily implement the contract and also to access additional methods that aren't available for nonprivileged users. This was probably the idea behind `javax.swing.text.Document` and its support pair class `javax.swing.text.AbstractDocument`. It more or less worked, because subclassing `AbstractDocument` is simpler than trying to implement all its methods in the plain `Document` interface. Also, `AbstractDocument` contains methods accessible only to implementors, such as **protected** `writeLock` and `writeUnlock`. This looks reasonable, but it restricts access only to subclasses. So, it's common to find code like the following, which exposes the additional "creator only" methods to all the code in the same package, which is often needed:

```
public class MyDocument extends AbstractDocument {
    public MyDocument() {super(new StringContent());}

    final void writeLockAccess() {
        writeLock();
    }
}
```

It isn't nice to force API users of `AbstractDocument` to duplicate methods such as this one. A better-designed API might eliminate this verbosity. However, as this is just a stylistic issue, it isn't the main problem.

The biggest problem with `AbstractDocument` is that it contains a handful of other useful methods that are of interest to "nonprivileged" API users. These include the publicly accessible `readLock`, `readUnlock` (why use `render` and create an unnecessary `Runnable` anyway?), `getListeners` (why not find out whether I am the first listener, and if not rearrange all listeners so that I am?), or methods such as `replace` that were probably added too late to fit into the original `Document` interface. In short, there are several interesting methods that the clients calling into the `javax.swing.text` API might want to call. What are such users to do? They take an instance of a document and cast it to `AbstractDocument` and call those methods. Where is the security? If it was as easy for a nonadministrator to log in to a server as it is to call a "privileged" method on `AbstractDocument`, every server on the Internet would already have been hacked. That's why this pattern of an API interface with a support class doesn't solve the "privileged" access problem.

NETBEANS FILESYSTEM API

You might well ask how I can claim to know so much about Swing's text document API problems. In fact, to be honest, I don't! I know a lot about the NetBeans FileSystem API, where I made a similar mistake. I then searched the JDK sources for similar patterns, and `AbstractDocument` was a nice and handy anti-example.

The NetBeans FileSystem API introduces the concept of a virtual filesystem. You can build such a filesystem around a plain `java.io.File`. Alternatively, it can wrap access to HTTP or FTP servers, or it can represent completely virtual files that reside only in memory. In each case, the base API interface is `org.openide.filesystems.FileSystem`, which is intended for regular API users. However, because implementing a filesystem isn't easy, we also have a support class that helps implementors, called `org.openide.filesystems.AbstractFileSystem`. This, by chance, used to have several interesting methods not available in the base `FileSystem` interface. Moreover, there was a public `LocalFileSystem` derived from it with additional useful public methods.

Users of that API were supposed to work with plain `FileSystem`, but one day I found to my horror that they weren't doing that! Because the NetBeans IDE works almost solely with plain `java.io.File`, it was quite safe to cast to `LocalFileSystem`, after which some fancy methods could be called on it. These methods were intentionally not available to the public. They were intended to be accessible only to "privileged" users. At the time, I shortsightedly believed that no one else would call them. However, API users are quite inventive, especially when they stick to the cluelessness principle while doing whatever it takes to get their job done quickly.

We needed to prevent people from calling these methods. The first step we took was a little bit of bytecode patching. Our bytecode patching converted these methods to protected while retaining backward binary compatibility. Later, we stopped using `LocalFileSystem` for the representation of local files. We replaced it with a different implementation not derived from `AbstractFileSystem`, which wasn't part of any API. Users had no need to cast to it, as it didn't offer anything worth calling.

A common way of customizing objects in Java is to turn them into JavaBeans and then to use setters and getters. However, this provides no security and no "privileged" role for an object's creator. However, with a surprisingly simple addition, you can turn this setter-based pattern into a nicely working solution supporting the "privileged" mode. All you need to do is add the method **public void** *setReadOnly*() and then modify all setters to work only before the method is called. Then throw an exception; for example, `PropertyVetoException` or `IllegalStateException`. You can find an example of this pattern in `java.security.PermissionCollection`, which allows the collection's creator to add new permissions to it and then make it immutable by calling `setReadOnly`. Every other piece of code that gets hold of such objects later can only read the state of the collection, without the right to modify it. In effect, it is executed in nonprivileged mode. This approach works fine and the only complaint you can have about it is that it isn't elegant. Of course, as discussed in the section "Beauty, Truth, and Elegance" in Chapter 1, software design isn't about beauty. Nevertheless, this solution does have some practical drawbacks. First, it mixes the API for two groups of people. Both privileged as well as regular users need to read the API of the same class, which might be distracting. Second, it introduces a state-based API. The same sequence of method calls might work or might throw an exception, depending on whether the object is still in privileged mode or has already been switched to regular mode. This makes the object's semantics more complicated than necessary. Last but not least, the switch to regular mode can be done just once and definitively. Once an object is switched, there is no privileged code anymore. This might be an unwanted restriction in certain situations. Due to all this, let's continue our investigation of the other available solutions.

There is a member of every class in Java, as well as in other object-oriented languages, that can be called just once by the object's creator. It's the *constructor*. This fact gives us the basis for another straightforward separation for the privileged mode: everything the privileged code can control needs to be passed in when an object is created. Of course, as suggested in the section "A Factory Is Better Than a Constructor," it's better to have a factory method than a constructor, although the principle remains the same. In contrast to the previous "setter-based" solution, this solves the semantic problems, as it isn't stateful. Everything the privileged code can do is injected into the object at the time of its creation. Also, it partially solves the problem of mixed APIs. When users of an API have a reference to an instance of an object, they usually don't read documentation for its constructor, and it isn't offered to them by code completion in modern development environments. Also, factories and constructors are well-understood concepts. This solution is natural because it doesn't invent anything new. In short, this is probably the most appropriate solution.

However, is this solution ready for evolution? What if someone needs to add new methods to the privileged code? In such cases, you need to add a new constructor or factory method that accepts the additional arguments. This is backward binary compatible, but each such addition increases the size of the factory class. But that isn't the problem. The more complicated issue is that potentially the number of arguments in such methods can be significant. Long lists of arguments, especially of the same type, aren't pleasant to fill in. It's easy to make a typo and misplace an argument. This is usually not an issue in the beginning. However, as the API evolves it can get quite complicated. It's desirable to have a solution ready for such situations, such as mixing the factory style with the setter-based approach. Simply write the following:

```java
public static Executor create(Configuration config) {
    return new Fair(config);
}

public static final class Configuration {
    boolean fair;
    int maxWaiters = -1;

    public void setFair(boolean fair) {
        this.fair = fair;
    }
    public void setMaxWaiters(int max) {
        this.maxWaiters = max;
    }
}
```

With this approach you can stop adding new factory methods, and if evolution requires it, add new setters to the Configuration class instead. Adding such methods is safe, as the class is final and the only use for it is as an argument to the create factory method. Its usefulness is restricted outside this scenario, as it intentionally has no public getters. That's why adding new methods to it can only affect the internals of the factory method, which are under the API writer's control. You can therefore extend the internals to handle the additional variations in the input configuration.

Moreover, introducing the Configuration class solves the last outstanding issue—that is, the ability of the privileged code to perform its privileged operation after the nonprivileged code has already accessed the object. This was impossible with the setReadOnly pattern, as well as with the plain factory method. Now, the privileged code can continue to keep a reference to the Configuration instance and call its methods to modify parameters of Executor instances already given to nonprivileged users. Such users' code has no chance to get a reference to the Configuration instance; casting doesn't help because these are two different objects. The Configuration acts like a secret token, which cannot be obtained through an API. So, this solution is completely safe and secure.

MUTEX AND PRIVILEGED ACCESS

We used to face similar issues with the NetBeans APIs. We had our own homemade read/write lock called the Mutex, whose methods took `Runnable` and could execute them in read or write mode. This worked fine. However, we found that in some situations the high number of newly created runnables impacted performance. We considered adding the following typical methods:

```
lock.enterReadAccess();
 try {
  // do the operation
 } finally {
   lock.exitReadAccess();
 }
```

However, we were afraid that this could allow malicious code to forget to release acquired locks, thus breaking the consistency of the whole subsystem coordinated with such a lock. But we were sure that our own code would contain no such bugs, so we decided to use the *privileged creator* pattern.

We kept the original signatures of Mutex that only worked with `Runnable`, but added a `Mutex.Privileged` static inner class that had the `enter` and `exit` methods and supported the more efficient "enter/try/perform/finally/exit" lock access. We added a new constructor to Mutex to take the `Mutex.Privileged` instance:

```
 private static final Mutex.Privileged PRIVILEGED = new Mutex.Privileged();
 public static final Mutex MUTEX = new Mutex(PRIVILEGED);
```

Now, any creator of a public Mutex can create a back door giving its code a faster—but more error prone—access to synchronization, while ensuring that nonprivileged code isn't able to maliciously spoil the consistency of locking.

Although Java doesn't have a special access modifier for the creator of objects, it's possible to create an API that ensures such a contract. There are many solutions, ranging from the simplest and ugliest to the most complex and elegant. The most promising option, in my opinion, is to have two classes: one giving privileged access to the creator and the other providing a public API for common use.

Do Not Expose Deep Hierarchies

Some people argue that object-oriented languages are good because they support code reuse. It's true that certain code patterns are better expressed in object-oriented programming languages than in plain old C. However, that doesn't improve the code's "sharability," because the main problem faced when sharing code is communication. There has to be someone offering something to share and someone else absorbing and reusing it. This isn't going to happen simply by using object-oriented languages. Instead, you need to think about reuse and prepare for it, while bearing in mind that it will never automatically happen simply as a by-product. My advice here is to be careful, and on top of everything else, to be aware of deep hierarchies.

Classic object-oriented programming languages are said to be inspired by nature and its evolution. Everyone knows the example defining a Mammal class with basic methods describing the behavior of every mammal, and various subclasses such as Dog or Cat overriding the methods to do what cats and dogs do differently. This example not only demonstrates what object-oriented languages do best, but it also justifies their whole purpose. By showing how easy it is to describe nature, the object-oriented concept is also elevated to be the right programming technique to describe the real world. Just like physics is better for reasoning about the real world than plain geometry, object-oriented languages are supposed to be more suitable than traditional, procedural ones for coding and capturing real-world concepts.

After maintaining a framework in Java for more than ten years, I don't buy this. It's fine that something (usually a class) reacts to messages (in Java method calls) and that there might be someone who can intercept that message and change its meaning by overriding some of the methods and reacting differently to them. However, honestly, this is nothing other than an intricate switch statement. A method call isn't a direct invocation of some code but rather a switch that chooses from multiple implementations. The switch is based on the list of subclasses and can potentially grow as various developers create more and more subclasses. But it's still a switch. Of course, explaining object-oriented programming as an enhanced switch is much less fancy than presenting it as a technology that helps us model the real world. That's why computer courses are likely to stick with the Mammal example. However, I'll use the switch explanation to reveal an important hidden catch: when writing an API, the size and behavior of the switch is unknown to the writer of the code. This can be seen as an advantage, increasing the number of ways that a piece of code can be reused. However, a few releases later, if you don't know the actual participants in the switch, you can have a nightmare on your hands. Simply allowing an unknown party to participate in your code "switch" can be too open to be maintainable.

So, simply exposing a deep hierarchy of classes is unlikely to improve an API's usability. When writing an API, the term "subclass" shouldn't be used for someone who can "participate in a switch," but for someone who behaves exactly like me, plus adds some additional behavior. True, many would agree that a Human is a subclass (a specialization) of a Mammal. But how much can you use this fact in an API design? Do you really want to claim that a JButton is a specialization of AbstractButton and that it's a specialization of JComponent, which is a specialization of a Container, which is a specialization of a Component? Of course not! The subclassing here is simply an implementation detail. That is, it's a switch statement enabling you to code things in a simple way. However, it has nothing to do with the notion of an API. If it did, it would be normal to use a JButton as a Container. In other words, you could add additional components to it. Even though it might be possible to code in this way, this isn't at all the intended API usage of JButton.

Here we can identify a common API flaw in object-oriented languages. If your implementation can benefit from subclassing another class, don't expect that everyone else, and eventually the whole API and its clients, can benefit from exposing that class. If the subclass is there only to implement the switch statement, this is unlikely to happen. The advice here is: instead of big, rooted families, try to define the real interface of the application and let users implement it. Always remember that if something is a subclass or a subinterface, it can inherently be used in place of the original superclass or interface.

Be aware of situations similar to Frame indirectly extending Component. Given all the API rules, this relationship should mean that you can use a Frame in all places where Component is used, even though this isn't true at all. The fact that the frame inherits from the component is just an implementation detail, just a switch statement to reuse some of the component code. However, it has nothing to do with the actual API. This type of *object-oriented reuse*, which would better be called *misuse*, is common, especially in cases of deep class or interface hierarchies. That's why if the inheritance hierarchy is deeper than two, it's useful to stop and ask yourself, "Am I doing this for the API or just for the code reuse?" If the answer is the latter, rewrite the API to be stricter or to be explicitly ready for subclassing.

■ ■ ■

CHAPTER 6

Code Against Interfaces, Not Implementations

An old and true rule of thumb useful for every piece of code is to "separate your code into interface and implementation and then let other parts of the system rely just on the interfaces." This advice is much older than Java, but it's so true that it's valuable to investigate its implications for writing Java APIs. This chapter provides an overview from various angles.

First, this rule of thumb implies that if you have a working application and want to provide some APIs to allow others to access it, it's not reasonable simply to make a few classes public and then pretend it is an API. Without refactoring, you're likely to be exposing the internals of the implementation and not the real API. Therefore, don't treat your code as an API. It's better to spend some time polishing it. Think about the reasons that you're creating the API. Then make sure the amoeba model of your API won't be shaken up whenever you change a line in your implementation.

CREATION OF NETBEANS OPEN APIS

The coding of the NetBeans APIs started in 1997, with the vision of having a well-defined set of APIs and separate implementations of them, along with several modules communicating with one another through those APIs.

This was a solid design back in those days—much better than cluelessly using a bulldozer to put everything into one big pile of dirt in the form of a monolithic application. We were able to make it all work. However, the separation into APIs, the implementations, and the user modules was more logical than physical. For example, we only had one build script that compiled everything. Simply by looking at package names you couldn't tell whether a package was part of the API or not.

Someone on our mailing list complained about how hard it was to distinguish between API and implementation. Our initial answer was simply to help the person find the API then and there. However, after reflecting on the situation, we realized that we had a problem. A thousand thanks to the person who brought that problem up. Only because of his help, our API was separated and repackaged completely in 1999. We put the APIs of that time into `org.openide` and subpackages, with their core implementations into `com.netbeans.core`. Yes, `com.netbeans`, as this happened before NetBeans become open source. The rest of our noncompulsory modules were put into `com.netbeans.modules`.

During the rewrite we found how messy our original source code had been and how many interdependencies there were between the APIs and their "independent" implementations. A moral to remember? Simply claiming that part of your application is an API isn't enough. You need to underline the parts that are the API—that is, separate the interfaces from their implementation.

Another argument that can be used to explain the "code against interfaces and not the implementation" perspective is the view of an honest API user. Don't try to cheat when you need an API! Don't fall back on reflection if something that you need isn't publicly available and accessible. Don't rely on undocumented properties and files. Ask the author for a proper API! It's in the long-term interest of the API users as well the API provider to understand each other's needs and to satisfy them. Any kind of hacking is fragile. It's much better to clearly formulate the need of an API, define its use case, and help the API writer with the implementation. Cooperation in creating a real API is much better than coding against the implementation.

A slightly more technical point relates to the practical application of the advice for coding APIs in Java. Such advice suggests to code against interfaces, but as that advice is much older than Java, it doesn't use the word "interfaces" in the *Java* sense. Without meaning to speak for the author of that advice, it's clear that the common languages of that time were C, C++, and maybe CORBA. Although the interfaces in CORBA's interface definition language (IDL) are reminiscent of interfaces in Java, there's nothing like a "class" versus "interface" there. Similarly, there's no such separation in C++. That language knows just classes—that is, types with methods and fields—and yet still the advice to code against interfaces was valid in C++. Similarly, this advice applies to CORBA, even though its IDL knows only interfaces—that is, types with nonstatic methods and no fields.

Can the same advice be brought up to date with Java? Sure, you just need to understand that coding against interfaces doesn't mean using the Java interface keyword, but coding in a way that separates the abstract definition of an API from its actual implementation. You can achieve this in multiple ways, and indeed some of them benefit from the use of Java interfaces, while some of them profit from the use of Java classes.

Should Java interfaces be used for coding an API or should you use Java classes instead? This is an excellent question to start a never-ending flame war. This isn't the intention of this chapter at all. People often have strong opinions on the topic of interfaces versus classes, probably because some of them have successfully used interfaces and some of them have successfully used classes. The experience might vary, but in fact it might just signal that for certain situations it's better to use classes, and in others it's better to rely on interfaces. The goal of the rest of this chapter is to understand the API and especially the evolution characteristics of both solutions, and know when each of them is the appropriate one.

Removing a Method or a Field

Can you remove a method or a field from an interface or class that is publicly exposed in an API? Well, if anyone can call it, then no. First of all, such a change isn't source compatible. The code that calls that method or accesses such a field wouldn't compile. Also, such a change isn't binary compatible: if you compiled against the older version of an API that contained the method and executed against the newer version, you would get a runtime exception either during linkage, or during the call to the method. That's why removing elements from publicly visible classes or interfaces isn't a good idea.

Hypothetically, the field or method in a class could have restricted access and not be public. If it was private or package private, then it would be hidden to the outside world and as such wouldn't be accessible. Removing it wouldn't hurt anyone—except people using reflection. As has been explained before, using reflection in places not designed for it—which generally means in almost any API—is a violation of good habits. That's why those who violate them deserve to get hurt.

Can you remove a protected method? Well, it cannot be called from any code, but subclasses can call it by using **super**.*theMethod*(), so removing it is not a good idea. Perhaps you can remove it only if there can be no subclasses, such as when the class is final. However, if that's the case, there's no reason to make that method protected! Indeed, some APIs contain protected methods in final classes, but that is often an oversight rather than a useful design. If there's anything to advise here, perhaps it is to generate a Javadoc of your API and read it to discover and eliminate such trivial mistakes before the first release.

But what if the protected method is abstract? Nobody from outside can call it, as it's protected and subclasses can't do that either. If they try, the compiler complains that the "abstract method cannot be accessed directly." As a result, it's source compatible and binary compatible to remove a protected abstract method. Everything will still compile and run with a new modified version. However, a change of this kind is unlikely to be functionally compatible. The method was probably there for a reason and subclasses expected to be called at certain points in time. Now their implementations won't be called at all and the semantics will also be different. Though a removal is possible, it's potentially dangerous. It's inadvisable to plan for this scenario as a reasonable alternative to the evolution of any API.

Removing or Adding a Class or an Interface

If a class or interface is accessed—that is, if its methods can be called or its fields referenced—then removing that class creates an incompatibility on both source and binary levels. There seems to be no difference between interfaces and classes—once put into an API they are like stars and they simply have to be kept around.

Adding new interfaces or classes is fine from a binary point of view. Source compatibility can get broken when using wildcard imports, as I already discussed in the section "Source Compatibility" in Chapter 4. I also discussed the fact that to allow some evolution, it is very likely acceptable to break source compatibility and add new classes and interfaces into existing packages while keeping binary compatibility.

That means adding classes or interfaces is okay. However, it's necessary to say that there's no difference in adding a Java class or a Java interface. Both behave the same way when introduced into an API.

Inserting an Interface or a Class into an Existing Hierarchy

In certain situations it might be beneficial to insert new classes or interfaces into an existing hierarchy of types. For example, imagine there's a type with two different abilities to say hello:

```java
public abstract String sayHello();
public abstract String sayHelloTo(String who);
```

In a subsequent release, the author decides that it's reasonable to simplify the API and provide yet another type that can handle just the "no argument" request to say hello:

```
public abstract class SimpleHelloClass {
    public abstract String sayHello();
}
```

Nevertheless, the old type needs to be maintained. It should now extend the new simple type and simply add the more complicated way of saying hello to its definition:

```
public abstract class HelloClass extends SimpleHelloClass {
}
```

This change is backward compatible for source and binary files, and functionally as well, irrespective of whether the refactoring is performed on Java classes or Java interfaces. The only constraint is that the overall set of methods visible (that is, inherited or defined) from the original and new Hello types stays the same, or at least doesn't decrease.

Adding a Method or a Field

Now we'll talk about methods and fields, and we'll start with fields first. In the section "A Method Is Better Than a Field" in Chapter 5, I argued that fields shouldn't be added to an API. They are much more restricted in evolutionary terms than are methods. That's why you shouldn't even consider adding a field to an API, unless it is a static final constant. Adding such constants is acceptable and supports binary compatibility.

Adding a static method is acceptable from the binary point of view. However, it is clear that static methods can only appear in classes. They can cause source incompatibilities, such as when an overloaded variant of a similar method is already present, even in nonpublic subclasses. Also, certain calls result in compiler errors, as the compiler doesn't know which of the variants to call.

Adding an abstract method to a class that is subclassable is an incompatible change. It's also source incompatible, because the compiler refuses to compile subclasses that aren't abstract and that don't implement all the abstract methods. Surprisingly, such a change might or might not be binary incompatible. The reason for this is that the virtual machine uses a different way of dispatching and representing classes and their methods from the way it represents interfaces and their methods. As a result, the virtual machine complains during class-loading about classes not implementing all their abstract methods. It defers the check for interfaces until a method is called.

However, this is only a slight advantage of interfaces over classes, because any call to a method added later can result in a runtime exception. It's not very nice to have to put the following words into the Javadoc: "Whoever calls this method must catch UnsatisfiedLinkError, as older clients may not implement it." In fact, that leads to the development of a rather ugly API, and on top of that, leads to functional incompatibilities.

As a result, you should try to minimize the addition of abstract methods to subclassable classes and interfaces. Alternatively, try to ensure that they cannot be subclassed.

Can you add a nonabstract method without risk? First, you can only add a method with an implementation to classes, so this paragraph isn't about interfaces at all. It's important to realize that subclassable classes can easily cause problems relating to source compatibility. For example, when JDK 1.4 was about to released, the NetBeans APIs had an exception that defined the method **public** Exception *getCause()*. Though this worked fine with JDK 1.3, JDK

1.4 introduced the new method **public** `Throwable` `getCause()` to `Throwable`. We were in big trouble, as the compiler refused to compile our APIs! Thankfully, we caught the problem a few hours before the release and were able to rename our method. However, if we hadn't done that, our APIs written against JDK 1.3 would no longer have been compilable against JDK 1.4. But this was simply a source compatibility problem and on a binary level everything was fine. Because the virtual machine encodes the return type in the method signature, our method and that provided by the JDK would be treated as different methods, so there would be no interference.

However, accidental interference remains the biggest problem when adding methods to existing classes. Imagine the NetBeans getCause() method had been defined with the `Throwable` return type. It would have ended up exactly matching the signature added to `Throwable` in JDK 1.4. Surprisingly, things would still work, but only by chance! The NetBeans getCause method would exactly match the signature of a method introduced later into a superclass. It could therefore be invoked in moments that were never anticipated. Of course, this can break semantics, so it's semantically, functionally incompatible.

ADD A NEW METHOD AND A NEW TYPE

A trick eliminates this "interference." When adding a new method, you can also add a new type and use that type in the method signature. If it's one of the parameters or the method's return type, it's encoded into the method's binary signature.

This is acceptable from a binary and semantic point of view, as this method signature cannot match anything compilable in the previous version. That's because one type in its signature did not exist at that time. This completely prevents accidental interference, because there's no way any subclass's method can be called by accident. Therefore, adding a method of this kind is a binary and functionally compatible change.

The likelihood of running into accidental interference varies with the number of users of some class and also with the name of the newly added method. Adding a new method into `java.awt.Toolkit` is likely safe, as there are only a few implementations of this class anyway. Adding a method called **public boolean** `isValid()` into java.lang.Object is going to break someone's code for sure.

In summary, let's say that adding a method to a class or interface that can be subclassed cannot be a 100 percent compatible change. It's not source compatible, though possibly binary compatible. It's nearly always semantically incompatible. If you want to be careful, you should never try to add methods into subclassable API elements.

Comparing Java Interfaces and Classes

After the analysis of the previous sections, it might be the right time to resolve the never-ending fight between Java interface lovers and Java class lovers.

The most profound feature of Java interfaces is multiple inheritance. In fact, many claim that it's also the most important one. However, the NetBeans API experience shows that multiple inheritance in APIs is almost never actually needed. The only real reason to strive for it is performance—that is, to minimize the amount of occupied memory. With multiple inheritance, you need just one object to implement an unlimited number of interfaces from an API.

In the case of classes, you would need to create one subclass for each API class, and if these classes are related to one another, join their instances by means of delegation. This can significantly increase the amount of occupied memory: a single instance of an object implementing an unlimited number of interfaces can fit into 8 bytes of memory on most common 32-bit JVMs on Intel processors. However, in the other case, where API classes are implemented by different instances interconnected with references among one another, you need at least 16 bytes per instance to implement each API class. The whole collection of implementation objects could require significantly more memory than if you were using interfaces. However, this only has a significant effect if you create many objects, certainly more than one or two. For example, the abstract syntax tree data structures used in compilers might benefit from this. For most existing scenarios, performance considerations aren't significant enough to outweigh the evolution problems of interfaces.

In Weakness Lies Strength

From the perspective of interface evolution, it's clear that it's rather difficult to add a method into an existing interface. It's not just hard, but almost impossible, if you're striving to honor backward compatibility. However, such a weakness in evolutionary capabilities can easily be turned into an interface's greatest strength.

Often, you need to provide versioned interfaces. For example, there might be a need for an interface expressing the capabilities of the Java language in versions 1.3, 1.4, and 1.5. In fact, that set of capabilities is frozen, cannot change, and is different across versions. Here an excellent opportunity is provided for the use of interfaces. Define the Language13, Language14, and Language15 interfaces and let anyone implement them. By selecting the implemented interface, the user also selects the capabilities that are supported, and does so consciously. During the writing of the code and during compile time, it's determined which language level is supported. Interfaces are an ideal tool for communicating such messages through the medium of the API.

However, there's one hidden catch. The proliferation of interfaces can severely complicate client code. NetBeans once faced this with the case of an instance provider interface. Imagine the following:

```
public interface InstanceProvider {
    public Class<?> instanceClass() throws Exception;
    public Object instanceCreate() throws Exception;
}
```

Later we found that one of the most frequently used operations involved getting the class from the provider and testing whether it can be assigned to another class. NetBeans performed this query so often that we considered it a performance bottleneck. We needed a way to avoid the loading of actual instance files into memory. That's why we created the following:

```
public interface BetterInstanceProvider extends InstanceProvider {
    public boolean isInstanceOf(Class<?> c);
}
```

Now all the clients around our code, as well as in all modules written by third parties, are supposed to check if the provider they have reference to is "better" by doing instanceof, and if so, cast and invoke its isInstanceOf method.

This creates new problems. First of all, all client code using just InstanceProvider will be rewritten. This is not possible, as the code is spread all over the world and nobody has complete control over it, so it's still likely clients will be using the old approach and thus performance won't improve. Also, the client code is getting more and more complicated. Every client has to do the instanceof check and handle both alternatives. If it's true, it needs to use the new method; if it fails, it needs to revert back to the old behavior of myClass. isAssignableFrom(provider.instanceClass()). Also, spreading such "if" statements throughout the entire code base isn't nice at all.

```
if (instance instanceof BetterInstanceProvider) {
    BetterInstanceProvider bip = (BetterInstanceProvider)instance;
    return bip.isInstanceOf(String.class);
} else {
    return String.class.isAssignableFrom(instance.instanceClass());
}
```

That's why I prefer Java interfaces to clearly specify an interface that isn't about to change. However, be careful not to spread huge switches of instanceofs throughout the clients of an API and force them to select the right interface from the many that are available. There are better ways, as will be shown.

A Method Addition Lover's Heaven

While Java interfaces are completely immutable with respect to method addition, there's the opposite extreme. In this scenario, it's not only possible to add methods, but it's also possible to make them completely binary compatible. In Java this can be expressed in the form of the *final* class.

By making a class final, you prevent others from subclassing it. As a result, there's no need to worry about the problems that typically need to be solved when a method is added to an interface or abstract class. The only threat to compatibility occurs if a method of that class is called. However, as the class file format fully identifies called methods by their name, parameters, and return type, no compatibility problems can occur on a binary level. However, as usual, there can be compatibility complications on the source level. Imagine that there's a method **void** *add*(Integer i) and someone decides to add **void** *add*(Long l) in the next version. Some existing sources might no longer be compilable. For example, code such as theObject.*add*(null) will throw a compiler error, as the call is ambiguous. However, you can easily prevent this by not adding methods with the same name and the same number of arguments.

Therefore, when you need to add a new method to a class or interface, select the final class. With the final class, you won't encounter the problem of complicated client code that was described in the interfaces section. Say the InstanceProvider is a final class:

```
import java.util.concurrent.Callable;

public final class InstanceProvider {
    private final Callable<Object> instance;

    public InstanceProvider(Callable<Object> instance) {
```

```
        this.instance = instance;
    }

    public Class<?> instanceClass() throws Exception {
        return instance.call().getClass();
    }
    public Object instanceCreate() throws Exception {
        return instance.call();
    }
}
```

Then, it's easy and safe to add new methods to it and provide a default implementation, so that the class becomes the following:

```
import java.util.Arrays;
import java.util.HashSet;
import java.util.Set;
import java.util.concurrent.Callable;

public final class InstanceProvider {
    private final Callable<Object> instance;
    private final Set<String> types;

    public InstanceProvider(Callable<Object> instance) {
        this.instance = instance;
        this.types = null;
    }
    /** Specifies not only a factory for creating objects, but
     * also additional information about them.
     * @param instance the factory to create the object
     * @param type the class that the create object will be instance of
     * @since 2.0
     */
    public InstanceProvider(Callable<Object> instance, String... types) {
        this.instance = instance;
        this.types = new HashSet<String>();
        this.types.addAll(Arrays.asList(types));
    }

    public Class<?> instanceClass() throws Exception {
        return instance.call().getClass();
    }
    public Object instanceCreate() throws Exception {
        return instance.call();
    }

    /** Allows to find out if the InstanceProvider creates object of given
     * type. This check can be done without loading the actual object or
     * its implementation class into memory.
```

```
 *
 * @param c class to test
 * @return if the instances produced by this provider is instance of c
 * @since 2.0
 */
public boolean isInstanceOf(Class<?> c) throws Exception {
    if (types != null) {
        return types.contains(c.getName());
    } else {
        // fallback
        return c.isAssignableFrom(instanceClass());
    }
}
```

}

The difference with the interfaces example is that the clients of the API in version 2.0 don't need to care about whether the actual instance handles their call to isInstanceOf in a better way or if it's a fallback to the old implementation. The switch inside isInstanceOf handles such decisions for them. The switch might seem similar to the previous example with interfaces, but the main difference is that all the switch logic is hidden from the client and concentrated in one place, which is a place that can easily be maintained.

Are Abstract Classes Useful?

Up until this point, it has been argued that you should use Java interfaces when you want to define an immutable contract and that you should use Java final classes when you want to have the ability to add methods. So it's reasonable to ask, "Is there actually any reason to use abstract classes?"

The short answer is "No." Abstract classes in an API are suspicious and often indicate an unwillingness to invest more time in the proper API design. The longer answer is, "Well, there might be reasons to use abstract classes in APIs after all."

First, sometimes you don't need a 100 percent binary compatible API. Sometimes the amount of implementors of a class is so limited that it doesn't make sense to optimize for safe subclassing. An example could be java.awt.Toolkit. There are three or four implementations of that class and millions of clients that call its methods. The API owner more than likely gave up on compatibility for subclasses and even adds new abstract methods to that class. For 99.9 percent of clients this is acceptable, and therefore this is probably an acceptable approach. The only downside is that NetBeans used to fall into the 0.01 percent of users that implement the class! We experienced problems with every new version of the JDK that added new methods to it. But, again, this is completely about attitude. If being 99.99 percent compatible is good enough for you, then using abstract classes such as this might be acceptable under the circumstances.

The other advantage of Java abstract classes versus Java interfaces is that Java abstract classes can include static methods. Even if you want to specify clear interfaces with all methods abstract, it might make sense to work with abstract classes if there's a need for static factory methods that the user can easily discover while reading the Javadoc for the interface class. You can also have an interface and a separate factory class that creates it, but this is ultimately a matter of preference.

A third useful feature of Java classes over Java interfaces is the possibility of *restricting access rights*. Every method in a public Java interface is public and everybody can implement or call it. This might be the right time for the use of an abstract class. For example, you can make all methods protected abstract and in this way declare an interface that others can implement, but that nobody outside your code can call. This might be an advantage in certain situations. However, bear in mind that this prevents delegation—you cannot create a decorator that adds additional capabilities, such as logging, on top of an existing instance. Sometimes this might be quite a painful restriction.

Yet another possibility with abstract classes is to restrict those who can implement them. You can make all your methods public abstract, while either providing a package private constructor or restricting creation to certain subclasses during runtime:

```java
public abstract class InterfaceThatJustJoeCanImplement {
    protected InterfaceThatJustJoeCanImplement() {
        if (!"impl.joe.JoesImpl".equals(getClass().getName())) {
            throw new IllegalStateException(
                "Sorry, you are not allowed to implement this class"
            );
        }
    }

    public abstract void everyoneCallThisJoeWillHandleTheRequest();
}
```

Though the runtime check isn't pretty, it does the job of restricting the set of possible implementors. This wouldn't have been possible with interfaces.

Getting Ready for Growing Parameters

One of the most frequent questions you need to solve when changing an API is how to enhance your existing methods with additional parameters. This is a common scenario, especially if the requirements for the API are in flux. For example, say you have a method that was called by the framework to compute the content of a UI list. Later you realize that you not only need that content, but you also need some additional text to describe or classify the computed data.

If that happens, you can add a new method that calls the previous one, as follows:

```java
public abstract class Compute {
    /**
     * @return list of strings to work with
     * @since 1.0 */
    public abstract List<String> getData();
    /** Computes the strings to work with together with their
     * associated descriptions. Shall be overriden in subclasses.
```

```
 * By default delegates to {@link #getData}
 * and uses the provided strings as both, the string
 * and its description.
 *
 * @return name to description pairs to work with
 * @since 2.0 */
public Map<String,String> getDataAndDescription() {
    LinkedHashMap<String,String> ret =
        new LinkedHashMap<String, String>();
    for (String s : getData()) {
        ret.put(s, s);
    }
    return ret;
}
}
```

This is possible, but only if the method is inside a class. On top of that, giving clients a class to implement isn't as clean a solution as giving them an interface. Also, adding methods into a class that is often subclassed is slightly dangerous. That is why it's preferred to use a Java interface for the Compute class. However, then you can give up on the need to add new methods. Although it's possible to create an extended interface, a much better situation, with respect to evolution, can be created by means of the response/reply pattern:

```
public interface Compute {
    public void computeData(Request request, Response response);

    public final class Request {
        // only getters public, rest hidden only for friend code
        Request() {
        }
    }

    public final class Response {
        // only setters public, rest available only for friend code
        private final Map<String,String> result;
        /** Allow access only to friend code */
        Response(Map<String,String> result) {
            this.result = result;
        }

        public void add(String s) {
            result.put(s, s);
        }

        public void addAll(List<String> all) {
            for (String s : all) {
                add(s);
```

```
            }
        }

        /** @since 2.0 */
        public void add(String s, String description) {
            result.put(s, description);
        }
    }
}
```

In this setup, you can easily achieve any extension to the method parameters by adding
new getters into the Compute.Request class, which is immutable and final, and therefore its
methods can only be called. That means that you can add more methods there without any
risk.

On the other hand, if there's more to return from the method, you can add new setters to
the Response class. There can be an add(String) method or a setMessage(String) method, and
so on. Again, as the class is final, it's acceptable to extend it with new methods. Notice that this
pattern also solves the lack of support for multiple return types from a method in Java. Each
setter in the Compute.Response method is in fact one return type.

When using this pattern, it's important to make the request and response classes final. If
you make them interfaces, the system won't be able to evolve safely. Others might implement
those interfaces in one version; adding new methods to them would break their code. This is
what happened to the Servlet API. This API is also based on the request and response style;
however, Java interfaces represent both these types. That means those servers that implemented the API in version 1.1 cannot simply replace it with the next version because their
code wouldn't compile. If you happen to need this coding trick, remember that the parameters
should be able to evolve safely; that is, you should make them final classes. You should also
consider the use of the friend accessor pattern to tell people clearly that they aren't supposed
to read anything from the response and write anything to the request objects.

Interfaces vs. Classes

In summary, always code against interfaces and not implementations. Remember, this doesn't
mean Java interfaces, but abstract definitions. When coding in Java, use Java interfaces to
specify immutable types and use final classes as the type where methods can be safely added.
When designing more intricate structures, think about extensibility and choose the appropriate style, just like in the request and response example. Sometimes it's acceptable to use
abstract classes. However, remember that if the goal is 100 percent binary compatibility, never
add methods to classes or interfaces that someone else can implement.

CHAPTER 7

■ ■ ■

Use Modular Architecture

Few should be surprised that operating systems, and distributions built on top of them, are coded in a modular way. The final product is assembled from independently developed components, enabling distributed coordination and workflows across time zones in a reasonably reliable way.

However, a similar change is happening to individual applications. As they increase in complexity, they are moving toward being assembled from independently developed pieces. The way to attain this end is to code applications in a *modular way*.

As applications grow in size and functionality, it becomes increasingly necessary to separate them into individual pieces, components, modules, or plug-ins. Each of these separated parts then becomes one element of the modular architecture. Each part should be independent and provide well-defined exported interfaces so that the other parts can use them. In NetBeans we call such pieces *modules*, and as this chapter refers to a modular architecture, let's call them modules as well.

Splitting an application into modules can greatly improve its design. It's not difficult to understand that a monolithic piece of code, where each statement can access each other statement, is much more interconnected and less readable than code that introduces modules, especially if the architecture only allows such uncontrolled calls to happen within each individual module.

Comparing modular applications to object-oriented applications is similar to comparing spaghetti code to structured programming in the '60s. The concept of spaghetti code used to apply to unwieldy FORTRAN or BASIC programs, where every line of code could use GOTO to jump to another place in the program. This tended to be done in a chaotic way, which only the program's writer could understand, if at all. Structured programming tried to reduce the chaos by introducing blocks of code: for loops, while loops, if statements, procedures, and calls to procedures. Indeed, this improved the situation: the application's readability and maintainability improved. If nothing else, you could be sure that a call to a method had to return once, aside from corner cases.

The plain object-oriented style of programming, in some ways, resembles the situation before structured programming established itself: an application is full of classes and virtually any method can call any other method. Even though there are public, private, and protected access modifiers, most of the granularity is achieved at the class level. However, this is simply too small of an entity to serve as a basic building block for applications. It's also certainly too small to create a unit of evolution.

Modular applications, in the sense used by NetBeans, are composed of modules, where one module is a collection of classes. Some of these classes are public and thus serve as an exported API to other modules, while others are private and cannot be accessed from the outside. Moreover, a module has a set of dependencies on other modules, clearly stating on a high level the functional environment required for execution. Of course, within a module you can still apply the worst coding practices. Nevertheless, an application's architecture can be well observed by checking the dependencies among all its modules. If one module doesn't have a dependency on another, it's clear that its classes cannot directly access those in another module. This serves to clean up the architecture significantly, because it prevents accidental GOTOs between unrelated parts of the code.

Some developers claim their application is too small to benefit from a modular architecture. Well, it might be too small right now, but if it's not simply a student project, it will almost certainly evolve. As it evolves, it's likely to grow. Rewriting a messy and interconnected application to use a nicer modular design is often such a complex task that many are not willing even to try it. Instead, they prefer living with the old, monolithic code that is harder to maintain, but known to work. For an example, take a look at the JDK! Classes from the java.lang packages implement interfaces from the java.io packages, and sometimes from the java.util packages. Moreover, everything is wired with the sun.* packages. It's nearly impossible to imagine someone splitting the JDK into modular parts that are not mutually interconnected in vicious circles. This is a natural result of the JDK having been coded in the "spaghetti object-oriented style."

SPAGHETTI DESIGN IN NETBEANS

Similar spaghetti-related problems happened to NetBeans. Though the application was always designed to be modular, it used to have one huge module called OpenAPIs, which contained all the APIs for communication between the other modules. From today's point of view, this was ridiculous. However, in those days, from 1997 to 2000, no project in Java was as modular as NetBeans. It took time for us to realize that there would be scalability problems in terms of maintaining such huge and monolithic APIs. In 2000 or so, it became clear that each module would need to be able to export its own API. Modules created after that date now do exactly this. However, some of the large monolithic OpenAPIs remained.

The situation gradually worsened. In each release, something needed to be fixed. Developers started adding inner dependencies between logical parts of the OpenAPIs, instead of leaving them separated. The situation was becoming comparable to java.lang referring to java.awt. Sometimes this was done as an implementation detail inside the body of methods and sometimes this was even exposed in the APIs! By 2003, we'd had enough. We took the first important step: we cleared out unwanted cross references and split the compilation of the OpenAPIs into logical parts. However, the resulting binary was still more or less one big module. This at least prevented further spoiling of the code with unwanted dependencies among logical parts. However, it took another two years for the whole monolithic module to completely disappear.

The section "Incremental Improvements" in Chapter 4 introduced the concept of the *entropy of software*. The degradation of architecture, where ("as a workaround") each part of the code base starts talking to each other unrelated part, is inevitable. It has to happen, unless explicitly prevented. Modular programming is here to help prevent such entropy. However, modular programming doesn't make each line of the code beautiful. Naturally, you can continue using a horrible coding style within a module. However, a modular approach can enforce the architecture on a higher level, on a level of larger components, which is also likely to provide real results. Once again, this follows the *selective cluelessness* vision of identifying and working with the key parts of the system that are essential for success.

It's crucial to start projects with modularity in mind from day one. Modularity gives a clearer design, better control of dependencies, and far more flexibility in maintenance. Regardless of the size of the project, designing it in a modular way is a boon right from its inception.

Types of Modular Design

Not all modules need to export an API. For example, they might simply contribute to the user interface. This is likely to be the simplest form of module: *completely closed*, without public classes and only with some kind of user interface. If other modules depend on these modules, they just do so to make sure that certain functionality is available somewhere in the user interface. This is the case with the NetBeans Favorites module, which provides an "explorer" window to browse local files. If an application needs that functionality, it can depend on the Favorites module, which is all that is needed to ensure that the Favorites window will be available to the user. However, no direct API communication to that module is likely ever to take place.

Another simple case is one of a *simple library*. Such a library is easy to understand and is a common type of module that is used by developers writing open source projects and reusable libraries, such as the Apache Commons Collections. It's simply a JAR with some public classes, interfaces, and so on. Others can depend on it, call its classes, override those classes, and subclass and override their methods. However, there is no attempt to support multiple "vendors," because it's assumed that if any improvements are to be made, such as optimizations, they should be made in the main source base on SourceForge, or wherever the module is hosted, and all the clients will automatically benefit.

Sometimes even multiple "vendors" would make no sense because the library provides controlled access to the functionality of a part of an application's user interface, such as a scripting API for a word processor. Again, the module would have some public classes, along with a lot of private ones, but on a general level the physical packaging and usage is similar to the case of a simple library.

The next level is to support multiple "vendors." Some specifications prefer to release public documentation of an API in the form of a PDF file with descriptions, specifications, and code snippets. It's then up to the individual providers of the API to write the API classes and make sure that they comply with the specification. Most importantly, they also provide an implementation that complies with the specification. Sometimes the actual specification JAR or complete system is then released as a "reference implementation." Other "vendors" can then make copies of the interfaces, bind their internals with different back ends, and distribute their own self-contained JARs or frameworks, which contain both the interfaces and the implementation classes. The client code compiles and runs against one or the other of the vendor's copies. Presumably, client code compiled against one vendor's copy—that is, the reference implementation—could then run against another vendor's copy because the interface names and signatures should match, although you need to trust that this is true.

Although all this is possible, it's not very modular. The biggest problem here is that multiple implementations of the same API cannot be used simultaneously. As the API portions of the vendor's JARs will overlap, they can either be loaded once into the virtual machine or multiple times by different classloaders. None of this can actually work. If the classes are loaded only from one vendor's JAR and the other is of a different version, the two implementations might not link and can throw missing method errors at runtime. On the other hand, if the classes are loaded twice, every piece of client code needs to decide in advance which of the vendor's modules it will use. It cannot use both without the use of reflection. The only hope in this situation is to load both implementations and only one—the newest—API that will be shared between them. This can work, and indeed it is an approach used by some modular systems. On the other hand, this doesn't happen automatically; you need to carefully design and evolve the APIs so they can be linked and can work with both implementations. From this perspective, it's more honest to admit that the API is special—not part of some implementation—and separate it into its own module.

That is why we can solve the multiple "vendors" problem with a real *modular library*. This approach puts the specification and implementation into different modules and enforces their separation with a module boundary. One module contains the specification; that is, the actual interfaces, abstract classes, and so on, as mentioned in its documentation. There might be one or more separate modules, possibly from other vendors, which implement that specification. Typically there is at least one small "entry point" constructor or static factory method in the specification packages that allow clients to acquire an implementation.

It's possible to find many different ways to obtain and register an implementation in the JDK, as there was no clear approach that set out how to do it in the JDK's early days. For example, SecurityManager has the setSecurityManager setter, which can be called only once without throwing an exception. URLStreamHandlerFactory is a similar case, with one setter method to register one factory class. Allowing the registration of only one implementation might be fine in certain situations, but for other use cases this doesn't make much sense. Actually, both SecurityManager and URLHandlerFactory would benefit from multiple registrations. NetBeans is an example of that: the NetBeans code needs multiple SecurityManagers, as security concerns can be split across multiple modules. Similarly, we need multiple URLStreamHandlerFactorys, because many modules want to provide their own URL schemes.

That is why it's better to allow multiple factory classes to be registered. For example, JEditorPane.registerEditorKitForContentType allows the registration of a kit for each MIME type, because it was anticipated that multiple modules would be trying to register their own kits.

Other parts of the code use the property-based solution. For example, Toolkit checks the value of the java.awt.Toolkit property. The value of the property contains the name of a subclass of java.awt.Toolkit with a default constructor. Such a constructor is then called to get an instance of the Toolkit. This is quite a bit nicer, because the API is not polluted with useless (for the majority of its users) setter and registration methods. However, it's necessary to configure the JVM's runtime correctly. You need to initialize the properties either at its start or early during the execution of the program.

That is why the most modern (well, JDK 1.3) style of registration comes with a solution based on the classpath. You can simply put a JAR file with an implementation on the classpath and then the API can find its implementation(s) immediately. The Java API for XML Processing (JAXP) is an example of this approach. Most of the API consists of interfaces in public packages. In addition, there are also a few factories, such as DocumentBuilderFactory. The factories look for the implementations using a documented search procedure: scanning for META-INF/ services/pkg.name.ClassName entries.

Clients compile against the interface module, and can express a request that at least one implementation module must be available at runtime so the factories work. Alternatively, the API module itself might raise such a request. Moreover, there can be multiple versions of the "vendor" implementations; each can automatically be registered and can then be found by the API module.

A real modular architecture is likely to encourage a *modular library* design and probably also uses the simple library approach, where appropriate. Solving the multiple vendors problem by copying the classes is simply not good design in a modular world, because you duplicate the actual .class files of the specification across vendors.

Furthermore, the copy-based approach doesn't permit easy publishing of a revision to the specification independently of updates to vendor implementations. You need to use special semantics such as, "This JAR provides such-and-such specification version such-and-such implementation," which the module system has to interpret somehow.

By contrast, the *modular library* approach is straightforward in a modular system, and you don't even need special semantics for "specification" or "implementation." A "specification" is simply a module that exposes some packages with interfaces and a factory or two, and is accompanied by documentation explaining its permissible behavior. An "implementation" is simply a module without exposed packages that depends on the specification module and registers implementations of the factories into your service registration system (whatever that is). A "client" is a module that depends on the specification module and calls the factory methods.

INDIRECT DEPENDENCIES VIA THE NETBEANS RUNTIME CONTAINER

There is a need for some sort of "indirect dependency" declaration permitting either the client or the specification to request that at least one implementation be loaded before the specification can be used. The NetBeans module system uses "provide-require tokens" (similar to RPM require lists) for this purpose. Clients can require a particular version of a specification simply by using module versioning. Implementations can declare that they implement a particular version of a specification by using module versioning to link against the new specification classes and by providing a new token, such as `org.w3c.dom.v3` in addition to or instead of `org.w3c.dom.v2`. Specifications might require the presence of such an implementation.

By the way, JDBC tries to use the *modular library* style, but its usage is a bit flawed in its original form. A client needs to know the class name of the driver implementation in order to load a driver and needs to be able to locate the `ClassLoader` that can load it. That is no problem in a flat classpath application, but can be a significant hindrance in a complex modular system. Also, the registration of drivers is static, using some sort of hash table, which means an unused driver cannot be unloaded. So, don't emulate this example! A later revision of JDBC might solve these problems using `ConnectionPool` and JNDI, which is great for a J2EE application but probably cumbersome when not using an application server.

Intercomponent Lookup and Communication

The sole purpose of modular design is to decouple individual pieces of an application from one another. Two modules shouldn't know about each other if we want them to be independent. Instead, as discussed in Chapter 6, they should talk to each other using well-defined interfaces.

It's much nicer for a module that requires a database to talk to an AbstractDatabaseService rather than talking directly to jdbc://mysql.mycompany.com. By defining the AbstractDatabaseService, the module code clearly defines the environment it needs. If it's written correctly, as soon as someone writes an implementation of the service and passes it to such a module in its environment, the module can work with any database, which increases its configurability and testability. In fact, it reduces its potential for an object-oriented spaghetti mess.

However, at the end of the day, we want the module to talk to jdbc://mysql.mycompany.com! So, by coding against interfaces, we've made the code nicer, though we need to solve the *configuration problem*. Someone is needed to prepare the module environment. There needs to be a way for our module to query its environment and obtain the correct implementation of the AbstractDatabaseService that will talk to the correct database.

Usually this is a task for a framework. Spring; Java Platform, Enterprise Edition 5 (Java EE 5); and so on call their system *dependency injection* and often use additional configuration files for this purpose. Each module defines its required environment, either by using annotations, by defining setters, or by defining classes with constructors. Then the assembler of the application configures the database service, its parameters, and other services. These are then put in the framework's pool of services. The framework then scans each module for a list of its environment slots and populates them. In other words, it "injects" the appropriate implementations of the abstractly defined services.

To illustrate the point on a real example and also show various approaches that can solve it, their benefits, differences and similarities, let's convert the *Anagram Game*, an example that is distributed with NetBeans IDE, to a modular style. The point of the application is to play a game that shows the user a randomly scrambled word, which the user must attempt to unscramble. Following the advice to code against interfaces and not implementations, you'll define contracts for the three major parts of the system: the library that produces the original words, the business logic that knows how to scramble them, and the UI that presents the game to the user:

```java
public interface Scrambler {
    public String scramble(String word);
}
public interface WordLibrary {
    public String[] getWords();
}
public interface UI {
    public void display();
}
```

As our goal is to demonstrate proper usage of modular libraries, these APIs are put into separate, individual JARs. The actual implementations of these interfaces are then placed in various other modules that depend on the API and provide classes that implement them.

There can be various implementations—even multiple implementations of the same inter-face. However, for purposes of this example, it's enough to have one module that defines StaticWordLibrary, one that defines SimpleScrambler, and one that offers Anagrams—implementations of the UI with the use of Swing components. You might define other imple-mentations: a library that reads the words from a file; a scrambler that obfuscates the word more than just exchanging the position of two letters; and instead of the Swing UI, you might have a command-line interface for the game. However, having these additional modules would only complicate the example, as what you've defined already is enough to demonstrate various ways of injection. Notice that here clearly is a need for injection! The UI desperately needs references to the word library and for the scrambler to work. The base Anagrams class doesn't prescribe how to get them; it simply predefines the need for them by creating two abstract methods that need to be implemented to work with various technologies:

```
public abstract class Anagrams extends javax.swing.JFrame implements UI {

    protected abstract WordLibrary getWordLibrary();
    protected abstract Scrambler getScrambler();

    public void display() {
        initWord();
        setVisible(true);
    }
}
```

The simplest solution to implement these methods, while making sense for modularity, is to create a few registerXYZ methods in the API or in the integration module. To maintain modularity and allow multiple instances of the configured system, let's make these methods accept a class. They expect that the class for the word library and for the scrambler provides a default constructor. Meanwhile, to inject these instances into the UI, the class for the UI has a constructor with two arguments. Exposing a constructor with additional parameters is a common practice in various injection frameworks. In addition to this, frameworks often also support setters. However, for the purpose of this registration example, the constructor with arguments is simpler to call, so let's use it:

```
public final class Launcher {
    private static Class<? extends WordLibrary> wordLibrary;
    private static Class<? extends Scrambler> scrambler;
    private static Class<? extends UI> ui;


    private Launcher() {
    }


    public static void registerWordLibrary(
        Class<? extends WordLibrary> libraryClass
    ) {
        wordLibrary = libraryClass;
    }
```

```java
    public static void registerScrambler(
        Class<? extends Scrambler> scramblerClass
    ) {
        scrambler = scramblerClass;
    }
    public static void registerUI(Class<? extends UI> uiClass) {
        ui = uiClass;
    }

    public static UI launch() throws Exception {
        WordLibrary w = wordLibrary.newInstance();
        Scrambler s = scrambler.newInstance();
        return ui.getConstructor(
            WordLibrary.class, Scrambler.class
        ).newInstance(w, s);
    }
}


public class AnagramsWithConstructor extends Anagrams {

    private final WordLibrary library;
    private final Scrambler scrambler;

    public AnagramsWithConstructor(
        WordLibrary library, Scrambler scrambler
    ) {
        this.library = library;
        this.scrambler = scrambler;
    }

    @Override
    protected WordLibrary getWordLibrary() {
        return library;
    }

    @Override
    protected Scrambler getScrambler() {
        return scrambler;
    }
}
```

If the Launcher is part of the API, together with all the interfaces others can code against, you get quite a nice example of a modular library. Various implementations of the API interfaces might be independent, and only the launcher knows how to bind them together and can do it flexibly. The only condition is that, before using the launcher, someone registers the appropriate factory classes. For this to happen, the person who puts the whole application together—its assembler—needs to execute initialization code and correctly call all the registerXYZ methods. This is not hard; however, it diminishes coding style beauty, as the assemblers usually prefer not to write code in a particular language. They'd rather write nothing at all, or if necessary, they simply tweak external configuration files.

Also, this kind of registration comes with all the drawbacks of procedural registration, as analyzed in Chapter 12. This style can also slow down startup. Imagine there are many more registration methods and that there are even more implementations of each of their interfaces. All the implementing modules need to be triggered at startup of your application. They need to call the appropriate methods and register their implementations. This can be inefficient, as it requires classes from various modules to be loaded, linked, and executed. This doesn't happen for free.

GENERIC REGISTRY

The use of the registerXYZ methods is natural and almost obvious. That is why it's probably the first solution you choose when solving the "configurability problem." In fact, the NetBeans project started with this approach as well. However, as we needed many of these registration methods, we soon realized that most of their internal implementations were identical. Except for the type that they were supposed to hold, the rest was almost identical boilerplate code. That is why we investigated the possibility of replacing the individual registration methods with one generic method instead:

```
private static Map<Class<?>,Object[]> instances =
    new LinkedHashMap<Class<?>,Object[]>();
public static void registerClass(Class<?> impl) {
    instances.put(impl, new Object[1]);
}


public static <T> T find(Class<T> whatType) {
    for (Map.Entry<Class<?>, Object[]> entry : instances.entrySet()) {
        if (whatType.isAssignableFrom(entry.getKey())) {
            if (entry.getValue()[0] == null) {
                try {
                    entry.getValue()[0] = entry.getKey().newInstance();
                } catch (Exception ex) {
                    throw new IllegalStateException(ex);
                }
            }
            return whatType.cast(entry.getValue()[0]);
        }
    }
    return null;
}
```

Instead of many registration methods, we decided to have just a single one that can hold the registration of everything, thus eliminating repetitive code. This solution provided a nice unification of all the registrations and was, in fact, the basis of NetBeans' current solution.

It's better to perform a kind of call-less binding. This doesn't require any binding code to run and performs the registration in a more declarative way. An often used solution of this kind is based on System.*getProperty*("...") calls. It's common even in the JDK and is quite nice, as it allows not only call-less registration, but also late bindings. The implementation class is loaded into the virtual machine only at the time of execution, when it's really needed:

```java
@Override
protected WordLibrary getWordLibrary() {
    try {
        if (wordLibrary == null) {
            String implName = System.getProperty(
                "org.apidesign.anagram.api.WordLibrary"
            );
            assert implName != null;
            Class<?> impl = Class.forName(implName);
            wordLibrary = (WordLibrary)impl.newInstance();
        }
        return wordLibrary;
    } catch (Exception ex) {
        throw new IllegalStateException(ex);
    }
}

@Override
protected Scrambler getScrambler() {
    try {
        if (scrambler == null) {
            String implName = System.getProperty(
                "org.apidesign.anagram.api.Scrambler"
            );
            assert implName != null;
            Class<?> impl = Class.forName(implName);
            scrambler = (Scrambler)impl.newInstance();
        }
        return scrambler;
    } catch (Exception ex) {
        throw new IllegalStateException(ex);
    }
}
```

In this solution, the assemblers of the final applications still need to provide some kind of configuration. However, in contrast to the registerXYZ solution, they don't need to write code. Instead, they only need to create a property file that will then be read by the application, or before the application is started, and influence its selection of various components. This is much more comfortable for the people creating the final shape of the application, as editing properties files can be done much more cluelessly than writing, compiling, and executing pre-setup code. Still, the assemblers need to know the name of implementation classes, which might be too much detailed information for a person who just wants to get the whole system working with just minimal knowledge.

Various other registration formats can replace the property-based configuration. One of the most famous is provided by the Spring Framework, based on an XML configuration file:

```xml
<beans xmlns="http://www.springframework.org/schema/beans"
       xmlns:xsi="http://www.w3.org/2001/XMLSchema-instance"
       xsi:schemaLocation="http://www.springframework.org/schema/beans
       http://www.springframework.org/schema/beans/spring-beans-2.5.xsd"
>

    <bean
        id="wordLibrary"
        class="org.apidesign.anagram.wordstatic.StaticWordLibrary"
    />
    <bean
        id="scrambler"
        class="org.apidesign.anagram.scramblersimple.SimpleScrambler"
    />
    <bean
        id="ui"
        class="org.apidesign.anagram.gui.AnagramsWithConstructor"
        autowire="autodetect"
    />
</beans>
```

The XML file also supports the cluelessness of application assemblers. It can be edited with as much knowledge as when editing the property file, and despite providing a richer set of configuration options—including configuration via setters or constructors, autowiring, and so on—it's still easy to edit, as its format is specified by an XML schema. Common IDE editors can provide hints and text completions, so that even assemblers with a minimal knowledge of the exact format can tweak the file and change it to suit their needs. This file is then read by Spring's ApplicationContext implementation, which does all the bean instantiations and mutual wirings necessary for creating the desired, configured instance:

```java
public static void main(String[] args) throws Exception {
    ApplicationContext context = new ClassPathXmlApplicationContext(
        "org/apidesign/anagram/app/spring/conf.xml"
    );
    UI ui = (UI)context.getBean("ui", UI.class);
    ui.display();
}
```

Spring provides greater flexibility than the property-based solution, yet it seems to require the application assemblers to know the name of the bean classes that should participate in the wiring. Sometimes this is useful, especially if the wiring is also done with the developers who provide the beans implementing the interfaces. On the other hand, knowing the class names is still a significant amount of knowledge for external assemblers. Also, it makes the names of implementation classes part of the API, as they are exported to external users who make the final assembly. And, as has been argued while talking about separating interfaces and implementation in Chapter 6, you should not need to directly refer to implementation classes.

THE PUREST COMPONENT INJECTION

The Spring Framework's approach is the effective standard, and when somebody says "dependency injection," they often refer to the solution provided by Spring. This is an example where a single product has become synonymous with a complete technology. This has two implications. First, it has a defining purpose: it helps to define the meaning of dependency injection, as many of us immediately envision Spring when hearing such terms. However, it also has a limiting role. As soon as we create the association between injection and Spring, we might be unable to see other possible solutions to the original problem.

This kind of definition and limiting association between meaning and representations is not restricted to programming. It happens all the time in all kinds of situations. In my country, Lux is synonymous for all vacuum cleaners, and not simply for those produced by the company whose name ends in "Lux." Coke could be the name for every dark soda. To add an example from physics, just think about the meaning of "time." Can it be expressed and counted in seconds? That is exactly how Newton presented it, and how most of us see it! It's a useful definition for everyday use. However, this definition of time almost prevents us from understanding that the real world treats time quite differently, as illustrated by Einstein's theory of relativity and many other modern works. Newton's definition is so defining, so useful, that it prevents us from perceiving the meaning of time in other contexts.

It's useful to have an understanding that goes beyond abstract meanings. It's helpful to envision Spring whenever injection is mentioned. However, we should be aware of the potentially limiting nature of this kind of synergy. The fact that we've successfully used Spring to solve our *component injection* problem should not blind us and prevent us from discovering other viable alternatives.

That is why our search for the most clueless way to perform component injection is not over yet. We'd like to have a solution that imposes even less required knowledge for assemblers. Luckily, Spring 2.5 takes a huge step in this direction by providing you with the option to annotate implementation classes:

```
@Service
public class SimpleScramblerAnnotated extends SimpleScrambler {
    public SimpleScramblerAnnotated() {
    }
}
@Service
public class StaticWordLibraryAnnotated extends StaticWordLibrary {
    public StaticWordLibraryAnnotated() {
    }
}
@Service("ui")
public class AnagramsAnnotated extends AnagramsWithConstructor {
    @Autowired
    public AnagramsAnnotated(WordLibrary library, Scrambler scrambler) {
        super(library, scrambler);
    }
}
```

You use an indication that identifies the exported beans, their names, and potentially also their dependencies on other APIs that need to be provided for the implementation to work correctly. The final assembler no longer needs to write a configuration file with references to all names of implementation classes, but rather can instruct the Spring Framework to use the provided annotations:

```
<beans
 xmlns="http://www.springframework.org/schema/beans"
 xmlns:xsi="http://www.w3.org/2001/XMLSchema-instance"
 xmlns:context="http://www.springframework.org/schema/context"
 xsi:schemaLocation="http://www.springframework.org/schema/beans
   http://www.springframework.org/schema/beans/spring-beans-2.5.xsd
   http://www.springframework.org/schema/context
   http://www.springframework.org/schema/context/spring-context-2.5.xsd"
 >
     <context:component-scan base-package="org.apidesign.anagram.app"/>
</beans>
```

It's still necessary to know the name of the packages that contain all the implementations. However, that is significantly less knowledge than knowing all the classes and their parameters. This is almost the situation where we wanted to be at the start. Assemblers simply pick up the necessary libraries, some providing the APIs, some providing the implementations. The assemblers then write the configuration file and launch the application in the created configuration. That is a significant step forward compared to the original approach of the registerXYZ methods. On the other hand, the assemblers still need to write the configuration file. Can we eliminate the need for that?

It's possible to extend the solution provided by Spring to work without the configuration file at all. Maybe future versions of the framework will provide such extensions themselves. However, it's a good time to shift focus and look at other ways to do component injection. Let's look at a solution that takes the good things from the "Generic Registry" and from the property-based registration. One such solution is based on the Java Extension Mechanism, in use in JDK since version 1.3, and made available to clients with Java 6's java.util.ServiceLoader class or the NetBeans Lookup framework.

INJECTION TERMINOLOGY

As you can see from the list of examples given so far, the range of possible solutions is broad. I used to include all these solutions in the dependency injection category. However, the specification of dependency injection is stricter than I had originally thought. It's said to be a special case of *inversion of control*, which means that the infrastructure calls the library and does the injection without being asked for it. This might be true for the Spring-based solution. However, in the other cases, including registration methods, property-based configurations, or the Java Extension Mechanism, there is no inversion of control at all. Still, the injection of implementations is handled successfully. That is why I've decided to call these technologies component injection. The first part of the name describes what it does and the other contains a buzzword, which is important, as technologies with good names help attract the attention of the right developers.

In 2001, we submitted a proposal for JavaOne called "Intercomponent Lookup and Communication," talking more or less about the topic of this chapter, which we considered important for all modular applications. However, the JavaOne selection committee simply was unable to imagine how "cool" the original topic was, or, probably, what it was about, because the term "component" is so overloaded. Nearly anything can be imagined under that term. The proposal was rejected. Later, in 2006, my colleague Tim Boudreau and I submitted a talk on the same topic, named "Discovery and Dependency Injection Patterns in Modular Architectures." To nobody's surprise, it was accepted this time around. This is just another example proving the need to find terminology that is close to your target audience. When using the "dependency injection" term, we seem to have struck a chord. Just like an API, proper naming is about communication. The easier it is for the user of the API to understand your intentions, the sooner it will be accepted.

There is not much difference in the general principle of component injection. You define abstract services, request their implementations, and let others register their own implementations into the pool. However, in the case of Spring, the injection is done from the "outside." Somehow, you need to identify slots of abstract service types that need to be filled with instances of real services. Then you hope that the framework will fill those slots before execution begins. This can be done either with annotations on fields or with configuration files describing setters and constructors that are then invoked during initialization. You end up with the feeling that the framework surrounds the application, providing a safe cushion so that the application gets all the resources it needs.

The Java Extension Mechanism used in NetBeans is different. Compared to Spring, it feels as if things are "inside out." Instead of having a framework around it, Lookup is a small library that needs to be called. That is, the whole application is built around it and calls it as needed. Instead of inspecting the class files or configuration file to find where the slots are to insert the implementations, you define the slots by calling the lookup methods:

```java
import org.openide.util.LookupEvent;
import org.openide.util.LookupListener;
class AnagramsWithLookup extends Anagrams {

    public AnagramsWithLookup() {
    }

    @Override
    protected WordLibrary getWordLibrary() {
        return Lookup.getDefault().lookup(WordLibrary.class);
    }

    @Override
    protected Scrambler getScrambler() {
        return Lookup.getDefault().lookup(Scrambler.class);
    }
}
```

This presents us with all the pros and cons of nondeclarative APIs as covered in Chapter 12. Specifically, it's difficult to statically analyze an application for a list of all its injection slots.

On the other hand, you are in charge and you now have more control over them. Each dynamic call to the lookup establishes a service slot. The library then consults the environment, builds the pool of available service implementations, and returns them for each request. Embedding the API in a library simplifies setup, as you don't need to execute any special code prior to running the actual application and executing the queries. Because a slot is simply a method call, you don't need to do the injection prior to executing the code. That means the setup is as simple as it can be.

In addition, the setup of the service implementation pool, which is performed by whoever assembles the final application, is as simple as possible. Because the default implementation of Lookup.*getDefault*() is based on the JDK's extension mechanism, you don't need to generate any configuration files. Instead, you simply need to set up the classpath correctly. Say a piece of code searches for a service such as org.apidesign.anagram.api.WordLibrary by means of a call to the following:

```
Lookup.getDefault().lookupAll(org.apidesign.anagram.api.WordLibrary.class)
```

As soon as that happens, the implementation discovers the current classpath, reads all the resources located at META-INF/services/org.apidesign.anagram.api.WordLibrary, analyzes them for the names of classes, instantiates the classes, and returns their instances.

COMPONENT INJECTIONS OR SERVICE LOCATOR

Purists might argue that this is no more than a service locator pattern. True, the call to the Lookup API looks like that. If that was all it consisted of, it would not deserve to be called injection at all. However, the important part is having discovery based on the classpath configuration. With it, the component is genuinely injected into the libraries, simply by inclusion in the application.

This makes it easy to create and register alternative implementations of a given service type and specify which implementation is to be used via final application configuration, without any change to the objects that use the service. This is especially useful in unit testing, because it's easy to inject a mock implementation of a service into the object being tested:

```
@Test public void testInjectionOfServices() throws Exception {
    Anagrams ui = create();

    assertNull("No scrambler injected yet", ui.getScrambler());
    assertNull("No scrambler injected yet", ui.getWordLibrary());

    MockServices.setServices(
        ReversingMockScrambler.class, SingleMockLibrary.class
    );

    Scrambler s = ui.getScrambler();
    assertNotNull("Now we have scrambler", s);
    assertEquals(
        "It is the mock one", ReversingMockScrambler.class, s.getClass()
    );
    WordLibrary l = ui.getWordLibrary();
```

```
        assertNotNull("Now we have library", l);
        assertEquals(
            "It is the mock one", SingleMockLibrary.class, l.getClass()
        );

        ui.display();

        assertEquals(
            "The word from SingleMockLibrary is taken",
            "Hello World!", ui.getOriginalWord()
        );
        assertEquals(
            "The word is rotated using ReversingMockScrambler",
            "!dlroW olleH", ui.getScrambledWord()
        );
    }

    public static final class ReversingMockScrambler implements Scrambler {
        public String scramble(String word) {
            return new StringBuilder(word).reverse().toString();
        }
    }

    public static final class SingleMockLibrary implements WordLibrary {
        public String[] getWords() {
            return new String[] { "Hello World!" };
        }
    }
```

These are exactly the requested features of pure dependency injection. The fact that Lookup fulfills them as well qualifies it as a variant of injection.

This kind of component injection is not only straightforward and easy to configure, it's also a Java standard. As stated earlier, JDK 1.3 defined the registration format in the META-INF/ services namespace, and since then, the JDK has used this for its own purposes, such as for XML parsers and transformers. However, since JDK 6, there is also the public API to query the list of all registered implementations of a service:

```
class AnagramsWithServiceLoader extends Anagrams {

    public AnagramsWithServiceLoader() {
    }

    @Override
    protected WordLibrary getWordLibrary() {
        Iterator<WordLibrary> it;
```

```
        it = ServiceLoader.load(WordLibrary.class).iterator();
        return it.hasNext() ? it.next() : null;
    }

    @Override
    protected Scrambler getScrambler() {
        Iterator<Scrambler> it;
        it = ServiceLoader.load(Scrambler.class).iterator();
        return it.hasNext() ? it.next() : null;
    }

}
```

As a result, you can practice this kind of component injection in any application based on Java 6. There is no need for additional libraries or frameworks at all.

SPRING AND LOOKUP

It's clear that you can build a real dependency injection framework on top of Lookup. In some senses, Lookup is an enabling technology. It's like an assembly language for injection, on top of which various solutions can add a bit of syntactic sugar and get something that really can be classified as injection, as well as inversion of control.

In fact, we have a bridge between Spring's ApplicationContext and Lookup. If you have an instance of Lookup, you can wrap it with ApplicationContext, and vice versa. This clearly shows the same expressive power of these technologies. Not only that, it means that you can use a part of one and mix it with another. For example, you can have beans' definitions described with Spring's configuration XML file and access them via Lookup. Or, you can have META-INF/services registrations and use them with Spring's dependency injection framework. The possibilities are endless and if you want to know more about them, visit http://injection.apidesign.org.

As the JDK already contains the ServiceLoader API, it's reasonable to ask why we continue to offer Lookup. There are three reasons. The first applies to particular versions of Java. ServiceLoader is available only for JDK 6, while NetBeans provides Lookup versions for all JDKs since 2001. So, if you need to run on an older JDK, you might consider Lookup for this reason.

The other reason is because of the dynamic nature of NetBeans-based applications: modules can be added and removed at runtime, so it's common for the effective classpath of a NetBeans-based application to change. That also means that the resources registered in the META-INF/services/ namespace might change as well. When they change, they can influence the results provided by Lookup.getDefault queries. When the set of available services changes, many things might need to be refreshed. For example, when someone uninstalls a module providing support for CVS version control, you need to refresh and redraw the state of all the files that have been under that module's control. This means you need to be informed about changes. For this purpose, the Lookup library introduces support for listeners:

```
private Lookup.Result<WordLibrary> libraries
    = Lookup.getDefault().lookupResult(WordLibrary.class);
```

```
private LookupListener listener = new LookupListener() {
    public void resultChanged(LookupEvent ev) {
        initWord();
    }
};
{
    libraries.addLookupListener(listener);
}
```

So, the listening capability is the second reason to prefer Lookup over ServiceLoader. The JDK is still imprisoned in a world of static applications, where tricks with dynamic class-loading are possible (as NetBeans shows) but are not considered mainstream. Therefore, there is no way to listen to any changes in the ServiceLoader API. Also, listeners are not easy to implement or support with traditional dependency injection frameworks. These frameworks are more mentally oriented toward the initial setup phase, followed by execution where all services are set and ready for use. On the other hand, with listeners and dynamic models, you can expect changes at any time, and you should always be ready to handle them. In situations where this style of behavior is needed, Lookup is probably the right choice.

The third and final reason favoring Lookup over ServiceLoader is that Lookup provides both sides of the API: the API for clients to query for registered services, and the API for providers, meaning those wanting to write their own pools of services and to define new ways of registering and obtaining them. That means that the Lookup API can be seen as a generic framework for independent communication between two distinct components. In fact, this is another example of a teleinterface, as shown in Figure 7-1.

Figure 7-1. *Teleinterface in Lookup*

On one side of the picture you see the callers that search for services and use the general Lookup API to get them. On the other side, you see the provider that maintains the pool of services. In the middle, you see the Lookup API. It doesn't know anything about the queries or anything about the service pool provider, but it can connect these two together and can do so while maintaining full type safety. The type traverses from one side of the universe to another while being hidden, and invisible during the journey. This lets you define APIs that are fairly extensible while not knowing anything about the extensions.

Writing an Extension Point

One question that people often ask is how to use Lookup to define an *extension point*: an abstract service that other modules can implement and extend functionality at a certain point of execution of the base module.

Let's imagine that we have several modules, one providing the core functionality and the others wanting to extend that functionality. What is the right way to implement it? How does the NetBeans Lookup declare an extension point?

The first step is to declare an extension interface in the core module and to make it part of an API. That means to make it public, and in the case of the NetBeans Runtime Container, to also include it in the module's public packages. Let's say the module wants to display various tips of the day provided by other modules. So, it defines the following interface:

```
package org.apidesign.extensionpoint.api;

public interface TipOfTheDay {
    public String sayHello();
}
```

When the core module is about to display the tip of the day, it can ask the system for all registered instances of the TipOfTheDay and randomly select one of them:

```
Collection<? extends TipOfTheDay> all =
    Lookup.getDefault().lookupAll(TipOfTheDay.class);
List<TipOfTheDay> arr = new ArrayList<TipOfTheDay>(all);
Collections.shuffle(arr);

String msg;
String title;
int type;
if (arr.isEmpty()) {
    msg = "I do not know what to say!";
    title = "No provider registered";
    type = JOptionPane.WARNING_MESSAGE;
} else {
    msg = arr.get(0).sayHello();
    title = "Selected from " + arr.size() + " providers";
    type = JOptionPane.INFORMATION_MESSAGE;
}
```

Then it simply displays the tip. Simple. Trivial. Simply by using the Lookup interface, you've created a registry that other modules can enhance. However, such enhancement obviously requires work on the other side. Each module that would like to register its TipOfTheDay implementation needs to have a dependency on the module providing the TipOfTheDay class and have it on its compilation and execution classpath. Only then can it write a class with its own implementation of the provider:

```
package org.apidesign.extensionpoint.impl2;

import org.apidesign.extensionpoint.api.TipOfTheDay;


public class HelloWorld implements TipOfTheDay {
    public String sayHello() {
        return "Hello World!";
    }
}
```

At this point, all that is left is to register the class in a standard Java Platform, Standard Edition (Java SE) way: create a plain text file called META-INF/services/org.apidesign. extensionpoint.api.TipOfTheDay to go in the module JAR. The file should contain only the following line:

```
org.apidesign.extensionpoint.impl2.HelloWorld
```

Your modules are now ready to communicate using your own extension point. Their configuration is fully in the hands of the final application's assembler, as the behavior depends on the actual runtime classpath. If you compose it with JARs providing different implementations of the TipOfTheDay service, you'll get different behavior.

The Need for Cyclic Dependencies

Some runtime systems allow cyclic dependencies, which is quite useful, especially when dealing with legacy code. On the other hand, using this feature for newly written code is just like creating one big dish of spaghetti consisting of references between your classes and modules. That is why the NetBeans Runtime Container doesn't allow cycles at all. Not everyone likes this. However, the stricter nature of the container helps people to create a cleaner architecture. In fact, disallowing cyclic dependencies is one of the biggest contributions the NetBeans modular system provides to fight object-oriented spaghetti code. Especially for new code, you should avoid them. However, even legacy code can be rewritten not to need them, as the following paragraphs explain.

It's not good to have mutual dependencies among modules full of messy object-oriented spaghetti code. Regardless of how people try, the entropy of software is always around the corner and cannot be completely avoided. If things get out of hand, each piece of the system starts to refer to each other one. After a while you are left with what in graph theory is called a *complete graph*, where each piece is interconnected with every other piece. Not only that, but in bad situations the dependencies can even be bidirectional. The whole system becomes progressively harder to maintain, compile, and understand. You effectively end up having to treat the whole code base as a single package, which completely nullifies the benefits of having a system of distinct pieces.

The NetBeans Lookup, or Java 6's ServiceLoader and component injection, form a system that is carefully designed to eliminate the need for cyclic compile-time dependencies between individual modules in an application. I can't guarantee that you won't shoot yourself in the foot—you could still create a single huge module and inside it adhere to the spaghetti design, if that's what you really want to do. However, as soon as you decide to split the application into multiple modules, you'll be guided to make your classpath dependency graph acyclic.

People migrating from an existing monolithic application might want help splitting the application into modules. Let's practice a bit on the following example. Imagine a piece of legacy code that is split into two packages:

```java
package org.apidesign.cycles.array;

import java.io.IOException;
import java.io.OutputStream;
import org.apidesign.cycles.crypt.Encryptor;

public class MutableArray {
    private byte[] arr;

    public MutableArray(byte[] arr) {
        this.arr = arr;
    }

    public void xor(byte b) {
        for (int i = 0; i < arr.length; i++) { arr[i] ^= b; }
    }

    public void and(byte b) {
        for (int i = 0; i < arr.length; i++) { arr[i] &= b; }
    }

    public void or(byte b) {
        for (int i = 0; i < arr.length; i++) { arr[i] |= b; }
    }

    public void encrypt(OutputStream os) throws IOException {
        Encryptor en = new Encryptor();
        byte[] clone = (byte[]) arr.clone();
        en.encode(clone);
        os.write(clone);
    }
}
```

```java
package org.apidesign.cycles.crypt;

import org.apidesign.cycles.array.MutableArray;

public final class Encryptor {
    public void encode(byte[] arr) {
        MutableArray m = new MutableArray(arr);
        m.xor((byte)0x3d);
    }
}
```

The example is simple and a bit artificial, but it gets the point across. You see two independent packages that need each other. The package for working with arrays needs to encrypt its data, to which end it uses the Encryptor class. The crypt package then works on arrays and uses MutableArray to simplify its work. This is an excellent example of spaghetti object-oriented design, by the way!

Can this example be split into two NetBeans modules? Can these modules eliminate its mutual cyclic dependency? Yes, this can be done. Just use Lookup to replace the mutual classpath dependency with component injection! One module can keep its classpath dependency on the other; that is completely acceptable. So, the initial step is to decide which of the modules will depend on the other. In the preceding example, it seems like the Encryptor is some kind of service, and as a result, it might seem more natural to let the org.apidesign.cycles.crypt module depend on org.apidesign.cycles.array, as mapped out in Figure 7-2.

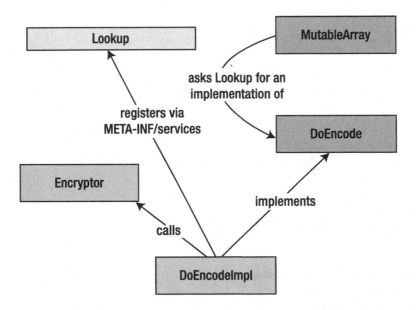

Figure 7-2. *Application split into two modules*

No changes are needed in Encryptor; its use of MutableArray is allowed, because the class is on its compile classpath as well as its runtime classpath. However, MutableArray can no longer refer to the Encryptor directly, during compile time. It can and in fact has to have access to the Encryptor during runtime, as it's a necessary part of its execution environment. Without it an essential piece of the functionality, the encrypt method, cannot be implemented. How can you create such an environment/runtime dependency and not refer to the class during compilation? You need to create a facade and wrap the calls to the Encryptor in it. The facade interface is defined in the org.apidesign.cycles.array module and implemented by the org.apidesign.cycles.crypt module. You can find the implementation using Lookup. Here is the rewritten code sample:

```
public class MutableArray {
    private byte[] arr;
```

```
    public MutableArray(byte[] arr) {
        this.arr = arr;
    }

    public void xor(byte b) {
        for (int i = 0; i < arr.length; i++) { arr[i] ^= b; }
    }

    public void encrypt(OutputStream os) throws IOException {
        DoEncode en = Lookup.getDefault().lookup(DoEncode.class);
        assert en != null : "org.netbeans.example.crypt missing!";
        byte[] clone = (byte[]) arr.clone();
        en.encode(clone);
        os.write(clone);
    }
}

package org.apidesign.cycles.array;
public interface DoEncode {
    public void encode(byte[] arr);
}

package org.apidesign.cycles.crypt;
import org.apidesign.cycles.array.DoEncode;
public class DoEncodeImpl implements DoEncode {
    public void encode(byte[] arr) {
        Encryptor en = new Encryptor();
        en.encode(arr);
    }
}
```

The DoEncode interface is the facade that isolates the actual calls into the Encryptor class. The new version of the MutableArray code uses Lookup.*getDefault*().*lookup*(DoEncode.**class**) to locate the actual implementation of the facade and communicate with it. The implementation is provided by the org.apidesign.cycles.crypt module that can refer to the Encryptor class. As you can see, the cyclic compile-time dependency is avoided.

At runtime, both modules have to be present, because they cannot work independently. An assert check in MutableArray.encrypt ensures that an implementation of the DoEncode facade is provided. This is an important architectural restriction defining the execution environment for the modules. Because our goal is the clueless assembly of individual modules into working units, it's highly desirable somehow to express such a dependency on a higher level, not just as an assert in the code. The NetBeans Runtime Container allows you to specify the environment with "needs/provides" tags in the module manifests. Those can then easily be consumed and analyzed during application assembly, and the entire set of modules can be automatically verified for the consistency of its whole execution environment. To demonstrate that in this example, the module with MutableArray should specify that it needs an implementation of the facade by adding the following line in its manifest:

```
OpenIDE-Module-Needs: DoEncode
```

The module providing the `Encryptor` should tell the NetBeans Runtime Container that it provides the implementation:

```
OpenIDE-Module-Provides: DoEncode
```

By doing this, the NetBeans Runtime Container knows that these modules need each other and always enables both of them, or neither.

You can apply similar refactorings to all cyclic dependencies between modules that need each other to perform their internal functionality. As a result, by using component injection, you are allowed to clean up your architecture to be acyclic and effectively clean up the object-oriented spaghetti mess and replace it with cleaner module dependencies. Using component injection helps to improve the architecture of Java applications!

Lookup Is Everywhere

I've talked about component injection, a concept that is found in other frameworks. You might ask what's so special about that. So far you've seen several good aspects of the Lookup repository. However, there is much more to it. Imagine that there was more than just one Lookup. Imagine tens, hundreds, thousands, millions!

That's exactly what you have when working with Lookup. In contrast to the JDK's `ServiceLoader` class, the NetBeans Lookup can have multiple instances, each serving as a separate pool. As Tim Boudreau used to say, "Lookup is a pool with objects swimming in and out." As a result, you can create adaptable objects, meaning objects that can extend their behavior and functionality by providing additional interfaces from their pool. Let's demonstrate this by creating an enhanced Swing icon that can also offer additional capabilities:

```java
public interface ExtIcon extends Icon, Lookup.Provider {
    public void paintIcon(Component c, Graphics g, int x, int y);
    public int getIconWidth();
    public int getIconHeight();

    public Lookup getLookup();
}
```

The `ExtIcon` class is a place to look for interfaces that can provide additional optional functionality or that temporarily mark the icon as having some capability. For example, imagine that there is a need to convert the icon into a `java.awt.Image`. You can provide an optimized way to do so if the icon already knows its image, and also provide a default fallback implementation if it doesn't:

```java
public static Image toImage(ExtIcon icon) {
    Image img = icon.getLookup().lookup(Image.class);
    if (img != null) {
        return img;
    }
    BufferedImage buf = new BufferedImage(
        icon.getIconWidth(),
        icon.getIconHeight(),
        BufferedImage.TYPE_INT_RGB
```

```
    );
    icon.paintIcon(null, buf.getGraphics(), 0, 0);
    return buf;
}
```

Each icon can now influence its own destiny and provide an optimized way to convert itself into an image. If that optimization is not provided, the icon is printed via the default conversion through BufferedImage. This is an example of a static way of enhancing an interface with a new type, because the ability to convert to an image is likely to be permanent. Either the image has the ability or it doesn't. However, there are other more dynamic examples, such as the modified state of an icon. If the icon represents an object inside a graphics editor, it often is in a modified state when it needs to be saved or reloaded. Let's model that with the following interface:

```
public interface Modified {
    public void save() throws IOException;
    public void discard() throws IOException;
}
```

The implementation of this interface can swim in and out of the icon's lookup to notify its observers about its state. For example, if an icon supporting this contract is modified, it can add an instance of the interface into its lookup by calling ic.add(new ModifiedImpl()), just like in the following:

```
public final class ModifiableIcon implements ExtIcon {
    // AbstractLookup is a helper implementation
    // so that people do not need to write their own
    // lookup from scratch
    private AbstractLookup lookup;
    // InstanceContent is an interface that gives the
    // "creator of the lookup" more rights, such as
    // ability to modify the content
    private InstanceContent ic;

    ModifiableIcon() {
        ic = new InstanceContent();
        lookup = new AbstractLookup(ic);
    }

    public Lookup getLookup() {
        return lookup;
    }

    public void markModified() {
        if (lookup.lookup(ModifiedImpl.class) == null) {
            ic.add(new ModifiedImpl());
        }
    }
}
```

```
        private final class ModifiedImpl implements Modified {
            public void save() throws IOException {
                // save somehow
            }

            public void discard() throws IOException {
                // discard changes
            }
        }
    }
}
```

When it's saved, it can again remove the implementation of the Modified interface. Any foreign code, such as a save action or revert action, can listen on the content of the lookup and update its state accordingly.

SELECTION IN NETBEANS

Lookup is used inside NetBeans-based applications for various purposes and one of the most intricate is to track selection between different UI components. Here the Lookup represents a global UI context, a place where interesting objects appear and disappear. The global actions, such as those in the toolbar or main menu, can enable or disable themselves.

The global context is only a proxy that delegates to the component currently selected by the user. This component can either provide its Lookup to represent its state, or it can continue to delegate to the currently selected element inside itself. At the end the delegation might end up at our ExtIcon. When that happens, the global toolbar save action inspects the current context, which after a bit of proxying and delegation is the Lookup of our icon, and re-enables its state according to the presence of the Modified interface.

In this scenario, you can think of Lookup as an *event bus*. An event bus is also a place that "objects swim in and out of." It's used to drive what the user interface shows. In this approach, your first step is to create an instance of a Lookup and call it the event bus. Next, make the user interface elements attach listeners to the Lookup and then listen for your known objects. Finally, you need to define a way of placing your objects into the Lookup. And there you are. You now have a generic and type-safe event bus. There is room for various improvements and additions. For example, it's completely doable to support the merging of events or network access.

Yet another of the patterns considered useful is the *query pattern*, which mixes both aspects of Lookup: its ability to be a facade over component injection, as well as its ability to be an API for the adaptable pattern.

You often find your code holding an object while wanting to find out something special about it. For example, you have an icon and need to find out whether it represents a cat or not. Some icons might know what they represent themselves. However, most of them only know the values of their own pixels. Understanding their own content is beyond their domain. However, there might be various external algorithms that can inspect the pixels and guess whether they represent a cat or not. These algorithms are independent of the individual icons and can work with any of them. Moreover, there might be many different implementations of each algorithm. Can we create an API to make this whole system cooperate?

We need a single method in the API that allows the users to ask the "cat question" for any icon. The icon itself might or might not know the answer to your question. If it doesn't, let's consult the registered oracles and find out what they think. Although there is a need for a simple API that everyone can query, the decision needs to be extensible and needs to be injected into the API by the modular add-ons. This is where Lookup comes into play nicely:

```java
public class CatQuery {
    private CatQuery() { }

    public static boolean isCat(ExtIcon icon) {
        for (CatQueryImplementation impl :
            Lookup.getDefault().lookupAll(CatQueryImplementation.class)
        ) {
            Boolean res = impl.isCat(icon);
            if (res != null) {
                return res;
            }
        }

        for (CatQueryImplementation impl :
            icon.getLookup().lookupAll(CatQueryImplementation.class)
        ) {
            Boolean res = impl.isCat(icon);
            if (res != null) {
                return res;
            }
        }

        return false;
    }
}
public abstract class CatQueryImplementation {
    protected CatQueryImplementation() { }

    protected abstract Boolean isCat(ExtIcon icon);
}
```

Each add-on can register and inject its own implementation of the CatQueryImplementation. When asked, each add-on can decide whether or not an icon represents a cat, or it can leave the decision for another registered query implementation.

This is an example of component injection. The API opens the door and lets extensions register their enhancements that it then uses. However, this example can also benefit from the adaptable pattern. From time to time people might need to implement their own icon and want to decide for themselves whether their own icon is a cat or not. You can achieve this easily by adding your own CatQueryImplementation into your icon lookup. Once it's called, decide and return the right result.

THE LESSER OF TWO EVILS

Close readers may ask why, especially after the discussion in the section "Are Abstract Classes Useful?" in Chapter 6, the `CatQueryImplementation` is an abstract class and not an interface. Didn't I claim that interfaces are to be preferred over abstract classes? Yes, I did, but I also mentioned that under certain circumstances the access control offered by abstract classes can be useful. The "cat query" is an example of that.

My biggest fear, as an API writer, is that a client of the API won't use the `CatQuery.isCat(ExtIcon)` method, but rather will directly find the query implementations by calling `Lookup.`*`getDefault`*`()`. *`lookupAll`*`(CatQueryImplementation.`**`class`**`)` and talk to them directly. That would bypass my mediating code in the `isCat` method completely, and prevent me from evolving the interface in the future. We'll talk more about that in Chapter 8. By making the query implementation methods protected, I've eliminated this danger.

On the other hand, nothing comes for free and this is not a win-win situation. Making the methods protected effectively prevents delegation. It's not possible to create your own `CatQueryImplementation` that would delegate to another such implementation. This might be limiting in certain situations. However, there is not much to be done about that. Either you stay in charge and keep the future of the API in your own hands, or you put more freedom in the hands of API users, limiting your API's evolution capabilities. I've chosen to stay in control and that is why I used an abstract class with protected methods.

The whole setup reminds me once again of a teleinterface. In the middle, in "hyperspace," is the object containing the Lookup. Around it is an observer on one side and a provider on the other. The Lookup itself doesn't know anything about the objects traveling through it. However, it can type-safely transmit them from one side of the cosmos to the other.

Query patterns can smoothly merge injection with the adaptable pattern, synchronizing them and achieving unlimited extensibility. If needed, they can also provide a single local place to "fish for" the implementations of the enhanced interfaces as they "swim in and out." The beauty of the NetBeans Lookup is that it unifies injection on a global scale with an adaptable pattern (thus also showing how similar they are) and creates a consistent and unified approach to injection and adaptable APIs.

Overuse of Lookup

The dynamic nature of Lookup is so interesting and inspiring that those who start to like it in appropriate places are liable to use it even in places where more type-safe variants exist. This overuse can lead to an increased amount of empiricism in your API design: the Lookup itself acts as a "magical bag" full of interesting objects. Users of such an API then put their hands into that bag and blindly search for a given interface. Either it's there or it isn't. If so, things work; if not, things fall apart. The result is probably not the best basis for pleasant coding experiences, which is why this section will talk about various ways to replace the use of Lookup with alternative API coding styles.

I once saw an API proposal that used Lookup as a factory. It contained a set of interfaces that you might pass into a factory method. Based on their presence, the factory created the desired object:

```java
public interface NameProvider {
    public String getName();
}
public interface URLProvider {
    public URL getURL();
}
public interface ResetHandler {
    public void reset();
}
```

```java
public static AServerInfo create(final Lookup interfaces)
```

This relied on the "magical bag" feature of Lookup, and it did all feel a bit magical! Simply by looking at the API you could hardly guess what possible instances could be fed into the interfaces parameter. The motivation behind this approach was not bad, because it optimized for future extensibility. Whenever you needed to improve the factory methods with a new interface, there would never be a need to add new methods. You would simply change the implementation of the create method to recognize a new interface and then tell users of the method to provide it. Nevertheless, this usage completely lacks the teleinterface aspect. There is no bottleneck for tunneling type information. The factory method needs to know all the interfaces that it recognizes. Therefore, it would be better to list them directly in the method signature:

```java
public static AServerInfo create(
    NameProvider nameProvider,
    URLProvider urlProvider,
    ResetHandler reset
)
```

This is more explicit and easier to use with the modern code completion features of Java IDEs. It also supports a greater degree of cluelessness, because you don't need to read documentation to discover what to implement or what not to pass to the factory method when creating server information. Also, the evolution aspect is fine: as soon as you need support for shutdown, you can add a new interface and factory method:

```java
/** @since 2.0 */
public interface ShutdownHandler {
    public void shutdown();
}
```

```java
/** @since 2.0 */
public static AServerInfo create(
    NameProvider nameProvider,
    URLProvider urlProvider,
    ResetHandler reset,
    ShutdownHandler shutdown
)
```

The only drawback is the proliferation of the many overloaded create methods with a potentially long parameter list. This is especially visible when you want to support all the variations of the method parameters, from 1 to N parameters. There can be up to 2^N factory methods. This might not be a problem all the time, but when it is, there is a way around this. I call it the *cumulative factory* pattern:

```
public static AServerInfo empty() {
    return new AServerInfo(null, null, null, null);
}


public final AServerInfo nameProvider(final NameProvider np) {
    return new AServerInfo(np, this.url, this.reset, this.shutdown);
}
```

The pattern introduces only one factory with minimal arguments, which creates a "default" implementation of the object, along with a set of "cloning" methods. The latter methods all take the state of the already existing instance, modify one of its aspects, and return the newly created instance that then has the new combined values, while leaving the original instance untouched. As a result, you are not bothered with parameters that are not important. Also, you can choose any combination of these methods, while keeping the amount of methods linear to the number of useful interfaces:

```
inf = AServerInfo.empty().nameProvider(p).urlProvider(p).reset(p);
```

TUNING A DVB-T SIGNAL

For my DVB Central project, which I created to be able to capture digital video broadcasting on my computer, I needed a way to tune to the right TV channel. However, DVB is more complex than the previous, soon-to-be-switched-off classic TV broadcast signal. It's not enough to specify a *frequency* to tune into. You also need to set *bandwidth*, *transmit mode*, *code rates*, *modulation*, *spectral inversion*, *guard internal*, and maybe even more.

Originally, I wanted to have a Tune class and classic factory methods to create its instances. However, the enormous number of configuration parameters scared me. It would have to be a long list of parameters for the most detailed factory method. At that time I realized the possibility of using a cumulative factory and Tune was then simplified.

Moreover, this solution allowed one nice feature. The DVB signal, in contrast to the classic broadcast signal, usually shares one common frequency for a state. This is possible because signals broadcast from two transmitters can use the same frequency and strengthen themselves, while the classic broadcast signal transmitters interfere. How that is possible is far beyond my cluelessness level. However, based on the locale of the country the caller of the default factory is living in, the API can create an instance of Tune with appropriate values for the caller's location. Some of the values might be off. However, it's very likely that most of them are correct. As a result, it's usually enough to get the default Tune and only change its frequency, leaving all additional parameters untouched. This would not be easy to achieve with a classic factory method.

It helps if the AServerInfo class is final and immutable. There are several helpful suggestions relating to this point elsewhere in this book, such as the section "Make Objects Immutable" in Chapter 12. For purposes of this Lookup-oriented chapter, you simply need to keep in mind that Lookup is not always the best solution. In particular, when its teleinterface capabilities are not needed, you should consider an alternative API style.

CHAPTER 8

■■■

Separate APIs for Clients and Providers

Is there more than one type of API? Is an API for clients different from an API for implementors? "Yes" is the simple answer to both questions. This chapter explores why this is so and what the implications are for API design.

As an example, let's imagine a fictitious API for Winamp, or in the Unix world, for the X Multimedia System (XMMS). The related player can play audio files, skip to the next song, return to the previous song, and offer a playlist. The playlist provides the possibility of adding, removing, and reordering songs. The functionality is provided for users, but is also accessible to other programs through an API. The program can call xmms.*pause*() or xmms.*addTo-Playlist*(filename). As you can see, communication is initiated by the other program: the one that uses the player's API to instruct it to perform an action. After execution of the command ends, control returns to the caller. Let's name the caller a *client* and the API a *client API*.

At the same time, the XMMS APIs allow third parties to register *output plug-ins*. You can extend the functionality of the default player by providing a utility method that writes the played data to disk, broadcasts it over a network, and so on. The player itself initiates the communication in such cases. After collecting enough data for playback, the program locates the current output plug-in and sends it the data to process: plugin.*playback* (data). After finishing the playback, execution is returned to the player, which can then continue gathering more data, and the whole process continues. Is the plug-in a client? Well, it's in a completely different position from the client in the previous paragraph. It doesn't instruct XMMS to do anything. It increases the list of activities that XMMS can perform. Therefore, the plug-in is not a client. The XMMS ability to register plug-ins is an example of a Service Provider Interface (SPI).

Expressing API/SPI in C and Java

To show how client APIs and APIs for service providers differ, let's now try to express the difference in two different languages. First, let's write an API in procedural C, without any object-oriented extensions. Then you'll create a version of the same interface in Java.

The C language is perfectly suited to expressing a client API. You simply write the methods and announce them in the header file. Then, others can compile against them and call them:

```
void xmms_play();
```

```
void xmms_pause();
void xmms_add_to_list(char *);
```

The Java approach is not very different:

```
public class XMMS {
    public void play() { doPlay(); }
    public void pause() { doPause(); }
    public void addToPlaylist(String file) { doAddToPlaylist(file); }
}
```

However, you have more choices. It's possible to declare these methods static, to leave them as instance methods, to make them abstract, or to make them final. Each of these options has slightly different semantics. However, let's suppose these methods are without any additional modifiers and clients just somehow obtain the predefined instance of the XMMS object. Then it's clear that the way C and Java handle client APIs is similar. However, the situation is completely different when writing an SPI.

To write your own plug-in for XMMS in C, you must start with a function that will perform the playback. The plug-in must define the following:

```
void my_playback_prints(char* text) {
 printf("%s\n", text);
}
```

Also, the player itself has to have a registration function accepting a pointer to some other function, such as the following:

```
void xmms_register_playback(void (*f)(char*));
```

The plug-in should call this method to register itself:

```
xmms_register_playback(my_playback_prints)
```

XMMS then calls its playback function whenever necessary. In Java, instead of playing with pointers, the contract starts with the definition of a playback interface:

```
interface Playback {
    public void playback(byte[] data);
}
```

Then the plug-in has to implement the interface and register that instance to the player:

```
class MyCallbackPrints implements XMMS.Playback {
    public void playback(byte[] data) {
        System.out.println(new String(data));
    }
}
xmms.registerPlayback(new MyCallbackPrints());
```

That's all. The player can make its calls to the plug-in as it would in the case of C. The behavior is the same, but the logic you use to obtain it is quite different. In the case of Java you use only language constructs learned in the first semester of a Java course, such as classes and interfaces, and how to subclass and implement. In the C version, you'd need to use a pointer to a function, which is something that most first-semester students haven't even heard of.

In the case of C, the amount of work to produce an SPI, such as a callback, is enough to prevent a beginner from even trying it. Your knowledge has to grow significantly to attain a state where you can—or need to—design an SPI. However, in Java any declared method that is not private, final, or static is an invitation for someone to provide a callback and thus create an accidental SPI. Often programmers and teachers don't clearly understand this. It's not part of conventional wisdom. Although Java books introduce public, nonstatic, and nonfinal methods in their first chapters, or at least as soon as they start talking about applets, they don't provide proper warnings about all their consequences. Though that might be fine for simple development, when you start to design APIs, all the bad habits learned at the start come back to haunt you in the form of mistakes.

API Evolution Is Different from SPI Evolution

Evolution is a natural part of any contract. Over time, everything becomes obsolete, insufficient, or broken. APIs and SPIs are not exceptions. It's better to be prepared for evolution and to plan for it, avoiding the mistakes that would otherwise be difficult to undo.

In the case of an API that offers methods to clients, there are no problems with additions. Adding new methods to remove a file from a playlist cannot break binary compatibility. It can simply please clients of the new version of XMMS's API. They have more possibilities, more choices, and they can either use them or not. This is a win-win strategy for extending client APIs.

In the case of APIs for providers, the situation is exactly the opposite. Adding new methods to an interface that others must provide effectively breaks all existing implementations because they have not implemented them! On the other hand, it's acceptable and valid to stop calling, thus essentially removing a method from this kind of interface. If the operation flow was not part of the contract, not calling one method would not break much.

BINARY VERSUS SOURCE COMPATIBILITY

The JVM can load classes that don't implement all methods of the interfaces that they implement without linkage errors. The error occurs later, when a missing method is called. Then a `java.lang.AbstractMethodError` is raised when the call to the undefined method is made. Although not recommended by this book, this can be acceptable if the caller of the method is also adding it. Then it can always surround the call with a proper exception catch.

The path of evolution depends on the type of interface: additions to an API are acceptable, while removing functionality is not. In SPIs removals are allowed, while additions are not. When producing a contract, you must understand which pieces form part of the API that clients will call and which pieces are part of the SPI that will extend the functionality that you are writing. The biggest mistake that you can make is to mix *API and SPI together* within a single class. If you do that, you have not created any room for evolution. Adding a method is forbidden because of the contract for SPIs and removing is forbidden because of the contract for APIs. *Always separate your API from your SPI.*

Writer Evolution Between Java 1.4 and 1.5

Let's imagine java.io.Writer with its API in Java 1.4 and let's replay what happened to it in the subsequent release of the JDK. The class started to implement java.lang.Appendable and needed to provide implementations for its methods, especially Appendable *append*(CharSequence csq). The new method could not be left abstract, because several subclasses already implement the Writer class without knowing about the new method added in the 1.5 version. So, the method has to have some kind of implementation. Let's now think about various options that might have been taken when implementing it. Of course, we already know what implementation has been chosen in JDK 1.5, but let's pretend we don't and let's search for the best alternative.

We already know that it's not possible to make the method abstract. However, could we make it throw an exception?

```
public Writer append(CharSequence csq) throws IOException {
    /* throws an exception as this method is new and
     subclasses need to override it */
    throw new UnsupportedOperationException();
}
```

Yes, it can throw an exception. This is reasonable behavior for implementors because those who subclassed Writer have not implemented the new write method. Letting it throw an exception might seem like correct behavior from the point of view of a provider of a Writer subclass. However, from the more common—that is, client—point of view, the Writer's new method with no implementation is nonsense. Nobody can reliably use it, or at least everyone has to write defensive code and get ready for possible failure:

```
try {
    bufferedWriter.append(what);
} catch (UnsupportedOperationException ex) {
    bufferedWriter.write(what.toString());
}
```

This is indeed a ridiculous API. Instead of a simple call, there is a need for four lines of code. If I were a user of this API I would rather rely on the old methods and always use the conversion to String, rather than trying to mess with the new call! Throwing an exception therefore doesn't appear to be a good choice. It's much more reasonable to provide a default implementation of the new method:

```
if (csq == null) {
    write("null");
} else {
    write(csq.toString());
}
return this;
```

Here we have an excellent solution from the point of view of Writer class clients, and actually this is the one the JDK uses. The clients can rely on the method being implemented, either by the default implementation or by a subclass that can provide a more efficient implementation. So far, so good.

However, we have one problem. Even if there is a highly optimized writer that can process the characters from the sequence without converting it into a string, you might not get the optimal performance that you are looking for. How is that possible? Well, what do you do if you want to speed up the output stream? You wrap it in a BufferedOutputStream. If you want to speed up the operations with writers, what do you do? You use BufferedWriter. Alas, this will no longer work once the Writer has been enhanced with new append methods. The problem is that while implementing the new methods in BufferedWriter, you need to choose between efficient delegation and compatibility. There is no simple way of implementing a fast and correct implementation of BufferedWriter. If you don't override the new *append*(CharSequence seq) method, there will never be a performance benefit for anyone optimizing their own code with a BufferedWriter:

```java
/** Writer that counts the number of written characters.
 */
public class CountingWriter extends Writer {
    private int counter;


    public int getCharacterCount() {
        return counter;
    }

    @Override
    public void write(char[] cbuf, int off, int len) throws IOException {
        counter += len;
    }

    @Override
    public Writer append(CharSequence csq) throws IOException {
        counter += csq.length();
        return this;
    }
}
/** A "lazy" sequence of characters, for example one that can represent the
 * content of a CD, read it lazily, does not fit all into memory at once.
 */
private static final class CDSequence implements CharSequence {
    private final int start;
    private final int end;

    public CDSequence() {
        this(0, 647 * 1024 * 1024);
    }

    private CDSequence(int start, int end) {
        this.start = start;
        this.end = end;
    }
```

```
    public int length() {
        return end - start;
    }
}
//
// testing code from BufferedWriterOnCDImageTest:
//
CountingWriter writer = new CountingWriter();
 CDSequence cdImage = new CDSequence();
 BufferedWriter bufferedWriter = new BufferedWriter(writer);
 bufferedWriter.append(cdImage);
 assertEquals(
    "Correct number of writes delegated",
    cdImage.length(), writer.getCharacterCount()
 );
```

Even if the client application is rewritten to use the new method, as in the preceding case, the potentially optimized method w.append(CharSequence) is not going to be called. The implementation in BufferedWriter renders all these optimizations useless. The sequence is always converted to String, which might sometimes require so much memory that the successful computation is not possible. Is there a better way? Yes; let's reimplement the new append methods in BufferedWriter to delegate without losing performance:

```
// efficient, yet dangerous delegation skipping methods unknown to
// subclasses that used version 1.4
if (shouldBufferAsTheSequenceIsNotTooBig(csq)) {
    write(csq.toString());
} else {
    flush();
    out.append(csq);
}
return this;
```

This change provides the desired effect; that is, computing the number of characters on enormous sequences succeeds, just as shown by BufferedWriterOnCDImageTest. However, this is not the end of our journey; there is another problem to solve. BufferedWriter is subclassable and its methods can be overridden to change the behavior of its inherited peer methods. For example, you might use the following to do some cryptographic operations:

```
public class CryptoWriter extends BufferedWriter {
    public CryptoWriter(Writer out) {
        super(out);
    }

    /* We need to override all known methods of BufferedWriter
     * and do conversion of the argument char, string, or char array.
     */
```

```java
@Override
public void write(char[] buf, int off, int len) throws IOException {
    char[] arr = new char[len];
    for (int i = 0; i < len; i++) {
        arr[i] = encryptChar(buf[off + i]);
    }
    super.write(arr, 0, len);
}

@Override
public void write(int c) throws IOException {
    super.write(encryptChar(c));
}

@Override
public void write(String str, int off, int len) throws IOException {
    StringBuffer sb = new StringBuffer();
    for (int i = 0; i < len; i++) {
        sb.append(encryptChar(str.charAt(off + i)));
    }
    super.write(sb.toString(), 0, len);
}

private char encryptChar(int c) {
    if (c == 'Z') {
        return 'A';
    }
    if (c == 'z') {
        return 'a';
    }
    return (char)(c + 1);
}
}
```

Such a class overrides all the known methods at the time of writing (for example, JDK 1.4) and correctly encrypts all the data sent to it using any of the old write methods. However, the developer creating the class knew nothing about the append methods, as they were to appear later. Using them makes the text appear to be unencrypted:

```java
CryptoWriter bufferedWriter = new CryptoWriter(writer);
bufferedWriter.append("VMS");
bufferedWriter.flush();
assertEquals("Converted", "WNT", writer.toString());
```

We expect the preceding code snippet to work. However, with the efficient delegation of the *append*(CharSequence) method to the underlying out.*append*(CharSequence), it's not going to encrypt anything. None of the methods known previously in the JDK 1.4 implementation is called, and as such from the point of CryptoWriter, we have introduced an incompatible behavior. The intention of the CryptoWriter class was to wrap all writes, which is not happening in this version of BufferedWriter.

This is getting complicated! For certain purposes, such as processing of enormous sequences, it would be better to delegate to the underlying writer directly. In other situations it's necessary to call BufferedWriter.*writer*(String); otherwise, backward compatibility is compromised. This is a tough situation, but not unsolvable. With a little bit of reflection magic, you can find out when to do what, by inspecting whether the class is subclassed or not and whether it overrides the write method or not. The code that satisfies both conditions exists and works correctly. It looks like this:

```java
boolean isOverriden = false;
 try {
    isOverriden =
        (
            getClass().getMethod(
                "write", String.class
            ).getDeclaringClass() != Writer.class
        ) ||
        (
            getClass().getMethod(
                "write", Integer.TYPE
            ).getDeclaringClass() != BufferedWriter.class
        ) ||
        (
            getClass().getMethod(
                "write", String.class, Integer.TYPE, Integer.TYPE
            ).getDeclaringClass() != BufferedWriter.class
        );
 } catch (Exception ex) {
    throw new IOException(ex);
}

if (isOverriden || shouldBufferAsTheSequenceIsNotTooBig(csq)) {
    write(csq.toString());
} else {
    flush();
    out.append(csq);
}
return this;
```

This third version is the final one. It's a bit complicated due to the introspection, but it works. It finds out whether the behavior of all the write methods is expected; that is, if they are not overridden. And if they are not, it delegates the processing of the CharSequence directly to the underlying writer. This is why this version can efficiently process even a sequence representing a CD image. On the other hand, if there is a danger that the default behavior of BufferedWriter might be somehow altered, it resorts back into delegating to its own write methods to ensure proper compatibility for those who subclassed this class in the previous version. This kind of delegation is slower, but ensures that the code such as `CryptoWriter` continues to work.

The use of reflection makes this kind of code much less nice than it used to be, but at least it works and does its job right. As backward compatibility is often a constraint, and evolution is needed from time to time, hacks such as this might be found necessary, especially if you do a poor job when releasing the first version. This is the price you have to pay because the API was not ready for evolution in its first version. The `Writer` class mixes the API for clients together with service provider APIs. As these kinds of API impose different restrictions on the evolution, and particularly the service provider API is not happy when new methods are added to it, you can get into pretty obscure situations. This was clearly illustrated when discussing the `BufferedWriter` and `CryptoWriter` cooperation.

NODE AND FILTERNODE IN NETBEANS

Some of you might think that the `Writer` and `BufferedWriter` are a rather artificial example and that the problems with cryptography and processing of a whole CD are unlikely to happen in real life. True, I made the example up and decided to use `Writer` and `BufferedWriter`, both because they are widely known and also because they underwent the process of being extended with new methods delegating to already existing ones. So the example is artificial; however, the situation is not. I have faced it in the NetBeans Nodes API and when I saw it I could not believe my eyes.

The NetBeans Nodes API is an abstraction over the JavaBeans API that allows you to represent a node—that is, a bean—with its properties, name, display name, a few additional extensible attributes, and a hierarchy. The hierarchy was inspired by `java.beans.beancontext` and it allows completely unknown nodes and beans to be arranged into a tree hierarchy and cooperate with one another.

NetBeans uses this API a lot for displaying the content of files on disk, the logical organization of projects, the structure of databases, the elements in Java sources, and so on. The pattern is almost always similar: someone defines the skeleton, such as a structure of a project, and then he picks individual nodes/beans and inserts them into the structure. As a result, nobody controls the whole tree. Everyone is responsible just for its part, delegating the rest to unknown peers in the system.

The preceding would not be that big of a problem. However, from time to time, the default structure of a project might not be good enough. For example, you might want to filter out all non-Java files from it. For that situation we have something called `FilterNode`. That class can decorate another `Node`, including its name, properties, and hierarchy. As a result, when you use `FilterNode` or its subclass, you can get two layered structures of nodes. Underneath is the tree of original nodes; on top of it is a tree of `FilterNodes` that delegate to the nodes below. These two trees need not match exactly; the filtering can leave some original nodes out of the hierarchy or add a few additional ones. However, from time to time a `FilterNode` delegates to some original `Node`. Due to the way we composed the original hierarchy, it might be a completely unknown node, provided by a completely unknown module. This all forms a situation like `BufferedWriter` and `Writer`, just a bit more complicated, because you cannot control the underlying objects that the calls are being delegated to at all.

Once I needed to add an alternative method to get the actions for a pop-up menu shown on top of the `Node`. Originally there was `SystemAction[]` *getActions*(), created a long time before Swing became widespread. As such, it returned our own NetBeans type. We decided to change this and use real Swing actions, so I introduced `javax.swing.Action[]` *getActions*(**boolean** b). As our `SystemAction` implemented `javax.swing.Action`, I just delegated from the new method to the old one, just like JDK 1.5's `Writer.append` delegates to `Writer.write`. Also, I modified all the code that displays the pop-up menu to use the new method. This all seemed natural and correct: all nodes could stop supporting NetBeans' private actions and instead they could directly empower the existing or homegrown Swing ones.

However, in a week or less I got a bug report complaining that the pop-up menu on some node wasn't correct. After some investigation I found out that the problem was in `FilterNode`. As soon as users decorated an existing `Node`, then the `FilterNode`'s new `getAction(boolean)` method delegated to its old `getAction()` method, which then called the old `getAction()` method on the node being decorated, completely skipping its new `getAction(boolean)`. That's just like if you tried to optimally write out a `CDSequence` using `BufferedWriter`.

I was surprised to find out the cause of all the troubles. As a result I took two actions. First, I put the reflection checks into `FilterNode` to optimize the delegation if the old method was not overridden, or to delegate properly to the original method in case it was provided by a subclass. Second, I invented the `Writer` and `BufferedWriter` example to illuminate my adventures as something closer to users of plain Java libraries.

Now that we know the problem, and also know how to recover from such a situation when it appears, we might also think about preventing it from even occurring in the first place. From a higher-level point of view, the cause of all the problems seems to lie in the mixing of subclassing and delegation. While subclassing is an example of using a class as a service provider API, with all its implications to evolution, the delegation is making just client API calls, but into the same interface, restricting its ability to evolve in different ways. Mixing these two types of API usage doesn't go as smoothly enough as one would wish. I'm not sure if there is a way to merge these two approaches together to work well in Java and also support evolution. However, I know how to prevent the mixing situation: either prevent subclassing, or prevent delegation.

Let's see what it would take to prevent subclassing. All we need to do is follow the advice from this section and split the client API from the subclassable API implemented by others. Say the original version of `Writer` looked like the following:

```
public final class Writer {
    private final Impl impl;

    private Writer(Impl impl) {
        this.impl = impl;
    }
    public final void write(int c) throws IOException {
        char[] arr = { (char)c };
        impl.write(arr, 0, 1);
    }

    public final void write(char cbuf[]) throws IOException {
        impl.write(cbuf, 0, cbuf.length);
    }
    public final void write(char cbuf[], int off, int len)
    throws IOException {
        impl.write(cbuf, off, len);
```

```java
    }
    public final void write(String str) throws IOException {
        impl.write(str, 0, str.length());
    }
    public final void write(String str, int off, int len)
    throws IOException {
        impl.write(str, off, len);
    }
    public final void flush() throws IOException {
        impl.flush();
    }
    public final void close() throws IOException {
        impl.close();
    }
```

Tip The API is in the final class with methods similar to the original `java.io.Writer`. Here comes the service provider part of the whole interface with a few factory methods to build various implementations of the API.

```java
    public static Writer create(Impl impl) {
        return new Writer(impl);
    }

    public static Writer create(final java.io.Writer w) {
        return new Writer(new Impl() {
            public void write(String str, int off, int len)
            throws IOException {
                w.write(str, off, len);
            }

            public void write(char[] arr, int off, int len)
            throws IOException {
                w.write(arr, off, len);
            }

            public void close() throws IOException {
                w.close();
            }

            public void flush() throws IOException {
                w.flush();
            }
```

```
        });
    }

    public static Writer createBuffered(final Writer out) {
        return create(new SimpleBuffer(out));
    }


    public static interface Impl {
        public void close() throws IOException;
        public void flush() throws IOException;
        public void write(String s, int off, int len) throws IOException;
        public void write(char[] a, int off, int len) throws IOException;
    }
}
```

Then, the addition of the new method would be easily done compatibly. Adding a method to a final class is completely binary compatible, and introducing a new interface is also binary compatible. So the following additions would be made in version 2.0 to introduce support for CharSequences:

```
public final class Writer implements Appendable {
    private final Impl impl;
    private final ImplSeq seq;

    private Writer(Impl impl, ImplSeq seq) {
        this.impl = impl;
        this.seq = seq;
    }
    public final void write(int c) throws IOException {
        if (impl != null) {
            char[] arr = {(char) c};
            impl.write(arr, 0, 1);
        } else {
            seq.write(new CharSeq(c));
        }
    }

    public final void write(char cbuf[]) throws IOException {
        if (impl != null) {
            impl.write(cbuf, 0, cbuf.length);
        } else {
            seq.write(new CharSeq(cbuf, 0, cbuf.length));
        }
    }
    public final void write(char cbuf[], int off, int len)
    throws IOException {
        if (impl != null) {
            impl.write(cbuf, off, len);
```

```java
    } else {
        seq.write(new CharSeq(cbuf, off, len));
    }
}
public final void write(String str) throws IOException {
    if (impl != null) {
        impl.write(str, 0, str.length());
    } else {
        seq.write(str);
    }
}
public final void write(String str, int off, int len)
throws IOException {
    if (impl != null) {
        impl.write(str, off, len);
    } else {
        seq.write(str.subSequence(off, off + len));
    }
}

public final void flush() throws IOException {
    if (impl != null) {
        impl.flush();
    } else {
        seq.flush();
    }
}

public final void close() throws IOException {
    if (impl != null) {
        impl.close();
    } else {
        seq.flush();
    }
}
```

■**Tip** So far the code just mimics the original APIs. However, each method contains a switch. It either calls the old implementation or it converts the arguments into a single CharSequence and calls the new implementation interface. Now comes the set of newly added API methods. The calls to the new implementation are simple; the calls to the old one need to convert input parameters.

```java
public final Writer append(CharSequence csq) throws IOException {
    if (impl != null) {
```

```java
            String s = csq == null ? "null" : csq.toString();
            impl.write(s, 0, s.length());
        } else {
            seq.write(csq);
        }
        return this;
    }

    public final Writer append(CharSequence csq, int start, int end)
    throws IOException {
        return append(csq.subSequence(start, end));
    }

    public final Writer append(char c) throws IOException {
        write(c);
        return this;
    }
```

■**Tip** Here comes the service provider part. We have a new `ImplSeq` interface for implementors and a new factory method to convert it. The rest of the API remains the same; just notice that the implementation of `Writer create(java.io.Writer w)` is now simpler due to the use of `ImplSeq`.

```java
    public static Writer create(Impl impl) {
        return new Writer(impl, null);
    }

    public static Writer create(ImplSeq seq) {
        return new Writer(null, seq);
    }

    public static Writer create(final java.io.Writer w) {
        return new Writer(null, new ImplSeq() {
            public void write(CharSequence seq) throws IOException {
                w.append(seq);
            }

            public void close() throws IOException {
                w.close();
            }

            public void flush() throws IOException {
                w.flush();
```

```
        }
    });
}

public static Writer createBuffered(final Writer out) {
    return create(new SimpleBuffer(out));
}


public static interface Impl {
    public void close() throws IOException;
    public void flush() throws IOException;
    public void write(String str, int off, int len) throws IOException;
    public void write(char[] arr, int off, int len) throws IOException;
}
public static interface ImplSeq {
    public void close() throws IOException;
    public void flush() throws IOException;
    public void write(CharSequence seq) throws IOException;
}
}
```

Now compile time checks completely replace the problems with the default implementation of *append*(CharSequence) that so complicated the runtime behavior when BufferedWriter was subclassable. You can implement a Writer.Impl and use an appropriate factory method to create the instance of Writer. Alternatively, you can implement Writer.ImplSeq, use the new factory method, and provide the new method *append*(CharSequence). The decision is fully done during compile time and doesn't require any runtime checks.

Indeed, using final classes for client APIs, using interfaces for provider APIs, and bridging them with a factory methods pattern might sound complicated, but it is built from the basic patterns that are commonly used, well understood, and accepted. The new API uses "factory methods," it "hides as much as possible," and it clearly defines interfaces for clients (the final class) as well as for providers (those two implementation interfaces). So, it's not that complicated to use such an API. Moreover, it solves a lot of evolution problems pretty well. Although writing the initial version might require more work, *separating client APIs from provider APIs* greatly simplifies future evolution and prevents problems created by the fact that delegation and subclassing don't work well together.

Split Your API Reasonably

The previous section talked about the importance of splitting the API that people call from the API that people implement. Its motivation to separate the APIs for clients from those intended for service providers was mostly motivated by evolution problems. However, there is another interesting approach to looking at the separation of APIs: readability.

Any API—especially an API written in Java—exhibits signs of locality: related things are expected to be defined next to each other. They should either be defined in the same class, in the same package, or as in the NetBeans case, in the same module. Locality is encouraged by the object-oriented nature of the language. For example, the core runtime libraries in the java.* namespace follow this principle. When you're looking for methods that query information about a String object, it's a good start to look into the Javadoc of the String class. Even though other usages of String are all over the APIs, those that manipulate the content of String are mostly, or even exclusively, declared as members of the String class.

Let's take streams as another example. The basic streams are defined as java.io. InputStream and java.io.OutputStream. These two classes are related to each other. Probably due to their relationship, they are found in the same package: java.io. They define the basic interface to any stream, but found together with them are several other classes that complement the stream offering. For example, they provide subclasses with useful functionality, decorators, and classes that can join input streams and output streams together. All of these are in the java.io package. As a result, they're easy to find, and API users are able to make a safe bet by starting their hunt for the appropriate stream API in the java.io package. Though other streams are in other packages, such as ZIPInputStream in the java.util.zip package, those are specialized. On top of that, anyone working with ZIP files is likely to search the package containing the name "zip" before anything else. Also, people who don't care about ZIP files aren't bothered by the presence of the ZIP stream classes in the main starting point for all the stream classes.

The two preceding examples mentioned can—and probably should—be generalized. Nearly every API that people design should follow them. Think about your users and provide them with the *locality* that they expect from your API:

- Place related methods into the same class.

- Don't put unrelated methods where they don't belong just because you cannot think of a better place to expose them.

- Put related classes into a single package.

- Move extra classes that are useful in special situations to other places.

Following these simple rules will increase your API's locality. As a result, the orientation of users in the API will increase significantly.

Often an API is in fact a set of APIs for different groups of people. This is also true in the case of the java.io package. The basic package is for everyone, but the ZIP utilities are only for people interested in the ZIP format, while the cryptography streams are intended for a different set of people again. Each of these groups is likely to have different interests. It makes sense to provide specific entry points for each of them. People interested in ZIP files start at java.util.zip, from where they can be directed to java.io if needed. The likelihood of distracting their attention by something related to cryptography is minimized by the chosen packaging. So, bear in mind that different groups of people will probably be using your API. Structure the API in such a way that they will all feel comfortable and be able to navigate around its packages with ease.

The NetBeans project has indeed come a long way in understanding that there are multiple types of APIs. Mistakes have been made learning this lesson. A good example of this relates to the org.openide.filesystems library. This is the award-winning library providing an abstraction over any kind of virtual filesystem. Its primary purpose, and the one that has had the biggest target audience, was to provide an API for access to any file-based resource. We achieved this aim by creating a FileObject class that could represent any file, whether on disk, in a ZIP file, an imaginary file in memory, or a remote file on an FTP server. This was the interface 99 percent of people were interested in. However, our mistake was to put the generic implementation next to it. We put `LocalFileSystem`, `JarFileSystem`, and so on, into the same package. This completely broke the locality of the API: these interfaces were supposed to be used by 1 percent of the people who wish to write or tailor their own implementation of the virtual filesystem. However, this is not what happened. People found these interfaces in the same package, and instead of using the `FileObject` class, a significant percentage of those 99 percent of users started to do crazy and unexpected things with the API. They tried so hard that they got a reference to one of the implementation classes and could call methods that were never meant to be called by the clients of the API. We concluded that it would be better to put implementation classes into a separate package, to make them harder to find and to possibly prevent API users from having the chance to get to such classes at all.

That was the day we decided to use two kinds of packages: `org.netbeans.api` and `org.netbeans.spi`. If we could design the filesystem library again we would likely put the `FileObject` class into the API package, with the rest of implementation classes in the SPI package. That way, the actual implementation would be hidden from the 99 percent of users who don't need it. They would then be less likely to invent ugly tricks for using them. However, we couldn't make this change when the library was already in widespread use without breaking binary backward compatibility. That's why we've simply put large warnings into the documentation to navigate people to the right classes for their interest. Also, we've learned from our mistake and subsequently have created split packages, as described earlier, for each newly designed API. For example, when we designed a `masterfs`, which is the most commonly used filesystem type in NetBeans today and represents files on local disks, we separated the implementation into its own module, with a single separate API intended for version control providers—that is, for the 1 percent of users who need it. The 99 percent of regular users can now focus on the good old `FileObject` class, without being distracted by everything that the `masterfs` package offers.

Separating API from SPI didn't solve all our problems. New questions appeared, as people could not agree on the difference between API and SPI. This is natural; you can try it yourself. Simply ask two of your colleagues the difference between these terms, and their answers will differ. At least, that was our situation on the NetBeans project. The basic problem lay in the perception that an API is something that people call and an SPI is something that people implement. In general, this is a good observation that would match the FileSystem API as well. In the case of the FileSystem API, the `FileObject` is there to be called, while the `LocalFileSystem` and `JarFileSystem` are there to be implemented. However, a conceptual problem soon transpired. The problem applies to any API based on JavaBeans that makes use of listeners. Although an implementation of a listener does, in fact, implement an interface and could therefore be classified as an SPI, listeners' locality is usually close to related API interfaces. In fact, they do belong to the same package.

It took the NetBeans project a great deal of time to sort through this confusion. Fortunately, there was one aspect of the API versus SPI separation that NetBeans has always tried to stress: classes in the API package should be *self contained* and should not refer to classes in the SPI package. This clearly draws the boundaries of the possible separation. It includes listeners and other callback interfaces related to the API classes within the same location as those classes. In fact, this rule is a specific case of the "locality" criterion described in this chapter. It anticipates two groups of potential users. The first group is a majority that will use the API by making calls to it, while needing to know only about the API package. The second group is a minority that needs to perform special operations, such as the registration of their own implementation. The second group needs to understand a much wider contract, including both the API and the SPI parts. If this situation applies to your library, then splitting the interfaces into separate API and SPI parts is a good idea. A perfect example of the usefulness of this approach is the javax.naming package versus the javax.naming.spi package. Most people care only about the first package, while only those who need to hook into the process of creation or name context resolution need to study the latter package.

But why should only two groups of people approach your library with certain needs? Sometimes there could be more *localities*, at which point it makes sense to split the interfaces of your library into even more parts. There is an example of a NetBeans module that defines four different categories for its APIs:

- *Core API*: Usually of interest for the group of users who want to perform some essential operations with the library that cannot be done without using this core API.

- *Support API*: A set of utility methods that make the use of the API easier. These don't need to be used, but just provide comfort for the API user. We found that it makes a lot of sense to separate this kind of API from the core, as it clearly communicates that these interfaces are not needed for the work of the library—they are simply helpers.

- *Core SPI*: A set of interfaces for a different group of users, who want to plug in to the library. This might not need to be present at all if plugging in is not supported.

- *Support SPI*: Sometimes implementing the interface to plug in to is a bit complex. Therefore, again, you can provide helper interfaces. Once again it makes sense to separate the two types of SPI interfaces, as it's good to clearly describe what needs to be implemented and what is simply helper utility support.

This set of API categories is not intended to be final. It only shows what works well for certain modules in NetBeans. Other projects and libraries might find different separations as useful as we have found ours. However, there is a general observation to make from the NetBeans mistakes described earlier: it improves the life of your API users if the API follows the *locality* of usages. When designing an API, think about the groups of users you are targeting and then organize the API in a way that most closely suits their needs. And remember: few libraries are composed of a single API. Often there are multiple purposes and multiple groups that the API tries to address. Structure your API according to your users' needs.

CHAPTER 9

■■■

Keep Testability in Mind

Software design practices are changing. People are developing software in completely different ways now compared to the end of the '90s, even though they are still using Java. I've already suggested that one reason for this change is the rise of freely available and usually open source libraries that turn developers of new code into assemblers of existing functionality.

Another important and related change is the rise of modular applications. Composition was always a dream, but today it's increasingly a reality. Successful products are built on top of modular containers, proving the benefits of modular architecture. Modular applications can be delivered with acceptable integration of individual components, while continuing to provide a coherent user experience. Ten years ago this scenario was no more than a dream.

The change is huge and affects various aspects of a developer's daily life. However, one of the most important changes that has occurred since the end of the last century is the increasing popularity of testing. Developers have come to realize the importance of testing relative to all the other tasks common to day-to-day development cycles. Increasingly, automated tests are being written. When developers start down this path, they tend to never leave it. In short, testing is addictive.

It's not the intent of this book to argue the importance of automated testing. For these purposes, I direct you to other sources, the most important of which is "Test Patterns In Java" (`http://openide.netbeans.org/tutorial/test-patterns.html`), which gives detailed motivations, together with in-depth examples. However, for purposes of this API design book, let's stick with those aspects of testing that influence the way people evaluate and write APIs.

There is only one explanation for why you might disagree with my assertion that testing is addictive: you haven't tried it yet! Primarily, testing is effective. For example, you can improve your planning skills if you make sure that tests are written early, together with or even before the rest of your code. You can eliminate the "feature freeze" effect—that is, the effect of developers announcing they are finished with features only to find themselves spending the last week adding more and more new pieces to the application. What's worse, they're not even trying to execute their application at all anymore. Early automated testing prevents this self delusion and gives each project a clear way of measuring its current state. Let's not forget to add that testing is religious! The roots of testing are related to the Extreme Programming (XP) movement, and to be honest, it's difficult to be "extreme" without becoming "religious" in the process. It's often the case that people who get addicted to testing become religious about it. Sometimes they refuse to write any application code at all without writing tests!

API and Testing

Here we arrive at the first meeting point between API design and testing. According to a recent poll on Javalobby, about 45 percent of developers write tests. Because they write tests, they are likely to be more productive. They started testing sooner than others and therefore are also early adopters of new enhancements. From every point of view, these are the people that no writer of a library wants to miss. These are the creative and enthusiastic adopters who are crucial to your library. However, there is an easy way to discourage those developers: write your library in a way that prevents testing. In one fell swoop, those highly creative developers will simply refuse to use it.

The testing lifestyle is so addictive and religious that developers can easily refuse to use an API simply because it's too difficult to test. Of course, this attitude can be outweighed by marketing pressures or by eliminating all the other possible alternatives to your API. However, to be honest, this is not easy to achieve. There are so many open source choices that your success won't last long if you succeed in eliminating alternatives. If there is a need for a solution that supports testing, someone will find it, and tough luck if that solution is provided by one of your direct competitors.

The basic strategy for most testing, and especially unit testing, is related to *mock objects*. There are many polemics and lengthy explanations as to the nature of mock objects. However, for the purposes of analyzing the influence of testing on the design of API, it's enough to note that a mock object is little more than a fake implementation of an interface that is used for testing purposes. For example, when the real application is supposed to connect to a database through an implementation of the Connection interface, the tests use a mock implementation that doesn't actually make a connection, but reliably simulates the behavior of a real implementation. By using this kind of dummy implementation, you can concentrate on the logic of the application and eliminate the random effects of a network connection to a database. This also simplifies the test setup, because its execution doesn't require a real database populated with data, but only its reliable simulation in memory.

From the point of view of an API writer, the most important aspect of an API is to provide a way of creating mock objects for the most important interfaces. Either it has to be possible to write an implementation of those interfaces, or the API has to provide some default implementations. Of course, this applies only to APIs where implementing mock objects makes sense. For example, nobody will write a mock object for String, partly because String is a pure and simple library. It does its job and it does it right. The other reason is that the execution of all String methods is self contained. It doesn't need to be surrounded by any environment, and therefore is well suited to being tested in isolation without any mock objects.

On the other hand, there are definitely cases where mock objects are needed. Besides the aforementioned database connection scenario, there are other examples. URLStreamHandler can be useful for providing fake implementations of a URL that handles the http: protocol by serving local files or data instead of connecting to a network. As another example, a fake implementation of java.awt.Toolkit is sometimes useful, and I could name various other examples.

When APIs correctly expose no more than what is needed, there can be a problem in the testing phase: sometimes an API's users don't need the capability for subclassing. Consequently, subclassing might not even be possible. This means that you're not able to create your own mock object for the concepts in the API, which seriously limits testability of applications using the API. As explained, this might seriously discourage the interest in your API, which is why it's good to come up with some kind of solution.

Sometimes this might be the reason why people tend to prefer using interfaces in an API. However, remember that interfaces might encounter problems evolving, because they disallow the addition of methods in future revisions. So, having the ability to create mock objects is important, but not more important than having an API that can recover from the mistakes it contains and grow to satisfy user needs.

The first way to overcome this obstacle is simply to face up to it. Admit that the use cases for the API should include the ability of clients to create their own implementation of the API classes. This is a fair approach that lets anyone implement his own mock object. On the other hand, it also increases the constraints that you need to follow when evolving the API. That is why this solution might not always be desirable. You can easily paint yourself into a corner by opening up the API. Writing tests and mock objects might be easier, but there is a high price to pay for that. Improvements of the API might be hard to make, or completely prevented. That is not the best trade-off.

The solution to all this is to provide not only a regular API, but also a *testing API*. The testing API is an extension to the regular API. It's not intended to be used in regular products and applications, but only for writing tests. The testing API can contain its own implementations, or at least the means for creating mock objects for the API classes. It can also contain other useful utilities that expose the internal details of the API implementation. This is possible because the tests usually reside in the same package as the API classes. The tests can use package private methods that are not available to regular API users.

DIGITAL VIDEO BROADCASTING FRONT END

I've been in similar situations with my Saturday project dvbcentral (http://dvbcentral.sf.net). It's a fully modular, nonvisual application based on the NetBeans Runtime Container for capturing, saving, and broadcasting digital TV transmissions—*DVB-T*.

One of the modules is called frontend, which is a Java wrapper around a /dev/dvb/adapterX/ frontend Linux device. It contains the Frontend class with the find(int X) factory method, which locates the X-th Digital Video Broadcasting (DVB) device and returns an instance that can control it. If followed to the letter, the suggestions presented in this book would result in as little as possible being exposed: just enough to satisfy my use cases. That means that the Frontend class is final. It cannot be implemented by anyone else. The only implementation delegates to the Linux device file. Though this is perfectly fine for the running application, it creates some serious restrictions when writing tests.

Many other modules are built around the Frontend API. Tests need to be written for these modules and need to run in an isolated environment. I don't want them to access the real TV capture device. This was impossible because of the "never expose more than you must" rule, which was used when I designed the Frontend API. For this reason, I needed to add additional APIs for testing.

First, I simply tried to mimic the device files on disk. I added a frontend.root property that defaulted to / and was used for locating the device file. Inside the test setup, I created a dummy structure of dev/ dvb/adapter0/frontend, and so on. I did this in a temporary test directory and set the property to that directory. The tests didn't use the real device, but rather a prepared fake. This worked fine for certain tests. It even served the file content well, although it didn't allow me to write tests simulating latency errors in the delivered data—where some reads fail or are blocked—because on a local disk all reads are fast and reliable.

After a few doubts, I decided to add a "test-only method" to the API itself. This is a new factory method called createVirtual(...), which takes arguments and allows tests to create their own implementation of the virtual Frontend. I don't expect this approach to be useful for anything other than tests. Nonetheless, it's in the API and I need to guarantee the same stability category as for other APIs, which so far hasn't been a big problem.

However, a more defensive and flexible solution would be to put the same method, with the same implementation, in the `FrontendTest` testing package, instead of being directly in the `Frontend` class. The API would then remain unchanged. All tests would include the testing classes on the classpath and make use of them.

You might well ask how it's helpful to split an API from a testing API. Why can't the API users simply include the testing JARs on the classpath and then use its backdoors in their regular applications? Of course, they can do exactly that. There is no way to prevent them from doing so. However, subtle differences might warn them not to do so. First, you can declare that the stability of the real API is higher than the stability category of the testing API. For example, in NetBeans the real API would be "stable," and the testing API would be, at most, "under development." More likely it would be a "friend"—that is, requiring or asking each of its users to send a note to the API's author to notify the author that the API is in use.

The other difference is that the testing API is likely to be more "hidden." For example, if it's in a different JAR, it's also likely to be documented in a different Javadoc. Developers using only the library API might not care or even know about the testing API. They shouldn't be distracted by the presence of a method in the API that has unclear and mysterious purposes. This all sounds fine. However, it still doesn't prevent developers from using the testing API in a regular application. As already mentioned, that is hard to prevent completely. However, you can exploit a trick: the testing code usually runs with assertions on, while the production code has assertions turned off. As a result, you can guard the methods in the testing API with a check for assertions being enabled and otherwise throw an exception. One way to do so is as follows:

```
boolean assertionsOn = false;
assert assertionsOn = true;
if (assertionsOn) {
    throw new IllegalStateException("This is a testing method only!");
}
```

Too obscure and too paranoid? Maybe. You don't need to use that trick. However, keep in mind that testing is increasingly becoming popular. Creating a framework without testability in mind will likely repel the most talented and careful programmers—exactly those you need to recruit. Making applications based on your untestable framework is like telling them to select a competing offering immediately.

The Fade of the Specification

There used to be a time when every software project was supposed to start with a major planning phase that analyzed the requirements and put out a solid plan describing the system's expected behavior. Only then would the programming start. Skeptics would add that it could start just to find out that the plan was all wrong. Today more and more projects use agile methodologies, where the plan is taken as a living document and is updated as the coding takes place. Sometimes this works, sometimes it doesn't. My feeling is that a similar shift toward more agile methodologies is happening to libraries, frameworks, and programming languages.

There used to be a time when a language—especially when designed by those who prefer a rationalist approach—was first specified in a paper, and only then would developers try to implement it. There was a clear difference between the specification and the implementation. Each of them was written at a different time, usually by a different group of people. Often there were even multiple implementations trying to fit into a single specification. This was a common approach when designing languages such as ALGOL, Pascal, and Ada, as well as their standard libraries that handled operations with streams, their data structures, common algorithms, and so on. As rumor has it, this was as successful as trying to plan a software project before any coding starts. In some cases, especially with ALGOL and Ada, the specification has been found to be unimplementable, or at least hard to implement, during the implementation phase. Of course, in such a situation, you need to do another round—rewrite the specification and try to implement it. It's a lot like switching to agile development mode, except unintentionally and with a long round trip.

With common libraries the situation was similar. There is the `libc` library, which contains the basic methods every C programmer needs, such as `printf`. Signatures of functions that it's supposed to contain are specified in header files, but there are multiple implementations of them. Each Unix vendor has one. There is also the GNU `libc`, and there is probably something for Windows as well. The program can then be written against one library and its headers, and compiled and linked against any of them. The situation is similar with standard C++ libraries. However, the languages and libraries developed recently don't seem to expose this proliferation of various implementations.

The explanation for this seems to lie in the fact that most of the useful libraries developed these days are available under liberal open source licenses. As such there is not a need to reimplement them from scratch. Trying to do so is usually tedious, costly, and ultimately useless. Why would you write another implementation of some library from scratch? It's much easier to take an existing implementation and *fork* it. The open source licenses allow that. That means the origin of the code is the same. Everything starts upon the same base and as such there is no longer a strict need for a detailed proper specification. The implementation itself becomes one. Indeed, forks by definition differ in some behavior. However, because maintaining a fork is costly, the most common outcome of a successful fork is that it merges its changes and enhancements back into the main product line. This seems to be the mode of operations for systems such as Perl, Ruby, and PHP, which are heavily unspecified except by the source code. Aren't those frameworks successful?

RUBY AND JRUBY

Recently Sun decided to build upon the increasing popularity of Ruby and provided its reimplementation called JRuby, which is being built upon the HotSpot virtual machine, the same one behind Java. As the virtual machine is well optimized and robust, the expectation is that JRuby will be more well-performing and reliable than plain Ruby, especially under a heavy load.

The guys who write JRuby seem to do as good of a job as possible in mimicking the original behavior. I'm sure they know the whole Ruby specification. I've heard that they run all the tests of Ruby on the old implementation as well as on the new one and compare the results. Also, they write their own tests and again run them on both systems and fix the JRuby side until the results are the same. However, although all their tests passed in the middle of 2007, they still could not run the most important Ruby framework—Ruby on Rails on top of JRuby—as it still behaved differently under certain conditions.

This clearly shows how underspecified the language is. There doesn't seem to be any independent specification; there is just the implementation. Still, the language is quite popular.

The "bulldozer" approach seems not only to be used when designing our applications, but it also seems to infiltrate the way we design our core frameworks. Why bother with a specification if you can make the implementation public? The more people who see it, the more bug fixes you get, and that's all you need, right? Specifications are rendered obsolete—at least it seems that way. Still, you need to stiffen the framework's (or the language's) amoeba shape as much as possible. In terms of cluelessness, this stiffening needs to be maximized, while the demands on understanding are minimized. You can do this by increasing the test coverage. If the tests are good, then the likelihood of a new version breaking existing programs is minimized. In fact, the tests become part of the informal specification and help compensate for the lack of a formal one.

When I see an attempt to provide multiple implementations of the same framework these days, then these attempts seem to be mere rewrites of proprietary technologies—such as Flash, C#, or Java—into open source versions. As the Java example shows, this is hard to get right. Certain parts of Java, especially the Swing library, are unspecified and documented only on the level of source code. Of course, having two implementations of the Swing library's signatures is almost useless. The behavior is always different, and any complex application, including NetBeans, is guaranteed not to run on anything other than the original implementation. Thank goodness those days are over and Java has been open sourced. These days we still have multiple versions, but the differences are minimized to an acceptable level. Hopefully Java will operate in the fork/merge mode from now on.

Does this have any impact on API design? Yes, it does. If you are writing an open source library with a liberal license, you can almost be sure that no other reimplementation of its APIs will be created from scratch. At most, someone will fork your version. As such, you can slightly shift the focus from absolutely proper documentation to ensuring proper behavior. Cluelessness based on proper usage of API patterns should get you ready for evolution. Testing should help you ensure that the runtime aspects of your API stay unchanged in future revisions of your library.

Good Tools Make Any API Easier

From time to time you might be willing to evaluate what to do to make your library or framework more attractive. We do that in NetBeans often, possibly due to the strong pressure on the rich client Java platform and IDE battlefields. As a result, I know various ideas people often come with and I can also see whether they will work or not.

Measuring the cost of ownership isn't the primary focus when you want to find out why you don't have as many developers using your library as you would like. It might be reasonable to analyze that, if you used to have developers and are now losing them. However, if you're just starting and you need to attract new ones, this is probably not the most important criterion to use. It helps to have a good reputation with respect to backward compatibility, which reduces the cost of ownership, but it's not the primary concern.

What matters the most is time to market—that is, the ability to get productive with your library as quickly as possible without knowing it. In other words, it needs to be optimized for developer cluelessness as much as possible. This is important. This is what makes an API or a framework attractive. The question is how to do it.

I often hear suggestions to create more documentation and more examples. Of course, there are never enough of these. But ultimately, we don't want our developers browsing with Google and downloading cool stuff. We want them to have the documentation instantly ready to do what they want to do the most—that is, create an application using the library. To achieve that, we need some kind of interactive examples that not only show tips, but do the work.

Ruby on Rails and Grails demonstrate that they are well aware of that when they offer a single command to be executed that generates a skeleton of the whole application. From a certain point of view, you are "almost" finished with your application as soon as you've started. You might not have a clue about what it does, but it obviously does something and looks cool, or at least it shows something in the browser immediately. How can a framework be bad when it's so easy to do this first step?

The NetBeans Platform has the advantage of being enveloped in the NetBeans IDE. As such, it doesn't need command-line tools like the aforementioned web frameworks do. It can provide deeper integration with the tool itself. Also, wizards are the primary subsystem in the IDE for creating new things. To make the NetBeans Platform more attractive, we didn't need to completely revamp our APIs, but we needed more "interactive examples." When we introduced the wizards, the platform's productivity barrier was reduced to a few mouse clicks. Any developer is willing to agree to that price when testing and evaluating a new framework.

It helps that every major NetBeans Platform technology has a wizard that generates a skeleton. If we just had documentation instead, we would have just a small fraction of people trying our platform. Reading is easy, but unzipping, setting up a project, and running the project is too much work for most.

A good tool can also help a lot with testing. Usually it's not so easy to set up the testing infrastructure by hand. Automated tests are often executed in a sandbox—an isolated environment—and creating the sandbox correctly might turn it into too complicated of a task. Moreover, it's a task that is unrelated to the actual use of the API. The good thing about wizards is that they can not only create a skeleton of the application, but also create the right environment for writing tests. With the proper setup being instantly available, it's just a matter of a few lines of code to test the API use case or modify the test to verify the added value. That is the real use of the API. Not all developers around the world are real fans of testing, so not all of them will use the test part of the generated skeleton. However, those people who cannot live without testing will immediately find the API much more pleasant to use.

From the time-to-market point of view, the most successful API is the one that is covered with good wizards. It doesn't matter how the API itself looks. A proper creation tool can present even an ugly and complex technology as a shining diamond. Now, this is just for getting up to speed. When things get complicated and people need to deal directly with the API, it's desirable for it to be approachable, easy to use, and compatible. However, this is about cost of ownership, which always takes a back seat to the time-to-market criterion. The best promotion for your API is a slick wizard! The best way to help people write reliable code on top of your API is to let the wizard also generate the skeleton of the tests.

Test Compatibility Kit

When you allow multiple implementations of the same API, such as when designing a modular library, it's important to help each implementor fulfill every aspect of the API. As the purpose of the API is to be an abstraction over implementation details, it's important that all the implementations are consistent. Only then can users of the API ignore the actual implementations they are talking to through the API. Only then can they be sufficiently clueless.

You can enforce the consistency of modular library API implementations in two ways. One is discussed in the section "Enforcing Consistency of APIs" in Chapter 10. The other is to provide a test compatibility kit (TCK)—that is, a set of tests that implementors can use to verify their implementations for correctness, especially in consistency with the expected functional behavior.

Writing a TCK for a modular library is more complicated than writing regular tests. When you write tests for your own code, you control the code and all its tests, from the initial setup, through to the calls to the tested code, up to the final check of behavioral correctness. However, with a TCK, you leave the initialization and potentially also the result verification up to the API's implementor. This requires more imagination, as you need to envision the potential implementations and their differences, and to write the test in a way that allows them to perform the necessary initializations and checking of results. This isn't easy. It requires a bit of training. On the other hand, this is desperately needed for well-designed APIs that people can easily implement. The better your TCK, the less users will need to study the actual source code of the API. The need to study source code is a clear sign of a badly written API. A TCK kit is a way of supporting the clueless usage of your API, while improving the consistency of its implementations.

To show the value of TCKs, think back to the days when you started writing a model for Swing. For those who have not done so yet, here is a short summary. Although Swing is easy to use when you "simply assemble its components," it is also powerful. When you use its more powerful features, things might get complicated. For example, every component defines a model. There is a `ListModel` for `JList`, a `TableModel` for `JTable`, and similar models for buttons, trees, and so on. When simply assembling components, you don't need to care about models much, because they all have default implementations. However, sometimes the defaults are not enough. At that point, you begin considering implementing your own. Immediately, you find you are in the situation of an implementor of an API. Simply implementing the methods of a model is not enough: there are strong semantic constraints, especially when it comes to the coordination of events. For example, there are various restrictions on the order and content of events delivered to listeners when the model changes. This is sometimes tricky, and is hard to get right without reading and debugging the Swing source code. It would be much easier if you could simply reuse an existing `ListModelTCKTest`. You'd simply take it, change its setup, instantiate your own implementation of the model, and then verify that its behavioral aspects are correct. Alas, as far as I know, there are no such tests. As a result, writing models for Swing is a task for experts, not clueless newcomers.

TESTING COMPATIBILITY FOR THE FILESYSTEM LIBRARY

A situation similar to Swing applies to the NetBeans FileSystem library. The NetBeans FileSystem library is relatively easy to use. However, it isn't easy at all to fulfill all the library's contracts when you want to write your own filesystem from scratch. We support notification events, atomic actions, locks, mutual exclusions of read and write, and so on. It's easy to miss one of these behavioral requirements. This is what you always find when you design an interface that others can implement. You're exposed immediately to potential problems caused by wrong implementations. More than likely, at least one implementor won't do everything correctly and something will go wrong. However, clients don't care whether they are working with regular filesystems, versioned filesystems, JAR files, FTP, or something else. They simply see a bug and they report it against the API that they used; that is, against the generic framework, regardless of the actual implementation that is often responsible for the faulty behavior. This increases the amount of work for which the maintainer is responsible while analyzing such bug reports. There came a point when we simply had enough of this useless work, so we implemented a TCK for our NetBeans FileSystem library. At its heart, it has a factory class with one create and one cleanup method:

```
public static abstract class FileSystemFactoryHid extends NbTestSetup {
    public FileSystemFactoryHid(Test testToDecorate) {
        super(testToDecorate);
    }


    protected abstract FileSystem createFileSystem(
        String testName, String[] resources
    ) throws Exception;
    protected abstract void destroyFileSystem(
        String testName
    ) throws IOException;
}
```

However, a good TCK needs to count on different requirements for various implementations. For example, some of our filesystems are read only, so it doesn't make sense to test modification operations. They would fail if executed, which would be unsurprising. That's why a TCK usually needs to come up with configurations. In the FileSystem library, there are a number of "suites." Every implementation can choose which suite to use. For example, the code that wraps access to ZIP and JAR archives uses the following:

```
public static class JarFileSystemTest extends FileSystemFactoryHid {
    public JarFileSystemTest(Test testToDecorate) {
        super(testToDecorate);
    }


    public static Test suite() {
        NbTestSuite suite = new NbTestSuite();
        suite.addTestSuite(RepositoryTestHid.class);
        suite.addTestSuite(FileSystemTestHid.class);
        suite.addTestSuite(FileObjectTestHid.class);
        return new JarFileSystemTest(suite);
    }
}
```

```
    protected void destroyFileSystem(String testName) throws IOException {
    }

    protected FileSystem createFileSystem(
        String testName, String[] resources
    ) throws Exception {
        JarFileSystem fs = new JarFileSystem();
        fs.setJarFile(createJarFile(testName, resources));
        return fs;
    }
}
```

Other types of filesystem plug-ins do similar things, simply creating different instances of the filesystem.

As usual, this helps to fight application amoeba shapes. Moreover, a TCK helps to improve the regular activities a software engineering organization needs to solve. For example, it simplifies the life cycle of a bug report, it makes it much easier to find which part of the system is buggy, and it lowers the number of reassignments for which a bug needs to find the right owner. At NetBeans, we really lowered the number of "assigning to you for evaluation" bug transfers by introducing TCKs. In some senses, a TCK supports the best incarnation of a programmer's "arrogance": if you have an implementation, also use the TCK, or your bug reports won't be taken seriously.

I believe it is the responsibility of an API provider to support cluelessness as far as possible, which in turn means providing a TCK. Not everyone will use it, but those who do will probably be the most valuable users of your API. Because they are concerned with quality, they don't want to hack something that works temporarily. They want to write a system that functions correctly in the long term. These are the users who might be able to contribute back to the original library, by means of reports and bug fixes, or even by implementing new features. In other words, it's smart to let these kinds of users spend as much time as possible on improving your API.

■■■

CHAPTER 10

Cooperating with Other APIs

APIs are unlikely to live alone. They don't do anything interesting on their own; they need to be called. That means the primary concern for an API is to be designed in a way that allows smooth incorporation into a bigger application and easy coexistence with other APIs.

Only a minimal set of APIs is designed to live alone, without needing others in its environment. Knowing how to use and consume other APIs properly without painting ourselves into unwanted consequences is an important aspect of a system designed to properly evolve independently, isolated from the changes in its surrounding environment.

This chapter discusses the most important things to be aware of when consuming, reusing, exposing, and re-exporting APIs.

Beware of Using Other APIs

There are two ways to use a foreign API: either you can use a library provided by someone else internally without exposing it to clients of your API, or you can expose interfaces provided by a library to your own clients. The following paragraphs analyze the risks associated with using foreign APIs.

Exposing the API of another library, usually through its signatures, is called *re-export*. This can happen when a method returns a type defined by the other library or when it accepts this kind of a type as its argument. This can became tricky with respect to backward compatibility, because as soon as an API is re-exported, it in essence becomes part of the re-exporting library. In fact, if there is an API change in the underlying API, such as a new method added to an interface, it's immediately visible in the re-exporting API as well. This also means that if there is an incompatible change in the underlying API, certain usages of the main API might no longer be valid. That is why re-exporting always has to be done with care and you always have to think about the stability of the main and the underlying re-exported API. If the main API is intended to be more stable, it's almost a requirement to replace the re-export with some kind of wrapper. Otherwise the API cannot hold up to its own stability promise. This is especially true if the underlying API that is less stable decides to perform an incompatible change.

There is also the so-called *transitivity* of an incompatible change. For example, say an API uses some imported API and re-exports it like this:

```
public final class String {
    private final char[] chars;

    public String(char[] chars) {
        this.chars = chars.clone();
```

```
        }

    public int length() {
        return chars.length;
    }
    public char charAt(int i) {
        return chars[i];
    }
}
```

Then someone decides to remove a method from the String class (this is just an illustrative example—it should never happen, as String is a part of java.lang classes, which are developed compatibly). Let's then suppose that you decide to make String consistent with the Collections API and replace **int** *length*() with **int** *size*(). When you switch to a new version of Java, its usage of the Query library could be broken. For example, the following code would no longer compile:

```
Query query = new Query();
String reply = query.computeReply();
assertEquals("Length is correct", 5, reply.length());
```

This can happen even without changing a single line in the Query library! Simply because the underlying re-exported library is changed incompatibly, now all other libraries become incompatible as well. The incompatibility transitively spreads through all its re-exports and effectively ruins any effort to develop your own library compatibly.

There are only a few ways to avoid this kind of problem: accept the incompatibilities, deny the incompatibilities, or use wrappers.

First, you can accept the incompatibilities. If an API is re-exported and it changes incompatibly, the simplest approach is to accept that and announce that the main library has also changed in an incompatible way. That means releasing a new version with an incompatible version identification that depends on the new incompatible underlying library. Essentially, this means that you accept the release cycle, the development style of the underlying library, and the library's stability category. As with every incompatibility in the underlying API, another incompatibility is introduced to the main API.

Second, you can deny the incompatibilities. The simplest way of preventing incompatibilities is to avoid producing them, both in your own library and in the re-exported underlying libraries as well. This is easier said than done: you need to have enough influence on the underlying library to prevent unwanted incompatibilities. You can achieve this by establishing a closer relationship with the development teams of the underlying library. In the case of commercial libraries, you can become a partner and test the preview releases of new versions. If you are dealing with an open source project, you can join its mailing lists, become a contributor, and influence the direction of the library's development.

However, this prevents the problem, not fixes it when an incompatibility is actually released. The only fix in such cases, other than accepting it and transitively re-exporting the incompatible change, is not to upgrade to a newer version. Stick with the older, compatible version instead. Though this works relatively well, it has its drawbacks: usually the most interesting developments happen on the edges. Only occasionally are important fixes backported to older versions. However, this is possible if the need is strong enough: I've heard about people maintaining Linux kernel 2.4 and even 2.2, because some users don't want to risk stability-related problems when migrating to the latest 2.6 versions. Experience shows that sticking with an older version of a library is a possible and acceptable solution. However, this works only as long as there is no second user of the same library—someone who needs a different incompatible version from the one you're using. At that point, you encounter the problem of the mutual coexistence of multiple versions of the same library. This is sometimes possible, especially if the two instances of the same library are well isolated and don't know about each other. However, sometimes this approach might not work at all.

Even the decision about whether there is a nonconflicting configuration to enable all modules in the system when multiple incompatible versions of a library are re-exported by other libraries seems to be an *NP-complete* problem—a problem that is hard to solve. The details are beyond the main topics of this book; in case you are interested visit http://reexport.apidesign.org.

Third, you can use wrappers. A possible solution—one that eliminates the re-export problems completely—is to create a wrapper around the imported API and not to show it in your own API signatures at all. The library can still be used internally, but it is invisible from the outside, where it is a hidden implementation detail:

```
public final class Query {
    public static final class Sequence {
        private String data;

        Sequence(String data) {
            this.data = data;
        }

        public int length() {
            return data.length();
        }

        public char charAt(int i) {
            return data.charAt(i);
        }
    }

    public Sequence computeReply() {
        char[] hello = { 'H', 'e', 'l', 'l', 'o' };
        return new Sequence(new String(hello));
    }
}
```

If the initial version of the Query library is rewritten not to re-export String at all, and instead uses its own type, then the aforementioned fictional incompatible changes in the base Java String class would have no compatibility impact. Even if the string is used internally, the version of the Sentence class would initially use the length. When a new, incompatible String library is released, it would simply update its own internal and nonexported dependencies and change its code to the following:

```
public final class Query {
    public static final class Sequence {
```

```
    private String data;

    Sequence(String data) {
        this.data = data;
    }

    public int length() {
        return data.getSize();
    }

    public char charAt(int i) {
        return data.charAt(i);
    }
}

public Sequence computeReply() {
    char[] hello = { 'H', 'e', 'l', 'l', 'o' };
    return new Sequence(new String(hello));
}
}
```

Wrappers effectively eliminate the transitivity of incompatible changes. However, they increase the amount of APIs your users have to learn. If every library defined its own wrapper around String and named it differently, it would be very difficult to learn to program against the various APIs of these libraries. It would be difficult even to exchange strings between those produced by one library and those consumed by another.

COMPILING NETBEANS AGAINST NEWER VERSIONS OF JAVA

For a long time, the NetBeans project has tried to support the execution of the NetBeans IDE on top of the latest two major releases of Java. With NetBeans 5.5x, we ran on Java 1.4 and Java 5, while with NetBeans 6.0 we support Java 5 and Java 6. This is usually done by compiling and developing on the older version of Java, while testing on it as well as on the newer version. This works relatively well, except for the fact that developers tend to like living on the edge. They normally want to develop on the latest version of Java. That means that our source code must be compilable on the older as well as on the newer version of Java. Often this is not the case. Whenever we try to compile the NetBeans IDE against a new major version of Java, we face potential problems, as parts of the Java libraries are not developed in a compatible way.

I can accept that our code breaks when we provide our own implementation of java.awt.peer interfaces. I can also accept that our code no longer compiles as a result of new abstract methods having been added to these classes. In fact, java.awt.peer is not declared as part of the Java API and we should not be using it, although we need it for our Matisse GUI builder.

On the other hand, I'm not happy when we have to play tricks with the compilation of our own implementations of javax.sql.RowSet. That class forms a standard API that everyone can use. So, you'd think that "to use" also means "to subclass." This is exactly what we do, because we want to intercept the calls to methods provided by this interface. However, this leads to uncompilable code, because providers of the API love to add new methods into interfaces. This is often difficult to work around. It's difficult to make the code compilable against two different versions of Java. The good news is that our usage of `javax.sql.RowSet` is at least self-contained and we don't re-export it.

At the same time, we do re-export the `org.w3c.dom` interfaces. These exhibit the same problem: their maintainers love to add new methods to them. In contrast to the `RowSet` case, we expose methods returning these interfaces in our own classes. Moreover, we need to return our own decorator implementations for performance reasons. This was tricky to handle, but with a bit of help from `java.lang.reflect.Proxy`, we managed to get around the compilation problem. We don't compile at all; instead we dynamically dispatch. As a result, the underlying implementation can add methods as frequently as it wants. Our proxy will always mimic its current state and dispatch all of them. The code works, but it's not the most pleasant thing to write and maintain.

Therefore, it's better and simpler to develop compatibly. Projects that are verifiably able to produce compatible APIs are then easier to reuse. You don't need to play tricks with wrappers, propagate transitively incompatible changes of the underlying libraries, or suffer with the use of older versions of a library when development has already shifted focus to newer versions.

Leaking Abstractions

The section "Beware of Using Other APIs" warns about re-exporting foreign APIs. However, not only foreign APIs can cause problems. You can also face problems when exposing your own APIs. After all, the more you expose, the less flexibility you have when using or evolving the APIs.

NETBEANS CODE COMPLETION API MISTAKE

In NetBeans we have a code completion API. The code completion API lets anyone plug a code completion API implementation into the editor, and the implementation may offer various hints when typing. This API operates on Swing's text document. It finds all registered providers and sends them a context—that is, the document—along with the position where the hints should be displayed.

For some reason, the context also has a `getTextComponent` method that returns `JTextComponent`. This immediately opens the door to a never-ending set of additional APIs, including the hierarchy of Swing components, all their methods, whole AWT libraries, and so on. As a result, the API for code completion has become extraordinarily large, and the possible usages of the API go far beyond the original horizon of the API designer's imagination. What can you do with `JTextComponent`? Anything. Anything at all.

Unlimited APIs can be problematic. We discovered that when we started to embed languages into each other, such as JavaScript inside HTML and Java inside JSP. We had code completion providers for each of these languages and we wanted to eliminate the surroundings, such as HTML and JSP. We wanted to create its appropriate context. However, part of the context is the `JTextComponent`. Can we return a context for the whole document? Unlikely. Can we create a fake context? Maybe, but what methods that return `JTextComponent` do we need to "fake"? Will *getParent()* work, does the component need to be visible, and so on?

If we had hidden the component from the API and explicitly enumerated the methods developers might need when computing the completion hints, we would have been in a much better situation.

Just imagine what can happen when a method in your API exposes java.io.File: your API users can read the content of the file and they can write to that file, which is usually acceptable. However, they can also perform various searches to find the existence of relative files. As a result, as soon as you give a file to some API method, you completely lose control. Maybe your goal was to provide someone a stream so that they could simply read something. However, with a file they can do much more than that.

FAKE ENCAPSULATION

Let's look at another API in NetBeans: the Task List API. This particular API allows developers to add individual tasks to a *task list* window. These tasks are associated with user files. When a user double-clicks a task, a file is opened and the cursor lands on a specific line, which the user can modify or fix to complete the task.

When we prototyped this API, we defined the concept of a Resource. A Resource is the object representing a file. That class had a method to get the name and input stream, which was enough for most API usages. However, there came a point where we realized that this would not be enough. We also needed to add a getter for FileObject, which is the NetBeans-enhanced wrapper around java.io.File.

However, FileObject itself already has a way to obtain a stream and a name. The original concept of Resource had become overcomplicated already. In fact, it didn't encapsulate anything, as it had a getter for FileObject. That is why we decided to remove the "resource" abstraction completely and directly use the FileObject class. This was not a compatible change, but we were allowed to do it, as it happened prior to the first release.

In the end, this still made encapsulation possible, as the NetBeans FileObject, unlike java.io.File, allows independent implementations unrelated to physical files on disk. As a result, you can still create a task for a completely virtual file residing only in memory. Though simplified, the Task List API remained well encapsulated and reusable.

Encapsulation of an API—that is, the ability simply to configure the environment needed for an API to perform its operations—greatly increases the potential of its reuse. If it was easy to invoke code completion on a simple string or CharSequence, it would be used much more frequently than if you needed to create your own JTextComponent. When defining an API's environment, it's important to think about proper encapsulation, and balance between the ease of use in common cases and the ease of setup in uncommon invocations of the API. Remember that when defining an API, you are optimizing for unknown users who have unknown goals. It's unwise to limit the use of an API by overcomplicating its use in strange and uncommon environments. Simply bear in mind that often "less is more." The less you expose from an API, the easier it will be to reuse.

Enforcing Consistency of APIs

Some APIs provide more than a single way to obtain a similar result. Often, these ways are related. They are expected to yield the same—or at least related—results. This is the expectation of the author of the API and reflects the API's original vision. It might even be the expectation of the users of the API, although the actual implementation might not live up to the dream.

When there are multiple ways to obtain the same result in a simple library, it's easy to know what needs to be fixed. Remember that by "simple library" I mean a library that contains its only implementation, as defined in the section "Types of Modular Design" in Chapter 7. Say for some reason you use the following:

```
URL url = new URL("http://www.apidesign.org");
assertEquals(url.toString(), url.toExternalForm());
```

If you expect the toString and toExternalForm of the URL to return the same result, then you need to write an automated test to ensure this is true and then change the implementation. This is easy because java.net.URL is a final class containing its implementation, and you can be confident that its implementation matches your expectations.

However, the modular lifestyle requires us to design more than "simple libraries." We also need to design modular libraries; that is, those that define only APIs, while their implementation is provided by independent modules. In this case, our expectation of the API needs to be enforced for all implementations. It's no longer enough simply to fix the code of the library itself. It's necessary to force every provider of an implementation of the library to fix the related code.

INCONSISTENCY IN NETBEANS LOOKUP

NetBeans provides a general API for the discovery of implementations of various services, as described in the section "Intercomponent Lookup and Communication" in Chapter 7. NetBeans has various ways of querying registered services:

- *Call for one implementation—usually the most prominent or first one.* For purposes of this sidebar, let's call this method the following:

  public abstract <T> T *lookup*(Class<T> clazz);

- *Call for all implementations.* This is a method that returns a collection of instances. For purposes of this sidebar, let's call this method the following:

  public abstract <T> Collection<? **extends** T> *lookupAll*(Class<T> clazz);

- *Call for a list of all implementation classes.* This is a method returning a set of java.lang.Classes. For purposes of this sidebar, let's call this method the following:

  public abstract <T> Set<Class<? **extends** T>> *lookupAllClasses*(
    Class<T> clazz
  );

From the context of the API's usage, it's reasonable to expect that if *lookup*(clazz) returns a non-null result, the collection provided by *lookupAll*(clazz) will contain at least one instance. Also, you would expect that the set of classes computed by *lookupAllClasses*(clazz) contains all the implementation classes of objects in the *lookupAll*(clazz) collection. It's natural to expect this, and as an author of that API, I can confirm that this was my vision as well.

There are many instances of this Lookup class in NetBeans, and thankfully, most of them are derived from one of our support classes (AbstractLookup, ProxyLookup) or created by using our well-tested factory methods (Lookups.fixed, and so on). These implementations are well tested and guarantee consistency among all their methods. It took me a while to get to this state. However, now, after a few years of development, almost all corner cases seem to have been verified and tested. The implementation is stable enough to work as expected. From this point of view, the Lookup API behaves as a "simple library."

However, the Lookup API is also part of NetBeans, which is extremely modular. So, it can also be seen as a "modular library"; that is, certain parts of the system can completely skip the support classes and provide their own implementations of the Lookup class written from scratch. It's up to them to guarantee consistency among all their methods. Although it might seem simple, in some situations, especially during delegating, filtering, and merging of multiple other lookups, this might become quite complex. As a result, some implementations of Lookup in NetBeans don't implement the original API properly and don't fulfill the API contract to its full extent.

Having broken implementations of an API is never good. However, in this case, it's even more complicated. Supposedly 95 percent of all lookups in a running NetBeans-based application behave consistently, although the rest might be broken from time to time. However, clients calling into the Lookup API don't expect that or know that. It's not always possible to discover which lookup you are calling into, because the implementation classes are usually package private and often are also hidden behind decorating lookups. Also, because the majority of implementations are correct, you might not even notice that some functionality is broken. During testing, everything might work perfectly. When it's deployed into a real environment, you might query a broken implementation of Lookup, and then the inconsistency among its methods might cause unexpected failures.

There aren't many ways of fixing problems of this kind. First, you might try to define a "policy"; that is, add into the Javadoc a huge warning that the implementors of the class have to guarantee consistency. In fact, this is better than nothing at all. I can assure you, though, that this doesn't really help. Maybe it will lower the number of broken implementations by half. A huge number will remain and potentially your problems will increase. Whenever a client encounters a broken instance, its code is broken, usually with a nondescriptive exception, such as NullPointerException or ArrayIndexOutOfBoundsException. To maximize your despair, any information about the broken implementation will be missing, even the relevant class name. So, you receive a failure message, but discovering what actually failed might take hours, or sometimes years. That's how it goes all the time. Defining policies is good for the blame game, but not for fixing actual problems.

A more promising approach is to write a TCK. As advocated in the section "Test Compatibility Kit" in Chapter 9, every modular library should be equipped with a test suite that implementors can use to verify that their provided implementations are correct. This works, but under one condition only: that all implementors actually run the tests. I don't want to sound skeptical, but I'm fairly certain that a significant portion of an API's users simply provide the implementation and skip running the tests. In the end, they want to be clueless and they want to ignore instructions as far as possible. They simply want to get their job done. Learning how to set a TCK up is an additional and annoying obstacle, the first to be ignored. Only those who have burned their fingers in the past know the danger of playing with matches. However, in this context you need to spend several days hunting a mysterious bug and then finding that it would have been discovered after only a few minutes by running a

TCK. As a result, a TCK is a good and workable option, but only for those who are diligent. As at least some of our API users cannot be described as diligent, there is no guarantee that all implementations will be consistent. There is simply only one way to ensure consistency: enforce it!

CONSTRAINTS AND ASPECTS

I can imagine that, at this point, many readers can guess the right solution: use a constraint language, or even better, use aspect-oriented programming (AOP). This means that you need to define an additional way to annotate a method or class with a consistency constraint. With the use of a special compiler or with bytecode manipulation, this would then enhance the generated code to perform the consistency checks and guarantee them for all implementations.

This is a possible solution. However, as outlined in the section "Learning to Write APIs" in the Prologue, we want to stay in the context of Java, using it as a language for API design. Inventing constraints in an enforceable way goes beyond this horizon. It feels like we would then be inventing a new language altogether, with new concepts. And that is why, dear AOP fans, we need to enforce consistency without recourse to our favorite tools!

The best way to enforce the behavior of a method is to prevent it from being overridden. The best approach to ensuring the consistency of a set of methods is to make their defining class final and to check consistency in their bodies. This turns the class into a simple library schema and puts everything that clients can do with it under your control. In fact, this restricts modular extensibility. Extensibility is only allowed by implementing additional interfaces and using factory methods that turn such interfaces into the final class representing the API for clients:

```java
public abstract class Lookup {
    /** only for classes in the same package */
    Lookup() {
    }

    public <T> T lookup(Class<T> clazz) {
        Iterator<T> it = doLookup(clazz);
        return it.hasNext() ? it.next() : null;
    }

    public <T> Collection<? extends T> lookupAll(Class<T> clazz) {
        Iterator<T> it = doLookup(clazz);
        if (!it.hasNext()) {
            return Collections.emptyList();
        } else {
            List<T> result = new ArrayList<T>();
            while (it.hasNext()) {
                result.add(it.next());
            }
            return result;
        }
    }
```

```
    }

    public <T> Set<Class<? extends T>> lookupAllClasses(Class<T> clazz) {
        Iterator<T> it = doLookup(clazz);
        if (!it.hasNext()) {
            return Collections.emptySet();
        } else {
            Set<Class<? extends T>> result =
                new HashSet<Class<? extends T>>();
            while (it.hasNext()) {
                result.add(it.next().getClass().asSubclass(clazz));
            }
            return result;
        }
    }
}
```

This is a genuinely bulletproof solution. All the checks are concentrated in a single place, guarding all client access, because all client calls pass through it. The single place can contain the much-needed consistency checks, argument verification, and so on. Moreover, the tests can be conditional; that is, they can be enabled only in testing mode and turned off for production, which is especially useful if they are expensive in terms of performance. However, because they are all collected in a single place, for one API we have one place that guarantees its consistency.

As described in Chapter 8, you can achieve this by separating clients from their API providers. Separation is a powerful concept that allows the API provider to intercept calls from clients and perform checks before or after passing them to unknown implementations. It's a suitable style for unifying and eliminating those "little differences" between implementations provided by currently unknown modules written by members of organizations that operate in distributed environments.

Delegation and Composition

Object-oriented languages are built around the concept of inheritance. Inheritance is a first-class citizen of C++, Java, Smalltalk, and most of today's object-oriented languages. Inheritance is usually expressed with its own keyword or other language construct. It's advertised to such an extent that you might think that inheritance should be used as much as possible. It's true that inheritance provides a convenient way to reuse code. However, its usefulness for good API design—that is, the creation of libraries that can be cluelessly used by others—is highly questionable. In the section "Do Not Expose Deep Hierarchies" in Chapter 5, I argued that it might not be good to expose deep hierarchies to a library's API. This section will look more deeply into this problem and will also discuss suitable alternatives.

Let's start with an example showing a relatively good API. The API looks so simple that it cannot cause much of a problem. Let's define a simple class to encapsulate basic arithmetic operations:

```
public class Arithmetica {
    public int sumTwo(int one, int second) {
```

```java
        return one + second;
    }

    public int sumAll(int... numbers) {
        if (numbers.length == 0) {
            return 0;
        }
        int sum = numbers[0];
        for (int i = 1; i < numbers.length; i++) {
            sum = sumTwo(sum, numbers[i]);
        }
        return sum;
    }

    public int sumRange(int from, int to) {
        int len = to - from;
        if (len < 0) {
            len = -len;
            from = to;
        }
        int[] array = new int[len + 1];
        for (int i = 0; i <= len; i++) {
            array[i] = from + i;
        }
        return sumAll(array);
    }
}
```

This is an example of code—potentially also of an API—that many of us write daily, me included. I would not publish it to others as a stable API because it breaks a few of the "never expose more than necessary" rules discussed in Chapter 5. However, at least it gives you the opportunity to see what can happen when you don't follow those suggestions.

Do you see anything wrong with the Arithmetica class? Let's check its behavior from the point of view of the amoeba model. First, note that it does what we would expect it to do. All three public methods add all their parameters and produce the expected results:

```java
public void testSumTwo() {
    Arithmetica instance = new Arithmetica();
    assertEquals("+", 5, instance.sumTwo(3, 2));
}

public void testSumAll() {
    Arithmetica instance = new Arithmetica();
    assertEquals("+", 6, instance.sumAll(3, 2, 1));
}

public void testSumRange() {
    Arithmetica instance = new Arithmetica();
    assertEquals("1+2+3=6", 6, instance.sumRange(1, 3));
```

```
assertEquals("sum(1,10)=55", 55, instance.sumRange(1, 10));
assertEquals("sum(1,1)=1", 1, instance.sumRange(1, 1));
assertEquals("sum(10,1)=55", 55, instance.sumRange(10, 1));
}
```

Therefore, the vision of the application that we have in our minds is fulfilled. We know that we wanted to write a class to add some numbers. It seems that it does that correctly. That means the actual behavior of the library is at least as good as expected. Its amoeba shape covers our expectations. Where is the problem, then? Well, the problem is that the application is able to do much more than just add a few numbers. Surprisingly, it's a good library for computing a factorial:

```
public final class Factorial extends Arithmetica {
    public static int factorial(int n) {
        return new Factorial().sumRange(1, n);
    }
    @Override
    public int sumTwo(int one, int second) {
        return one * second;
    }
}
```

This is indeed a strange and unexpected use of the original API! However, it's a possible usage and it works perfectly. By overriding the sumTwo method in the Factorial class, you've changed the behavior of all the other methods in the class. As a result, sumRange multiplies all the numbers in the range. That is, it does exactly what is needed to compute factorials.

SIGNING BLANK CHECKS

It always helps to express the magic hidden beneath language keywords by means of the actual implementation that lies behind it. In the case of subclassing, the technology behind it is a virtual methods table, which I introduced in the section "Binary Compatibility" in Chapter 4.

Whenever you define a class and add a subclassable method to it, you're adding new entries to the virtual methods table associated with the class. Whenever you call a method on the object of that type, the caller first looks into the table to find the method that should actually be called, and only then are the actual code instructions executed.

The virtual methods table is inherited from the superclass. Whenever you inherit from a class, you inherit its virtual methods table, with its content prepopulated with the exact values found in the superclass. By adding new methods to your class, or by overriding the methods defined by superclasses, you alter the content of the table by adding new slots or by pointing existing slots to your own methods. This is from the standpoint of a subclasser.

Looking at the process from the point of view of someone who exposes a class to be subclassed, this means that whenever you leave or define a public or protected nonfinal method, you're signing a blank check for the subclasses to do whatever they wish. So, it's superfluous to remind you that signing checks without knowing what the amount payable will be is a bit dangerous. And if blank checks do need to be signed from time to time, it should always be done with care.

Subclassing is more or less the same. If you need to allow it, do it carefully.

In terms of the amoeba model, this means that the actual shape of the application is much wider than our original expectations. You might well argue that this is not a problem. In fact, this is beautiful! We wrote a class, put it into an API, and then someone else just built upon our shoulders and used that class to create something new, extraordinary, and creative. This is the perfect success story of code reuse. Without object-oriented programming, such code reuse would not have been possible, and this is evidence that object orientation is sound, that it helps people produce better software. Code reuse needs to be encouraged!

The truth is that we do need code reuse, which is why we're trying to learn about writing APIs in the first place. However, reuse needs to be planned. Simply exposing something without knowing what it is, and letting others use it, harms reuse more than it helps. For example, imagine that in version 2.0 you discover a better way to compute the sum of a range. You then rewrite the method to the following:

```
public int sumRange(int from, int to) {
    return (from + to) * (Math.abs(to - from) + 1) / 2;
}
```

This significantly speeds up the computation. However, it's not a backward compatible change. Although the vision of our application didn't shift at all, the 2.0 version significantly changes the shape of the application from what it was in 1.0. The new implementation doesn't delegate to sumTwo anymore, and the previously functional implementation of Factorial doesn't work anymore. The change is so strong that you might think of it as an earthquake: everything built on top of our library is in danger and quite a few buildings/applications are destroyed. Instead of seeing code reuse, we've been witness to a disaster.

My experience says that this is almost always the case when you allow subclassing. The reason is simple. Subclassing in object-oriented languages is heavily optimized for code reuse. In fact, it's so optimized that it almost always opens many more back doors than intended. As we saw with the Factorial example, it's bad to open up more than planned, especially when we do so without noticing it. One answer to this is to use delegation and composition rather than subclassing.

The problem with rich classes that define a lot of virtual methods (along with a lot of implementations) is that there can be various relationships between methods in the class. Each method can call its peers. Because these peer methods are virtual, any subclass can intercept the calls and replace them by overriding the methods and completely changing the meaning of the whole class. This has been demonstrated with the Factorial example, where we managed to twist the original purpose of the Arithmetica superclass. The most significant problem is that the interdependencies between various methods in a class are usually considered an implementation detail and are therefore not described anywhere. When subclassing a rich class with a lot of methods, you must resort to reading its source code. Otherwise it's almost impossible to understand which overriding method you are changing. Anyone who has ever tried to make sense of the intertwined methods of javax.swing.JComponent knows that they are impossible to understand without studying the source code. That is probably the reason why Sun had to release Swing with its source code. Without the source code, nobody would be able to know what is going on when subclassing its classes. With the source code, subclassing still requires a lot of work, but is at least possible. Of course, all this completely flies in the face of cluelessness!

If you need to read an API's source code, there is probably a problem in its design. In fact, I can guarantee that there are design problems in classes with a huge number of interconnected virtual methods. That's why I suggest the elimination of such classes from any good API. The first piece of advice, already discussed the section "Make Everything Final" in Chapter 5, is to use final classes. In fact, if you use final classes, you won't have any virtual methods to subclass. As a result, you won't need to deal with the `Factorial` problem. Surprisingly, the other solution preventing the confusion of interconnected virtual methods is to use Java interfaces. If you use Java interfaces, all the methods are virtual and abstract. In other words, they have no implementation, and they cannot be interconnected by the API. Obviously, this eliminates the `Factorial` problem as well.

If final classes are acceptable, and if Java interfaces are also acceptable, the only source of inheritance confusion would be when the API contains nonfinal, noninterface types—that is, classes or abstract classes with an implementation. If this is the problem, can it be avoided? Can an abstract class be replaced with a combination of final classes and interfaces? The answer is yes, and the trick is one of composition, which I'll discuss in the next section.

COMPOSITION IS NOT A FIRST-CLASS CITIZEN

There is no single keyword like `extends` to use composition easily in common object-oriented languages. You always need to type a lot of code by hand to organize your data structures in a way that they delegate to one another. This might seem discouraging and sometimes is. However, if you look at the problem more closely, then it's clear the burden of additional manual work is mostly on the implementor of the composition structures, not on the users who make calls to it. Composition is a less-supported concept than inheritance, so it might seem a bit unnatural and hard to implement in an object-oriented language. However, it's not unnatural for users of an API. Remember that there is only one API writer and many readers. That means there is nothing wrong with spending more time designing a more "correct" API, while giving its users a chance to be more clueless than they would otherwise be able to be.

The first step in the quest to eliminate the intertwining of virtual methods with abstract classes is to understand the meaning of methods in a regular class. Why do we use public or protected methods? Why do we annotate them with "final" or "abstract" keywords in the first place? Be aware that we can ignore package private and private methods, as they are not visible in the API. Aside from these, there are three basic motivations for introducing methods to classes. You can combine these motivations, because some methods might be in a class to fulfill more than one need. However, in their purest form, there are three reasons for having a method in an API:

1. First and foremost, a method is something that can be called from the outside. Whenever a user has a reference to object of a type that defines a method, and this method is accessible, the user can call that method on the object. As mentioned before, this call looks up the appropriate entry in the virtual methods table and then calls the related method. The purest form of these methods is attributed with **public final** modifiers. These methods can only be called and have no purpose beyond that.

2. The other purpose of a virtual method is to be a slot that can be replaced with an implementation—that is, a method that can be overridden in a subclass. In this case, the new class replaces the existing implementation of a supertype method with its own. Whenever the method is invoked on an instance of the new type, the new method

is called, while completely skipping the code in the previous method. In its purest form, this means **protected abstract** methods. These can only be overridden: calling them from external code is not possible. Because they are protected, calling them from a subclass has no meaning, as they don't provide any implementation in the defining class.

3. The third style of calling a method is that a subclass calls the original implementation of some method inherited from the superclass using **super**.`methodName` constructs or by simply calling such methods without overriding them. The cleanest way to define methods of this kind is to annotate them with **protected final** access attributes. These methods are accessible only for subclasses and can only be called because they are not virtual.

These three motivations for introducing a method into an API cover only a limited set of method access modifiers available in object-oriented languages. This means that the object orientation is richer, but also that it doesn't carry a clean message with respect to API design. If you see protected abstract methods in the API of a class, it's clear what you should do with them: override and implement. Such an API construct carries a clean message. The same applies to the other types, such as the public final and protected final types. These clearly communicate to the user of the API what can be done with them. As an API is about communication between its producer and user, and as using clean messages is better than those that are hidden behind clouds, we might conclude that the more methods from these three categories that are used, the better. However, object-oriented languages both use and prefer other modifiers. These modifiers usually carry more than one meaning (see Table 10-1 for a cumulative overview). The problem with methods that can be interpreted in more than one way is that they can easily be misused, as extensively demonstrated in Chapter 8.

Table 10-1. *The Meaning of Java Access Modifiers When Designing an API*

Access Modifiers	Primary Meaning	Additional Meanings
public	Method to be called by external clients of the API.	Can be overridden by subclasses. Can also be called by subclasses.
public abstract	Method has to be implemented by subclasses.	Method can be called by external clients.
public final	Method to be called.	None.
protected	Method can be called by subclasses.	Method can be overridden by subclasses.
protected abstract	Method needs to be overridden by subclasses.	None.
protected final	Method can be called by subclasses.	None.

To increase the purity of an API and remove its unwanted side-effect messages, it can be desirable to eliminate methods with access modifiers that have potential side meanings. This is always possible. Table 10-2 describes recipes to use when you embark on this task. These recipes clearly show what you are in fact offering to users of your API when you declare a method with a certain access modifier. This might be much more than you would expect. Often the side meanings of various modifiers are so hidden that we don't think about them at first when we see such modifiers. That is why it's important to understand how to decouple these meanings into clear side-effect–free constructs.

Table 10-2. *Rewrite of Multipurpose Methods*

Original Code	Cleaned-up Version
```public abstract void method();```	```public final void method() { methodImpl(); } protected abstract void methodImpl();```
```public void method() { someCode(); }```	```public final void method() { methodImpl(); } protected abstract void methodImpl(); protected final void someCode() { }```
```protected void method() { someCode(); }```	```protected abstract void method(); protected final void someCode() { }```

Now, we know how to rewrite classes that have methods with multiple meanings into classes with methods that have clear single meanings. Next, we can concentrate on the act of converting such classes into even cleaner versions—that is, into types that each have a clean meaning. And here we finally arrive at the topic of composition. Instead of having one class mixing various types of single-meaning methods, such as the following:

```java
public abstract class MixedClass {
    private int counter;
    private int sum;

    protected MixedClass() {
        super();
    }

    public final int apiForClients() {
        int subclass = toBeImplementedBySubclass();
        sum += subclass;
        return sum / counter;
    }

    protected abstract int toBeImplementedBySubclass();

    protected final void toBeCalledBySubclass() {
        counter++;
    }
}
```

. . . you can use two classes and an interface. The first class is dedicated to clients of the API, the interface is dedicated to implementation by "subclasses," and the second class allows these "subclasses" to talk back to the infrastructure:

```java
public final class NonMixed {
    private int counter;
    private int sum;
    private final Provider impl;

    private NonMixed(Provider impl) {
        this.impl = impl;
    }
    public static NonMixed create(Provider impl) {
        NonMixed api = new NonMixed(impl);
        Callback callback = new Callback(api);
        impl.initialize(callback);
        return api;
    }

    public final int apiForClients() {
        int subclass = impl.toBeImplementedBySubclass();
        sum += subclass;
        return sum / counter;
    }

    public interface Provider {
        public void initialize(Callback c);
        public int toBeImplementedBySubclass();
    }

    public static final class Callback {
        NonMixed api;

        Callback(NonMixed api) {
            this.api = api;
        }
        public final void toBeCalledBySubclass() {
            api.counter++;
        }
    }
}
```

Although this looks more complicated than before, and even though it's more complicated to write for the creator of the API, it's much cleaner and more understandable by users of the API. Those who don't need to "subclass" now only see the *apiForClients*() method, especially if the factory method is moved to another class. For users, the API is now simple and understandable. Those who want to subclass know exactly what they need to implement— that is, all the methods in the Provider interface. They also clearly know what they can call—that is, all the methods in the Callback interface. As a result, for every user of the API this separation of concerns significantly simplifies the meaning of things:

```java
@Test public void useWithoutMixedMeanings() {
    class AddFiveMixedCounter implements NonMixed.Provider {
        private Callback callback;

        public int toBeImplementedBySubclass() {
            callback.toBeCalledBySubclass();
            return 5;
        }

        public void initialize(Callback c) {
            callback = c;
        }
    }
    NonMixed add5 = NonMixed.create(new AddFiveMixedCounter());
    assertEquals("5/1 = 5", 5, add5.apiForClients());
    assertEquals("10/2 = 5", 5, add5.apiForClients());
    assertEquals("15/3 = 5", 5, add5.apiForClients());
}
```

However, the code does look more complicated than the plain Mixed class. The reason is simple: we've replaced inheritance with composition. Because composition isn't a first-class citizen in current object-oriented languages, the code needs to be more verbose when creating the API.

Composition is a powerful tool if the goal is to make an API as correct as possible and let each API class have one purpose with one exact meaning. It clearly and elegantly separates the interfaces for various types of users of an API, without complicating its use. In NetBeans, we advise API designers to give preference to this approach to the extent that it's possible. If you are writing an API in Java, I suggest you do the same.

Prevent Misuses of the API

I've argued that an API consists of more than only the signatures and Javadoc. An API ranges from the entry-level tutorials all the way up to the functional behavior of the library at run-time. All these levels of an API are important. If even one of them is broken, end users are likely to suffer the consequences. If the entry level is high, users are discouraged even before they start. If the Javadoc is missing, they are unlikely to understand the individual API elements. If the runtime is broken, they'll complain and probably give up. However, one thing is more important than any of these things: all levels should be consistent with one another. One API level shouldn't promise something that another level of the API rejects.

Indeed, if the project description promises heaven on earth and your users only find ruins, they are unlikely to be pleased. Tutorials are hard to get wrong, at least if they work. Tutorials at least guarantee that the code produced by following them will execute and do something. However, that still doesn't mean the API will be easy to use—that it will lead the user to the good results achieved by the tutorial. This might not be true at all, especially if there are big discrepancies between the source and binary levels and the runtime level.

If you want to achieve consistency between these various levels, everything that is correctly typed when using a library should also function correctly when executed. This isn't possible all the time. However, for the sake of consistency, you should try to achieve that. Again, this can help cluelessness a bit, as the API user can rely on the semi-automated code completion in an IDE to produce code that actually runs, which isn't true if the difference between type level and execution is large.

My favorite example of this discrepancy is the fact that `javax.swing.JFrame` is also a `java.awt.Component`. As a result, the frame might be used in places where a component is expected, such as being added to a `java.awt.Container`. Clearly this won't work. You cannot add a top-level window to a dialog. Still, the type system allows this mistake. This particular case is well known, and nobody—at least nobody with at least a little bit of experience with Swing—will do anything like that. However, that doesn't mean newcomers won't be hurt by this inconsistency between the Swing library's type system and runtime.

Another similar but more complex example is taken from JDBC drivers. The `java.sql.Connection` class is able to produce, and also consume, an instance of `java.sql.Savepoint`. You can get a savepoint instance by calling the `setSavepoint` method, which despite its name is not a setter. It returns an instance of the savepoint that can then be later returned to the connection's `rollback(Savepoint)` method. Because `Savepoint` is an interface, the type system suggests that you can create its own implementation of `Savepoint` and pass it to the `rollback` method. Take note of the fact that this doesn't work! Also, you cannot transfer instances of `Savepoint` between two different connections. Doing so yields runtime errors. The difference between the signatures of the API and the actual behavior is significant. One of these layers of the API is incorrect. Given that the runtime semantics more or less match the expectations people have about databases, the fault appears to lie on the side of the signatures. They should have been designed to match the runtime characteristics of the system; for example:

```
public interface Connection {
    public Savepoint setSavepoint();

    public interface Savepoint {
        public void rollback();
        // and other useful operations
    }
}
```

This new version doesn't allow a mismatch between the type system and the runtime. You cannot try to roll back a connection to a wrong savepoint, as the savepoint is supposed to know the connection it works with. When the savepoint is asked for a rollback, it rolls back just the one with which it's associated.

PROJECT CONFIGURATION

In NetBeans, we designed an interface that any project in the IDE can implement if it supports various build and run configurations. This interface was then used by a UI component that displayed the list of configurations and allowed the user to switch between them. If that happened, the UI needed to tell the project which configuration was now active. The original API proposal looked like this:

```java
interface ProjectConfigurationProvider {
    public ProjectConfiguration[] getConfigurations();
    public ProjectConfiguration getActive();
    public void setActive(ProjectConfiguration c);
}
interface ProjectConfiguration {
    public String getDisplayName();
}
```

This suffered from similar inconsistencies between the type level of the API and the runtime level, as in the JDBC example. You might get a false feeling that it's okay to create your own configuration and use it as an argument to setActive. Of course, we might fix it as outlined in the previous case, by moving the activation method into the configuration itself. For some reason we didn't do that. Instead, we decided to use generics:

```java
interface ProjectConfigurationProvider
    <Configuration extends ProjectConfiguration> {
    public Configuration[] getConfigurations();
    public Configuration getActive();
    public void setActive(Configuration c);
}
interface ProjectConfiguration {
    public String getDisplayName();
}
```

This is more beautiful. However, as already discussed, beauty has no value in software engineering (see the section "Beauty, Truth, and Elegance" in Chapter 1). The example uses a new language feature of Java 5, favors composition, and brings the type level and runtime level as close together as possible. Correctly typed programs are now guaranteed to be semantically correct. There is just one drawback. Ninety percent of our users, including the engineer who made the change, were unable to correctly write the typed program against this API. For example, the following won't type correctly:

```java
ProjectConfigurationProvider<?> provider = null; // obtain elsewhere;
provider.setActive(provider.getConfigurations()[0]);
```

The reason is the ?, which is treated as something unknown. If there are two ?s, they are certainly different. In the preceding example, setActive takes one, and getConfigurations()[0] returns one. However, these two are different for the compiler. You need to try harder to convince the compiler to accept code like that:

```java
{
    ProjectConfigurationProvider<?> provider = null; // obtain elsewhere;
    resetToZero(provider);
```

```
    }
    private static <C extends ProjectConfiguration> void resetToZero(
        ProjectConfigurationProvider<C> provider
    ) {
        provider.setActive(provider.getConfigurations()[0]);
    }
```

Now the types are correct. The change is that both provider methods now work with one type. C and the compiler can verify that they are typed correctly. As you can see, it's not easy to convince the compiler that a type of a provider is the same. You need to make a so-called *open operation*—open the unknown type ProjectConfigurationProvider<?> and turn it into a known ProjectConfigurationProvider<C>. There is no syntactic language sugar for that in Java, and the only way to do so is to separate the "opened" code into a separate method. It's no surprise that most API users are not able to realize that. Moreover, the situation is even more complicated, as we need to feed the UI, display it to the user, and only after the user action can we call the setActive method. That means we cannot use the open method, but we need the "open class":

```
static void workWithProjectConfigurationProvider(
    ProjectConfigurationProvider<?> p
) {
    ResetToZero<?> rtz = ResetToZero.create(p);
    rtz.obtainFirst();
    // after a while
    rtz.apply();
}

static class ResetToZero<C extends ProjectConfiguration> {
    C active;
    final ProjectConfigurationProvider<C> provider;

    ResetToZero(ProjectConfigurationProvider<C> provider) {
        this.provider = provider;
    }

    static <C extends ProjectConfiguration> ResetToZero<C> create(
        ProjectConfigurationProvider<C> p
    ) {
        return new ResetToZero<C>(p);
    }

    public void obtainFirst() {
        active = provider.getConfigurations()[0];
    }

    public void apply() {
        provider.setActive(active);
    }
}
```

Elegant, isn't it? I'm showing this here as an illustration of where a search for a correct solution can lead. No wonder none of our API users were able to use this API properly. You need to spend a few years listening to type system theories to write this kind of program correctly. On the other hand, I still believe that consistency between type and runtime levels should be a goal. However, in the previous case, we should have stayed with the `ProjectConfiguration.activate()` method rather than requiring our users to have completed several semesters on type theory.

Other less academic but trivial examples of type and runtime inconsistency can be seen in the usage of int versus enums. Whenever a method takes an int and accepts a few values that mean various states, you are immediately at risk of losing synchronization between type and runtime consistency. After all, int means natural numbers, doesn't it? Yet the runtime has to contain additional checks and accept only 1, 2, 3, and a few more. This topic has probably been beaten to death in *Effective Java*,[1] where enums just like those in Java 5 were suggested as a more type-safe replacement.

The cases where runtime and type level of an API can desynchronize are probably endless. They have to be, because execution has the computational power of a Turing machine. Regular languages usually have a type system that is not Turing complete, in that they are not able to express everything the runtime can. Differences cannot be prevented all the time, but they are clearly unfortunate. With every occurrence, the differences require the API user to know and learn more, and find that out at an unexpected point in time—during execution. In the name of cluelessness, these discrepancies deserve to be minimized. Keep that in mind when designing your next API.

Do Not Overuse the JavaBeans Listener Pattern

The theory described in the section "Comprehensibility" in Chapter 3 suggests that you can simplify the life of an API's users by reusing terms already known to them. For example, theoretically it's a good idea for an API to use concepts such as "factory method," "singleton," and "JavaBeans." However, sometimes less is more. Sometimes it's better not to try to fit into existing API types and instead to choose styles that are less common and more suitable.

JavaBeans is a popular design pattern, described in a specification that has existed for a long time. Virtually every Java developer has encountered JavaBeans components at one time or another while using Java. In their most common form, JavaBeans are relatively easy to understand. For example, it's safe to assume that every Java developer knows what a "setter," "getter," and "listener" is.

THE SPECIFICATION IS MORE COMPLEX THAN YOU THINK!

NetBeans, as a Java IDE, had the opportunity to look at the JavaBeans specification from the other side— that is, not only to provide beans, but also to understand them and to be able to use them. As a result, the NetBeans IDE can recognize and correctly use every existing JavaBeans component around the world.

To achieve this goal, it was not enough to read and learn just parts of the JavaBeans specification, but all its details, and especially all its darker corners. For example, did you know that there are indexed

---

1.   Joshua Bloch, *Effective Java* (Upper Saddle River, NJ: Prentice Hall, 2001).

properties? Did you know that you can use java.util.Vector to represent properties in JavaBeans components? Have you heard about vetoable setters?

The specification is not simple at all! However, in its most common form—the one understood by most developers—the specification is straightforward.

Because the specification is so well understood, many people try to twist their APIs to look like JavaBeans components. This is generally a good idea. However, one case reaps more problems than benefits: the Editor Highlighting API designed for the NetBeans editor, allowing modules to register their own HighlightsContainers. Such containers can compute a set of highlights for a document, and as highlights can change from time to time, the containers also report when changes happen. This can be easily expressed with a JavaBeans pattern:

```
public interface HighlightsContainer {
  public void addHighlightsChangeListener(HighlightsChangeListener l);
  public HighlightsSequence getHighlights(int start, int end);
  public void removeHighlightsChangeListener(HighlightsChangeListener l);
}
```

The preceding code is correct, until you realize that in this particular case there will never be more than one listener associated with the container! In fact, this listener is always the same, provided by the editor infrastructure and never deregistered. At most, the HighlightsContainer is garbage collected, but its removeHighlightsChangeListener is never called—not even once! When I realized this, I immediately started to think something was wrong with the use of the JavaBeans listener pattern in this situation and that a simpler API might achieve the same purpose.

The first complication a user of this API has to work with is the listener handling implementation. Though this is not rocket science, it's at least ten lines of Java code that needs to be uselessly duplicated by each user. The common JavaBeans-like solution is to define AbstractHighlightsContainer, which implements the interface, adds support for methods adding and removing listeners, makes them final, and provides an additional protected final void fireHighlightsChanged(). Now everyone is supposed to subclass the AbstractHighlightsContainer. The question to ask is, "Why is there a base interface?" Although standard, this is just too complicated. Too many classes and interfaces, too many methods. Too many options. Too many things to learn and understand. Where is the much-desired cluelessness? All this needs to be simplified.

First of all, let's get rid of AbstractHighlightsContainer. One option, again following the JavaBeans specification, is to mark a method to show that it supports just a limited set of listeners—in this case one—by throwing a TooManyListenersException:

```
public void addHighlightsChangeListener(HighlightsChangeListener l)
  throws TooManyListenersException;
```

Then implementing the proper semantics for the add and remove listener methods becomes much easier:

```
final class MyHighlightsContainer implements HighlightsContainer {
  private HighlightsChangeListener listener;
```

```
    public synchronized void addHighlightsChangeListener(
        HighlightsChangeListener l
    ) throws TooManyListenersException {
        if (listener != null) throw new TooManyListenersException();
        listener = l;
    }
    public synchronized void removeHighlightsChangeListener(
        HighlightsChangeListener l
    ) {
        if (listener == l) listener = null;
    }
    public HighlightsSequence getHighlights(int start, int end) {
        return null; // implement
    }
}
```

This is a simplification. However, the code still contains a useless implementation of a remove method that is never called. Plus, the code to generate the right events and deliver them properly to the listener can still be quite complex. Moreover, the JavaBeans specification dictates that listener types are interfaces. This means it's not really compatible to add new methods into listener types, which might be needed in future versions of the API. This is an unwanted restriction, as the listener is in fact implemented only by the API infrastructure itself. Then, of course, the API knows what events it can expect from the listener and there are no evolution blockers when evolving the event class, as it is final. However, anyone can implement interfaces, and it's not a good idea to extend them with new methods.

DELEGATION

You might ask, "Why would an API client try to implement a listener that is good enough only for the infrastructure?" However, remember that if something is possible, someone is more than likely to do it. Always bear in mind that API users are quite "inventive."

One of the most common reasons to implement these *infrastructure-only* objects is delegation. When you want to write a HighlightsContainer that wraps another HighlightsContainer and changes its computed HighlightsSequence, you might need to filter the events the container produces. For these purposes, you need to implement the HighlightsChangeListener.

As a result, NetBeans API design conventions prefer to use non-JavaBeans "callback" patterns in such situations:

```
public interface HighlightsContainer {
    public void initialize(Callback callback);
    public HighlightsSequence getHighlights(int start, int end);
```

```java
public static final class Callback {
    Callback() { /* only for the infastructure */ }

    public final void highlightsChanged() {
        // refresh everything
    }
}
}
```

This is an API that clearly communicates the intention to its user. There is a
HighlightsContainer interface that needs to be implemented. It has two methods, where
one of them is supposed to "do the work." The other will be called—guess when? During the
initialization phase. It provides a parameter. What can be done with it? I see a final class. That
means it can only be called. Okay, what methods does it have? I see a notification of changes.
So, let's call this method whenever the potential results of my "do the work" method change.
This is simple, less verbose, more straightforward, and almost understandable without any
additional documentation. It's clearly designed for clueless users, exactly as a well-designed
API is supposed to be.

Moreover, the "callback" style is much better set up for the API's future evolution. Whenever you need a new way to communicate with the infrastructure, you can add a new method
to the Callback class. This is a safe approach, as the only implementation is provided by the
API itself and will always be in sync with the methods in the API.

DOES NOT WORK ALL THE TIME

During the review of HighlightsContainer, we found that things weren't as simple as they looked: more
than one listener could potentially be attached to the container. As a result, we stuck with the JavaBeans
pattern in the end. However, there are other APIs in NetBeans where the "callback" design style was chosen
over the JavaBeans pattern.

Although adapting an API to existing patterns is desirable, it should never be done at the
cost of verbosity or complexity. The less you need to understand the API's details to use it, the
better.

CHAPTER 11

■■■

Runtime Aspects of APIs

So far, the chapters in this book have concentrated mostly on source or binary compatibility. Suggestions usually advise exposing fewer classes, methods, and fields and thereby help their evolution. This is indeed desirable, because if we want clueless assembly of applications built on top of our libraries, we need the applications to link and not throw UnsatisfiedLinkErrors. However, API design doesn't end when applications link. At that point the real quest is just beginning! Then you need the linked pieces of an application to continue working together. Also, they shouldn't only work once. Instead, they should continue when modular parts of the application are replaced by their newer versions. Only then are you aligned with the clueless application assembly approach. And you can only achieve this if you know and understand the implications of *functional compatibility*.

PERFORMANCE IMPROVEMENT ADVENTURES IN THE NETBEANS FILESYSTEM API

Our effort to speed up operations with java.io.File through the NetBeans FileSystem API brings up an interesting story about the implications of functional compatibility.

We found that some common operations, such as finding out if a file exists on disk, are much slower with the FileSystem API than when the check is done directly via java.io.File. As there was no architectural reason for that, we decided to investigate the problem and speed things up. The first area that needed optimization was caching and synchronizing the state of caches with the state on the local disk. The FileSystem API keeps some information about the disk in memory. Whenever you create or delete a file, the API updates not only the real files on disk, but also the caches in memory. So far, so good. However, users of our API are used to the bad habit of mixing the filesystem calls with java.io.File ones, bypassing the cache updates. They especially like to create a file using **new** *File("...").createNewFile()* and then immediately access it via FileObjects. Though this is a discouraged technique, malicious code uses it from time to time, because the previous versions of the java.io.File to FileObject mapping allowed this kind of conversion.

This is just another example of API users engaging in "empiric programming." They don't care about what is right or wrong, but only what works and what doesn't. Because this coding style simply used to work, API users exploited it without any problems. However, we then needed to prevent this synchronization, because its frequent checks verifying that the state of cache still matches the state on disk were the reason for the FileSystem API being terribly slow.

The other reason for the slowness was that all drives on Windows systems, such as C:\, D:\, and even floppy drives and mapped network drives, were presented as one virtual filesystem. As a result, when you executed an external tool and needed to synchronize the caches in memory with the state on disk, you could only request a refresh of all the drives. This was inefficient, because a small change on the local hard drive might trigger extensive checks on all the network drives. Obviously, this was not a fast process. That is why we decided to change the mapping and create one virtual filesystem for each Windows system's disk. No changes in signatures or new methods were needed. Just a small shift in internal implementation. At least, that's what might have been assumed . . .

However, users of the API had a different opinion. We received many bug reports because a lot of code using that API was suddenly broken. Its maintainers were quite upset: "I haven't touched this module for months and now it has suddenly stopped working! How can you do that to me?", and so on. It was no help to show them their code and prove that it was incorrect to start with, or that it had violated the documentation all along. "It used to work; now it doesn't. And it's your fault!" We tried to fix the most visible misuses of the API ourselves. But we couldn't find them all, because just like a star that doesn't know who is observing it, we were unable to find all the places that incorrectly mixed `java.io.File` with `FileObject`. Instead, we provided a migration guide that explained how to map the old bad code patterns to new and better ones. It still wasn't enough and the complaints were endless.

In the middle of the release cycle we decided to give up. We didn't want to lose our performance enhancements. However, the complaints had become overwhelming. We needed to achieve the performance enhancements in a more compatible way. We then chose two different techniques to do that. In case of potential divergence between caches and the state of the disk, we performed the refresh. If there were no signs of such a distinction, we kept the new behavior; that is, we didn't touch the disk at all. To do so, we needed to identify the symptoms of potential improper combinations of `java.io.File` and the FileSystem API. We did that with a little help from `java.lang.SecurityManager`. Desynchronizing caches can only occur if you create or delete a file on disk. You can do this either from inside the Java runtime or with external tools, such as `/bin/rm`. However, Java provides a sandbox execution environment and can prevent these two operations if unsecured code performs them. Therefore, there is a way to detect them. It's enough to override `checkWrite(String file)` and `checkExec(String cmd)` in your own security manager and register it. We did exactly that. When developers worked with their files without the use of the FileSystem API, we noted in the cache that this file, or even the whole cache, was potentially no longer accurate. When, later in those circumstances, developers asked for such a `FileObject`, we did the refresh. In this way, we managed to retain our performance improvements compatibly with previous behavior.

However, we were unable to use the trick with the security manager to solve the problem with one versus multiple virtual filesystems on Windows systems. We decided to resolve to the compatible extension of the API. We returned to the previous behavior, where one virtual filesystem represents all the drives. We added a new method for a more optimal refresh. Then we identified all the places that caused excessive refreshes and modified them to use the new method. The old API stayed compatible, while simultaneously performance was enhanced.

Was this a happy ending? Yes, probably. Behavior is again compatible, while performance is improved. The only remaining irritant is our bad reputation. Recently, I was sitting in a meeting with a senior executive of a group building on top of the NetBeans Platform. I listened to his complaints about the need for stability and compatibility. "Some time ago," he said, "our whole system was completely broken by some of your changes." Of course, I immediately knew what he was talking about. Rather than explaining the technical details and informing him that his programmers probably never read a single line of our API documentation, I tried something like, "That might have been caused by your use of the development version of the NetBeans Platform. As soon as you migrate to the stable version, everything will be okay again!" My response was well received. And, in fact, it was also true, especially after our recent fixes.

We can try to master our skills and learn several API design patterns that can improve runtime compatibility. However, simply knowing what to do is not enough. You need to prevent the amoeba of your library from changing; that is, you need to prevent runtime differences between the shape of the application in one release (as described in Figure 4-2 in Chapter 4), and its functionality in a subsequent release (as shown in Figure 4-3 in Chapter 4). To do so, you need to take note of one important piece of advice: you need to be *responsible*.

Although this is not the primary topic of this book, and although it's not directly related to API design patterns, this chapter will talk in detail about the relationship between selective cluelessness and the making of *reliable* code; that is, how to match the vision of your library's functionality with your library's functionality in real life. However, as there are many other good books on this topic, such as *Pragmatic Unit Testing in Java with JUnit*,[1] I'll concentrate as much as possible on the API aspects of the symbiosis between cluelessness and reliability.

Fixing Odyssey

The amoeba model described in the section "Functional Compatibility—the Amoeba Effect" in Chapter 4 is one way to capture the problems that you can face when designing a library. It puts the emphasis on the differences between various releases. However, you can also look at software engineering problems related to releases from the point of view of time and evolution. I call this model "the path of the lost warrior," as it sometimes resembles the long and almost never-ending journey of Homer's Odysseus.

At the beginning of a software project, we always know where we are and where we want to go. At least, this is true in most cases. We more or less know our current state. We can dream about improvements of the current state and where we'd like to be. As shown in Figure 11-1, we know that getting from our current state to the dreamed state will be simple. In fact, it will all be a piece of cake!

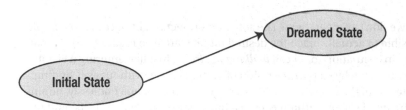

Figure 11-1. *The project will be a piece of cake!*

Obviously, things are never as simple as they seem. It's usually almost impossible to hit your target state completely accurately. For example, you can try to develop a solution on a branch. However, as soon as you merge it into the main product line, it becomes clear that not everything will work as expected. There are bugs and missing features, some people are not happy with the new behavior, and so on. As a result, it's unrealistic to expect that the dreamed state of a project can be reached in one cycle. However, that is acceptable. We can count on being able to perform multiple iterations, as illustrated in Figure 11-2. We know where we are heading. Certainly, sooner or later we'll get there with just a few small steps.

---

1. Andy Hunt and Dave Thomas, *Pragmatic Unit Testing in Java with JUnit* (Raleigh, NC and Dallas, TX: Pragmatic Bookshelf, 2003).

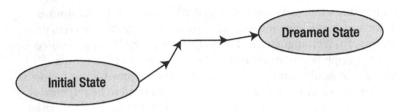

Figure 11-2. *Maybe it just needs a few iterations!*

We believe we'll get there—one day. However, these steps might not be straightforward at all. As shown in Figure 11-3, there can be regressions. Each regression puts us further from our idealized dreamed state. Still, we might believe that one day we'll get there. One day all the regressions will be eliminated! I am afraid that they won't. That is simply not a realistic perspective. Though their effect can be minimized, regressions are here to stay. We need to learn to live with them. Let's simply accept that our path from the initial state to the dreamed state won't be straightforward. Let's count on there being a number of regressions. That still gives us a chance, doesn't it? It can take us a bit of additional time, but we'll get there, eventually.

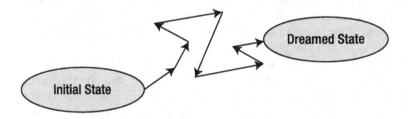

Figure 11-3. *We'll get there—one day.*

Unless . . . What if we don't ever get there? The software project might become so complex that it becomes impossible to actually reach the desired target state (see Figure 11-4). At that point, we find ourselves in a situation that I call *walking in circles*. Just like entering a vicious circle, we can move forward step by step with a vision of getting closer, without ever finding our way to the end. In terms of the amoeba model, we might push its shape endlessly, hoping that it will match our dreamed vision, without ever reaching that state. Real projects tend to be like that!

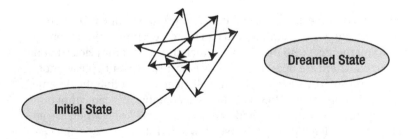

Figure 11-4. *Oops!*

In fact, real projects are worse! The model of an endless "fixing odyssey" follows only a single feature of a project. Real projects tend to have tens, thousands, or even more individual features. Those features can be watched individually. However, they don't change synchronously and they don't live in a vacuum. They influence each other. As a result, a fix that moves one feature closer to the dreamed state can cause a regression in another feature. That means that a single feature might even get to the target state, though it might leave that state as soon as you fix another feature (see Figure 11-5).

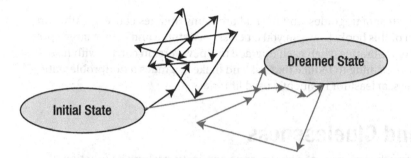

Figure 11-5. *Real projects are more complex.*

PREVENT UPDATES AS MUCH AS POSSIBLE

My wife used to work as an accountant in a company that used an accounting system produced by a software factory named after a wizard. They paid a lot of money for hotline support. After a few years of observing them, I realized that the hotline had only one piece of advice to give its users: "Okay, that is a bug. You can work around it like this. However, it's better to wait for a new update; then it will be fixed." That is advice perfectly in keeping with their wizard name: "Wait, I am preparing a magical update!"

I believe there were at least three updates while I was watching and as far as I can tell, they always fixed something, but simultaneously caused a number of regressions. My wife told me that she needed to spend hours on the hotline to learn how to perform various SQL `selects` and `updates` to fix the databases to work with the updated versions.

Software projects tend to walk simultaneously in many vicious circles. The amoeba model is an accepted reality. If there is a huge outstanding problem, it can always be fixed. You simply have to accept the collateral damage caused by regressions all around. That is why people are generally afraid of updates. Most of our experience tells us that it's better to live with something that is sort of working than to risk an update to a new version, with unknown behavior: "Oops, just don't touch that part of the application!"

UPGRADE X SERVER OR NOT?

All users running Linux on their own notebooks, two years before or after 2006, know the following feeling: "Okay, I have a sort of working system. It works. It can hibernate and most of the time it can also awake from hibernation. It doesn't suspend, but that is probably acceptable. Should I risk an update to a new version of X server with the hope that suspend starts to work as well, while risking that I'll lose the ability to hibernate?"

Needless to say, the fear of upgrades, and the real problems updates cause, greatly hurt the cluelessness motto of this book. How can you cluelessly assemble and evolve large applications based on modular libraries when each upgrade to a new version carries with it such large risks? Can we do something to reduce that risk and make upgrades a nonproblematic, semi-automated process, at least for frequently used libraries?

Reliability and Cluelessness

The problem of changing the behavior of a library or an application where its functionality shifts and shakes like the amoeba shape has not only technical, but also sociological implications. Nonprogrammers—that is, the users who consume our software—will become increasingly suspicious about the quality of the products we deliver. Though their expectations vary, they all share this belief: "If something worked in a previous version, it will continue to work in a later version." The fact that almost all software projects fail in fulfilling this basic assumption results in users losing faith in our software products.

This is a bad situation. In fact, it's even worse than that. Almost every upgrade of a software project is accompanied by the promise of more advanced features and improved behavior. Nobody promotes an update as a completely incompatible rewrite of an existing version, because that is unlikely to be the right strategy for selling a product. As a result, most development teams either promise compatibility or don't mention it at all. Later, when users actually try the product, they usually find a range of incompatibilities that cause software engineers to lose a significant amount of credibility. We are seen as unreliable. We are seen as people who cannot perform their work correctly, as people who cannot deliver on their promises.

A side effect of this attitude is that our users are constantly expecting their pessimism to be reflected in reality. Instead of embracing us and our products, users are almost forced to build walls around their software products and departments, so that they can isolate themselves from our failures and incompatibilities. I don't know about you, but I'm not very happy with this situation. I certainly don't want to be considered unreliable and untrustworthy!

BAD REPUTATION!

As the original author of most of the NetBeans Platform APIs, I was one of the first NetBeans engineers to "enjoy" the full effect of having a bad reputation. As my APIs are at the heart of the whole NetBeans infrastructure, and every other module relies on them, they also become the central source of amoeba changes. Whatever change is made in the API, regardless of how small and gentle that shift in functionality is, the impact multiplies with every module that uses that API. In the end, a gentle tweak can result in a complete earthquake for the whole system.

There once was a period of time where I was notorious for breaking builds in a variety of ways. Not that I was a bad engineer, but code that many developers and their projects depend on deserves a lot of attention. It deserves a lot more careful treatment than a buried dialog without an API that is used by only a few faithful end users. However, at that time we used the same coding techniques for our APIs as we did for our almost "hidden" features. We found that this simply didn't work. As a result, I deserved the bad reputation that I had at that time.

However, I didn't like the bad reputation I had acquired much. I believed it was a bit unfair and that I could do a lot better. That is why I worked on ways of eliminating the amoeba shifts in our APIs completely. I believe I succeeded because these days I can make changes without fearing earthquakes all around me or walking in endless vicious circles. How is that possible? Am I smarter now than before? No, not at all. The only thing that I had to change was my attitude. I needed to be more careful and selective in choosing what to care about. I needed to become selectively clueless.

Software development in general, and the development of sharable libraries with APIs in particular, needs to earn more credibility. We need to become more reliable and we need to earn back the trust of the people around us. We need to prove to people that there is no longer a need to be afraid of future updates. We can achieve that by following the spirit of this book: by increasing our selective cluelessness!

Whenever we need to make a change in our libraries, we need to concentrate on the most important aspect of the change. What is it? It's the changed behavior. We are likely making a change with some purpose. After all, we want to modify or extend some specific behavior, or we want to create new behavior. The most important aspect of change is that the modification will actually be achieved. This is even more important than the actual implementation of the change. In fact, the code that we create to do something is not important in and of itself if the "something" is really done—actually achieved.

It's important to invest our energy, our time, and our intellect into ensuring that the change satisfies its purpose. For the rest, including the implementation, we can act completely cluelessly. The only aspect that matters is the creation of a *guard*. A guard is an objective: an automated entity that allows us to verify that there really is a problem that requires a change. In other words, it helps us determine whether our current situation initially differs from the dreamed state. After we move toward the target state, it enables us to verify that we are closer to where we want to be. Figure 11-6 illustrates that if you write a guard first and add an implementation afterwards, you cannot find yourself wandering in vicious circles. If with every new change, we ask our previous guards to verify that we are still closer to the dreamed state than we were before creating that guard, we can never regress to the state that we were in before.

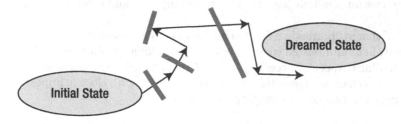

Figure 11-6. *Writing guards*

However, this doesn't guarantee that we have reached the dreamed state. We can always move just a step closer to it, while never getting to it completely. However desperate this sounds, it's much better than endless walking in vicious circles, and in fact, it probably reflects the reality of software projects. There are always some bugs; there is always a difference between the actual and the dreamed state. However, the important point is that guards can help us get closer with every step and even give us hope that we'll get near our ultimate goal.

At this point I must apologize to people who might have become bored by the Odyssey and guards analogies, because they know the final point of this story. Yes, guards are automated tests. If you want to prevent unwanted changes in the runtime behavior of your libraries, simply write tests. If you want to increase the reliability of your code, selectively concentrate on writing good tests and then cluelessly write the implementation. The result will be much better than if you put 100 percent of your intellect into creating beautiful, elegant, and correct APIs. In fact, thinking about API design is good and is also the reason why this book talks about design patterns. However, nothing can replace careful engineering work. Only careful engineering work leads to reliability, which is why you should adopt cluelessness and write good tests.

Synchronization and Deadlocks

Parallel behavior of programs and systems is one of the most difficult aspects to get right. There doesn't seem to be a consistent theory or methodology for achieving deadlock-free programs. Of course, there are solutions. For example, it's difficult to deadlock with pure functional languages, such as Haskell. However, for the rest of us—those who work with more traditional languages such as Java—the threat of deadlocks and improper synchronization is real. Still, it's desirable to write multithreaded applications. Modern computers come with multiple processors, or at least multiple cores. If you need better performance, which is almost always the case, you cannot rely on single-threaded execution anymore.

It's difficult to create a deadlock-free application when you control all its sources. In these "in-house" cases, you can enforce certain "good habits" and organize the whole application in a way that minimizes the likelihood of deadlocks. However, you can only know that there are no known deadlocks, not that there are no deadlocks at all. The source code of a system that has been successfully deployed for a few years without a single deadlock is worth its price in gold. Such sources are to be kept in a safe deposit box and modified only minimally and carefully.

However, we see the world from the point of view of a bulldozer. We assemble our applications from big modular pieces provided by others. We don't want to know, and in fact cannot know all the synchronization details hidden within each library. We rely on the authors of the libraries to know what they are doing and to handle their synchronizations correctly. Moreover, we believe that when we mix multiple libraries, they will fit together and continue to stay deadlock free.

All this puts writers of shared libraries in a difficult position. They are supposed to design their APIs to work correctly in multithreaded environments, without knowing the whole of it. At the same time, they shouldn't expose unnecessary levels of detail to API users, because those users want to remain as clueless as possible. This is not easy. In fact, it's close to impossible, but a few design patterns and suggestions might prove useful.

Document the Threading Model

The first and most common suggestion is to document the threading model properly—in other words, describe the assumptions that need to be fulfilled to use a library. In fact, this is something library writers neglect more than anything else. You can only add this info into the Javadoc's prose section, as currently the Java platform doesn't provide standard annotations or other Javadoc elements to document threading behavior of a class or method. Many libraries don't do that at all. Those that do so suffer from the fact that the information is no more than free-form text that can be overlooked, missed, or ignored. There is also no way to enforce conformance to such informally described threading policies with automated tools.

FINDBUGS & CO.

There are tools that provide annotations for the threading behavior of a library and for verification that the threading behavior is being obeyed. As of this writing, these tools also need to define their own library with annotations. As these annotations are part of the documentation, they need to be visible at least in the Javadoc. Sometimes they are also present in the resulting binaries, which means that your library re-exports APIs of the testing tool. Because re-exporting foreign APIs should not be done lightly, as explained in the section "Beware of Other APIs" in Chapter 10, few people want to use these annotations until they are stabilized.

Recently we investigated this for the NetBeans APIs. We decided that we definitely didn't want to leak these annotations into a binary class format. We wanted to keep things as they are today. However, as these "behavioral annotations" are handy, we decided to write our own, with source retention level only: they can be in the source and so the compiler validates them. However, they are removed before the class file is generated. We hope this is an acceptable tradeoff, before Java adopts a real, official, and stable alternative.

People say that a threading model should be easy to explain. They say it's bad if it cannot be described in one sentence. I have to admit, I've always been a bit skeptical of being forced to condense it to that extent. However, this is probably possible with a certain level of cluelessness—by ignoring the details, at least in some cases.

An API is thread safe. That is the best description of a threading policy for every client making calls to an API. It means that you don't need to care, or restrict the code from calling the API. Calling it in any state is acceptable. The API claims to be able to accumulate and handle such calls. On the other hand, this is slightly difficult for those who need to implement the API. A provider of the API needs to be ready to handle calls from anyplace, while the calling code holds any lock or resource. Nevertheless, the implementation needs to work. This can be complicated to write. That is why requiring a provider's API to be thread safe doesn't help toward the cluelessness of your providers at all. In fact, they need to be aware of what they're doing and they also need to be very skilled to do so well, because even a small mistake can result in a deadlock of the whole system.

An unsynchronized API is usually only handy for objects that are not shared. These are objects that your calling code creates and keeps private. It's fine not to synchronize anything and to delegate access control into the hands of the API's user. An example is the java.util Collections API, and it seems to work well there. The client code only needs to be aware of the need to keep objects private and not to leak them out via method return types or calls.

Swing uses a dedicated thread policy. This is a relatively good balance for an API that is both client API as well as provider API, which is the case with Swing. Clients need to be aware of the restriction and always transfer control to the dedicated thread before making calls to the API. On the other hand, anyone who writes listeners or implements client components can expect the calls to be made from one thread. Then there is no need for synchronization and no need to worry about parallelism.

Pitfalls of Java Monitors

When two people do the same thing, the results are often quite different. The same can be said about Java synchronization primitives, called *monitors*. In fact, they are not monitors in the way the original authors intended them to be. This is partially caused by the difference between theory and reality and partially because of differences among object-oriented languages. Simply transferring the same solutions that worked in procedural languages might reveal surprising problems.

THE APRIL 2001 DEADLOCK

In April 2001, we ran into a problem with one of the NetBeans APIs. It deadlocked, suddenly and inexplicably. After a bit of investigation, I found a clash between our API locks and the locks used by the users of those APIs. This revealed that the standard synchronizations in Java have certain caveats that you have to be aware of when designing APIs.

The deadlock was quite obscure. Our API's `Children` class used `synchronized` methods to keep its own private fields in a reasonable state. The synchronization of these structures was well thought out and there was no chance that this could deadlock, until we found the API being used in the definition of the `EJBClassChildren` subclass. There, it also used `synchronized` methods to protect the class's own internal data structures.

However, according to the Java specification, defining a synchronized method is like synchronizing on `this`. Because the `this` for the `Children` class and its `EJBClassChildren` subclass was the same object, the two "monitors" accidentally merged into one. The two classes interfered with each other, and this unexpected interference resulted in a deadlock.

Per Brinch Hansen, who is one of the authors of monitors and who created Concurrent Pascal in the '70s, wrote a paper called "Java's Insecure Parallelism" in 1999.[2] In the paper, he objected to Java's attempt to call its synchronization model "monitor-based." According to Hansen, a real monitor should allow a compiler to verify that the code is correct and thus help to eliminate programming mistakes. However, Java simply uses something that looks like a monitor, but doesn't provide any of a monitor's benefits. The Java compiler knows almost nothing about synchronization.

His primary objections were about insecurity, because you can mix synchronized and nonsynchronized methods into a class. So, it's easy to allow access to internal structures without proper synchronization. Also, compared to the original monitor-based extension of Pascal, only private fields in a class are guarded from accidental unsynchronized access coming from outside the class. As a result, the amount of work put on a programmer's shoulders is the same as when using the lowest synchronization primitives, such as semaphores. His

---

2.   Per Brinch Hansen, "Java's Insecure Parallelism" (1999), http://brinch-hansen.net/papers/1999b.pdf.

argument is correct. Those of you who know what it takes to maintain a class that uses synchronized methods can only confirm that Java offers no comfort in this area.

When you maintain a class for a few years, over a few releases, you can easily forget to synchronize newly added methods. The only way to prevent this is always to use getters and setters, even for private fields, and to guard them with asserts:

```java
private int counter;

private int getCounter() {
    assert Thread.holdsLock(this);
    return counter;
}

private void setCounter(int c) {
    assert Thread.holdsLock(this);
    counter = c;
}
```

This can guarantee that the field is never accessed without having a lock on the right object. It's easy to see that this version lacks all the beauty and simplicity of the original Concurrent Pascal monitors. I know, yes, beauty is not important. However, here it also verifiably increases the likelihood of errors in multithreaded Java code.

Hansen was right. It's easy to leak out internal data structures from an object that's likely to be synchronized. This shouldn't be compared to monitors at all. As far as I can see, Hansen didn't know, or at least doesn't mention, the most significant leakage, which is the fact that subclassing shares locks.

The original monitor design was done for a procedural language that had no concept of subclassing. Nobody even expected that if you have a monitor (a data structure with access methods) that it's possible to extend the declaration. It's quite the opposite, in fact. The monitor is supposed to be self-contained. All the data and all the operations are declared together, written in one place, by one person, completely isolated from the rest of the system.

THINGS ARE NOT HOW THEY SEEM

When I saw the synchronization approach in Java for the first time, I thought it was based on a monitor model that I knew from school. As far as I remember, it was explained as an extension to the Pascal record structure. You could create a new record and in its definition list all methods that should be synchronized with it. That is similar to Java synchronization. You define a class and can then synchronize its methods.

In Java there are two ways to synchronize: either you create a synchronized method or you use a synchronized block:

```java
synchronized (anObject) {
    // do the critical stuff
}
```

Ask yourself which of these ways is preferred. I have to admit that I used to think it was better to synchronize methods.

The suggested way is to use synchronized in the definition of a method. Fine, that can work for me. I am able to write my code in one class without deadlocks. But what if somebody subclasses my object and also uses synchronized methods? Well, in that case it uses the same lock as mine, usually without any knowledge as to how I should use the lock, because my synchronized methods can be private and thus not of interest to subclasses. The result? Deadlocks everywhere.

Subclassing and using synchronized methods sneaks into the superclass's own synchronization model. That can completely invalidate any synchronization assumptions the superclass has made. Doing so is just plain dangerous. It can happen in any Java program. However, when writing APIs, this is almost a killer. APIs must be designed for simple, almost clueless use. By interfering with a subclass's locking scheme, you expose the poor users of your API to many more details than necessary. You inherently hurt your own reputation, as your library is then known to be full of deadlocks.

The only way to prevent this is never to synchronize with a class that is visible in the API. That also means that you shouldn't use any synchronized methods in classes exposed in the API. This is especially harmful in the case of subclassable classes, as users might still believe that synchronization in Java is monitor-based and that when writing a class they have the right to add their own synchronized methods. The only way to prevent such interference is to use internal locks, as follows, or similar locking mechanisms from the java.util.concurrent packages:

```java
private final Object LOCK = new Object();
private int counter;

private int getCounter() {
    assert Thread.holdsLock(LOCK);
    return counter;
}

private void setCounter(int c) {
    assert Thread.holdsLock(LOCK);
    counter = c;
}
```

These are all low-level techniques, far from the concept of a monitor, but they at least guarantee that privileged synchronized sections won't collide. This is not nice and a bit complicated. However, unless Java provides some syntactically nicer and still correct synchronization model, it's more important to get the synchronization in an API right than to do it in a simple and comfortable way.

Deadlock Conditions

Fighting with deadlocks is the sad destiny of any multithreaded application. The problem field has been extensively researched because it causes huge problems for every writer of an operating system. Most applications are not as complex as operating systems. However, as soon as you allow foreign code to run in your application, you have to fight with the same set of problems.

In spite of the huge research efforts, no simple solution has yet been found. We know that a deadlock is created under four conditions:

- *Mutual exclusion condition*: There has to be a resource (lock, execution queue, and so on) that just one thread can own.

- *Non-preemptive scheduling condition*: It is not possible to take away or release a resource already assigned by someone other than its owner.

- *Hold and wait condition*: A thread can wait for a resource indefinitely and can hold it indefinitely.

- *Resources can be acquired incrementally*: You ask for a new resource (lock, execution queue), while already holding another one.

If we write code that breaks at least one of these conditions, then we know that we'll get a deadlock-proof system. However, writing such code is not easy; there is no standard coding technique in Java to follow. From time to time we resolve to code breaking mutual exclusion—sometimes the hold and wait condition, sometimes the others. Then we merge our libraries and find out that they deadlock anyway. Moreover, we also don't know how to do a static analysis over source code to check whether a deadlock can or cannot appear. It's not easy to fight with deadlocks.

The basic advice for a programmer using a language with threads and locks, such as Java, is *do not hold a lock while calling foreign code*. If you follow this rule, you eliminate the *fourth* condition. Because all four conditions must be satisfied to create a deadlock, you might believe that you have now found the ultimate solution to deadlocks! However, it can sometimes be difficult to satisfy the restriction. For example, can the following code deadlock?

```java
private HashSet<JLabel> allCreated = new HashSet<JLabel>();

public synchronized JLabel createLabel () {
    LOG.log(Level.INFO, "Will create JLabel");
    JLabel l = new JLabel ();
    LOG.log(Level.INFO, "Label created {0}", l);
    allCreated.add (l);
    return l;
}
```

This piece of code feels safe, because the only real call is to HashSet.add. HashSet doesn't use synchronized at all. In fact, though, there is a lot of room for failure here. The first problem is that JLabel extends JComponent. Somewhere in JLabel's constructor, you acquire the AWT tree lock: JComponent.getTreeLock(). Say someone writes a component that overrides:

```java
public Dimension getPreferredSize () {
    JLabel sampleLabel = createLabel();
    return sampleLabel.getPreferredSize ();
}
```

Then, you are in danger of a deadlock, because the getPreferredSize method is often called when a component is painted while the AWT tree lock is held. Even though you tried hard not to call foreign code, you've just done so. The second and even less visible problem is the implementation of HashSet. It uses Object.*hashCode*() and Object.equals, which again can call virtually anywhere because any class can override them. So, if the implementation acquires another lock, you can get into similar problems that are even less expected.

The advice here is simple: where possible, don't hold locks while calling foreign code, especially if the code is "above" your library. What do I mean by "above"? Well, you cannot code without depending on other libraries. For example, in many cases you need to read files, manipulate strings, and use collection utilities. However, all these classes are on the "bottom" of the library hierarchy. The JDK's rt.jar provides them, and their default implementations don't call anything outside the JDK's boot classpath. Your library is "above" the rt.jar, because it sees the JDK's classes on the classpath and can make direct calls to them. This cannot deadlock unless the JDK is buggy or it calls back into some higher level, outside the JDK's own classes.

Users of your library are in a similar position. They can see your classes on the classpath. They can make calls to you. However, unless your library is buggy or you make a call from outside your classes, there cannot be a deadlock. You've created a hierarchy of locks and you can guarantee that they are always obtained in the same order. There are two basic threats to this hierarchy ordering: subclassing and listeners.

If you allow subclassing, you essentially create one slot for each nonfinal method that can be filled in with foreign code. Therefore, in classes that allow subclassing, you should never call a method that can be overridden while holding a lock. Alternatively, as suggested in the section "Delegation and Composition" in Chapter 10, you should replace subclassable classes with more interfaces and you should replace delegation with a clear separation of concerns.

Listeners are just another path to creating slots. Whoever registers a listener into your object injects a piece of code in the middle of your methods' execution. That code is completely unknown to you. You shouldn't make assumptions about what the code will do. Moreover, in almost all cases, this code is "above" your library in the hierarchy created by the classpath dependencies. That code can likely see your classes, because it can call your addXYZListener methods. Therefore, it has full rights to call back to you at any time. As a result, you are asking for trouble if it's called while you are holding some of your locks. Always make sure that you call your listeners without holding locks.

RUN ATOMIC ACTION

Fixing your code to never call a listener with a lock might not be enough. Let's take as an example the NetBeans FileSystem library. As has already been noted a few times, NetBeans uses the FileObject abstraction to access files instead of directly using java.io.File. The advantage is that FileObject supports listeners. So, code in NetBeans can observe changes to files and adapt its views to reflect their state.

Listeners are notified synchronously. This is an advantage that simultaneously has negative side effects because it's a huge source of deadlocks. Initially, our implementation of the library was buggy. Our implementation called back to the listeners while holding our own locks. This continually caused problems that we needed to fix. However, to our surprise, it wasn't enough to fix the code of the FileSystem library to eliminate deadlocks.

The problem is that whoever calls the FileSystem API to write or remove a resource can trigger its listeners. Because listeners are unknown code, it's not reasonable to call the FileSystem API methods under a lock. On the other hand, this is inevitable in certain situations. People need to keep their internal structures synchronized. Writing to disk is occasionally necessary. Calling an API at a "lower" level (on someone's classpath) is safe and acceptable. However, because of listeners and the fact that in the NetBeans IDE almost everything listens on file changes, this was not safe at all.

Our solution to this problem is called *atomic action*. No, our filesystems don't support transactions. However, they allow any code to postpone notifying listeners. You can enclose code within a `Runnable`, pass it to the `FileSystem` library, change the files, and remain sure that no events will be delivered from this thread while the runnable is not finished. Any code can start an atomic action, grab its own listener, and create or remove resources on disk, without the danger of unknown code being called.

It seems to me that almost any low-level library that supports synchronous listeners should provide support for atomic actions, similar to how our filesystems do. Otherwise, the risk of deadlocks exists. The danger increases with the number of users of the library. However, the support for atomic operations is not really straightforward. That is why if I had the chance to write the FileSystem API again, I would support only asynchronous listeners.

The other option, and according to our NetBeans experience probably the better one, is to always call a listener asynchronously in a dedicated dispatch thread. This is safer. The dispatch thread doesn't hold locks. However, events are delivered "later," when the state of the model might already be quite different. As a result, such events don't need to—or even shouldn't be able to—carry much information about the state when they were generated. The presence of this information is at least misleading, because the state of the model can already be quite different. A plain "I am changed" event is enough for the rest of the listeners to query the model.

Asynchronous execution is a powerful approach to fighting deadlocks. Just like the spooling of print jobs can prevent deadlocks when operating system processes want to use a printer, posting a piece of code to be executed "later" can prevent competition between threads for sparse resources. However, deferred execution is never as clean as deferred printing. The advantage of a printer is that processes cannot wait for the pages to be printed. Once the print job is sent, it's up to humans to pick up the results, while programs continue to run without waiting for that to happen. This is not always true with deferred execution. There are situations when code needs to, and wants to, wait for successful completion of such deferred code. Then we are back where we started: at risk of deadlocks.

A nice example of the pros and cons in this area is the `SwingUtilities.invokeLater` method versus the `SwingUtilities.invokeAndWait` method. Both methods schedule a `Runnable` to be executed later in the AWT dispatch thread, which is the thread dedicated to operations on Swing components. While `SwingUtilities.invokeLater` is generally safe because it simply schedules execution and returns immediately, `SwingUtilities.invokeAndWait` could be renamed "invoke and deadlock." It schedules execution and then blocks. If the calling thread already holds locks, especially an AWT tree lock, a deadlock is almost inevitable. Of course, bad code in a `Runnable` that is sent to `SwingUtilities.invokeLater` can also deadlock. However, in that case you need to make a conscious effort to create deadlocks. For example, you need to perform a few tricks with synchronization yourself. `SwingUtilities.invokeAndWait` causes deadlocks without much trouble at all. Such methods shouldn't be a part of an API that is supposed to eliminate deadlocks. Sometimes they are necessary, such as in tests where it's necessary to wait for asynchronous deferred execution to finish. In these cases, the method should look completely different and not be a sibling of safe methods such as `SwingUtilities.invokeLater`.

SCHEDULE VS. WAIT

The Java 5 concurrent utilities include support for deferred execution in the form of the `ExecutorService` class. This class makes it clear that posting code is different from waiting for it:

```
ExecutorService service = Executors.newSingleThreadExecutor();

// scheduling is quite different
Future<?> task = service.submit(someRunnable);

// compared to waiting
task.get(1000, TimeUnit.MILLISECONDS);
```

This builds on the expected knowledge that waiting is something that can cause deadlocks and that developers should do so with care.

However, it's difficult to completely eliminate waiting. That would turn the whole system into a kind of message-based program. Various Java Messaging Servers prove that this kind of program is possible. However, it's difficult to adopt this style with programs that are not message-based, or with libraries. You can defer as much execution as possible. However, there comes a time when it's necessary to wait. The only way to prevent deadlocks while waiting is to allow only time-out waits: to allow a thread to block for a certain amount of time only. This breaks the third deadlock-creation condition where a thread can wait for a condition indefinitely. It prevents deadlocks as well, unless someone puts the wait into a while loop, of course.

EASY CLIENT API, DEFERRED PROVIDER API

The time-out trick can be useful if you want to create an API for callers that can be used from any thread and you want to bridge that into a more simple threading model for providers. Providers can then be sure that everything is processed in a single thread. This, in turn, minimizes parallel execution problems on the provider's side.

Remember to create a single processor thread that is used to handle requests from clients. Whenever a client calls into the API, simply post a future task to the processor. Then either return immediately if the method has no return value or block for a certain time-out period, during which time the processor should handle the request. If the time-out period is exceeded, simply throw an exception to the caller to signal the cancellation of the request.

I prototyped this behavior when I tried to eliminate deadlocks in the NetBeans DataSystem API. Because almost all methods in that API deal with files, they can throw `IOException`. So, it was easy to create `TimeoutException` **extends** `IOException` and throw it after the time-out period. People already needed to check for `IOException`, so this code didn't complicate anything further.

This solution would eliminate deadlocks as well. However, it might also increase the unpredictability of the system's behavior. After all, sometimes the time-out can occur when there is no deadlock. That is why this code is currently not used in NetBeans. However, I am sure it can effectively, and together with proper testing, reliably eliminate deadlocks if needed in the future.

Another way to break the indefinite waiting (the third deadlock condition) is to take away a resource from a thread from outside. This is difficult to do when a thread is waiting for entry to a synchronized block or method. On the other hand, it's possible in the case of SwingUtilities. invokeAndWait. For the latter, the AWT event dispatch thread is a resource as well, and various other threads compete to enter it. It's possible to write a watch thread, or change the behavior of the invokeAndWait method itself, to watch for deadlocks. Do this by inspecting the stack traces obtained from Thread.getAllStackTraces. If the deadlock is observed, you can interrupt the thread, thereby breaking the deadlock.

As you can see, the possibilities when fighting deadlocks are endless. That, in turn, is probably because none of them are guaranteed to succeed. All of them can easily be violated, making them insufficient. We faced this problem with NetBeans too. Because deadlocks are fatal, we continued to search for a solution to prevent them. We gave up on beauty and elegance and instead focused on finding a consistent methodology. We applied the bulldozer by exterminating known deadlocks through writing tests.

Deadlock Test

Although it's difficult to prevent deadlocks, analyzing them in Java is easy. In contrast to native C, whenever a Java application freezes you can still produce a thread dump. From the thread dump, you can get a picture of the problem. From there, it's just a small step to fix the code, lock on another lock, or use the SwingUtilities.invokeLater method to reschedule the code from the dangerous section sometime "later." We used this style for a few years, resulting in unpredictable code. We didn't exterminate many of the deadlocks. When we modified the code to fix a deadlock, we often created a new one somewhere else. My favorite example is the change we made in our classes on June 26, 2000 and February 2, 2004, as shown in Figure 11-7. Both tried to fix a deadlock. The second returned us to the state that we had prior to the first integration. We had successfully shifted the amoeba shape of our code to fix a deadlock in 2000; four years later we simply shifted it again. We improved in one part, but regressed with respect to 2000's fix. This would never have happened if, together with the first fix, we had acted in a selectively clueless manner by also writing and integrating a test!

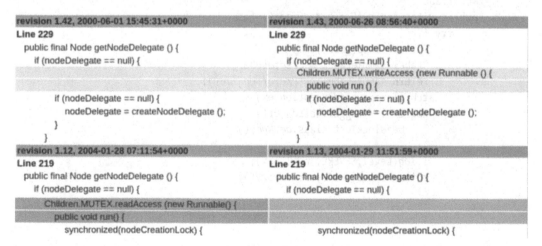

Figure 11-7. *Shifting the amoeba one way in 2000 and back in 2004*

A test for a deadlock? Yes, a test for a deadlock. However surprising that might sound, it's possible and often not difficult to write a test for a deadlock. We often write a test for a deadlock in about two hours; we've never needed more than a day. Beyond the automated nature of this kind of test, it also gives the developer the confidence to say that something has been fixed, which is usually not fully obvious due to the "esoteric" nature of deadlock fixes: they usually cannot be reproduced—definitely not by our quality department—so also cannot be verified. In addition, when there is a test, you can choose a simpler solution that fixes the problem, instead of inventing something that is both intellectually elegant and overcomplicated. The result is that the *art of deadlock fixing* turns into regular engineering work. And we all want our applications to be developed by engineers, don't we?

Writing a test for a deadlock is not that difficult. In our imaginary situation with createLabel we could do that by writing a component, overriding getPreferredSize, stopping the thread, and waiting while another thread locks the resources in the opposite way:

```java
public class DeadlockTest extends NbTestCase {
    static final Logger LOG = Logger.getLogger(
        DeadlockTest.class.getName()
    );

    public DeadlockTest(String n) {
        super(n);
    }

    @Override
    protected int timeOut() {
        return 10000;
    }


    public static class StrangePanel extends LabelProvider {
        @Override
        public Dimension getPreferredSize () {
            try {
                Thread.sleep(1000);
                JLabel sampleLabel = createLabel();
                return sampleLabel.getPreferredSize();
            } catch (InterruptedException ex) {
                Logger l = Logger.getLogger(
                    DeadlockTest.class.getName()
                );
                l.log(Level.SEVERE, null, ex);
                return super.getPreferredSize();
            }
        }
    }
}
```

```
public void testCreateLabel() throws Exception {
    final LabelProvider instance = new StrangePanel();

    class R implements Runnable {
        public void run() {
            JFrame f = new JFrame();
            f.add(instance);
            f.setVisible(true);
            f.pack();
        }
    }

    R showFrame = new R();
    SwingUtilities.invokeLater(showFrame);

    Thread.sleep(500);
    JLabel result = instance.createLabel();
    assertNotNull("Creates the result", result);
}

}
```

The test works with two threads. One creates a component and shows it, which results in a callback to getPreferredSize under the AWT tree lock. At that point, we start another thread and wait a while for it to acquire the createLabel lock. Under the current implementation, this blocks in the JLabel constructor, and as soon as our thread continues (after 1000ms), we create the deadlock. There can be many fixes, but the simplest is probably to synchronize on the same lock as the JLabel constructor:

```
private HashSet<JLabel> allCreated = new HashSet<JLabel>();

public JLabel createLabel () {
    synchronized (getTreeLock()) {
        LOG.log(Level.INFO, "Will create JLabel");
        JLabel l = new JLabel ();
        LOG.log(Level.INFO, "Label created {0}", l);
        allCreated.add (l);
        return l;
    }
}
```

The fix is simple; much simpler than the test. However, without the test, we wouldn't make the shape of our amoeba more steady. The time spent writing the test is more than likely time well spent.

Often you can write the test by using an already existing API, such as in the case of the getPreferredSize method. Only in special situations do you need to introduce a special method that helps the test to simulate the problem. This is okay, as the tests are usually in the same package as the code and can use package private methods for communication, without exposing unnecessary details to the users of the API.

Deadlock tests are pure *regression tests*. You write them when a bug is reported; nobody will write them in advance. In the beginning, it's much wiser to invest in good design, but as I explained earlier, because there is no universal theory on how to prevent deadlocks, you should know what you want to do when a deadlock appears. For that reason, I suggest that testing is the best way with respect to our amoeba shape.

Testing Race Conditions

A similar yet slightly different set of tests that relates to parallel execution is able to check for problems with race conditions. Just like deadlocks, problems with multiple threads and their synchronization are difficult to anticipate. However, once you get a bug report that something is wrong, it's possible and useful to write tests to verify that various problems with parallel access to data structures are correctly handled. Sometimes it even makes sense to write these kinds of tests in advance.

We faced this problem when we were asked to write a startup lock for NetBeans. The goal was to solve the situation when a user starts the NetBeans IDE for the second time. Here, we needed to warn the user that another instance of the application was already running. After the warning, we needed the new process to exit. This is similar to the behavior of Mozilla or OpenOffice.org. We decided to allocate a socket server and create a file in a well-known location with the port number written to it. Each newly started NetBeans IDE can verify whether a previously running instance is active or not by reading the port number and trying to communicate with it.

DOES THIS HAVE ANYTHING TO DO WITH API DESIGN?

Yes, it does. The *startup lock* is an example of a file-based API, as well as a protocol-based one. It allows any process to communicate with an already running instance of NetBeans, and as such its proper behavior is an important factor that all third-party code can depend on. Moreover, in a recent version of NetBeans we also published a Sendopts API—a set of Java classes that allows each module in NetBeans to parse the command line. This API is more approachable by most developers, and as it relies on the *startup lock* to function properly, it makes it the subject of thorough testing.

The major problem we had to optimize for was to solve the situation where the user starts multiple NetBeans IDEs simultaneously. This can happen when the user clicks multiple times on the NetBeans desktop icon or when multiple files are dragged and dropped onto it. This causes multiple processes to start and compete with one another for the file and its contents. The sequence of one process looks as follows, but the system can interrupt it at any time:

```java
public static int start(File lockFile) throws IOException {
    if (lockFile.exists ()) {
        // read the port number and connect to it
        int alive = readPortNumber(lockFile);
        if (alive != -1) {
```

```
        // exit
        return alive;
    }
}
// otherwise try to create the file yourself
lockFile.createNewFile();
DataOutputStream os = new DataOutputStream(
    new FileOutputStream(lockFile)
);
ServerSocket server = new ServerSocket();
int p = server.getLocalPort();
os.writeInt(p);

return p;
}
```

Then, instead of executing as an atomic operation, control can be passed to the competing process that performs the same action. What happens when one process creates the file, while another tries to read it, before a port number is written? What if a file left from a previous execution has been killed? What happens when a test for the existence of a file fails, but when you try to create it, the file already exists?

You need to ask all these questions if you want to be confident about your application code. To get the confidence we were looking for, we inserted several checkpoints into our implementation of locking. The code became a modified version of the previous snippet, where the enterState method does nothing in the real production environment, while in the test environment it can be instructed to block at a specific checkpoint:

```
public static int start(File lockFile) throws IOException {
    enterState(10);
    if (lockFile.exists ()) {
        // read the port number and connect to it
        enterState(11);
        int alive = readPortNumber(lockFile);
        if (alive != -1) {
            // exit
            return alive;
        }
    }
    // otherwise try to create the file yourself
    enterState(20);
    lockFile.createNewFile();
    DataOutputStream os = new DataOutputStream(
        new FileOutputStream(lockFile)
    );
    ServerSocket server = new ServerSocket();
    enterState(21);
    int p = server.getLocalPort();
    enterState(22);
```

```
    os.writeInt(p);
    enterState(23);

    return p;
}
```

We can write a test when we start two threads and instruct one of them to stop at 22 and then let the second run and observe how it handles the case in which a file already exists but the port is not yet written.

This approach worked well, and despite the concerns of some initial skeptics, we got about 90 percent of the behavior right before we integrated the first version. Yes, there was still more work to do and bugs to fix after that. However, because we had well-automated tests for the behavior we had implemented, our amoeba edge was well-formed. We had enough confidence to enable us to fix all the outstanding problems.

Analyzing Random Failures

As is to be expected, the 10 percent of random failures mentioned in the previous section cause more work than simply the next 10 percent of additional tests and fixes. In fact, they have inspired this whole part of the book. Dealing with failures that happen randomly from time to time, and usually on a computer that you don't own, requires more sophisticated tracking techniques.

The problem with parallel execution is that there is not much information to help anyone to analyze what is not working properly. Existing methodology is either weak, missing, or just too concentrated on specific cases. Debuggers are not ready to push debugged applications to their "parallel limits." To really move somewhere, people resort to the oldest solution: to println and logging. This usually gives the best results. Just add log messages into your code, run it a few times, wait until it starts to misbehave, then try to figure out from the log file what went wrong and fix it. Luckily, testing can take a similar approach. Enhance the application code and also the tests with logging, and if the test fails, output all the collected log messages as part of the failure report.

We achieved this by writing our own implementation of Handler, which is a JDK class for processing log and error reports. Because the base API is in the JDK, in java.util.logging, it means that you can use this code in any test or application code, without the need to require any special libraries in your own execution environment. To capture the produced messages, just implement your own Handler. The implementation has to be registered at the beginning of the test and has to capture all logged messages. In case of failure, you must make them part of the failure message:

```
public class CLIHandlerBlockingTest {

    public CLIHandlerBlockingTest() {
    }

    @BeforeClass
    public static void initHandler() {
        Logger.getLogger("").addHandler(new H());
        Logger.getLogger("").setLevel(Level.ALL);
```

```
    }

    @Before
    public void setUp() {
        H.sb.setLength(0);
    }

    @Test
    public void start() throws Exception {
        File lockFile = File.createTempFile("pref", ".tmp");
        int result = CLIHandlerBlocking.start(lockFile);
        assertEquals("Show a failure" + H.sb, -10, result);
    }

    private static final class H extends Handler {
        static StringBuffer sb = new StringBuffer();

        @Override
        public void publish(LogRecord record) {
            sb.append(record.getMessage()).append('\n');
        }

        @Override
        public void flush() {
        }

        @Override
        public void close() throws SecurityException {
        }
    } // end of H
}
```

Logging can be done by the test to mark important sections of its progress. The main advantage of this approach is that your code won't contain any alien elements related to testing. At most it will be full of standard Java logging calls to java.util.logging.Logger.log. The test then collects all the messages, and in the case of a failure, provides a complete and detailed description of the failure. The problem can then be analyzed. You can then either fix the problem or make the logging more detailed to help track the problem more effectively.

Sometimes people are reluctant to analyze random failures in tests because these are assumed not to affect production code. While it might turn out that the problem is in the test and the code is okay, relying on this outcome is risky. Without a deeper understanding, you risk having a problem in the application code. Even if it's not reproducible all the time, it could have extremely negative consequences on the rare occasions it arises. If you want to trust your application's behavior, it's a good idea to add a logging message to the application code and to write logging-friendly tests.

Advanced Usage of Logging

The NetBeans project started to introduce tests that collect logged output. Only the most exposed places were focused on, meaning places where failures often occurred due to overly complicated usage of multiple threads. However, bear in mind that every application written in Java is nondeterministic, even if it consciously uses only a single thread. Depending on conditions external to the tested program, the garbage collector might start. When dealing with visual components, there is at least the AWT event dispatch thread, which can also receive events in a not strictly defined order. As a result, it turned out that logging support is useful in almost any test. The NetBeans project decided to support it in its NbJUnit extensions. This is a general library, not specific to NetBeans at all, that can be used in any project.

The simplest add-on is to support message collection during the running of a test. You can simply override the logLevel method in any subclass of NbTestCase. Let's look at the following example:

```java
public class CLIHandlerBlockingWithNbTestCaseTest extends NbTestCase {

    public CLIHandlerBlockingWithNbTestCaseTest(String s) {
        super(s);
    }

    @Override
    protected Level logLevel() {
        return Level.ALL;
    }


    public void testStart() throws Exception {
        File lockFile = File.createTempFile("pref", ".tmp");
        int result = CLIHandlerBlocking.start(lockFile);
        assertEquals("Show a failure", -10, result);
    }
}
```

Here the logging of all message levels is collected. If any of the test methods fail, the reported exception will contain the output of all messages logged during the program's execution, in the following format:

```
[name.of.the.logger] THREAD: threadName MSG: The message
```

The text in the exception message is truncated to a reasonable length. The full log report is also available. In NbTestCase.getWorkDir(), which would usually be /tmp/tests/ testLogCollectingTest/testMethodOne, a file called testMethodOne.log is found. The file contains the last 1MB of logged output. That should be enough for cases where you need a deeper analysis of complex logging code because most of the recently logged information will be available.

COMPARING FAILURE AND SUCCESS

Sometimes logged messages can get fairly long, and especially in cases of random failures, it might not be easy to analyze what happened in the test. Based on our experience, the best strategy for such situations is to add a $fail("Ok");$ line to the place in the test where the execution randomly fails. This will generate a log file, as well. The two log files—the one from the real failure and the one from the correct run—can then be compared and diffed against each other. It's wise to replace all @543dac5f messages in the output with something more neutral, because each run will have different memory locations. After resolving the difference, it's generally possible to understand the difference between the two runs and the root cause of the failure.

One of two reasons might explain why gaining an understanding of the differences between log files might not be possible. The first is that there might not be enough logs. Information recorded in a log file could simply be too coarse to provide meaningful information about what happened during the test run. Here the fix is to insert more logging messages into the test code. Using the NbTestCase.logLevel method, you can add more logging on various levels, such as Level.FINE, Level.FINER, and Level.FINEST. In different test cases, you can enable different test messages. When working with suspicious random failures that can potentially influence a critical piece of code, you might even need to log information about each line of code that is executed. You'll possibly need to send arguments to various methods and states of your local variables. Doing so should generate enough information to allow a detailed understanding of the reasons for the random failures occurring.

On the other hand, there is a subtle catch: the more log messages you add to your application, the further its behavior will change. Every call to Logger.log adds additional delays, and formatting your recorded messages also takes time. In fact, a failure that only occurs one-third of the time might almost completely disappear because of all the logging code added to your application. Increasingly, a failure becomes more difficult to repeat, and therefore more difficult to evaluate. Sometimes, you almost want to give up trying to emulate the problem, even with a debugger. However, from time to time the failure might reappear on someone else's machine. In NetBeans, we have a farm of machines that run tests on a daily basis in various configurations. This frequently helps to track down even the rarest of errors. Even when we don't find the bug on the developer's workstation, we tend to receive bug reports from the testing infrastructure, enabling us to hunt the bug down there.

Another problem arises when there are too many logging messages in your application. In this scenario, it's difficult to pinpoint where the messages are coming from. For example, if the test executes a series of steps that result in repeated calls to the same piece of application code, the same log messages are printed and you can find yourself completely lost. This is especially difficult if the application performs a computation in a loop, where it repeats the same or similar messages over and over again. In such cases, my advice is to put your logging messages into the testing code itself. Those messages anchor the base orientation in the log output. When comparing the differences between the successful and unsuccessful runs, you can first locate the test messages and compare the differences between the application messages inserted among them. The best advice when fighting random failures is to do a lot of logging, capturing your messages in tests, and printing enough messages from the application as well as from tests. As a result, the likelihood of understanding the root cause of the failure will increase dramatically.

A slightly different approach is to test that something has been logged. For example, when a new method in your API should be overridden by subclasses, you might want to let the existing classes (those that are compiled against a previous version of the class) know about it during runtime:

```
protected boolean overideMePlease() {
    Logger.getLogger(OverrideMePlease.class.getName()).warning(
        "subclasses are supposed to override overrideMePlease() method!"
    );
    // some default
    return true;
}
```

Anyone focused on testing wants to ensure that the warning will be printed only in the appropriate situations. You can either play the trick with your own logger, or you can use a special utility method in the NbJUnit library that will handle everything itself. So, you can simply do the following:

```
CharSequence log = Log.enable("org.apidesign", Level.WARNING);
OverrideMePlease instance = new OverrideMePlease() {
    @Override
    protected boolean overideMePlease() {
        return true;
    }
};
if (log.length() != 0) {
    fail("There should be no warning: " + log);
}
```

This is simply a small utility method, but it helps to easily access and analyze what is logged from inside the test case. Together with the rest of the support in the org.netbeans.junit. NbTestCase and org.netbeans.junit.Log classes, this should provide sufficient support to use logging when fighting the unwanted shifting of the amoeba's edges.

Execution Flow Control Using Logging

The earlier sections that discussed race conditions and the simulation of deadlocks implied a need for hooks in the code to allow the testing environment to simulate "obscure situations." The hooks would stop threads in critical sections while modifying internal structures either to corrupt internal data or to stop the thread in places that cause a deadlock with other executing threads. The previous sections suggested that you should insert special methods accessible from the testing code. These should allow for the execution control you need. Either you need to have your code filled with inserted statements such as *enterState*(10), or you need to provide overridable methods that let the tests provide the hook. However, you need to let these methods do something "insane" during the test, and who wants to have insane methods in their own code, anyway? Though this is possible, there is a small, and by this stage, obvious enhancement: instead of putting special methods into the code, simply insert logging messages!

Logging messages? Yes, logging messages! The beauty of this solution lies in the fact that logging is, or at least should be, a natural part of even the least complicated program. So, you don't need to obscure your code with enterState. Instead, you can simply use the following:

```
LOG.log(Level.INFO, "Will create JLabel");
JLabel l = new JLabel ();
LOG.log(Level.INFO, "Label created {0}", l);
```

These log messages are completely natural. Logging simply fits naturally into your programming work.

Now, the testing code can register its own Handler. In the Handler's publish method, it can do all the "wild" things. Instead of polluting your application code with all kinds of special hacks, you can achieve the same result by adding a logging handler. Then analyze the messages passed to your handler during the execution of your tests. Meanwhile, your application code stays clean and the test is as powerful as the messages logged in the application code. Each logged message is a chance for the test to influence the application's behavior. Taken to an extreme, it's possible to completely control a multithreaded program's behavior by suspending all threads other than the one that should be executed. For example, imagine the following program:

```
class Parallel implements Runnable {
    public void run() {
        Random r = new Random();
        for (int i = 0; i < 10; i++) {
            try {
                Thread.sleep(r.nextInt(100));
            } catch (InterruptedException ex) {}
            Logger.global.log(Level.WARNING, "cnt: {0}", new Integer(i));
        }
    }
    public static void main(String[] args) throws InterruptedException {
        Thread t1 = new Thread(new Parallel(), "1st");
        Thread t2 = new Thread(new Parallel(), "2nd");
        t1.start(); t2.start();
        t1.join(); t2.join();
    }
}
```

The program runs two threads, each counting from one to ten, while pausing for random milliseconds. The threads run in parallel. The speed of counting is random. You can easily verify this with a simple NbTestCase, with enabled logging:

```
public class ParallelTest extends NbTestCase {
    public ParallelTest(String testName) {
        super(testName);
    }

    @Override
    protected Level logLevel() {
```

```
        return Level.WARNING;
    }

    public void testMain() throws Exception {
        Parallel.main(null);
        fail("Ok, just print logged messages");
    }
}
```

When executed once, the output might be similar to the following:

```
[global] THREAD: 2nd MSG: cnt: 0
[global] THREAD: 1st MSG: cnt: 0
[global] THREAD: 2nd MSG: cnt: 1
[global] THREAD: 2nd MSG: cnt: 2
[global] THREAD: 2nd MSG: cnt: 3
[global] THREAD: 2nd MSG: cnt: 4
[global] THREAD: 1st MSG: cnt: 1
[global] THREAD: 1st MSG: cnt: 2
[global] THREAD: 2nd MSG: cnt: 5
[global] THREAD: 2nd MSG: cnt: 6
[global] THREAD: 1st MSG: cnt: 3
[global] THREAD: 1st MSG: cnt: 4
[global] THREAD: 2nd MSG: cnt: 7
[global] THREAD: 1st MSG: cnt: 5
[global] THREAD: 2nd MSG: cnt: 8
[global] THREAD: 2nd MSG: cnt: 9
[global] THREAD: 1st MSG: cnt: 6
[global] THREAD: 1st MSG: cnt: 7
[global] THREAD: 1st MSG: cnt: 8
[global] THREAD: 1st MSG: cnt: 9
```

However, subsequent executions create output that looks different. When the program is executed again and again, the output is unlikely to look exactly the same as in the previous iteration. That is acceptable. When two threads run in parallel, the result is obviously nondeterministic. However, imagine that one of the execution orders is "special" in some way. For example, imagine that an execution order is known to cause a race condition or a deadlock. Wrong behavior of this kind should be fixed. However, as discussed throughout this book, wrong behavior should also be simulated. Otherwise the struggle with the amoeba will never end. You should try to write a test that simulates the order of execution that is known to be broken. For example, let's try to generate a highly unlikely sequence where each thread increments and prints one number, goes to sleep, and then lets the other thread run. It's highly improbable for this kind of output to happen randomly. Therefore, it's reasonable to question whether this kind of test can be written at all. But . . . it can! With a little help from logging messages, here is the code that forces the threads to behave deterministically and always outputs only one number from the sequence:

```java
public class ParallelSortedTest extends NbTestCase {
    public ParallelSortedTest(String testName) {
        super(testName);
    }

    @Override
    protected Level logLevel() {
        return Level.WARNING;
    }

    public void testMain() throws Exception {
        Logger.global.addHandler(new BlockingHandler());
        Parallel.main(null);
        fail("Ok, just print the logged output");
    }

    private static final class BlockingHandler extends Handler {

        boolean runSecond;

        public synchronized void publish(LogRecord record) {
            if (!record.getMessage().startsWith("cnt")) {
                return;
            }
            boolean snd = Thread.currentThread().getName().equals("2nd");
            if (runSecond == snd) {
                notify();
                runSecond = !runSecond;
            }
            try {
                wait(500);
            } catch (InterruptedException ex) {
            }
        }

        public void flush() {
        }

        public void close() {
        }
    }
}
```

When the test is executed, you can see that each thread adds 1 to its counter and gives execution control to the other thread. This behaves deterministically in almost all cases. Nearly every execution of the test yields ascending output. The basic trick that allows the miracle to happen is the interception of the output messages. The special BlockingHandler, which the test registered before the application code started, analyzes the messages sent to it by the application threads. It suspends and then resumes the threads to simulate the execution order, where each thread adds one number and is then suspended by the operating system in favor of the other thread.

The beauty of this solution is that the application code doesn't know that the test controls its execution flow. If you were to look at the application code itself, you wouldn't be able to guess that a test does these kinds of "wild" things to the code, because the actual application code looks natural. Only due to the possibility of intercepting the logging messages is the test given the chance to influence the execution flow. As a result, the test is able to simulate even the "wildest" and least probable execution order.

Writing the BlockingHandler correctly might not be easy, especially when more than two threads need to interact. It's even more difficult if the messages that need to be analyzed are not simple. That is why the NetBeans JUnit extensions library contains a support method called Log.controlFlow, which registers the handler itself and performs all its own thread manipulations. You only need to specify the expected message order. A nice bonus is that the format of the expected messages is "THREAD: name MSG: message", which exactly matches the output reported by NbTestCase when you enable capturing log messages by overriding the logLevel method. You can simply copy the output and feed it to the controlFlow method, possibly without any modifications. However, as the real-world messages sent to a logger often contain some content specific to each run (such as @af52h442, which identifies the location of the object in memory), it's possible to use regular expressions to describe the expected messages. Here is one possible rewrite of your test that uses the Log.controlFlow method to simulate the "one by one" order of execution:

```
public void testMain() throws Exception {
    org.netbeans.junit.Log.controlFlow(Logger.global, null,
        "THREAD: 1st MSG: cnt: 0" +
        "THREAD: 2nd MSG: .*0" +
        "THREAD: 1st MSG: ...: 1" +
        "THREAD: 2nd MSG: cnt: 1" +
        "THREAD: 1st MSG: cnt: 2" +
        "THREAD: 2nd MSG: cnt: 2" +
        "THREAD: 1st MSG: cnt: 3" +
        "THREAD: 2nd MSG: cnt: 3" +
        "THREAD: 1st MSG: cnt: 4" +
        "THREAD: 2nd MSG: cnt: 4" +
        "THREAD: 1st MSG: cnt: 5" +
        "THREAD: 2nd MSG: cnt: 5" +
        "THREAD: 1st MSG: cnt: 6" +
        "THREAD: 2nd MSG: cnt: 6" +
        "THREAD: 1st MSG: cnt: 7" +
        "THREAD: 2nd MSG: cnt: 7" +
        "THREAD: 1st MSG: cnt: 8" +
        "THREAD: 2nd MSG: cnt: 8" +
        "THREAD: 1st MSG: cnt: 9" +
        "THREAD: 2nd MSG: cnt: 9",
        500
    );
    Parallel.main(null);
```

```
    fail("Okay, just print the logged output");
}
```

This might not look like a significant simplification. However, usually the key elements of the execution order are only affected by a single place in the code. If that's the case, the size of the script to replay the execution flow can be simplified further. For example, imagine that we only want the 1st thread to print 5 first, then the 2nd thread to print 2, and then the 1st thread to continue with 6. The script would be as follows:

```
public void testFiveAndThenTwo() throws Exception {
    org.netbeans.junit.Log.controlFlow(Logger.global, null,
        "THREAD: 1st MSG: cnt: 5" +
        "THREAD: 2nd MSG: cnt: 2" +
        "THREAD: 1st MSG: cnt: 6",
        5000
    );
    Parallel.main(null);
    fail("Ok, just print the logged output");
}
```

As you can see, log messages inside an application can be a valuable tool for preventing unwanted shifts of the amoeba's edge. Your messages can be enabled not only during the application's execution, but also when the code is executed in a testing environment. Having the log for failed tests not only helps in analyzing a failure's root cause, but if needed, the log can also serve as a script to control execution flow. It thus becomes useful in simulating the extreme situations that the application code can attain.

You can take this style of logging control even further with better log generation and better replay of log files. In terms of log capturing, it's good to know that tools such as dtrace can be helpful when a context switch is taking place; that is, when execution transfers from one thread to another. The interesting implication of knowing about context switches and being able to replay them is that this can turn a parallel, nondeterministic application into a deterministic one, though only on single processor machines. Another possible improvement might include the use of AOP, or any other bytecode patching technique, to insert logging code throughout your application. In the process, you'll receive information about the application even when it's not fully ready to provide it. Everything is possible, and only time can tell which of these improvements will be of use to you. For now, it's enough to say that NetBeans successfully uses logging, and controls flows based on logging, to fight the amoeba effect on its APIs.

Preparing for Reentrant Calls

Inconsistency due to parallel access to an API is unfortunate. However, this has an easy fix. It's enough to add the synchronized keyword and your inconsistency will be gone. Of course, you risk deadlocks, but the bigger problem is that even this doesn't guarantee consistency. You need to prepare to accept or prevent reentrant access.

ABSTRACT LOOKUP BROKEN DESPITE BEING SYNCHRONIZED

The Lookup class is at the heart of almost everything in NetBeans. It's queried about everything, all the time, from various locations, and for almost anything. I knew that when I wrote the implementation and that is why I correctly guarded all the manipulations inside the lookup with synchronized. At the time, I expected that everything would be fine and consistent. To my surprise, I was wrong, because from time to time we received mysterious bug reports with almost impossible stack traces showing that the internal structures had become corrupted.

After a few weeks of wondering what was going on, a colleague realized that the problem related to reentrant calls to the modification methods. He inserted the debugging asserts there, just like in the following:

```
private boolean working;
public synchronized int sumBigger(Collection<T> args) {
    assert !working : "Shall not be working yet in order to be consistent";
    working = true;
    try {
        return doCriticalSection(args);
    } finally {
        working = false;
    }
}
```

And, yes, instead of mysterious stack traces, we received several failed assertion errors. Good; at least we could now find out what was wrong. doCriticalSection could call into foreign code under certain situations. This code could then obtain the global instance of Lookup by calling Lookup.getDefault() and then call somemethod() on it again. As you can see, there was no mystery at all. It was simply a case of reentrant access.

The problem arises whenever you call into foreign code from inside a guarded section that would preferably run atomically. The foreign code can then call back to the same method. To complicate things, usually the callback occurs with different parameters and then almost all assumptions about atomicity are gone. There seem to be just two possible fixes. Either you need to use a non-reentrant lock to guard the critical section, or you make the section ready for reentrant access.

REENTRANT MISTAKES ARE COMMON

Mistakes with reentrant access are easily made. Even those who care about correctly synchronizing their code often forget to shield themselves from reentrant access.

For example, listeners and their listener support can often be a source of reentrant behavior. If you write a listener that, in reaction to a received event, calls a setter on a bean, does anyone know what the result will be and how many events have been received? This is not the first target to aim for, yet it's often the result.

Even if you define a reasonable threading policy, which is what Swing does, it's not true that you are shielded from the reentrancy because Swing is not reentrant. It's not wise to interrupt its own painting while inserting another call into the Swing APIs. When you ignore this advice, a magical thing usually appears on the screen because the painting buffer becomes completely confused by the additional injected reentrant access.

This solution with a non-reentrant lock has only two problems:

```
private Lock lock = new NonReentrantLock();
public int sumBigger(Collection<T> args) {
    lock.lock();
    try {
        return doCriticalSection(args);
    } finally {
        lock.unlock();
    }
}
```

First of all, you cannot do it after using reentrant locks first, as this would be an incompat-ible change. Before applying that solution, the clients of your API were able to call into your methods in a reentrant way and have something happen (although the result was mostly unpredictable). After applying that solution, such a call would be forbidden: it throws an exception now, which is an incompatible change in the behavior compared to the previous version. Of course, correctness of the API is probably more important than 100 percent back-ward compatibility, so you can justify a slight incompatibility. However, there is a more serious problem. If you prevent reentrant calls, then you can get unsolvable results and sometimes paint yourself into complicated unsolvable situations. That's because now the code's validity depends on which callers are on the execution stack:

```
@Test
public void testCriticalSectionWith15() {
    final CriticalSection<Integer> cs = create();
    testFor15(cs);
}
// if this runnable is called from inside the critical section
// and the locks are non-reentrant then it throws an exception
public void run() {
    testFor15(cs);
}
```

Calling the testFor15 method is fine by itself, but if called from code that is already hold-ing the lock, the call might fail. If this is in the same class, this can easily be prevented. However, if the lock is accessible to public code, even indirectly, foreign code might com-pletely destroy otherwise well-functioning code by enclosing its invocations within an additional critical section.

That is why it's probably better to allow reentrant access and make the critical method ready for it, as well as for mutual thread access. The trick is the same as with any code that would rather run in a synchronized block, but cannot as it calls external foreign code. At the beginning, obtain an immutable copy of the internal state, work with it, produce results, and at the end somehow merge the computed result with the global state. In case of an integer the merge is easy:

```java
private AtomicInteger cnt = new AtomicInteger();
public int sumBigger(Collection<T> args) {
    T pilotCopy = this.pilot;
    int own = doCriticalSection(args, pilotCopy);
    // now merge with global state
    cnt.addAndGet(own);
    return own;
}
```

In the case of more complicated internal structures than numbers, you cannot do much else than to repeat the execution again and again until it's not interrupted with a reeentrant or parallel call:

```java
public int sumBigger(Collection<T> args) {
    T pilotCopy = this.pilot;
    for (;;) {
        int previous = cnt.get();
        int own = doCriticalSection(args, pilotCopy);
        // if there was no parallel or reentrant change,
        // apply and return. Otherwise try once more.
        if (cnt.compareAndSet(previous, own + previous)) {
            return own;
        }
    }
}
```

However, this code can be potentially never-ending, because it contains an unlimited cycle. That is why there needs to be some additional attribute in the data structures that guarantees that with each reentrant call the internal structures get into a "more stable" state. Then the code repeats the given operation until it "stabilizes," meaning until there is a call to *doCriticalSection*(args, internalParam) that doesn't call the method once again in a reentrant way. The internal structure can be anything that represents the state of the object, but it's supposed to be immutable. If any operation needs to change the state of this structure, then it should create a new clone and work on it. With style like this and data structures that "stabilize" with each computation you can be sure that the code is absolutely ready for reentrant access.

Memory Management

Because Java has a garbage collector, memory management is different than in traditional languages. Unlike in C or C++, you need just a constructor. There doesn't appear to be a need for a destructor. As a result, you can say goodbye to X Window functions such as XCreateWindow and

XDestroyWindow and to C++ destructors. However, that doesn't mean you shouldn't pay attention to the memory management characteristics of an API. In spite of the common hope that the garbage collector removes the need to care about memory deallocation, this is true only in the simplest cases. For all the others you still need to care, especially when designing a shared library.

In contrast to languages with classical memory management where you need to design destructors or destroy functions, you need to pay as much attention as possible to runtime characteristics and the structure, mutual organization, and references between objects in memory. The API's designer needs to ensure proper runtime behavior, usually without any additional cleanup or destructor methods.

Let's start with the simplest possible cases. Classes that cannot be instantiated, such as java.lang.Math, appear not to need any cleanup. However, this is not absolutely true. There cannot be instances of the class, but still the class itself can be unloaded (garbage collected) from the virtual machine. That doesn't happen often, though, and I haven't come across many situations where an API would benefit from the unloading of one particular class.

NULLPOINTEREXCEPTION ON STATIC FIELD ACCESS

We faced a funny situation with class unloading in 1997. JDK 1.1 had just been released, and unlike the previous version, it knew how to unload classes when they were not needed. The central API of NetBeans at that time was a class called TopManager. It had a static field, a getter **public static** TopManager *getDefault()*, and an appropriate setter. During initialization, NetBeans injected the default implementation of this class via its setter. The other code then used the getter to gain access to all NetBeans functionality.

To our surprise, from time to time the getter returned null. "Impossible!" we said. We had definitely called the setter before and passed in a non-null value. Moreover, things sometimes worked and sometimes not. When we tried it in the debugger, everything worked. In normal execution, we received a NullPointerException from time to time. Why? It took us a few hours or days to find that the cause was the garbage collector. From time to time, the class was released from memory. Then, when it was needed later, it was loaded again. However, it was loaded without the field being initialized. That is why we received NullPointerExceptions.

So we knew what was going on, but it wasn't easy to find a fix. We somehow needed to prevent unloading of the class. At the end it was enough to hold the instance of the TopManager from a different class. However, the behavior was unintuitive, and as we later found out, it was also buggy. A week or two later Sun released an update to the virtual machine that prevented unloading of classes with static fields if their classloader was still in memory. That has remained the behavior since then. If you want to unload a class, you need to garbage collect all other classes loaded by the same classloader and the classloader itself at the same time.

However, sometimes it's necessary to garbage collect all a library's classes, such as when a module in NetBeans is disabled or about to be deleted. As each class has an internal reference to its classloader, this usually means getting rid of the classloader. For the classloader to be able to disappear, there cannot be any classes and their instances either. As you can see, this is a simple scenario.

The second simplest case happens when there can be instances of a class that don't have any special references outside themselves. As an example, let's imagine java.awt.Dimension or java.awt.Rectangle. These classes contain only a few integer fields and no references to other objects. This is the case where garbage collection works the best. The user of the API somehow creates these instances, keeps a reference to them, works with them, and when they are no longer needed, simply forgets the reference. As soon as nobody references the object, it can be collected from memory. There is no need for destructors; they cannot be called prematurely. Because of that, you cannot accidentally access memory that has already been deallocated. Memory management is greatly simplified. This is precisely the case in which garbage collection pays off in a big way.

However, this is the best scenario, and when designing an API with more complicated data structures, you can face far more complicated situations. The first happens when the data structure still remains relatively simple but is backed by a limited resource, such as an OutputStream file descriptor or an AWT window handle. In such cases, it's not possible to rely on the garbage collector to free the resource, as it might kick in too late or not at all if you have the reference to the object. In such situations, you need to add a kind of destructor. In the case of streams, there is the close() method, which closes the underlying file descriptor. AWT windows have the dispose method to release the handles behind the windows. Both these cases act like destructors. They don't release the object from memory, but force it to clean up its internal data. The object can then either become nonfunctional after calling the method, as in the case of streams, or it can simply release its data temporarily, and reallocate it if it's needed again. However, even in this case it's good to cooperate with the garbage collector. If a stream or window is no longer used and it disappears from memory, it should also do some kind of cleanup. For that purpose, it's necessary to be informed about the object vanishing from memory. Here you have two choices: either use finalize or use WeakReference with ReferenceQueue. The finalize method is a slightly worse choice. First, it's visible in the API. Second, it's logically unsound. How can a method be called on an object when it's not supposed to exist any longer? What if it makes itself accessible again? Also, the finalizers are called in a dedicated thread, but only "sometime later." It's not guaranteed that you'll really receive the information about the object being reclaimed. For all these reasons, the reference queue is a better choice. The essential information that needs to be cleaned up is kept in the reference. As soon as the object is garbage collected, the reference is put in the queue. You then poll the queue and do the cleanup.

These are simpler cases, because the API is encapsulated. Its users keep objects in memory and the API doesn't reference any external objects. When the API references external objects, the memory characteristics can get much more complicated. Many APIs, and especially those that mimic the JavaBeans specification, allow a kind of inversion of references. They allow the client of the API to inject a reference to itself into some objects in memory. For example, when you add a listener to a bean, in practice you are making the bean object hold a reference to your own objects. As soon as something like this happens, the life cycle of such objects becomes part of the API. If those objects have a long life, such as singletons that never disappear from memory, all the listeners added to them will be kept around the whole time as well. This can introduce memory leaks. If changed, it can also change the behavior of the code (shift the amoeba shape of the system), so things that worked before might no longer function correctly.

LISTENERS SHOULD HAVE BEEN HELD BY WEAK REFERENCES

Whenever we talk about the design of JavaBeans, we end up discussing the listeners and often come to the conclusion that it would have been much better if the specification stated that listeners are supposed to be held via weak references. This would remove the injection of references problem and also set a good example up for others to follow. Chances are that then all listeners and other callback interfaces would be held with weak references too.

However, the JavaBeans specification is silent on memory management. That's not quite surprising, as it was written for Java 1.1 and has since remained stable, whereas weak references were introduced in a subsequent version of Java. Rewriting the specification later would be likely incompatible or useless, as the change to weak references could only be suggested, but not enforced. In any event, no existing beans would use it.

The NetBeans project has faced these problems often. To address them, we created support for weak listeners:

```java
public static <T extends EventListener> T create(
    Class<T> type, T listener, Object source
) {
    return org.openide.util.WeakListeners.create(
        type, listener, source
    );
}
```

This method allows anyone to wrap an existing listener and create a new one that has a weak reference to the original. This in effect creates behavior you would get were the JavaBeans specification to be rewritten to use weak references. This is a useful method in certain situations. However, it doesn't solve all problems. You still need at least a bit of understanding of the basic life cycle of the objects and the behavior you want to get from their interaction with the garbage collector.

One of the least specified things in conventional project documentation is your application's memory model. It's not surprising, given the fact that there is no generally known methodology for designing an application's memory model. However, it's surprising, as you can hardly write an application that is supposed to run for days without ensuring that you manage your memory effectively.

Again, the classic model is to code the application, start the profiler, and search for possible memory leaks. When found, return to the code, fix it, and on and on and on, until the application is in releasable shape. Again, as described many times, this is not effective if you plan to release more than one version of the application. As time passes, all the improvements from the "profiler hunting" phase will regress, unless you make sure they are continuously tested.

The JUnit testing framework doesn't offer much in this area, so we've had to write a few extensions for our NbTestCase both based on, or supported by, our memory inspection library called Insane (http://performance.netbeans.org/insane).

The first memory management problem with which you have to cope in modern object-oriented languages such as Java is memory leaks. The problem is not that an application would address an unknown area in memory—that is not possible due to the garbage collector. Rather, sometimes (also due to the garbage collector), objects that you would like to disappear still remain in memory as somebody from somewhere continues to reference them. If a certain operation always leaves garbage after its execution, after a few executions you might find that the free memory starts shrinking and the whole application gets progressively slower. The NbTestCase offers the assertGC method for this:

```
WeakReference<Object> ref = new WeakReference<Object>(listener);
listener = null;
NbTestCase.assertGC("This listener can disappear", ref);
```

If you believe that after some operation an object should no longer be needed in memory, you just create a WeakReference to it, clear your reference to the object, and ask assertGC to try to release the object from memory. assertGC tries hard to force garbage collection of the object. It does a few iterations of System.gc, allocates some memory, explicitly invokes finalizers, and if the WeakReference is cleared, successfully returns. If not, it invokes the Insane library and asks it to find a reference chain that keeps the object in memory. A failure might then look like the following:

```
Of course, this listener cannot disappear, because it is held from long living
JavaBean:
private static javax.swing.JPanel
org.apidesign.gc.WeakListenersTest.longLivingBean->
javax.swing.JPanel@779b3e-changeSupport->
java.beans.PropertyChangeSupport@1e91259-listeners->
sun.awt.EventListenerAggregate@a553e2-listenerList->
[Ljava.beans.PropertyChangeListener;@16bc75c-[0]->
org.apidesign.gc.WeakListenersTest$PropL@11bed71
```

From this you can read that there is a longLivingBean static field, which points to PropertyChangeSupport. Through some internal Java implementation, it holds on to the listener that you wanted to garbage collect from memory.

Another thing that might affect performance is the size of its data structures. If you know that a certain object will be simultaneously kept in memory in thousands of instances, you don't want it to occupy 1,000 bytes or more. You want to minimize its size. Again, this might be observed in profiling, or this can be a decision thought out well in advance, but the usual problem remains: you need to ensure that from release to release the size constraint won't regress. Our NbTestCase provides the assertSize check for that:

```
private static final class Data {
    int data;
}
Data d = new Data();
NbTestCase.assertSize(
    "The size of the data instance is higher than 16", 16, d
);
```

assertSize uses the Insane library to traverse the graph of all objects referenced from the root instance passed in as an argument and computes the amount of occupied memory. Then it compares the value with the expected one. If lower or equal, it passes. Otherwise it fails and prints the sizes of the individual elements to let you analyze the failure.

The size of a simple java.lang.Object instance that has no fields is 8 bytes. When adding one field with an integer or a reference to another object, the size increases to 16 bytes. When adding a second field, the size stays at 16 bytes. When the third field is added, its size increases to 24 bytes. From that, it follows that it makes sense to round up the number of fields in an object to two. In fact, we do that in particularly sensitive places. However, note that the computed sizes are "logical" ones. The actual amount of occupied memory depends on the implementation of the virtual machine and can be different. However, that should be fine. The test of "logical size" expresses the programmer's intention, which is independent of the actual virtual machine architecture.

We've found both assertGC and assertSize to be valuable in stiffening the edge of our application's amoeba. By writing tests using these asserts we can *specify* and verify the expected memory model behavior of our application. So, these tests became part of the *functional specification* of our APIs. Not only that, as automated tests, they are an *active specification* that verifies its validity every time we execute them.

CHAPTER 12

■■■

Declarative Programming

An interesting way to minimize the problems that arise with runtime aspects of an API is to eliminate the runtime completely. For lack of a better name, let's call this *declarative programming*, though the term is overloaded with various meanings and it might mean different things to different people. With declarative programming, the basic idea is that users of your API don't describe step-by-step what they want your API to do. Rather, they "declare" what they want to have happen and then rely on your API to do it when necessary.

The power of declarative programming lies in its ability to define higher-level concepts and its ability to let someone else fulfill them, rather than specifying exactly what should happen in low-level details. For example, Lookup, as discussed in the section "Intercomponent Lookup and Communication" in Chapter 7, defines higher-level concepts for registration. You don't need to search for an existing registerXYZ method to register a factory to some API. Rather, you *declare* the registered instance by creating a META-INF/services/...XYZ file and leaving it up to someone else to pick it up.

Even though the Lookup example is simple, it already removes the need not only for the registerXYZ method, but also for its companion method, unregisterXYZ. Not only that, it also ensures consistency between these two, which is difficult to achieve in the case of a regular call-based API. Because many API users tend to engage in empiric programming—that is, "do something, try it, and if it seems to work, continue"—it's easier for them to find and use the register method than for them to care about the cleanup code. Indeed, this is wrong, because in a modular system container, we have a dynamic system where modules are enabled, disabled, and installed on the fly, and we don't want them to forget about the garbage they leave behind. Declarative programming is a solution to this problem: as soon as the developer describes what to register, proper cleanup can be provided for free.

INSTALLING AND CLEANING MODULE FILES

Since its beginning, the NetBeans Platform has handled cooperation between various modules in a system by reading their configuration files. For example, if you register files into the Toolbars directory, modules can influence which buttons are visible in the main toolbar. In the early days, we required each module to create its own files during the initial install. Nearly every module registered its own install hook. As soon as the infrastructure called the hook, it started to create its files by calling **new** *FileOutputStream*(**new** *File*(root, "Toolbars/my.button")). However, this was error prone, boring to write, and problematic at the time of uninstallation. People didn't bother to implement the cleanup code correctly.

We considered this a real problem that complicated the usage of the API. It made coding for NetBeans a painful process. I spent a lot of time trying to come up with a solution. As part of the project sandwich, also mentioned in the section "Files and Their Content" in Chapter 3, I invented the concept of "merging virtual XML filesystems." As a result, the API became more declarative. Each module simply exposed an XML file defining the layout of the files, letting the infrastructure do the rest.

This immediately solved the uninstallation problem. It's easy to write the infrastructure correctly—much easier than ensuring that hundreds of implementations have a consistent install and uninstall experience. Moreover, it allowed for interesting improvements. In fact, we didn't need to create files on disk at all, as it was enough to keep them in memory and simply merge them "virtually." Also, this was a completely compatible addition, as the merge happened over XML files as well as on the local disk, so that old modules that still extracted files on startup continued to work correctly.

Last but not least, when the number of modules in NetBeans grew to more than 500, we realized that the parsed XML files occupied far too much memory and that their parsing on startup took a significant amount of time. That is why we wrote a cache that remembered the result of the last merge. This kind of optimization wouldn't have been possible without the declarative nature of the APIs.

Consistency is not the only reason why the declarative approach is reasonable. The other reason is effectiveness. In Java, the amount of memory associated with the execution of a piece of custom code is not proportional to the size of the code. It's the opposite for small classes that have, for example, just one method. The virtual machine appears to have a 3KB overhead per class; that is, each class is likely to take at least 3KB. Moreover, although possible, it's not easy to force classes to be garbage collected. As a result, such loaded classes likely stay in the virtual machine forever and occupy valuable memory.

Also, loading a single class from a JAR file has significant associated overhead. You need to create a classloader for the JAR and load a list of its files into memory. None of this is free. For these reasons, you are not helping performance if on the start of an application you load a single class from each JAR and ask it to perform some kind of registration. It's much better to create a registration manifest—that is, a file containing the description of what should be registered where—and to load and process that file instead. Then you don't need to open a whole JAR and load a class into the virtual machine. Not only that, you can also provide intelligent caching, where resources may be released from memory when not needed and re-created on demand.

It might even be possible to store the caches computed on the first execution and keep their results for subsequent executions. This optimization is possible because most of the declarative approaches don't have side effects. The result of their processing is always the same on Monday as it is on Friday, neither being influenced by files on disk nor by the amount of occupied disk space. All these aspects often influence real code written in Java or another executable format. The fact that declarative approaches are more effective is exactly because of this incompleteness: if they were too expressive, they would be difficult to optimize later, just like the bodies of methods invoked in unknown classes or scripts in general purpose scripting languages. The more declarative your approach and the less general purpose the format is, then the more assumptions you can make, and the greater the optimizations that can be done as needed. Maybe this is the most important difference between traditional programming and declarative programming. It might also be the most important reason why you might want to create an API based on high-level declarations of the concepts you want to expose.

Make Objects Immutable

Because all four deadlock conditions introduced in the section "Deadlock Conditions" in Chapter 11 are necessary to create a deadlock, they can all be seen as being equal. Nonetheless, I would name the mutual exclusion condition (there must be a resource that can be owned by just one thread) as the most prominent. Why? Because this condition, in my opinion, attacks the heart of our understanding of computers and programming. Ask yourself this: why should there be only one thread that needs to own a resource? Taken to its extreme, there is just one reason: the thread wants to destroy it.

Of course, this is an extrapolation. Resources are not actually destroyed. In some senses, their potential future states are simply trimmed down. After a thread uses a printer, a piece of paper is filled with characters or pixels. At that point, it's no longer empty; it becomes "damaged." It can never be used again. When it was simply a blank page, it had great potential. Therefore, in some sense the future of the page has been destroyed by using the printer. In a similar way, you destroy a DVD when burning data onto it. Of course, it now contains a nice movie, which is not a bad fate for a DVD. However, before that point, the DVD could also have held a backup of this book or my music collection. By burning data onto it, the DVD's options have been destroyed. In a similar, though weaker sense, you destroy a hard drive when storing new data onto it. And, again taken to an extreme, you also destroy the options of an object in Java by changing one of its fields. Before an assignment, you could read the value of the field, or multiply it if it is an integer, and so on. After an assignment, the value is gone forever, and even if a part of the program might be interested in it, it's now too late because your object of interest is destroyed and replaced by a modified version of it.

"Well," you might say, "it's sad that my object's options are destroyed when I change its fields. However, there is nothing unnatural about that because that's what happens in the world all the time." True, yesterday my window had a whole pane of glass; today it's broken. (Similarly, when I started to write this book, I was enthusiastic; now I am tired! And again, I used to be young and handsome, now I am old and ugly!) Things in life change continually. We are used to that and can adapt. However, understanding the changing world is more diffi-cult than just taking a snapshot and studying it, especially if the world is changing right in front of us and bringing us new surprises. One day we might think we understand everything and the next day something changes and our understanding is gone. What is true today might turn out to be false tomorrow.

So, can we understand anything at all? Well, yes, if we simplify the model. From certain points of view, geometric cubes and spheres are abstractions of the shapes of stones in the real world. Similarly, we can try to improve our understanding by studying a state of the world where nothing changes, or at least where existing objects don't change. We can then seek out new objects. Actually, this is the approach that mathematicians have taken for centuries. Mathematical and especially geometric objects are immutable and are sometimes considered to have existed forever. We, their users, simply shine a light on them to see them, recognize them, and learn to understand the relationships between them. The more we illuminate, the larger the horizon we create and the more things we see. However, everything already discov-ered stays where it is and doesn't mutate. Maybe you are not watching anymore, but maybe someone else is. Maybe someone else is reading your proof or geometrical construction sev-eral hundred years later. They might still see the same objects exactly as you discovered them and brought them to the front of the horizon of your understanding.

The essential knowledge of mathematicians is built upon unmodifiable objects. We know how to study them and reason about them. There are methods to verify that our understanding is sound. Wouldn't it be beneficial if this knowledge was applied to computer programming as well? Imagine if we would read programs as proofs. We would be able to verify that they are cor-rect under all circumstances—not just today according to our own limited knowledge, and then broken tomorrow when we add a new synchronization lock, breaking the assumptions we made yesterday. The world of programming would then be a beautiful and truth-filled place!

You might see this as an impossibly distant dream. However, those in the know are aware that proven programming languages of this nature already exist. In functional languages such as Haskell, you cannot change objects that are already known. All you can do is throw new light on them via your computations, and based on your knowledge of existing objects, illumi-nate those that are new and currently unknown. The whole computation then illuminates newer and newer objects, while you obtain the result of your search somewhere at the end of the process. A naive implementation could then indeed easily exceed the capacity of a com-puter. However, these days we have garbage collectors, which can discover if objects are still needed or not. If not, they can be removed from memory, freeing space for new, yet to be illu-minated objects.

With this approach you exorcise deadlocks completely because there are no reasons to lock an object. The object is created—that is, discovered—at one point in time. From then onwards, the object can only be examined, but never modified. Indeed, there is no reason to lock an object if you only need to read its state. That can be safely done by many readers at once, so there is no reason for a resource to be exclusively owned by a single process or thread. This breaks the first condition of deadlocks and exterminates them forever.

As a result, you should make your data structure immutable if you want to eliminate deadlocks and prove that your programs are correct, while making them elegant at the same time. However, this is easier said than done. This programming style is indeed easy and natural in Haskell and other modern functional languages. However, when you mount that approach in Java, where the set of immutable objects starts with java.lang.String and java.lang.Integer and ends with java.lang.Class, then things are suddenly not straightforward anymore. Indeed, Java is based on mutable objects, in contrast with, for example, Concurrent Clean (a sibling of Haskell), which has a fully immutable API for GUI-based programming. Despite that, you can apply immutability at least locally, inside dedicated library APIs.

AM I REALLY CALLING FOR ELEGANCE?

When I finished my university studies by successfully defending my masters thesis about an object-oriented extension to a Concurrent Clean–like language, I didn't know whether it would be better to spend my time on my main hobby—that is, functional languages—or to use Java and create the NetBeans IDE. Then, as now, I considered functional languages to be the way to go in the future. Of the current solutions, only functional languages can provide full usage of multicore or multiprocessor machines, without the need for complicated parallel programming. This is because the compiler can effectively parallelize the code. Functional languages' time will come. I am just not sure when, exactly . . .

That is the reason I decided to work with Java and design the NetBeans IDE. The need for an IDE for the new language was clear and it was much easier to turn that into a business plan. Doing the same with functional languages would have been difficult, as there are too many unknown issues. The languages are different and they are still not taught in schools. As a result, the learning threshold is high, and unless the benefits of clueless parallelization outweigh this, it's difficult to estimate when the time for functional languages will come.

However, when and if their time comes, coding will suddenly become more beautiful, and much more elegant, like geometry, which is always stable and where truth is constant forever. Until then, we can get a sense of the time to come, by making at least parts of our APIs immutable.

The first thing to do to make an API more immutable is to remove all setters. Indeed, a setter is a way to set a field of an object, which effectively destroys its previous state. Instead, all fields need to be provided at the time of creation. That can work well. However, sometimes it might become impractical, at which point a cloning factory can be useful:

```
AServerInfo empty = AServerInfo.empty();
AServerInfo name = empty.nameProvider(prov);
AServerInfo urlAndName = name.urlProvider(prov);
info = urlAndName.reset(prov);
```

This style always creates a clone of the previous object, with one field differing from the original. This is an immutable version of setters and in some sense it can also be a more compressed version, because you can turn all the calls into a one-liner:

```
inf = AServerInfo.empty().nameProvider(p).urlProvider(p).reset(p);
```

The only drawback compared to setters is that this call appears to create two new objects that are used only as templates for cloning, and they can immediately disappear. Although this might not be well-performing enough for real-time applications, the Java garbage collector is so good that the temporary creation of an object should not influence anything. Moreover, should this programming style become more common, there is room for optimization in the virtual machine, as described in the sidebar "Unique Types and Escape Analysis."

UNIQUE TYPES AND ESCAPE ANALYSIS

One of the most frequently questioned features of programming with immutable objects is performance. If I need to create a new clone whenever I need to change something, can this be fast enough? The answer is, "Yes, it can," not only because we have a good garbage collector, but also because of a little trick that prevents cloning completely.

In certain situations, when you are sure that nobody else is observing an object, it appears to be acceptable to destructively change an object's state. If the object is known to have just one observer—you—the compiler can completely eliminate the allocation of a new object, and instead modify the previously existing instance, coming on par with the speed of the destroying executor, while keeping the immutable feel of the API.

Concurrent Clean has a construct of unique types for that, and the Java HotSpot machine is experimenting with the use of escape analysis that could be used for that purpose as well. For example, AServerInfo. *empty*() only creates an instance of the AServerInfo object that nobody else references. When you call a nameProvider method on it, it knows that the only reference to that object is passed to that method and then the method is free to update the object. The same is true for other similar methods.

Even if complete immutability might not be possible, it's beneficial for regular mutable objects to keep their internal state in immutable data structures, because that allows easier synchronization when the object is modified from multiple threads or in a reentrant way. I had the opportunity to see this with an implementation of the NetBeans Lookup class, which uses optimized, complex internal structures to speed up the computation of results. Originally, I wrapped the computation into a lock, but as it called out to foreign code, we experienced deadlocks. The best solution would have been to do something like the following:

```
public int sumBigger(Collection<T> args) {
    for (;;) {
        ImmutableData<T> previous;
        synchronized (this) {
            previous = this.data;
        }
        int[] ret = { 0 };
        ImmutableData<T> now = doCriticalSection(args, previous, ret);

        synchronized (this) {
            // if there was no parallel or reentrant change,
            // apply and return. Otherwise try once more.
            if (previous == this.data) {
                this.data = now;
```

```
            return ret[0];
        }
    }
}
}
```

This would use only top-level synchronization when updating the cache, while allowing the cache to be traversed and checked by multiple threads, without the risk of deadlocks.

SILENT NEED FOR IMMUTABILITY

Mutability has good support in object-oriented languages such as Java. In some senses, creating an immutable object in Java is more troublesome than simply defining it and its fields to be mutable. On the other hand, there are certain places where immutability is expected. This is especially visible in the Collections API. Its HashMaps and TreeSets expect a correct implementation of Object.hashCode and Comparable.compare, respectively. A necessary precondition is that the results of hashCode and compare are immutable; that is, that they are based on immutable aspects of the object. If they are not, and for example, a hashCode changes during an object's lifetime, it might easily happen that you insert an object into a HashMap without being able to find it later, although the object is still clearly present.

Although immutability is not a first-class citizen of Java and other languages that are currently used in a production environment, it makes sense to use it as much as possible. Although it might look like too rational an approach, it's in fact well aligned with selective cluelessness. It implies that you don't need to pay attention to a program's execution. The only important part is the creation of new immutable objects. This is good because it helps you to minimize your understanding while coding more reliable programs, which are coincidentally more beautiful and elegant as well.

Immutable Behavior

Immutability might have other incarnations than objects with final fields. Even if the objects in your API do change from time to time, it might be beneficial to minimize the frequency of their changes.

NETBEANS ACTION PERFORMERS

There is a single menu item for copy, cut, and paste in traditional NetBeans-based applications. Yet the menu item needs to have different functionality when the focus is in the editor than when it's in the explorer or in a Unified Modeling Language (UML) drawing tool. Although these pieces don't know about each other at all, they all need to control and react to user clipboard operations.

Originally we solved this problem with the use of "performers." Whenever a top-level element in the UI received focus, its componentActivated method was called. Now the code could locate the cut, copy, paste, or other actions. It could then attach its callback interface to them. From then on, all operations on the actions would be delegated to this UI element until another was selected and attached its own callbacks.

At first sight, this seemed like a reasonable architecture and it even worked in most cases. However, in certain less common situations we faced unsolvable problems. For example, on window managers that don't require a click to change focus, a user might invoke a cut or delete operation on a different element than expected. As you can imagine, it's not a pleasant surprise to find that the deleted node is not your backup file, but the content of your database. Sometimes this could happen even from inside a pop-up menu! Even if the focus behavior was acceptable, users might have experienced problems with broken modules that woke up randomly and attached their performers to copy, cut, and similar actions while another UI component remained selected.

We needed a fix. Luckily Swing in JDK 1.3 came up with the concept of `ActionMap`. Each Swing component has it and uses it to map generic keys to the actual performers. This looked ideal for solving our problems, and after a while, when we were struggling to find a backward-compatible solution, we started using it.

Right now, each top-level UI element has its own `ActionMap` and fully controls it. Most usages register the right callbacks at the time of creation and don't care about what happens next. The infrastructure then tracks the selection or the appearance of a pop-up menu and correctly binds the actions to those found in the `ActionMap` of the appropriate UI element.

Since that point, we haven't had any more random focus problems. The user code is more or less "immutable" and most of the dynamics are handled by the infrastructure, which is under our control and can be well tested, carefully written, and verified for correctness.

The more static the user code is, the greater the chance that it will be correct, even if written in clueless mode. If there is a need for dynamic changes, it's better to leave them up to the infrastructure, as that is a single point owned by us that we can focus on and write correctly.

Compatibility of Documents

Up to this point, I've mostly talked about signatures or the behavior of programs. However, as outlined in the section "Files and Their Content" in Chapter 3, the API of your library spans far beyond that point. For example, it includes the files your library writes and reads. The rules for such an API are the same as in the case of classes and methods: simplicity, robustness, correctness, evolution readiness, and so on. However, the techniques to achieve these might be different. Yet they are important, especially when you decide to empower declarative programming more and more.

"The first version is never perfect" was the mantra of Java API development. In fact, that is true for file-based APIs as well. Even the first format you write to disk needs to have some kind of identification because later you'll certainly have to enhance it and write a new one, while continuing to read the old as well as the new. The most important thing is to include a version number or some other version identification into every file your application or library stores to disk.

When evolution is possible, the next question that arises is how to simplify it: how to structure the file's content so that it can be enhanced from time to time. There are usually two options in this regard: a big bang change or incremental improvements. The big bang approach just changes the version identification in the file and then completely revamps the content. This is a kind of duplication of the format. It means that the code that reads the file to memory needs to be duplicated as well. That is bad because of the amount of code that you need to maintain. However, it's also good, because the old code that reads the old format can stay almost unmodified, which significantly lowers the risk of regressions.

On the other hand, the incremental approach prevents the complete duplication of the reading code. That's because it probably enhances the code that reads the format with additional if statements, so it might negatively affect the existing behavior of the old format. The good thing is that the code to read that file is not duplicated. However, you need to be more careful to continue reading the old format correctly. A few years ago this would have constituted a big risk. But these days, with automated testing being common, the potential for making everything work correctly for the old as well as the new format is high. It's just a matter of being diligent.

One important aspect can be realized only with the incremental approach: you can support not just backward compatibility, but also forward compatibility. This means that by knowing just the old version of the protocol, old versions of an application can partially understand its future version. Of course, they cannot understand all of it—that would be miraculous. But the old versions can understand the parts already present in the older version of the file, while ignoring the new additions. For example, imagine a file representing a text document that supports only black letters in its first version. In the new version you could add support for various font colorings. If done in a forward-compatible way, the format remains readable by the old version. It will ignore all the colors, but the result will remain useful, at least for viewing. Viewer-like applications are acceptable. Only editor applications need to care about this and warn users before making modifications to newer versions of their documents. Possibly all coloring will be lost if the document is modified in older versions of the editor.

BLACK-AND-WHITE TV VS. COLOR TV

The miracle of the forward-compatible extension of a protocol could be witnessed when black-and-white TV started to broadcast in color. In fact, the entire signal changed, yet the old black-and-white TV could continue to understand it and correctly display it in shades of gray, while the new TVs perfectly reconstructed its colors. This is a masterpiece in evolving formats that was not designed for evolution in a compatible way. As far as I know, TV sets from 1950 to 1960 can still display something reasonable even 50 years later! That is real compatibility. The trade-off is that we can't use the Red, Green, Blue (RGB) scale, but rather the obscure Yellow-Ultraviolet (YUV), as that was the key technology that allowed black-and-white TV sets to take only the Y and leave the colors in YUV for the newer versions. That negative was still greatly outweighed by the fact that the TV signal was kept compatible for such a long time. This isn't to say that I'm not glad the whole world is switching to the MPEG signal, as that is a huge step forward. Due to enhancements in video signal encoding, we'll have at least 4 times more channels than with this 50-year-old technology . . .

What is the best format that can contain additional data and yet be recognizable by those who know previous versions? To my knowledge, two are well suited for this task. One of them is a properties file and the second is XML. The properties file is composed of many name and value pairs. When a new version adds new keys, the old version can safely ignore them and still work acceptably. A similar case applies to XML: if designed well, it can contain additional attributes, comparable to name/value pairs, or additional elements. These might contain whole new subtrees. However, the old clients can completely ignore them and just pay attention to the elements known to them.

JUST ANOTHER BINARY FORMAT

In 2000, I was chatting with a friend and we were trying to figure out the benefits of XML over other existing formats. During long arguments, I tried to dismiss the format completely, while he, as a founder of Systinet, had completely the opposite view. After a few hours we decided to treat XML as a textual format. In that context, it has one big advantage over any other textual format: it inherently contains a hierarchical tree structure. As a result, when you are processing it, you can skip certain subtrees completely and still understand and even manipulate the rest of the document.

The other option we considered—that is, to treat XML as a binary format—didn't interest me much. On the other hand, my friend became quite interested in it, especially when we found that the only advantage of textual XML is the tree structure. When I had the chance to observe his later work in the area of web services, I always reminded myself of this discussion. Yes, Simple Object Access Protocol (SOAP) and similar formats don't take advantage of tree structures much. They seem to treat XML as yet another binary format.

The advice not to expose more than you need is difficult to achieve in the area of file formats. While classes have access modifiers such as private and protected, files offer nothing similar to help you. As a result, be prepared for files to be publicly readable. If you provide the opportunity, someone will potentially make use of it. The only way to make this less likely is to use the "security by obscurity" approach; that is, make the format of the file horrible, while investing in a good library that presents it in a nice way. In so doing, you can hope that developers will use the library, which will only expose those pieces that are supposed to be seen, instead of reading the files themselves. As there are always more programming languages than existing libraries, this is usually a false hope. It's better to expect that everything written to disk can be seen by anyone.

Another aspect of good API design is self documentation. In fact, both the properties format and the XML format push this in the right direction. Anyone who has ever tried to modify a configuration file written in one of these styles, especially when it allows for some kind of comments, knows that it's enough to stay with the file itself and that no other documentation should be needed under these circumstances. Of course, writing a whole new file from scratch is hard, but if you concentrate just on a small piece of it, the chances are high you'll understand its meaning correctly and will be able to perform local modifications correctly.

COMPATIBILITY OF ANT SCRIPTS

In the end, documents have meaning. Meaning can complicate evolution beyond the cases described in this section. For example, the NetBeans IDE is built around Ant scripts. An Ant script backs almost every project in the NetBeans IDE. The Ant script is partly generated by the IDE. However, users can also edit it in cases where they need to perform additional tweaks during their build processes. The IDE's features are continually evolving. In tandem, the format of the generated scripts needs to evolve too. However, because Ant supports a kind of inheritance and target overriding, targets in the script are continually being called or overridden. So, we need to pay close attention to the compatibility of our generated scripts. Deleting previously existing targets is a big no-no, and renaming them is not good either. This situation is especially problematic when we want to change dependencies between targets, as well as the properties they define or rely on. Moreover, the whole scenario is complicated by the fact that Ant build files don't support encapsulation; that is, every target is public and can therefore be called or overridden.

We have now almost switched from the world of file API compatibility to regular compatibility in object-oriented languages. Inheritance, overriding, and so on require us to face all these issues with Ant scripts, causing the same kinds of problems as with our Java APIs. This is magnified by the fact that the target group consuming this API includes all the users of the NetBeans IDE, not just those who write modules extending it. Fortunately, by no means do all these users modify their Ant scripts. As a result, not too many incompatibilities have been reported in this area thus far.

The area of files and their content has some specific complications with respect to APIs and clueless assembly. The number of the problems you can face depends on the amount of declarativeness versus imperativeness present in the document formats. For simple cases it's enough just to understand the version of the document. For complex ones, such as the case of Ant build scripts, you end up with complex implications similar to object-oriented API design. However, at least on the surface, the need for rules to measure successful design remains the same. The techniques you need to use might vary, but only slightly, when compared to Java classes and signature APIs.

PART 3

■ ■ ■

Daily Life

It's good when you understand how things are supposed to work, but it's better if you are able to make them work yourself. Unfortunately, the first doesn't automatically lead to the second! Understanding the theory is important: at least you now know the background of API design and can justify your day-to-day decisions. However, your common daily operations are even more dynamic and flexible than the theory describes. So, you need to apply the theory carefully, with an eye to the specific environments in which you are working at the time.

Theories are products of science. Whenever a science explores a world, it tries to describe it as comprehensively as possible. Only then can the science be understood to be precise. Only then can it be compared to the most admired science since that of ancient Greece: geometry. However, geometry is precise precisely because it doesn't talk about the real world. It talks about the world of geometric objects. In the purest form of geometry, it's moreover a static world where objects exist and can be discovered, but can neither mutate nor move. Indeed, this is very different from the real world, which changes from moment to moment. Still, there is great value in applying geometric truths to real-world situations. Computing the length of the fence I need to put around my property is just one example. On the other hand, not all geometric truths can be applied to real life that easily. Cutting a wooden stick one hundred times in the middle to create smaller and smaller "half-sticks" is easily imaginable in geometry, where scale is not important. However, this is harder to do in reality.

Real life is replete with compromises to which theory needs to adapt. You need to have a bit of experience to know what works and what doesn't. You need to know what needs to be done to make things work. This is as true for fence building as it is for API design.

This part of the book builds upon the general theory and motivation (as explained in Part 1) and the practical application of its rules to Java (as discussed in Part 2). However, daily life is imperfect compared to the world of science, as theories are always simplified projections of the real world. As our day-to-day decisions are full of compromises, you are unlikely to be able to apply the conclusions of the previous parts in their pure form. You'll need to adjust the advice to fit your real-life situations. This is the topic of this part of the book. It outlines the "gotchas" you should be aware of when living the life of an API designer. It explains when the theory works and what needs to be done to make it work. The suggestions presented here are on the level of "applied theory." Whenever possible, they are backed up by the design practices that we use when working on the NetBeans project.

We start with the expectation that the theory is known to us and that we understand how to apply it to the domain of the Java programming language. However, as that is definitely not enough for the real world, I'll explain what needs to be done to solve the everyday issues that arise when creating, publishing, bug fixing, and maintaining APIs. This is important, as most of your time is spent precisely with these boring tasks. The theory and the initial design are just the tip of the iceberg. The rest is the real work. This part tries to illuminate bits of it.

■ ■ ■

CHAPTER 13

Extreme Advice Considered Harmful

Part 2 of this book showed you how to make your APIs better. The worst thing you could do would be to follow those suggestions to the letter. That would be neither possible nor generally beneficial. Suggestions are no more than suggestions. Individual API problems need individual approaches. The suggestions given in this book are based on my personal experiences within the context of the NetBeans project. It's more than likely that other projects have different starting points. Even the slightest difference in initial factors can lead to a completely different set of suggestions. Still, the attempt to provide objective grounds for the decisions made in Part 1 is a good starting point for your own conclusions.

DO NOT LISTEN TO YOUR ELDERS

During JavaOne 2007, I overheard a conversation between two people designing part of the Java APIs. One was describing an API design case when his senior colleague told him to do something differently. The other said something like, "Yeah, I know that guy. When he wants something to be done his way, he insists quite strongly on that solution." The other responded, "No, it isn't like that. He convinced me his solution is better."

A story with a happy ending! However, I believe it was an exception. From time to time those two developers are forced to accept a solution without proper explanation as to how that solution is supposed to help. I would certainly not like to be in their situation. That might be one of the reasons why I try to avoid this kind of "suggestion" when telling others what to change in their own solutions.

In my opinion, it isn't useful to listen to people just because they are older or just because they have more experience. If their advice is genuinely useful, there should be evidence to support their assertions. I realize, though, that this is more or less an engineering approach. However, software engineering is a kind of engineering too, which is why this approach seems correct to me. Without it, we would be in a kind of gerontocracy: the older you are, the more valuable your advice is. While it's true that experience and instinct are important, basing all our operations on these criteria would be shortsighted. I suggest that you only adopt a suggestion if it makes sense under the circumstances in which you find yourself.

Some time ago, I tried convincing developers working on a JDK enhancement that their proposed solution would not be optimal to the end user. Their solution required the user to create three classes with various intrinsic inheritance relations, while mine needed one class only.

I did what I could to convince them that they should change the design. I referred to extensive analysis of user coding styles. I argued that the simpler the API is for the developer, the better. They seemed to agree with me. At least, they had no arguments against my approach. That path inevitably led to only one conclusion: that the solution with one class was better. To my surprise, they agreed, but they continued to insist on using their own solution, for no explicable reason at all. In other words, they exhibited unreasonable behavior. I was quite depressed at the time and I still carry the sad memory of those bitter discussions with me.

I am not advocating that extreme approach of declining to follow advice. When there is a justified reason for a change, with measurable benefits, you should simply follow the given advice. Only when someone wants you to do something without rational justification, for no reason other than being "older," for example, should you insist on your right to know and on the reciprocal obligation to explain the reasons for the suggested approach.

I'll now demonstrate a few examples of how a strict adherence to advice can turn API design into a painful experience.

An API Must Be Beautiful

Throughout this book we have taken note of the belief that truth needs to be beautiful. In Chapter 1, we attributed this to our deep, even mostly unconscious, respect of antique culture and science.

One of the most profound outcomes of the absolute glorification of beauty in API development is a complete rejection of deprecations. It seems there are people who would remove an element from an API rather than deprecate it. Indeed, having an API full of deprecations is not desirable. However, a deprecation is a small price to pay compared to the work that would need to be done to migrate to a new API when the old version is removed. The price associated with a deprecated element consists of a temporary distraction while reading the documentation. This is a significantly smaller price than the loss of trust that comes with removing something from an API. In fact, just like any other breaks of backward compatibility, removals amount to punishments for those using your library. This is the last thing a serious marketing agent wants to achieve, of course. You don't want to punish customers for using your product. From time to time, I have heard a defense based on the argument that "nobody uses the API anyway." Well, if that is true, you have a perfect reason to deprecate it, because no one will then be distracted by your deprecations anyway.

Let me repeat that beauty is nice, but not the most important attribute of an API. This is more than apparent when you start talking about money. Sponsors of development projects are typically obsessed with two factors: getting the product to market faster and reducing the cost of ownership. In addition to those factors, there is always a "coolness factor" in certain technologies. However, if "coolness" doesn't include one or both of those basic economic principles, I would argue that the technology's future use and adoption will be limited.

Yes, deprecations decrease coolness. However, deprecations don't influence time to market much, nor do they increase the cost of ownership. In fact, the opposite is true: the more deprecations, the more you show that you care about your existing user base and the more you help them lower the cost of ownership while showing that you value and preserve the investments they have already made. This is not meant to say that you should keep using deprecated APIs inside your own code. The deprecation is an important tool to encourage users of the API to migrate to a more modern replacement or to prevent newcomers from using already obsolete elements in the API. Still, it's better to use deprecations as a soft hint, then removals as a hard, hit-the-wall, wake-up-and-face-the-reality action.

An API Has to Be Correct

Another good piece of advice that you can violate from time to time is the myth that a good API must always be correct. A correct API is certainly more useful than one that is broken. An API that is naturally easy to use is also better than one that has many ways to be misused, requiring the API client to search through documentation to find the right way to use it. However, you can create a lot of problems for yourself by sacrificing ease of use for correctness.

If I were to be able to write one paragraph of this book instead of being forced to write a utility method to read the contents of a file to String or into a String array representing all lines in the file, this book would have been published years ago. I am sure I am not alone in finding that the way people have to read files from disk in Java is abnormally "verbose." On the other hand, I understand why they need to do so in that way: the verbosity mimics the way this has been done in C for years. With the C approach it's guaranteed that any file can be read regardless of its size or internal structure. Simplification would bring an added degree of incorrectness and randomness.

MERCURIAL VS. SUBVERSION

An interesting parallel to the case of Java APIs is something relevant to the NetBeans project: a comparison of various versioning tools. Some time ago NetBeans migrated from CVS to Mercurial, also known as hg. The hg workflow is quite different from what most of us had been used to. The result was no surprise: developers complained. A lot. It was not uncommon to hear the cry, "Why didn't we choose Subversion instead?"

The NetBeans engineer who managed the transition sent me an excellent explanation: "You should see CVS and Subversion as trying to present the world using classical mechanics, while quietly giving the wrong answers for speed or distance. On the other hand, hg presents the world directly, using special relativity."

That explanation is quite nice. In Subversion, the end result is completely unknown whenever you commit, just as if you were to send a light signal to the repository and think that it will reach it at a predictable time or in a certain order. The whole repository has a version of all the files, and if you commit, the repository might already contain integrations from other developers. First you need to do a checkout to determine the state of the repository that your integration created. This is similar to sending a beam of light from random stars and then hoping that some day someone on Earth will see them all composed in the form of the Mona Lisa! Obviously, this is unlikely to happen.

With Mercurial, things are different. First of all, you need to capture the state of the repository. You need to bring it to your system, merge your changes into it, and then push it back. Your push is accepted only if your vision of the repository is exact. If someone has changed the repository in the meantime, you need to start again: pull, merge, push. This guarantees that you know exactly what you are doing: you have the whole state of the repository on your own disk. In the "beam of light" example terms, this means that you need to get a light signal from a star that hosts the repository, modify it with your desired changes, and send both back while asking for changes from the previous state to the new state. Obviously if this is done from multiple places at once, only one such attempt can be successful. The others need to repeat the holy trinity of "pull, merge, push" again.

From the perspective of rationalism, the Mercurial approach is correct. It's also beautiful and elegant. Subversion is not, though it's easier to use. Guess what our developers are crying for? Yes, a clueless approach to committing their changes! So much for correctness and ease of use in the world of version control systems.

Let's take the perspective of a newcomer and imagine how to describe the Java approach to reading and parsing a file's content. Let's suppose you already have java.io.File in hand. You're searching for a way to process it. First of all, there is no method in java.io.File to help you. However, if you search long enough in the same package, you can find FileInputStream. Not every newcomer needs to understand the concept of streams. In other languages, you can solve file reading tasks completely without "stream" concepts. For the sake of simplifying this evaluation, let's suppose our newcomer knows what a stream is. It's easy to assume that FileInputStream is exactly what you need. Now that you have an instance of an input stream, you want to read from it. How can you read from it? Of course: use the read method. However, those available seem to be strange in some ways: one reads a single character, while another consumes an array. But I don't have any array! I want to read an array, but I don't have one yet! After a bit of searching you find that the right approach is to allocate an empty array and then repeatedly read it and process it. For someone coming from Perl it's a bitter pill to swallow that there is no simpler approach to achieving such a trivial task.

I've heard Java designers explain why the speed of change in Java is not as fast as in C#. They say that, compared to the producer of C#, Sun is committed to compatibility. If something is added to the language it needs to stay. That is why the development of new features needs to be slower: they need to be more comprehensively verified for correctness. Though that argument might be convincing, try to explain that to someone who needs to verify that the contents of a file on disk contain the text "OK." That is one of the most common actions when writing a unit test. Virtually all my modules contain a utility method to read a file to String, because it's such a typical requirement to do so. I know its implementation is not correct in the case of a large file, but I don't care! I know my files are small, and if they are not, I have no problem with an exception or error being reported. Although this behavior adds a certain amount of randomness and from a rational point of view it isn't correct, it's easy enough to use and works well in almost all use cases to justify the existence of such a simplified API.

Though unit tests are one of the more pertinent examples, file reading methods are needed all the time in regular code as well. When you read a configuration file, it's safe to assume that the file will fit into memory. Its lines are short, as it's likely to have been written by humans. That is why java.io.File should have the String asText(), **byte**[] asBytes(), and Iterable<String> asLines() utility methods. Not only would they be simple to use, they would also minimize the need for understanding, because you don't need to care about streams at all. They might not be absolutely correct, but they would certainly shorten the time to market. If they were to increase cost of ownership, you could always revert to defensive byte array feeding reads.

The next version of Java could add these methods. If that were to happen, I would say that it would be a great release, although about ten years late. These methods would let people concentrate on more important things than reading files and would prevent them from being confused by byte arrays and loops. Ease of use is sometimes more important than correctness. The C# designers have probably figured that out for themselves because their language has had these constructs for several releases already.

An API Has to Be Simple

A similar problem arises if you view the API only from a newcomer's point of view. That view is important. The feelings and attitudes resulting from the first encounter are influential. You don't want to disappoint or upset those who have just started using the API. Clearly, the entrance barrier shouldn't be too high. However, you shouldn't forget that most of an API's users will be using it a lot more than just the first time. They are likely to gain a much deeper knowledge over time, and their requirements will continue developing. The last thing you want is for them to hit a wall caused by your need for simplicity, right after they've made significant investments in your library. In short, when designing an API you should pay attention to making simple things easy, while letting complex things be possible.

A TALE OF TWO DIALOGS

Oversimplification happens frequently. A profound example in my life was not in the area of API design, but UI design. UI design is different from API design. A good UI designer is unlikely be a good API designer immediately, and vice versa. Nevertheless, on the meta level, these disciplines seem to have quite a bit in common. Most of Part 1, such as the need to be use case oriented and the need to know your user, can be generalized to be applicable to both.

In an e-mail by Linux creator Linus Torvalds (http://mail.gnome.org/archives/usability/2005-December/msg00022.html), he argues that the GNOME file chooser dialog is too hard to use. In the open source community, it's common for things not to be perfect, so the complaint is no surprise. The general idea is that if you want to make things better, you can make the necessary improvements yourself and donate the code back to the sources. However, the GNOME file chooser dialog is optimized for newcomers, while being too limited for power users. The main problem is that its maintainers refused to make the improvements that would have made it more suitable for complex use. Their excuse was that "it might confuse newcomers." As a result, anything more complicated than clicking with a mouse, even something as simple as using the keyboard to type a file name, is impossible or at least a hidden second-class citizen.

Torvalds' e-mail caused a lot of excitement. Those hoping for someone to create a bridge API that would allow users to see a file chooser of their choice, instead of GNOME's standard file chooser, could simply nod in agreement. Those who contribute to or use GNOME felt a bit injured, especially because Torvalds' words were strong.

However, Torvalds made an excellent and generally applicable point. Whenever you design anything, you don't want to treat your users as idiots. In striving to create a simple API, always avoid oversimplification.

It's acceptable to hide complex functionality. Those who need it are already likely to be your users anyway and will want to invest time in reading your documentation. Advanced functionality can therefore be hidden from newcomers. By hiding complexity, you avoid scaring them when they make their initial steps into your API. However, it's unacceptable not to give power users a chance to achieve their more complex objectives just because you want to keep things simple for newcomers. You can split complex functionality from simple functionality by putting them in different packages. For example, the basic network API can be in the net package, while the classes for working with the more advanced network streams can be in the net.stream subpackage.

An extreme example relates to what we did with the DataEditorSupport class in the Net-Beans APIs. This class guides the appearance of editors on the NetBeans Platform. In fact, it is an example of a complex API that is not intended for newcomers. It requires subclassing and a lot of glue code to let its users register a new editor in the NetBeans Platform. As a result, even a simple demo using it would be quite complex because of the amount of useless code that you would need to provide. We've been criticized about this by our tutorial writers and evangelists for a long time! As a solution, I've added the `DataEditorSupport.create(...)` factory method, which does all the "gluing" and eliminates about 100 useless lines. However, based on my experience, I would say that this method is only useful in demos. Since that time, nobody has complained about the complexity of registering an editor into the NetBeans Platform. Demo code looks slim and small to newcomers, while complex use cases remain possible (and complex). This is a perfect example showing how to make simple things easy (one method), and complex things possible (subclassing and adding glue code). This example also shows the benefits of the difference: demos are simple and are unlikely to scare an audience, while all the advanced functionality continues to be available to those who want to exploit it.

A last note on simplicity touches on a conflict with one of the most important principles of this book: "Do not expose more than you need." Throughout this book, I've argued the need to make things private, final, nonaccessible, and so on. This approach helps with the future evolution of your API and the incremental approach to API creation. This approach is tested and verified to work in NetBeans. On the other hand, because we expose as little as possible, from time to time we have users who write to our mailing list asking us to make a field public, a class subclassable, or a method overridable. Were we to comply with these requests, we would be painting ourselves into a corner by restricting our ability to handle future evolutionary changes. However, if we simply tell our users "No!" we might find ourselves being accused of being like the GNOME UI designers—sacrificing usability for simplicity. That would not be good. The last thing you want to tell your users is, "You are too advanced, so we don't support your use case!" Instead, I describe an answer in Chapter 14, which encourages your users to search for the solution themselves, design it, justify it, and document it. When they have done so, they can simply let you review it, accept it, and integrate it. We used this model in cooperation with Nokia when it used the NetBeans Platform as the base for its network monitoring application. Nokia's needs were unique and advanced. We didn't want to support them ourselves. Its requirements were not applicable to the NetBeans IDE at all. However, its contact person in our project created the changes for Nokia and pushed them through our review process. We only needed to verify that the changes fulfilled our API criteria. We also needed to verify that they didn't infringe on the "simple things should be easy" rule. Where Nokia's changes were acceptable, we integrated them into the NetBeans sources. That approach satisfied us, while the user of our API was satisfied as well because its "complex cases" were then supported by the NetBeans Platform.

An API Has to Have Good Performance

The main reason for breaking backward compatibility is performance. If your API is badly designed, its users might call methods that are inherently slow or that create many unnecessary objects. Performance might be hard to fix without changing some of the already existing behavior. On the other hand, when you design an API, you shouldn't overoptimize and violate the rules of good API design just to achieve benefits in performance. In that case, the gain might be illusory or only temporary. This is especially true when writing in Java or other dynamically compiled languages. The program that you get after compilation is still not exactly what the computer will see. It still needs to be interpreted or dynamically compiled. The machine code produced from such compilations is improving constantly. Allocating a lot of temporary objects was seen as a major threat to the garbage collector when Java started. However, because of the implementation of a generational garbage collector, these objects now stay in a "young generation" that is a part of memory from where they can be reclaimed pretty cheaply. If you've optimized your application or the API of your library not to need temporary objects, you've probably done a lot of useless work from today's point of view. Of course, the fewer objects you create, the less work the garbage collector needs to do. In that sense your work is not superfluous. However, if in the process of optimizing the allocation strategy, you've also limited your API by making it more difficult to understand, you've probably overoptimized.

The other case where performance optimizations can be premature, at least in the case of Java, is where you replace getters or setters with directly exposed fields. This might be a necessary technique in systems with fewer built-in optimizations, such as in .NET. However, in Java this is a completely useless activity. It fails to improve performance because the HotSpot dynamic compiler is able to eliminate the overhead of setters and getters by inlining their code, thus turning everything into simple field access. Moreover, if you directly expose a field, you limit future API optimizations, as discussed in the section "A Method Is Better Than a Field" in Chapter 5.

In short, beware of premature optimizations, because these could be seen as the "root of all evil" in the world of API design.

An API Must Be 100 Percent Compatible

Backward compatibility is the mantra of this book. If we have backward compatibility, we have no need to be wary about upgrading. End users and application assemblers alike need to rely on backward compatibility when gluing libraries together. Attaining backward compatibility is both desirable and necessary. However, with the current state of software projects, backward compatibility is not always achievable. One of this book's goals is to explain why every library or framework should be backward compatible and to describe techniques that help prevent the biggest mistakes that compromise it. However, whether you reach 100 percent compatibility is more a matter of attitude than a question of following the suggestions in this book.

One hundred percent backward compatibility is costly and hard to achieve. In fact, even a small bug fix can break compatibility. For example, you have an incompatible change if your API silently survives an exception where before it threw a NullPointerException. In this case the code that gets broken by such an incompatible behavioral change would need to be quite strange, as it needs to expect the NullPointerException to be thrown. However, it would be valid Java code and valid usage of the API. Not supporting that usage in a new version would mean that your API would no longer be 100 percent compatible.

Bug fixes are important. Bug fixes are the main reason for an upgrade. However, as the API Design Fest game that will be described in Chapter 17 shows, every bug fix that doesn't require a compile-time indication of whether it should be applied or not can compromise backward compatibility. In short, every bug fix is a threat to 100 percent backward compatibility. As a result, this level of compatibility is hard to achieve. Though the winners in the API Design Fest game show that such an amount of compatibility is possible, the question is how practical the attempts to maintain absolute backward compatibility are. If nothing else, they can prove costly.

As a result, in most cases, achieving 99 percent compatibility is enough! I know I am playing devil's advocate here. It's difficult to define what exactly falls within the range of 99 percent compatibility and what the remaining 1 percent refers to. Once some kind of incompatibility is permitted, I know people who are likely to sneak almost everything into that 1 percent, starting with returning null values from methods that never returned null before, continuing to throw exceptions in situations that previously worked without exceptions, starting to read the content of configuration files that were never properly documented to be read, and arriving at a complete revamp of functionality with the renaming of classes or the removal of some of their methods. For these kinds of people and your own sanity, it's better to pretend that the goal is to reach a 100 percent compatible release. On the other hand, some of my colleagues laugh when I ask them to be absolutely backward compatible. For these people, let me more strictly explain what I mean by "99 percent compatibility."

One hundred percent compatibility means absolute compatibility. Even someone or something that knows everything cannot break it. That inherently means that if there is a way for an API to be misused, it will be misused. However, when you know absolutely everything, you also have access to all versions of an API at once, before starting to exploit an incompatibility. Also, you can see not just the API, but also its internals. This is common in the case of users of open source libraries; however, it's not that common to study the source code for all the API versions at once. The only reason for this is to do line-by-line diffs between the various versions, hoping to examine every line for potential compatibility problems. If one is found, then by definition the API is not 100 percent compatible. However, this is not at all what API users typically do. They don't examine all versions of your API to find differences.

The following example shows a genuinely defensive style of evolution:

```java
public class Arithmetica {
    public int sumTwo(int one, int second) {
        return one + second;
    }

    public int sumAll(int... numbers) {
        if (numbers.length == 0) {
            return 0;
        }
        int sum = numbers[0];
        for (int i = 1; i < numbers.length; i++) {
            sum = sumTwo(sum, numbers[i]);
        }
        return sum;
    }

    public int sumRange(int from, int to) {
        if (Boolean.getBoolean("arithmetica.v2")) {
            return sumRange2(from, to);
        } else {
            return sumRange1(from, to);
        }
    }

    private int sumRange1(int from, int to) {
        int len = to - from;
        if (len < 0) {
```

```
            len = -len;
            from = to;
        }
        int[] array = new int[len + 1];
        for (int i = 0; i <= len; i++) {
            array[i] = from + i;
        }
        return sumAll(array);
    }

    private int sumRange2(int from, int to) {
        return (from + to) * (Math.abs(to - from) + 1) / 2;
    }
}
```

In the preceding code, in version 1.0, the sumRange method was using a slow algorithm, which was useful at most for computing Factorial after intrinsic subclassing. As demonstrated in the section "Delegation and Composition" in Chapter 10, just rewriting the implementation to use a more efficient algorithm is not backward compatible. So you decide to make the behavior compatible, unless consciously requested otherwise, and you add the property Boolean.getBoolean("arithmetica.v2"), which needs to be set to change the behavior of the method. This is at least 99 percent compatible, but not 100 percent. It's still possible to create an exploit and observe the differences in the behavior of the two versions.

The previous example illustrates the meaning and limitations of 99 percent backward compatibility: it's possible to show that the two versions are not compatible and therefore the API is not absolutely compatible. However, imagine how difficult it would be to write the exploit if only version 1.0 were known, without any knowledge of the future of the API's evolution, without knowing that in version 2.0 the author of that method will introduce a new property-based API, and especially without knowing the name of the property. The likelihood of that is not zero, although it's close to zero. For practical purposes, the 2.0 version is compatible with the 1.0 version.

SNEAKING EVERYTHING INTO THE 1 PERCENT

I need to repeat that this approach heavily depends on common sense. I know people who would argue that even if you were to negate the condition for new code by testing with !Boolean.getBoolean("arithmetica.v1"), you'd still obtain behavior that is 99 percent compatible. This is a false view, as the meaning of the class is changed completely, unless someone asks for the old behavior. Of course, this can be exploited "only" when developers try to write a factorial. However, the likelihood that some API user could discover that it's possible to use version 1.0 of the Arithmetica class to compute a factorial just by looking into its version 1.0 is not zero. It's not even close to zero. In fact, I can smell this kind of problem just by seeing a subclassable class with some implementation methods. That is why it's clearly and rationally a false view to present this as an unlikely usage. This kind of change is clearly not reaching 99 percent compatibility at all. But how can you explain that to an irrational person who has just one goal: to sneak his changes in?

The "99 percent backward compatible API" term tries to find an appropriate balance between the need for fixes and the practical impacts of their incompatibilities. The API change can be considered acceptable if the probability of someone exploiting the incompatibility while knowing only the already released versions is almost zero. However, this all depends on interpretation. As already mentioned, this kind of compatibility depends on common sense, so please use it with care.

An API Needs to Be Symmetrical

This is a specific rant against beauty. For some reason, things that come in pairs are considered more elegant if they are symmetrical. Somewhere deep within our minds, we connect beauty and elegance to truth. Sometimes similar judgments are applied to the correctness of APIs. Indeed, say you have two APIs that have the same qualities. They can evolve, are maintainable, and are easy to use—but only one of them is symmetrical. It's probably better to choose the symmetrical version. However, your attempt to make things symmetrical should not occur at the expense of other aspects of good API design.

As an example, let's look at a recent attempt by the NetBeans team to write a JavaScript Object Notation (JSON) reader and writer API. The engineer working on it asked me to help him review the API. He told me that he was not completely satisfied with its state. We looked at it for a while and tried to come up with solutions. The API became more meaningful, but still we were not satisfied. Something seemed to be missing. After a month we talked again about the API and my colleague told me what was missing: symmetry. His original API tried to provide similar functionality for writing and reading JSON objects. However, this is more than likely unnecessary. In the case of writing, you have a live set of Java objects on the heap. You want to store them to a stream. That can be done with a simple static method that takes the root object and an output stream. This use case needs to be reflected in the reading part of the API as well. There should be a method that takes a stream and returns a live Java object that is constructed on the heap. However, there is also the additional use case for reading. You might read JSON files that are too big, as they contain structures of a large size that cannot be fully constructed in memory at once. The solution to this is to create a callback event–based API, just like the Simple API for XML (SAX) for parsing XML files. That was an easy task. However, we then spent a lot of time trying to find out how to create the appropriate symmetrical API for writing the JSON object. That is not so easy and to nobody's surprise we failed to figure it out. We were embarrassed by that, until we realized that this is another symptom of the "truth, beauty, and elegance" dilemma: in fact, we simply didn't need the read and write APIs to be symmetrical at all.

Symmetry in an API might help its acceptance. Symmetry can even increase cluelessness because you need to keep only half the API in mind: the other matches it symmetrically and can be deduced from the first half. However, an API is not bad simply for not being symmetrical. Just like in the JSON parser case, remember that there can be setters without getters, or getters without setters. Or, setters might be protected, while getters are public. There is nothing wrong with being nonsymmetrical, especially if it improves another aspect of the API, such as its simplicity or its potential to evolve.

CHAPTER 14

■ ■ ■

Paradoxes of API Design

API design is different from regular in-house system design. That is why when we apply the same principles to it, we might come up with surprising results. These results may be slightly difficult to believe, because they might contradict our expectations. However, they need not be wrong. The scale makes the difference here. Just like there is a difference between describing a house and describing the whole universe, there is a slight difference when we talk about in-house software systems and those with APIs.

As we cross and expand our horizons, we enter unknown territory. However, that doesn't mean that we cannot envision what it will look like. We have two approaches to dealing with the unknown. The first is to let our fear of the unknown outweigh our desire to explore the new. In that case, we assume that the unknown is dangerous, wild, and unfriendly. Traveling there is unpleasant and difficult; better to stay at home. This is one way to see our attempts to expand our horizons. Indeed, it's not proactive. If we all preferred to stay at home, there would be no discoveries of new worlds and there would be no new inventions. Instead, we would build walls to defend ourselves from the unknown. However, from time to time, something seems to compel us to go out and reach toward the most unknown stars.

The second approach is to indulge the extreme but common opinion that the world beyond the horizon is similar to the one here around us. It posits that we already know everything. Indeed, pushing beyond the horizon with this expectation is much easier, because it feels safer. There is no danger of encountering something wildly unexpected. With this perspective, it's much more pleasant to leave home and undertake lengthy journeys to the end of the universe and back. We feel like we cannot get lost and that the rest of the universe is probably just like home.

These two approaches are never pure. They are constantly fighting within us and sometimes our fears outweigh our belief in an explorable universe. Sometimes it's the other way around. Both these situations have their pros and cons. In fear mode, you only slowly reach your horizons, expanding them carefully and with trepidation. This takes time, and in some cases, is not even possible because of all our fears of the unknown. However, in this mode we are never surprised by the strange behavior of newly discovered objects. We know that the world beyond the horizon is wild and we expect to find wild things. We are ready to expect the unexpected.

In the "I know it all" mode, we are much more reckless. We carelessly cross horizons, and whenever we encounter something there, we feel ready to explain it. Sure, it's exactly like something back home, maybe a bit bigger, maybe a bit faster, but otherwise behaving just like what we are used to. This often works, especially if we don't cross the horizon that much.

Likely the world just behind the horizon will be similar to what we already know. But the further we go, the more likely we will face something inexplicable—something that, according to our knowledge, cannot exist. Something "paradoxical." However, the paradox doesn't mean that there is something inconsistent with the world itself. Usually, it's only a conflict between our expectations and the world.

THE FEARLESS PHYSICS OF THE RENAISSANCE

The fear and adventure modes appear not just in the world of computer science, but also in that of physics. The fact that Newton's physics made such tremendous steps forward can be attributed to the mode in which many of Newton's followers operated. They were mostly in the "I know it all" mode. Only in this mental state were they able to believe in their actions. They were able to trust that whenever the inexplicable was encountered, it simply required time and hard work for it to be analyzed and understood. Only the belief that the whole universe is already known to us makes leaps such as that possible.

The blind trust and carelessness required to cross the horizon vanished as soon as the paradoxes discovered at the end of nineteenth century revealed that the world was quite different than expected. The fear of the unknown reentered our worldview and it took time to recover from that disappointment. It took time to work out reasonable explanations of the discovered paradoxes. Nowadays, the "paradoxes" are no longer viewed as unnatural. We have a technical explanation for most all of them. However, they are important from another point of view. They are here to remind us that once we falsely expected the universe to be the same as what we had encountered on our side of the horizon. We should be aware of this reminder, bearing it in mind for next time, when we again begin to believe that we know it all and that everything is as we believe it to be.

Most of this book has explored the world of API design slowly, step by step, hoping to enlarge our horizons smoothly. In this way, we can avoid getting lost, never needing to face anything that is strange or paradoxical. However, this chapter is a bit different. It's a little excursion beyond the horizon, showing things that seem to be true for API design but that contradict our knowledge gathered when building in-house systems. Enjoy the ride, and here's wishing you a safe return from the beyond!

API Doublethink

Sometimes API design can seem like *doublethink*. At least, some developers have told me that I sometimes require them to torture their minds in certain ways. Doublethink is a term introduced by George Orwell in his famous *1984*. Wikipedia defines it as "to simultaneously believe in two contradictory ideas, without considering the contradiction strange." For example, doublethink is something like saying "war is peace," or judging something as "insane and ingenious." A slight attack of doublethink can also be spotted in advice offering two completely contradictory outcomes from the same situation: this is a product that needs to be either "offered soon to the market or abandoned immediately." Or, as is common advice when judging the API before first release, either "expose the API as stable or discard it by hiding it as private."

How can you seriously advise stabilizing an API while at the same time requiring it to vanish and removing the API completely? Either the API is good enough and then it can be considered to be stable or as a candidate for being stable. Alternatively, the API is so horrible that it should be closed and not made available to anyone. How can both outcomes be applicable at once?

The process of designing an API has one important milestone: the first public release. Before that point, the library is in development mode. Fixes are allowed. You can freely change anything, even incompatibly, because there are no—or few—users of that API. The biggest effort at this point, aside from creating an API that satisfies the basic functionality requirements, is to shape it in a way that will be most suitable for future evolution. Complete refactoring of everything is acceptable because this only has limited impact. Potentially it will have a huge benefit, if doing so can limit incompatible changes in the future. However, this applies only until the first version is released.

As soon as the number of API users increases and effectively gets out of the author's control, the library switches to sustaining mode. At this stage, the highest desirable goal is to preserve backward compatibility. That is what will keep your existing users satisfied. As such, you should avoid removals, cleanup, and massive refactoring of externally visible classes, methods, or behavior. If there is a need for these radical changes, they should all be done before the API enters sustaining mode. After reaching sustaining mode, all changes have to be carefully evaluated for compatibility. You must make no negative impact (or preferably no impact at all) on the existing usages of the API.

The development and sustaining modes are commonly applied in all kinds of software engineering, not just in the design of APIs. In typical cases, these modes continuously alternate. After the development phase, the product is handed to the sustaining team, which writes or backports bug fixes. At the same time, the development team continues to develop the next version, operating in development mode. When the new version is done, it's again passed to sustaining, and so on. This is the mode in which most of the developers are used to operating, and they expect it to be applicable to API design as well.

However, it's not. Proper API design seems to have only one cycle: develop the API and release the first version, and then switch to sustaining mode. If a new feature is requested, it can be added, but only carefully and compatibly, just as sustaining mode is used to doing. Another detail of API design is that the two teams in question here are one. It's not the case that someone creates the API, passes it to someone else to maintain, and then designs a new enhancement to be passed to the maintainer. In most cases, maintenance as well as development of new features is done by the same author or the same group of authors. The same person needs to operate both in development mode and in sustaining mode.

The API contradiction exists as a result of the process duality of designing an API while playing the role of both a developer and a sustainer. You need to be aware of the contradictory requirements each of these roles presents. As a result, when the part of you that is a developer says, "Don't publish this API, it's not good enough," the part of you that is the sustainer can think at the same moment, "Release it, but just promise that you'll keep backward compatibility by declaring it stable."

ARCHITECTURE REVIEWS AT NETBEANS

Are there any customers yet? If nobody has yet observed a star, it does not need to follow rules of our world; it can undertake big, unexplainable changes. It can change size, color, trajectory, or even vanish completely. No observer can be surprised and complain. However, if we know we've already put the API into the universe to be observed by anyone, the whole review suddenly starts from a completely different perspective. The goal is to be as nondisruptive as possible.

I saw this when I tried to pass NetBeans through architecture review at Sun. In principle, it's expected that all Sun products should pass the review before being seen by customers. Indeed, this is not always the case, and NetBeans was not an exception. Before we were acquired by Sun, we had already had quite a few public releases. But the review still operated in the "before first release" mode. We were advised to completely change the layout of files in the distribution, rename the launcher, and so on. They were all pretty big and incompatible changes to existing customers. However, as this was Sun's first review, it was hard to explain that we already had some customers. They just operated in the "strive for beauty" mode.

Since then I've participated in at least five follow-up reviews. All of them were completely different from the first one. Instead of "rename-this-directory" kinds of advice, we usually got a few change requests influencing new functionality but not touching anything that had existed from prior releases. The biggest advice for older functionality was not to touch it if you didn't need to. You have your users and they might rely on existing behavior, so don't change it.

This is a clear symptom of doublethink, but well justified. Improve as much as you can prior to the first version, then just don't touch anything, if possible. It's a case of doublethink that clearly shows the difference between the development and sustaining modes of an API.

Although the thoughts of a developer and a sustainer are usually contradictory, they both move API design forward to the next step. One scenario prefers not to release the library yet, keeping it hidden and not making any promises to the public. This is the developer who wants to concentrate as much as possible on making the API good, better, or perfect. The sustainer recognizes that although the current state might not be perfect, the library exists to be used. Only that way can a library actually be useful.

This clash resembles that of rationalism versus empiricism, discussed in the section "Rationalism, Empiricism, and Cluelessness" in Chapter 1. Is perfection the sole purpose of a library and its API? Does striving to make the API more beautiful justify its incompatibilities? That is what the developer inside us wants to believe. Or is it more important for a library to be useful and serve its purpose well, and once used, not to change shape like an amoeba? That is the pragmatic approach seen from the sustaining point of view. The API contradiction introduced in this section specifies that prior to public release, rationalism's drive for beauty is desirable and useful. However, after crossing that point, beauty loses its special position and compatibility takes charge.

It looks like this API contradiction is a way of bringing the old rivals, rationalism and empiricism, back to the forefront: start with rationalism and prefer beauty and elegance in API design. Then, at a certain point in time, release your work to consumers, paying heed to usefulness from then onward. However, there is one important point to stress: although we know how to marry elegance and pragmatism, their connection should only have a short lifespan. The point where an API switches from development to sustaining should be short, such as one hour or one day. The worst you can do is to pretend both philosophies can be applied at once. That is why it's sane and justified to suggest two completely opposite types of advice at once:

"Expose the API as stable or discard it by hiding it as private." Give it to the public, or continue privately striving for elegance. But choose! The worst thing to do is to pretend you can operate in both modes at once. You cannot. Doublethink can only be thought, not practiced. You can hold two contradictory ideas at once and they can still make sense. However, you cannot operate without choosing which one is preferred. This approach doesn't work. You cannot serve both these goals at once. If you try, you'll achieve neither beauty, nor elegance, nor truth, nor compatibility.

The Invisible Job

Supervising the development of an API is a difficult task. First of all, a good API architect has to be like a Cassandra: always seeing possible failures, always knowing what might go wrong in the future, always proclaiming warnings of danger. Supervision is especially needed when design is done in a group. The better the architect you are working with, the further into the future the architect needs to be able to see. However, this creates a problem that makes the task particularly tricky. People only take notice when something goes wrong. For example, customers become upset by incompatibilities, refuse to migrate to a new version, and then switch to competitive offerings. On the other hand, if everything works as it should, then nothing happens, and it's difficult to present "nothing" as a big success.

The situation is comparable to that of security agencies. Until a plane is hijacked and destroyed, nobody likes the work of security agents. People complain about the security checks at airports, which seem complicated and unnecessary. Without a catastrophe, it all seems to be overkill. However, after the disaster it's too late to fix anything.

How similar this is to defending an API and fighting for its backward compatibility! Developers complain about review procedures, coding practices, and so on. However, API guardians need to be awake constantly, careful lest one small oversight bring catastrophe. On the other hand, a little problem from time to time at least proves that you are really doing something useful.

Whenever I find a problem in the evolution of an API, I point out that it violates one of the coding suggestions described in this book. However, that doesn't help much, as people might validly ask, "And what did you do during the review?" If you are so clever now, why didn't you warn us sooner? To that I have a solution called "minority opinion." Whenever we do a standard review, as discussed in the section "Organizing Reviews Before Committing Code" in Chapter 16, four reviewers vote. The majority decides, but the opinions of the rest are not ignored. The others have the right to record their opinion in a special section dedicated to them. I like to contribute to that part, especially by recording mistakes that are not catastrophic, just annoying. Then, when those problems actually arise, I can do more than simply complain because I've tracked the evidence that I predicted it from the beginning.

I can live with being outvoted. Typically my opinions and suggestions are extreme, as you can see from Part 2 of this book, and sometimes it's not necessary to follow all of them. In most situations, nothing bad happens—but sometimes it does. And yes, at those times I am glad to have the evidence of such foresight. Having such a case helps us recognize a similar situation in the future. We can then know that in this type of problem, it's better to strive for more extreme design suggestions, at which point I'll no longer be in the minority.

However, supervising API design continues to be a difficult long-term endeavor, the results of which might not be evident until many releases later. It's much more difficult to measure the usefulness of API supervision when compared to regular development tasks.

Recently I had the opportunity to work on improving the performance of the NetBeans IDE. Well, that was easy! Simply find a problematic operation, measure how much time it takes or how many resources it occupies, fix it, remeasure, and your task is done. Your success is expressed in terms of seconds or kilobytes, which everyone at least thinks they understand. The same probably applies to any end-user functionality. If a new dialog appears in your application and people can use it to do something useful, it's visible and real. When you provide a new API, nothing like that happens. The API is simply the first step. It then takes time to convince developers to use it and do something meaningful with it. This is measurable to some extent. On the other hand, backward compatibility of such a library, which is a key aspect of its API design, is difficult to explain in measurable terms. The goal is that "nothing" happens, and "nothing" is difficult to present as a success.

Overcoming the Fear of Committing to a Stable API

Typically, NetBeans engineers know how to write an API and how to document it. However, they are afraid of releasing an API into the public. While their API is not yet well baked, they are aware of the many known problems and ways to improve the code. Based on that feeling, they keep the API private or with "friend only" access. Remember that in NetBeans you can restrict the set of clients that can access the public classes of a module, as discussed in the section "Life Cycle of an API" in Chapter 4. If they make an API publicly available, they don't want to commit to it being "stable." They are afraid that it would then be impossible to fix bugs, implement new features, and so on.

The first thing to note is that "stability" is not about the static quality of the API. It's about the attitude of its maintainers. A stable API can change. It can evolve. However, if there are different ways to change a stable API, you should always prefer to choose the solution that doesn't hurt the existing users of the library or at least minimizes their suffering. For example, don't rename classes or methods simply to make them "nicer." This development style doesn't require significant technical skills, but the "attitude" is essential. The attitude entails preserving the functionality of the existing solution, even if it means making it uglier once in a while by deprecating its elements or introducing silly duplicated interfaces such as LayoutManager2. As you can imagine, this task is more moral than technical.

Many people I've met are hesitant to make this type of strong promise. That doesn't mean that those people are of bad character. Rather, it means that it's not easy to promise the unknown. Committing to a stable API is a lot like promising something unknown. The promise entails that whatever happens in the future, whatever new requirements you receive, whatever bug you'll need to fix, you'll always continue to support all the real and imaginary clients of the previous versions of your API. Clearly this is a strong promise. No wonder people are scared of making it.

After trying to convince a few developers to subscribe to compatible development, I've found that the best way to overcome the fear of the unknown is to make the unknown known. I've talked with developers about possible scenarios in relation to their library's future to make the unknown known to them. Then their fear has disappeared. Of course, you cannot know precisely what will happen in the future. However, you can predict it within certain boundaries, drawing limits as to what might happen. These limits usually represent the most extreme situations. If you know how to handle the extreme cases, you can be sure that you know how to deal with anything else too.

Let's imagine you've just decided to publish your API and declare it stable. What is the worst thing that can happen to you now? There are several things, of course, but a few stand out. Let's start with "lack of time." Priorities change. There are never enough engineers. Those who are available need to fix the most urgent problems. Once it might have seemed that your API was important for a particular release. Later, preferences changed and your API is not so important anymore. Possibly, you've created an API that you consider to be quite good, though it's more or less a byproduct of the work you had to do anyway. Publishing it was hard, but now it's out the door. You feel you might not have time to work on it in the near future. That scares you. Well, it shouldn't! The most stable API is the API that nobody touches. As the amoeba model shows, the most important problems in the use of an API are the changes in its shape and behavior from release to release. If nobody has time to touch the code of your API, if nobody can add new features or fix bugs, then the chance of the amoeba's shape changing is extremely limited. That is why there is nothing to fear in this case. Simply declare your API stable. If you don't touch it ever again, it will be stable in every sense of the word.

So, we've overcome our first fear. What else can go wrong with an API that we've just declared to be stable? You might find that something is not quite correct; that you need to enhance or change the functionality of your library in some limited way. Indeed, the details of this situation depend on the actual shape of your API. However, if you've followed at least some of the suggestions from this book, you should be in pretty good shape to make this change in a binary-compatible way. And if you have at least decent test coverage, you should be in a pretty good position to maintain functional compatibility.

However, what if you find that large parts of your API are wrong, requiring a complete rewrite? In such cases, you probably want to leave the old API alone. Instead, you would create a new one completely from scratch. You would need to do so in the right way, a way that allows the coexistence of the old and the new API, as is discussed in the section "Bridges and the Coexistence of Similar APIs" in Chapter 15. If you manage to let the APIs successfully coexist, you are in pretty good shape. Clients of the old API are fine, as you didn't touch their API at all or only minimally. Simultaneously, you can feel good about yourself, because you've created a shiny new version of your API from scratch. Possibly you have learned from your previous mistakes, without having broken any of the promises you made in previous versions.

MONEY OR TRUST?

Among the NetBeans API stability classification categories, one is special: the "official" category. This category includes all the APIs in the `org.netbeans.api` package. This category imposes certain rules relating to how to classify the libraries publishing these APIs. For one release, the libraries might be under development, but after the next release they should become stable. The hope is that this helps to solve the chicken and egg problem between the API not being ready, yet needing its users and their comments to become ready. This works in many cases, such as when NetBeans developed the new Project APIs. However, in most of these cases, it turned out that there was no need for incompatible changes at all. In these cases, the API could have been classified as stable to begin with.

However, in the case of other projects, this "future promise" didn't work at all, maybe because it was no longer socially necessary to keep our promises. I've been told that this is all the fault of mobile phones! In the Middle Ages, when two knights agreed to rendezvous in Paris after spending ten years on battlefields, they had no choice other than to be at the designated place at the designated time. Otherwise, there would be no chance that they would ever see each other again. Nowadays, when you want to meet with someone, you simply negotiate the approximate date and an hour of the meeting and phone the other to confirm validity and settle details. Mobile phones are the root cause of modern people being able to break their original promises!

In this context, it doesn't make sense to demand that modern people promise they will develop compatibly in the future. And, like Tracy Chapman's song "If Not Now . . ." says, a promise declared "for days to come is as good as none." If you are thinking about developing an API in stable way, which you should, commit to it now, during the first release. There is no reason to wait. Otherwise, you are at risk of not keeping your promises. What drives me mad is that some people are even proud of doing that! In one useless conversation, while trying to convince people to stick to their previous promise, I heard the claim that, "If there is a rule that says I should waste my money on something, then I am personally quite willing to ignore it and even congratulate myself for doing so." I have the feeling that nothing illustrates the current state of our society better than this quote. People are not willing to keep a promise if it's even slightly inconvenient.

However, there are still certain areas where promise and trust are more important than profit. I have a few friends working for various banks as stock dealers, where they all work with promises. If they want to make a deal, they call another dealer, negotiate the price over the phone, and as soon as they say "Done," the deal is made. Of course, no money is transferred yet. That is the work of the back office and is delayed by a few days. During that time, the deal might fall through and the bank might be tempted to cancel it. However, I have not heard about this ever happening. Even if the bank stands to lose money on the particular transaction, there is always a much higher cost: loss of trust. Because all the operations among the dealers are based on mutual trust, if you break your promise once, rumors spread and nobody is going to do business with you anymore. No bank wants to risk that.

Although I might be wrong, I see API design as another place where trust is more important than cost savings. The contract between the designer of an API and the API's users is built on mutual trust. Breaking that trust is the last thing you want to do, as that can only help you lose your biggest asset: the users of your API. That is why it's more efficient to spend a few bucks more to implement a compatible extension to your API, than to seek the most cost-effective solution at the expense of good relations with your users.

Still, in light of the erosion of promises in our modern society due to mobile phones, it's safer to eliminate "future" promises, replacing them with real and immediate actions. That is why I am trying to remove the exception for the temporary status of the NetBeans official APIs that allows them to stay unstable for one release. Those who care can produce good APIs without that exception anyway. If people want to make promises, they should do so immediately. Promising something for the future doesn't work.

The actual realization of these high-level suggestions might differ between different APIs. However, the general direction is clear: if you eliminate the unknown, you can be sure you are not doing anything wrong by declaring your API stable. Typically, it helps to have an *evolution plan* to know how you'll change your API if some specific, yet unknown, request is made. It takes some practice to envision what kind of requests might arrive in the future, but it's not impossible. If you are providing an API for clients, you might expect that they will request more methods to call, query, and configure your API. If you have an API for providers, expect that you'll find out that the interface they've used is insufficient and that you'll need to provide alternate ways for them to plug in their functionality. If your API can handle these requirements, then you have an evolution plan! With an evolution plan, it's a piece of cake to develop your API compatibly.

In summary, declaring an API stable is first and foremost a test of your moral skills. It's principally concerned with the will to develop an API in a backward-compatible way. First, you need to believe that having an API is good and that it's beneficial to preserve the investments made by its users. This has already been discussed elsewhere in this book. However, once you understand this point, finding the will to commit to a stable API should be a piece of cake as well.

Minimizing Maintenance Cost

A common concern is that creating and especially maintaining an API is costly. True: creating an API is definitely more work than not publishing anything at all for others to consume. However, sometimes there simply is no way around it. Our applications are built from components and these need to talk to one another. When there is that need, it's better to create the API properly, instead of sneaking around the problem by means of undocumented hacks. Although the initial design might take more time and work, the time and effort spent on it will be repaid in spades in the future.

I believe that maintenance of a published API can be reduced to close to zero. Let's analyze the possible situations. First of all, let's imagine that nobody is using your API. This is indeed not a desirable position. However, it has one significant advantage in that nobody will be reporting bugs. How could they? If your library is not in use, it cannot be exposed, even indirectly. Nobody can then actually know whether it's buggy or not. And if it's buggy, nobody cares. That means that the time needed for bug fixing is zero.

Now let's pretend that someone is using your library. As author of the library, you are immediately in a much better position. You know you are doing something good and you know that there are users who need you. Here there are two possibilities. Either your users are satisfied and don't complain, so that there is no maintenance cost, or they complain. The complaints might be a sign of interest and might be welcomed by the maintainers of the library. At that point there is some maintenance cost. However, the cost is voluntary, as the owners of the library are glad to be able to help.

Let's now imagine that the complaints are unwanted, or at least that the maintainers of the library don't have the time to address them. Again, there can be two cases. Either the users require support for the new, missing features, or they require a bug fix. Let's look at the bug-fix issue first. If the library has already been released to the public, then in light of the amoeba model introduced in the section "Functional Compatibility—the Amoeba Effect" in Chapter 4, you can argue that the existing behavior is not a bug, but a feature. This depends on the nature of the problem. If an unexpected `NullPointerException` is thrown from a piece of code, it's unlikely that this will ever be considered a feature. On the other hand, the fact that you use a slow algorithm can be considered an API feature, as shown in the section "Delegation and Composition" in Chapter 10, where we successfully piggybacked on this flaw to compute a factorial. This all boils down to how seriously you take compatibility. If compatibility is important, and this whole book explains why it should be, then it's necessary to minimize the changes in the application's amoeba shape. From this point of view, after a release every bug can in fact be treated as a feature request for a new API, because simply fixing a bug affects the previous behavior and someone can already be depending on it. With that said, let's leave the topic of maintaining bugs in an API for later and let's concentrate on complaints that revolve around requests for new features in an API.

Users are famous for requesting new features. APIs are no exception. However, most of the users are also famous for only complaining, not for doing anything helpful in response. Here API users are no exception either. On the other hand, open source really helps here, especially if you "live in a fishbowl." If it's well known and publicly documented how to integrate a change to the project's source base and your library is developed as open source, your reaction to an API user's complaint can be, "Okay, fix that yourself." Now the API user needs to take action. Complaints are no longer enough in this context. The user can either spend some time implementing the new features in the API or hack around it in his own code. Note that so far the maintainers of the library don't really do anything. At most they point a curious user to the guidelines that need to be followed before a patch to the source base is accepted.

Let's imagine that the API user has invested some time, has decided to create a patch, and has submitted it for integration. Now comes the time for review. Yes, someone needs to go through the submission and check if it's of good quality or not. However, based on my own experience, this is a pleasant task because you are reviewing work done by someone else that can improve your own creation. Of course, it's necessary to reject poor-quality patches as quickly as possible. Here I've learned a few simple tricks. The necessary precondition to measure if an API change is good or bad is whether there is a sufficient high-level description of what the API should do, as discussed in the section "The Importance of Being Use Case Oriented" in Chapter 4. Bad attempts to propose an API change usually miss this aspect, and it's easy to reject them simply by requesting a high-level use case to be added. The other concern you might have relates to the removal of buggy contributions. Nobody wants to accept code and then spend weeks fixing its bugs. Code reviews are good, but require a lot of time to understand the proposed changes. It's much easier to measure code coverage with an automated test. You don't need to count every line or branch, but you have sufficient grounds for rejecting the contribution if there is no test. If there is a test, the likelihood that the API change does something useful can be guaranteed at least on some basic level. You can always request more tests, which can only increase your confidence in the API change, as well as proving that the contributor is dedicated to making it. That is good, as dedicated contributors are more likely to fix bugs if they appear later. Even if they refuse to help with fixing bugs in their own donated code, you can use the trick described earlier—that is, for the sake of compatibility, treat a bug as a feature.

As can be seen, it's possible to integrate feature requests into an API with minimal effort. The only assumption is that the project is ready for doing reviews. There should be a mailing list and bug-tracking system. People should not let submissions fall under the table, and the project should have a clear description of how to write documentation. The project should use automated testing and can ask each contributor to use that as well. As far as I can tell, these assumptions are true for many projects. Certainly NetBeans and Apache's Ant use this approach when judging external contributions.

After the preceding environment is set up, we are left with only one problematic case: what if there are bugs in the API that cannot be turned into feature requests? Well, those bugs probably require maintenance on your part. However, you can still minimize their impact. The first effective approach is to ask the bug reporter for an automated test and add that it should be a minimal test case, not involving any other unrelated APIs. This is not always possible, but often is. When it's possible, it's helpful, as it eliminates the complainers and leaves you with the people who really use your API and are interested in contributing to it. If developers are able to write unit tests, they are skilled enough to locate the source code of your library, to understand how to build it, and to know how to run its tests. Moreover, they are willing to invest their own time to do so. It's usually a joy to work with those people and get bug reports from them. It's almost as easy to fix the problems they raise as it is to implement new features. That significantly lowers the cost of maintenance as well.

Are we left with any other cases that might increase maintenance cost? Yes, sometimes writing an isolated automated test is not possible. For example, you might have a paying customer who just wants you to fix the problem yourself. Or it might happen that there are no unit tests for the API to begin with. Then it would be difficult for an outsider to start writing them. Or the API behaves nondeterministically and problems are intermittent and hard to track down. All this is possible; however, all these situations could happen with any code you write. If your boss tells you to write something, you do it. If you don't write tests, well, then you can increase neither your cluelessness nor your reliability. If you have nondeterministic code, it's hard to track bugs down. This all applies to regular code; it's in no way special when writing libraries with APIs. If you write bad code, you'll have maintenance problems.

This is all that I wanted to prove. Maintaining a properly created API is not higher than maintaining regular code. In fact, it can be easier because with APIs you can rely on proper bug reports with automated tests, while users of your regular code are unlikely to be able to provide anything like that. The only condition is that you must start API development in the right way: prepare for evolution, suppress the amoeba effect with good testability, and use case-driven documentation. This needs to happen before the first version. Otherwise, especially if the API is not ready for evolution, it might be too late to do it then. That is probably the biggest motivation for reviewing or for asking for a review of the API as soon as possible. If an API is well-reviewed and well-designed, the maintenance from that point onward is a piece of cake.

CHAPTER 15

■ ■ ■

Evolving the API Universe

The previous chapter tried to prove that maintaining a library with an API is not more costly than maintaining code without an API. However, that doesn't mean that you'll simplify your life by adding an API to your code—not at all. All that has been proved is that if you are able to write code of a certain level of quality, you won't complicate your maintainer's life by adding an API to it, especially if you follow the evolution guidelines outlined in this book.

Still, from time to time, we aren't able to produce good-quality code. If that happens, the code won't improve by decorating it with an API. It will remain of poor quality. Moreover, as APIs are like stars, it will be poor-quality code that will shine for everyone and that everyone will see.

Bad code happens, as do bad APIs, for various reasons. Maybe we didn't reach sufficient reliability because we failed to concentrate our selective cluelessness on writing enough tests to cover the runtime aspects of our API. Maybe the original requirements no longer apply. Maybe the original project was ill-defined and doesn't make sense anymore. Whatever the reason, the outcome is clear: we have an API that we no longer like. We want to get rid of it, but properly, while preserving investments made by its users so far. The question is how to do it.

Many developers with experience building in-house software projects know that, while not always convenient, it's possible to close down a whole software code base. You can then completely remorph it and reopen shop a few days or weeks later. While the shop is closed and empty, you can apply many tricks to it, even some that are dangerous. It's even acceptable to remove all the elevators and tell everybody to use the stairs. It takes time to update all the floors, but if you know how many are available, you can estimate the time needed and fix them all before the "grand reopening."

Many people believe that scale doesn't matter: that if something works for an in-house system, it will also work for a skyscraper. However, they are wrong. APIs are like stars: once published, they are ready to be observed forever. The "stop the world methodology" doesn't work. You might be entitled to close shop for a while, but nobody has the power to stop the universe as a whole. That is why removing a whole API, together with all its usages, is not an option. An API, just like a star, cannot suddenly disappear. It can change its trajectory or it can turn into a supernova and explode. However, these things cannot happen all of a sudden. These events need to evolve over time by following the rules of good API design.

MASTERS OF THE UNIVERSE

You are unlikely to win your customers' hearts by punishing them. With the "stop the world," "big bang" rewrite, you are penalizing users of your API for using it. If the API simply disappears, nothing will work anymore and everything will need to be rewritten. Maybe the rewrite will be good for your users. Maybe it will help them to get rid of old code full of ugly hacks. Maybe you'll be able to replace their old code with a newer and shinier version. However, your users have a right to ask, "Why now? Can't that rewrite wait a bit?" They also have the right to complain that they have other and more important things to do. Remember that API users are famous for always having something better to do!

You can either listen to your users' wishes and defer big-bang changes or give them a long answer such as, "No, you shouldn't want us to wait. It's essential to the success of our whole project that we remove the old API and switch to a new version. Though you might have a conflicting opinion on this point, we believe, from a broader perspective, that it's important that you stop doing whatever you're doing and rewrite all your code right now!" Or you can offer its shorter version: "I don't care about you. Do as you're told!" Needless to say, an arrogant attitude is not going to win their hearts. Rather, the opposite is true. Your users will start to look for alternatives to your API.

You can argue that they have a good chance to clean up their code. However, as discussed in the sidebar "The Entropy of Software" in Chapter 4, you cannot expect the code to become automatically nicer just because of a rewrite. Maybe it will be initially, but not after a few years of additional maintenance. That can only happen if the developers also change their coding practices significantly. That is unlikely to happen when they are forced to do a massive rewrite under pressure.

I know a lot of people who tend to think that this is the best and most effective way. I've seen it applied a few times in the case of some NetBeans APIs, usually under the assumption that these APIs are not used by anyone except in internal NetBeans IDE projects; that is, that it's in effect an in-house project. However, as the NetBeans house is enormously large, the big bang has always taken longer than originally estimated, making the cost higher than expected. Moreover, this estimate has never included the cost of rewriting code produced by our partners, and except for one case that opened up new possibilities for NetBeans, I am afraid that the entropy of the software has always gotten us back to where we were before: with code full of hacks, or so-called release-only compromises.

That is why I am skeptical about this big bang strategy and tend to think of the stop-the-world evolution style for software projects as a negative thing. I see it not as something attributable to masters of the universe, but only to poor gatekeepers who don't know any better.

When a library and its API are in terrible shape, you have two options, just as with any other code: try to fix it, or give up and replace it with another version written from scratch. However, the second option is not followed by removing the old library. It might be deprecated, it might print warnings when used, but it needs to stay there, and just like a star, slowly burn out.

Resuscitating Broken Libraries

Of the two approaches to fixing a broken library, let's first look at repairing it. Repairing a library is a tough task. I've seen and maintained quite a few libraries that were not properly designed. They suffered from having interfaces that could not be evolved easily. They also didn't have much documentation and experienced nondeterminism during multithreaded access and use. I must admit that some of these libraries were my own creations. I created them when I was younger, without having the first clue about cluelessness.

The only way to fix the mess was to write tests. Here I applied total cluelessness: I didn't know what a particular library did, but whenever I touched it, I first wrote a test to prove that something was broken. Then I fixed the library's behavior. This is not a science, and it was a lot of boring work. But, at the end of the day, I had introduced many small evolutionary improvements. We ended up with libraries that were improved in terms of reliability, compared to the problematic original, while still providing backward compatibility. At least, each library maintained backward compatibility with the original vision and the spirit of the library. It didn't maintain backward compatibility with the original behavior because that was messy and more or less undefined. Indeed, I would have preferred to report that I applied my intelligence and fixed those libraries. However, that would be a lie. The only thing that helped me whip those libraries into shape was a strong will, hard work, and careful writing of guards to verify each change.

FIGHT FOR YOUR API

Every API can be fixed to a point where it's reliable. The question is how much effort needs to be spent on this task and whether the time spent pays off in the long run. The next problem is whether you can find and motivate someone to actually do the fixing. Developers are generally not enthusiastic about tasks that they perceive as being little more than fixing someone else's mistakes. It's difficult to ask maintainers of legacy code to do a better job than the original author of the API. However, if you are an author of an API accused of being unusable and unreliable, you have good reason to want to improve it yourself. Fight for your API! If you have the will, it can definitely be fixed.

I was in such a situation once. We had a NetBeans API that was wild, too rich, and suffering from random bugs and nondeterminism. Luckily for me, it was located in a central place and could not be removed easily, although many tried. That is why I was given the opportunity to try to fix it. With as much cluelessness as possible, while writing tests for even the simplest change in its behavior, I managed to make the API reliable. But it took two or three years to get rid of all the random bugs. Now, though, it no longer contains any wrong behavior at all. At least, no important bugs have been reported against it.

If you fight for it, you can fix any API, while keeping it backward compatible. However, that only means you can fix the "engineering aspects" of it. You can make it bug free; you can make it reliable; you can make it well documented; you can even relatively easily make it useful. However, you cannot make it "beautiful." Of course, beauty is not supposed to mean anything to engineers. Despite that, sometimes it does. The need for it is probably innate and our admiration of beauty is embedded deep within us. Although it's not measurable, we continually strive to attain it. By fixing an old API in a compatible way, we can only get more deprecations, but not more beauty.

That is why, when we know the infrastructure is reliable enough, it makes sense to start a new alternative API from scratch. We can then bridge its functionality with the old API. The new API can bring beauty back into the game, while retaining compatibility for all the existing users of the old API.

One of the most useful types of "guards" is a test that helps to verify compatibility against previous versions of an implementation. This is handy when you want to keep an API for a class while completely replacing the previous implementation with something less buggy. Imagine that there are maintenance problems with one class and you are looking for a more reliable implementation. Of course, in the spirit of this book, you know that incremental improvements might be slower but can cause much less concern among the users of the API. Therefore, in the terms of the amoeba model, the goal is to change the observable behavior of the API as little as possible. The old behavior is the specification. The goal is to mimic that behavior while completely changing the API's internals. You can see this as a minimalist version of a TCK. We want a set of tests to execute against the previous implementation and then again against the new one. If each test yields the same result on the old version and on the new version of the API, we've achieved our goal of reproducing the old behavior as closely as possible.

Our first step is to move the old implementation from the application code to the testing code. Instead of being deleted, the old unmaintainable class becomes the template for the expected behavior of the new code:

```
/** This is a copy of the implementation of Arithmetica from version 1.0 */
static class OldArithmetica1 {
    public int sumTwo(int one, int second) {
        return one + second;
    }

    public int sumAll(int... numbers) {
        if (numbers.length == 0) {
            return 0;
        }
        int sum = numbers[0];
        for (int i = 1; i < numbers.length; i++) {
            sum = sumTwo(sum, numbers[i]);
        }
        return sum;
    }

    public int sumRange(int from, int to) {
        int len = to - from;
        int[] array = new int[len + 1];
        for (int i = 0; i <= len; i++) {
            array[i] = from + i;
        }
        return sumAll(array);
    }
}
```

The testing code then contains a compare that executes a set of random operations on both the old and new implementations in parallel. If the test passes in both setups, the functionality of the old implementation has been preserved well enough to match the behavior in the new implementation:

```
private void compare (Arithmetica now, OldArithmetica1 old, long seed)
throws Exception {
    java.util.Random r = new java.util.Random (seed);
```

```java
for (int loop = 0; loop < r.nextInt(5); loop++) {
    int operation = r.nextInt(3);
    switch (operation) {
        case 0: { // sumTwo
            int a1 = r.nextInt(100);
            int a2 = r.nextInt(100);
            int resNow = now.sumTwo(a1, a2);
            int resOld = old.sumTwo(a1, a2);
            assertEquals("sumTwo results are equal", resNow, resOld);
            break;
        }
        case 1: { // sumArray
            int[] arr = new int[r.nextInt(100)];
            for (int i = 0; i < arr.length; i++) {
                arr[i] = r.nextInt(100);
            }
            int resNow = now.sumAll(arr);
            int resOld = old.sumAll(arr);
            assertEquals("sumArray results are equal", resNow, resOld);
            break;
        }
        case 2: { // sumRange
            int a1 = r.nextInt(100);
            int a2 = r.nextInt(100);
            int resNow = now.sumRange(a1, a1 + a2);
            int resOld = old.sumRange(a1, a1 + a2);
            assertEquals("sumRange results are equal", resNow, resOld);
            break;
        }
    }
}
```

It's appropriate to use randomized tests here, because they can simply generate a random sequence of calls, while applying them to both the implementations at once. In the process, you are verifying that they both produce the same results. You can use not only randomized tests, but also any other type of tests, and they'll still verify that the new behavior appropriately reproduces the old one. On the other hand, the randomized tests have a nice feature with respect to the amoeba model. As described in the section "Functional Compatibility—the Amoeba Effect" in Chapter 4, the actual behavior of an application is always different from the specification or our expectations. In general, testing is useful to automatically verify that the functionality requested by the specification is implemented. This is easy: if the specification says something will work, then write a test, run it, and if it fails, fix the implementation. If the specification requires that for some values a function should yield an exception, then write a test, verify that an exception is really thrown, and if not, fix the implementation.

On the other hand, our application can also do more than the specification says. This is dangerous as well, as this can create security holes or prevent future evolution of the library. That's because the future attempt to fix the library's behavior to match the specification is introducing an incompatible change against the previous—although unspecified—behavior. That is why finding out where the application does more than specified is important. However, this is not easy. The usual testing style won't help, as common tests can only verify expected behavior. This is exactly the place where randomized tests excel. To some extent, they are able to discover an unexpected behavior, as they are able to employ the randomness of its operations and create a sequence of steps no developer or quality engineer would write. These tests cannot cross their own shadow and invent a completely new way to use the API. The frame—the set of available operations—is given and the tests can only execute them in inventive sequences. Still, random exploration is useful as it can stretch the API to its limits.

THE TOTAL REWRITE OF THE COOKIESET

NetBeans used the approach described here during an attempt to rewrite CookieSet to a new and enhanced implementation. The old implementation was copied to a test called OldCookieSetFromFebruary2005. The test compared the behavior of the implementation of the class from February 2005 with the new code. It was able to confirm or deny that the new code behaved in the same way as the old code. This turned out to be a useful verification process, as it caused us to postpone the integration of the changes into CookieSet until full compatibility had been reached.

Having randomized tests might seem counterproductive. Any failure is a random failure, and it might be hard to track down. That's true, but this test is just pseudo-random. The compare method takes an initial seed and prints it in case of a failure. If necessary, you can reliably repeat every test run:

```java
public void testRandomCheck () throws Exception {
    long seed = System.currentTimeMillis();
    try {
        CountingSubclass now = new CountingSubclass();
        CountingOldSubclass old = new CountingOldSubclass();

        compare(now, old, seed);

        assertEquals(
            "Verify amount calls to of sumRange is the same",
            now.countSumRange, old.countSumRange
        );
        assertEquals(
            "Verify amount calls to of sumAll is the same",
            now.countSumAll, old.countSumAll
```

```
        );
        assertEquals(
            "Verify amount calls to of sumTwo is the same",
            now.countSumTwo, old.countSumTwo
        );
    } catch (AssertionFailedError ex) {
        IllegalStateException n = new IllegalStateException (
            "Seed: " + seed + "\n" + ex.getMessage ()
        );
        n.initCause(ex);
        throw n;
    } catch (Exception ex) {
        IllegalStateException n = new IllegalStateException (
            "Seed: " + seed + "\n" + ex.getMessage ()
        );
        n.initCause(ex);
        throw n;
    }
}
```

The previous test executes a random sequence of operations depending on the time seed. Every day it tests different behavior. If it fails, it will print the initial seed. As such, if you want to reproduce one of these test runs, it's enough to copy the seed and run the same sequence of operations again for eternity. Following is a test that used to work on April 13, 2008:

```
public void testSimulateOKRunOn1208120436947() throws Exception {
    CountingSubclass now = new CountingSubclass();
    CountingOldSubclass old = new CountingOldSubclass();

    compare(now, old, 1208120436947L);

    assertEquals(
        "Verify amount of calls to sumRange is the same",
        now.countSumRange, old.countSumRange
    );
    assertEquals(
        "Verify amount of calls to sumAll is the same",
        now.countSumAll, old.countSumAll
    );
    assertEquals(
        "Verify amount of calls to sumTwo is the same",
        now.countSumTwo, old.countSumTwo
    );
}
```

With an infrastructure like this it's easy to create as many nonrandomized tests as necessary. Just remember the seed and rerun the test as in the following case, which used to fail on the same day, just a few minutes later:

```
public void testSimulateFailureOn1208120628821() throws Exception {
    CountingSubclass now = new CountingSubclass();
    CountingOldSubclass old = new CountingOldSubclass();

    compare(now, old, 1208120628821L);

    assertEquals(
        "Verify amount of calls to sumRange is the same",
        now.countSumRange, old.countSumRange
    );
    assertEquals(
        "Verify amount of calls to sumAll is the same",
        now.countSumAll, old.countSumAll
    );
    assertEquals(
        "Verify amount of calls to sumTwo is the same",
        now.countSumTwo, old.countSumTwo
    );
}
```

This is a sustainable solution because it allows you to keep the old behavior for a long time. Whenever a new bug report or a new feature is to be added, you add a new test and verify that the code behaves in the same way as the older version of the API. With this kind of infrastructure, you can then become increasingly clueless because you don't need to spend a lot of time trying to understand, read, and improve the old implementation.

The previous approach is good for fixing the internals of an API, but it leaves the API itself untouched. How can you revamp the API itself, while not compromising the functionality it offers its existing users? You need to deprecate the old API somehow and introduce the new version. Moreover, the two APIs must be able to coexist and work together. Due to the distributed nature of development and the distributed nature of the acceptance of the new features in your library, not every team or API user is likely to switch simultaneously to the new version. Some have better things to do and might decide to stick with the old API for some time. Coexistence of different API versions is a necessary prerequisite for a correctly evolving API.

Conscious vs. Unconscious Upgrades

As you've seen in the previous sections, keeping backward runtime compatibility can sometimes be difficult. Even small changes in library behavior can cause radical shifts in the "amoeba shape" of the whole system. As argued earlier, such shifts can cause big earthquakes and can even destroy the faith of your users in your API, as well as in your development skills.

On the other hand, fixes are important. If there is buggy behavior in your API, it simply needs to be fixed. Keeping old bugs in your code without showing any effort to fix them can push your users away just as easily as the earthquakes caused by your upgrades. Compatibility is one of the most important goals when designing shared libraries. Delivering proper fixes is important as well. The art of API design is the ability to balance between the conflicting demands of these two goals.

COMPATIBILITY IS A CONSTRAINT

When I joined Sun, I was told that Scott McNealy, our former CEO, used to argue that "compatibility is not a goal, it's a constraint." These words could be seen posted all over Sun and many colleagues used to recite them out loud. However, nobody acted that way, at least not in the departments I interacted with. Don't get me wrong: compatibility was always considered good, but never more than a nice addition or at most a goal. It was never seen as a constraint.

It took me a while to understand this inconsistency. Now I believe that Scott's words were addressed to people using and developing Sun OS and Solaris at the time when they had to fight other offerings from large vendors such as IBM, HP, and so on. To convince users that the shift to a new operating system is reasonable, you can only bring improved quality to bear. In that context, compatibility is a strong sign of quality, as that means that you value the prior investments made by your customers. In this situation, compatibility becomes a constraint.

Since that time, the portfolio of products has grown and includes other types of software, including Java, NetBeans, and so on. It's clear that the quality of an end-user application doesn't need to achieve the quality of the operating system. In the case of your mail client, you accept that it shows the wrong number of messages from time to time. Mistakes of this kind are acceptable in this context. Similar mistakes in operating system code can be disastrous.

Scott never said compatibility is no longer a constraint, and it remained a constraint with respect to Solaris. However, for newly created or acquired groups and their products, nobody treated those words as absolutes. That is acceptable. Compatibility is about users, and if product quality matches their expectations, everything is probably in good shape. However, you need to know the limits. As soon as users indicate a fear of upgrading to new versions, something is very wrong.

I've observed that people are more likely to accept the consequences of incompatibilities if they consciously decide to incorporate them and use them. They somehow feel that they are part of the decision-making process and that nothing has been decided without them. This sense of participation can smooth the irritation that they might otherwise feel.

In some cases, such as when a NullPointerException is thrown, it's reasonable to expect that nobody actually depends on the exception being thrown. Users will happily accept a new version that, instead of throwing an exception, computes a result. In situations like this it's desirable to shift the shape of the library's behavior and to change it. This is the place for an *unconscious upgrade*. Simply give people a new version with changed behavior and let them accept the change without being aware of it. Of course, you should tell them that there is a change in a behavior, just in case someone actually cares. However, if your original evaluation was correct and nobody relies on the behavior, your users simply don't need to know. They can accept the new version cluelessly, without even caring about the changes you've made.

BACKGROUND LOAD OF EDITOR CONTENT

For NetBeans IDE 6.1, I needed to improve the way we loaded text into an editor. Instead of blocking the event dispatch thread, I changed the code to prepare everything outside in the background before switching to the event queue and showing the editor.

Indeed this was an incompatible change, and I properly marked it as such. However, my expectation and hope was that this was a minimal change with a small negative impact, comparable to the fix of NullPointerException. However, I was wrong. Soon I got tons of reports about incompatibilities. The trouble was that the editor class is subclassable and people can sneak into its behavior creatively. The examples of code using the API I've seen have far exceeded the horizons of my creativity, and indeed my change was not ready for such stretching of the original API to its limits.

At the end we managed to stabilize the code and keep the change in, as it looked like an important bug fix. However, if I could make the change again, I would provide the background loading as a new feature of the API and ask all clients to switch to it consciously.

Sometimes it's desirable to change faulty behavior even though that faulty behavior might be useful to someone. Possibly that means eliminating certain calls for performance reasons, asynchronously reporting events to listeners in another thread, changing the order of calls in a method, and so on. This might seem just as faulty as the previous case of throwing an exception. However, just because the code doesn't die miserably doesn't mean that you can be certain that some users might not find this behavior desirable. Someone might have written an application that depends on it. Obviously, if an upgrade changes it, the new version of the whole system will start to misbehave. Who is to blame? All that changed was the version of your library. The assemblers simply upgraded your library to a new version and now suddenly everything is broken. The conclusion is simple: the blame lies squarely on your two shoulders. This is not fair, as the only thing you did was fix a few faulty parts of your library. However, such is the life of an API designer.

The way to eliminate these problems while still fixing faulty behavior is to provide the fixes conditionally. This can take many forms. However, basically this means that unless the API user changes the source code, the old behavior is retained. If API users want the new behavior, they need to edit their code slightly. For example, if the authors of the Arithmetica API want to keep compatibility for the factorial example from the section "Delegation and Composition" in Chapter 10, they can do so by providing a new constructor and making the new, fast behavior conditional:

```java
public class Arithmetica {
    private final int version;

    public Arithmetica() {
        this(1);
    }
    public Arithmetica(int version) {
        this.version = version;
    }

    public int sumTwo(int one, int second) {
```

```java
        return one + second;
    }

    public int sumAll(int... numbers) {
        if (numbers.length == 0) {
            return 0;
        }
        int sum = numbers[0];
        for (int i = 1; i < numbers.length; i++) {
            sum = sumTwo(sum, numbers[i]);
        }
        return sum;
    }

    public int sumRange(int from, int to) {
        switch (version) {
            case 1: return sumRange1(from, to);
            case 2: return sumRange2(from, to);
            default: throw new IllegalStateException();
        }
    }

    private int sumRange1(int from, int to) {
        int len = to - from;
        if (len < 0) {
            len = -len;
            from = to;
        }
        int[] array = new int[len + 1];
        for (int i = 0; i <= len; i++) {
            array[i] = from + i;
        }
        return sumAll(array);
    }

    private int sumRange2(int from, int to) {
        return (from + to) * (Math.abs(to - from) + 1) / 2;
    }
}
```

This clearly preserves the investment of those who write strange code, such as computing factorials out of this class. Simultaneously, this allows those who wish to use the updated version 2.0 to get that version's performance benefits in computing a range. By default, when upgrading to version 2.0, they would get identical behavior to version 1.0. The improvement is available, but slight changes to the code are required. This is the conscious action that makes the difference. When your users decide to do it, they'll no longer complain about incompatibilities because they know they changed their code. Engineers are used to the fact that things can break when they touch their code.

There are many approaches to increasing the consciousness level of an API user to an upgrade. I'm not going to discuss them now. Simply remember that there is a significant difference in perception when you cause unconscious compatibility breakages on your own versus inviting your users to perform conscious upgrades themselves.

Alternative Behavior

From some points of view, designing a library and maintaining it in a compatible way always revolves around two options. Either we can enhance the library with new functionality or we can provide alternative behavior to the functionality that already exists. There is no sharp border between these two alternatives. In fact, adding new behavior is similar to adding new functionality. Adding a new class or method can also be seen as an extension to the number of alternative behaviors. Clearly, the line between these options is not an exact science. The question of whether changing a library means adding new functionality or an alternative behavior is psychological. The answer is probably related to the amount of danger there is of breaking previously existing functionality. When adding new features, the likelihood of breaking something that already works should be minimal. When introducing alternative behavior, we recognize the fact that we already have existing functionality, which now risks being negatively impacted.

So much for the philosophical introduction. Let's now look at the technical aspects of introducing new behavior while trying to minimize the impact on existing behavior. The simplest approach is to provide a new API that is completely unrelated to the previous version. Just make sure that both of them can coexist. An example of this approach is `java.lang.Math` and `java.lang.StrictMath`. However, the creation of these two classes is not an example of compatible development. In the early versions of Java, behavior provided by `StrictMath` was originally provided via `Math`. The need for strict precision was slowing down Java applications on certain platforms. It was considered more important to speed up the computation for everyone, even though some might have faced incompatibilities due to losing absolute precision. That is why Java 1.3 moved all the strict behaviors into `StrictMath` and introduced `Math`, which doesn't guarantee standardized precision, but can use the speed of a native coprocessor unit. Regardless of these "birth pangs," nowadays the `StrictMath` and `Math` classes are a fine example of completely safe alternative behaviors without mutual interference.

Creating a bug fix in a safe and compatible way is almost always the biggest motivation for wanting to create alternative behaviors. You can do so while being motivated by performance improvements, such as in the case of `Math`, or by a need to alter existing behavior. These concerns combine the need for improvement with the need for stability. Their technical realization might vary in terms of the merits of performing the change, as well as in the scope by which you can turn individual alternatives on or off. One of the biggest scopes is defined by the executed application, which in the case of Java is determined by the running virtual machine. Introducing environment variables is a natural way of letting behavior be turned on conditionally. In Unix applications, environment variables can influence the current user directory, the active language, and many other aspects. For Java, you can influence an even richer set of features. In this case, instead of environment variables, you can use Java system properties:

```
if (Boolean.getBoolean("arithmetica.v2")) {
    return sumRange2(from, to);
```

```
  } else {
    return sumRange1(from, to);
  }
```

If a bug fix is guarded by a condition that depends on a global property value, you can effectively eliminate any incompatibilities with the previous version. The user can set the property, which means that the user is aware of it being set. In this scenario, the user has made a conscious decision to accept the risks associated with the new behavior. Those unaware of the property continue to exist with the previous behavior, which remains compatible. However, there is always a risk that a property name has been used before for different purposes. Proper naming of the property can bring the risk close to zero.

ABSOLUTE COMPATIBILITY OF NETBEANS PLATFORMS 5.0 AND 5.5

The NetBeans Platform is usually released as part of the NetBeans IDE. However, that doesn't mean it fully shares the same release cycle as the IDE. For example, the difference between versions 5.5 and 5.0 of the NetBeans IDE was significant. There were many new features, including enhanced support for enterprise functionality. Despite that, it was claimed at the beginning of the release that no other part of the system would be impacted, aside from perhaps a few bug fixes. In this context, I felt it was the right time to try "absolutely compatible development." I convinced the NetBeans Platform team to sign up for doing all the bug fixes in an absolutely compatible way.

The situation looked favorable. Development was done in "high resistance" mode, which means that each commit was reviewed before integration. Things also looked favorable because the number of requested bug fixes was not high. We were able to evaluate each change with respect to compatibility. If it seemed compatibility would be compromised, we put safeguards in place to guarantee backward compatibility would be maintained.

One of our most frequently used guards was a trick with system properties. Each potentially dangerous bug fix was provided as an alternative behavior, enabled by the user through specifying a system property. The NetBeans IDE simply turned these properties on during startup. Users of the NetBeans Platform didn't need these properties and benefited from the default behavior, which was backward compatible. In this way, we released a completely new version of the NetBeans Platform, including new APIs and capabilities, while remaining completely backward compatible.

Clearly, while compatibility is important, bug fixes are important as well. Because of these two important requirements, we decided to make conditional alternative behaviors the default for subsequent releases of the NetBeans Platform. The NetBeans Platform 6.0 was a major release and we were not able to guarantee bug-to-bug compatibility all the time. By providing alternative behaviors first and then turning them on by default in the next major release, we successfully married the bug-to-bug compatibility with necessary quality improvements.

The system property solution might not be suitable for an acceptable coexistence between alternative behaviors. For example, if you need both behaviors at once, you need to start two JVMs. This might not be acceptable in a modular system, such as those based on the NetBeans Platform. There might be two modules in the same virtual machine, each requesting a different behavior.

In a modular system it can be more correct to let each module make its own individual choices. As shown in Figure 15-1, the idea is to let an API "guess" the user's intentions, calling the right implementation at the right time. To do this, rely on a module's versioned dependencies. For example, imagine that the API wants to support two alternative behaviors. The first has been present in the API until version 2.5, while the second was introduced in version 2.6. Versions 2.6 and later need to mimic the previous behavior for clients that might not be aware of the 2.6 changes. You can meet these requirements by inspecting module dependencies.

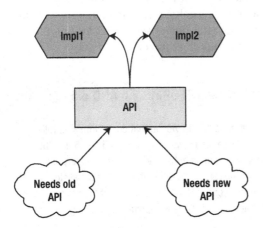

Figure 15-1. *Runtime implementation selection*

Users of version 2.5 or earlier create a module that has a dependency api >= 2.5, or api >= 2.4, api >= 1.7, and so on. The dependencies depend on when the user's module was created and compiled. In modular systems, such as the NetBeans Runtime Container (the engine behind all NetBeans-based applications), you can obtain and inspect a dependency at runtime because it's usually carried with the class loader that loads the individual classes:

```
StackTraceElement[] arr = Thread.currentThread().getStackTrace();
ClassLoader myLoader = Arithmetica.class.getClassLoader();
for (int i = 0; i < arr.length; i++) {
    ClassLoader caller = arr[i].getClass().getClassLoader();
    if (myLoader == caller) {
        continue;
    }
    if (RuntimeCheck.requiresAtLeast("2.6", "api.Arithmetica", caller)) {
        return true;
    }
    return false;
}
return true;
```

The calling class needs to have a dependency. If the dependency is lower than or equal to 2.5, the module will mimic the old functionality. As soon as the module defines a dependency on version 2.6 or later, it's clear that the module had to have been compiled against the newer version. Either there was a conscious decision to move to a newer version, or the module was written against the new version when it was initially created. In any case, there is no reason to try to simulate the old behavior present until version 2.5.

You can attain this kind of behavior by implementing a few class-loading tricks, especially when establishing the caller of the functionality and the requested version. Though this might sound a bit complicated, this is the common style used by the dynamic linker in the C world. You can specify two versions of an exported function and tell the linker to bind the right one, according to the version the shared library is requested to provide. In this way, you can fix the behavior of `printf` while preserving bug-to-bug compatibility. You can read more about that in "How to Write Shared Libraries."[1] Of course, there is a difference between using this style and Java introspection. While the linker does all the bindings once, and only at the time of linking the application, the Java version might have performance implications because it does the check during runtime invocation. However, you can still eliminate this unnecessary cost. The first option is to do some bytecode weaving, simulating the behavior of the C library loader, or play tricks with class-loaders as discussed in the section "The Importance of Module Dependencies" in Chapter 19. Or, for each runtime container, you can provide an infrastructure that optimizes the speed of queries by caching. The effectiveness of caches can vary. However, it's clear that you can easily and effectively optimize for the most desired state, which is the state when the system only has the modules that require the latest version of the alternative behavior. This situation can be decided globally at load time so that there is no need to check the caller at the time of method invocation. Actually, this is a nice example of finding the balance between the backward compatibility and the need to upgrade. If modules in the system are not upgraded yet, they get the environment that they expect. At the same time, the whole system might suffer from performance penalties. However, the lost performance is regained as soon as developers change the dependencies to the latest version and consciously accept the new behavior even without changing a line of their code, just module dependencies. This is a soft hint motivating people to upgrade, while not forcing them to do so. At least technically, if your project has a performance team, it's clear that upgrading will still be an urgent priority.

For the moment, let's leave the discussion of runtime selection of alternative behavior. Next we'll look at the range of choices you have when offering alternatives during compilation. The simplest approach has already been mentioned: simply copy the class and offer a new one. This approach works fine for `Math` and `StrictMath`, and should work well in other cases too. Just keep in mind that the case of "maths" is simple: there are two new classes that don't have anything in common. However, this is not always the case. Sometimes you need a common interface between the alternative behaviors, especially when you expect code will provide methods that work with all the alternatives. For example, the engineers working on JDK 5 realized that because `StringBuffer` is heavily synchronized, performance of string concatenations might not be optimal, even if it's known that the buffer won't be shared between multiple threads. This is common, because the Java compiler converts each string concatenation, such as `return "a" + "b" + "c" + "d"`, into code using the buffer:

```
return new StringBuffer().append("a").append("b").append("c").append("d").toString()
```

Removing the synchronization in the `StringBuffer` would not be a backward-compatible change. The designers decided to add a new class called `StringBuilder`. This class is almost an exact copy of the `StringBuffer` class, except that its methods are not synchronized. Up until this point, this is the same situation as with the "maths" example. However, as code might need to work with both the buffer classes, JDK 5 also introduced a common super interface,

---

1. Ulrich Drepper, "How to Write Shared Libraries (2006), http://people.redhat.com/drepper/dsohowto.pdf.

called Appendable. The interface abstracts the basic functionality of the two classes, together with a few others, such as the ability to append characters to existing text. In this setup, you can write code that uses either the synchronized version, the unsynchronized version, or both.

I am not sure if those who introduced the StringBuffer and StringBuilder classes considered this, but they could have introduced the alternative behavior without creating a new class. At the time of its construction, it might have been enough to specify whether the class was supposed to be thread safe or not. You would add a new StringBuffer(boolean threadSafe) constructor, store the value of the argument in an instance field, and in each method of the class decide whether it's supposed to be synchronized or not, depending on its value. In addition to keeping backward compatibility, it would allow the compiler to use the version without any synchronization.

At times, this constructor-based alternative might be a better solution than creating a whole new class, especially if the differences between the two behaviors are minimal. You only need to be aware of the potential danger of the increased number of constructors. If there are eight versions, each with different behaviors, you might find yourself with eight constructors, taking from one to eight booleans. In that situation it might be better to replace the boolean with a multivalue type, either int or enum. Then you might have code like the following:

```
public class Arithmetica {
    private final Version version;
    public enum Version { VERSION_1_0, VERSION_2_0 }

    public Arithmetica() {
        this(Version.VERSION_1_0);
    }
    public Arithmetica(Version version) {
        this.version = version;
    }

    public int sumRange(int from, int to) {
        switch (version) {
            case VERSION_1_0:
                return sumRange1(from, to);
            case VERSION_2_0:
                return sumRange2(from, to);
            default:
                throw new IllegalStateException();
        }
    }
}
```

One reason why this might not have been used in the case of StringBuffer is that if used in a constructor, this approach requires an additional field to be stored inside the class to keep the choice from the alternative behaviors. This might increase the memory requirements of one instance, which in some situations might not be desirable. The solution to this problem is the use of factory methods. Instead of adding a new constructor, there could be a new factory method. The factory method doesn't need to create the actual type it returns, but a subtype instead. So, in this case you would have the following:

```
public static StringBuffer createUnsynchronized() {
    return new StringBufferUnsynch();
}
```

This eliminates the need for internal field switching between the alternatives, as the switch is done inside the factory method by creating the correct subtype. Also, it lets you keep the code in the StringBuffer simple and free of any switches, because methods that are overridden by the package private subclass StringBufferUnsynch achieve all the required behavior adjustments. This is a good solution that shows the power of factory methods, except that it would not work too well for StringBuffer because it requires the class to be subclassable and StringBuffer is final. However, in other situations this approach can work well.

Alternative behavior is also often needed when you are using service provider APIs. For example, you need alternative behaviors for interfaces that people implement or extend and then pass around to some kind of infrastructure for processing. As has been discussed in the section "Adding a Method or a Field" in Chapter 6, adding a method to an existing interface is not compatible behavior. Adding a method to an abstract class is more or less acceptable, though usually not 100 percent binary compatible. That is why the best way to accommodate the new requirements that appear with the new version is either to add new factory methods, if they consume the provider interfaces before passing them to the infrastructure, or to add new interfaces such as LayoutManager2. This is a possible solution; however, if you really want to be sure that things remain compatible, remember that it is better to request new interfaces instead of existing ones. For example, sometimes people might be tempted to modify the contract to say, "By the way, if your interface also implements Runnable, its run method will be invoked at some point." It's not secure to modify the contract this way after introducing the API in a version, especially not in the case of Runnable. That interface can be used for many other purposes. Your service provider might already implement this interface for some other reason, and your modification of the contract will be a surprise because of the totally unexpected call to its run method.

Bridges and the Coexistence of Similar APIs

Sometimes it can be hard to allow two APIs to coexist. However, before arriving at that conclusion, let's start with the basics. For one type of library, coexistence is easy. If you have a "simple library" as introduced in the section "Types of Modular Design" in Chapter 7, it's easy to start a second library that does the same things, but with a different, hopefully better, API. The reason for that is that a simple library is just a collection of methods that can be called, such as those in java.lang.Math. These methods are well-encapsulated and do their job, but they never call any other code provided by the user of the API. It's easy to duplicate the class and introduce java.lang.StrictMath, which provides the same functionality but in a better way. These two classes can coexist without a problem, as the only way they interact with each other is that they consume and produce the same data (numbers in this case). Both are capable of performing operations on the same range of values. In other words, they consume each other's output, though from time to time they produce slightly different results when performing the same operation. There is no need to resolve compatibility issues in this case. You can simply leave the old API untouched and provide a new API without even thinking about the old one.

You can see this principle in action in Figure 15-2. In general, each user approaches an API with an idea of what he wants to do. Then he needs to figure out how to realize that use case with the API. He then calls the API, with an internal implementation handling the calls. In this case, when two simple libraries are performing the same task, with each providing its own API and implementation, the decisive moment arises on the user's side before anything is coded. The user needs to decide which API to use. After the decision is made, the APIs no longer influence or disturb each other. Each has its own way of handling the use case request.

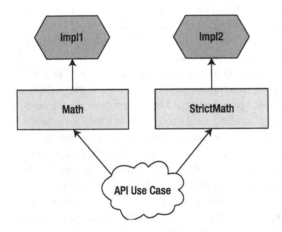

Figure 15-2. *Alternative yet completely independent APIs*

ENUM PACKAGE OR KEYWORD?

One of the oldest APIs written for NetBeans was a set of classes that provided support for high-level and lazy manipulation with enumerations. We wrote it in the late summer of 1997 and we packaged it into the `org.openide.util.enum` package, providing classes such as `SingletonEnumeration`, `ArrayEnumeration`, `SequenceEnumeration`, and `FilterEnumeration`.

There was no reason for us to replace the API until JDK 5 introduced a new keyword into the Java language: `enum`. The name of our package stopped being valid when source code was compiled against `-source 1.5`. We had to create a replacement, deprecating the old classes. As there was ample time between creation of the two APIs, I was able to apply many good API design practices to it, avoiding the various beginner mistakes of the early NetBeans days. As a result, we created one `Enumerations` factory class with methods such as `singleton`, `array`, `sequence`, and `filter`. The implementations could continue to exist, but only as private classes hidden by the consistent and compact API consisting of a few factory methods in a single class.

I used the "test for compatibility" trick to ensure that the behavior of our adequate old API class was the same as the new API. I created a set of tests that teased these enumerations in various ways, which I ran in two configurations. The first configuration was for the old API, the second for the new version. As soon as they started to pass, I could be sure that concepts in the old API had appropriate and compatible counterparts in the new factory methods.

I deprecated the old enumeration classes and advised people to migrate. However, I allowed the old classes to continue existing for those who were not able to follow the latest developments of our APIs and for those who didn't want to migrate. However, as it's always good to motivate your users to migrate to the latest version of your APIs, I added a small bonus for those who decided to switch to the new version: the new version used generics to improve the static type checking when using enumerations. The old version was left without them. Users were expected to appreciate the nicer alternative and upgrade their code accordingly.

It's always good to motivate migration by means of some kind of bonus. For example, offer functionality in the new API that cannot be achieved in the old version. Or refuse to fix bugs in the old version or cripple its implementation to be unacceptably slow. However, these cheap tricks were not necessary in the case of our enumeration APIs because JDK 5 provided sufficient motivation: anyone who wanted to use Java 5 language constructs needed to switch to `-source 1.5`. Then they immediately had to start treating enum as a keyword. They were then unable to refer to our old API classes and were forced to make the switch.

A more complicated situation occurs when the old version and the new version of a library fight for shared resources. "Shared resources" can mean almost anything. For example, it's hard to deprecate AWT and replace it with another graphical toolkit while allowing part of the application to use the old version and another part to use the new one. This is possible, but not easy, because at the end of the day the toolkits fight for a single shared resource: the screen.

The situation is similar for modular libraries, meaning those that contain mostly APIs, but without an implementation, as many providers can potentially provide that. If you need to deprecate the library and provide a new version, there is another scarce resource: the providers. In this situation, it's not enough simply to create a new API. You must also somehow make it cooperate with the originally registered providers. Moreover, as the APIs for clients and the APIs for providers are related to each other, with the new version of the API you can also introduce a new version of the providers for registration purposes. In this scenario, it's desirable for old providers and new providers to coexist. Both need to be available to serve the requests of clients using the old as well as the new API.

MULTIPLE FAILED ATTEMPTS TO REWRITE THE NETBEANS WIZARDS API

The Wizards API in NetBeans is an example of an API that was initially designed to meet the requirements of a certain period, after which it was rewritten to meet new and updated requirements. Originally the wizard was simply a plain extension of dialog handling. It had some additional buttons, such as Next, Previous, and Finish. Later, we learned that we needed standard handling of graphics, validation, and a steps overview. At that point we needed to rewrite it to accommodate these new requirements. However, the result was not very good. The original API violated nearly every principle suggested in this book: things that were supposed to be final were not, setters were everywhere, and so on. Not surprisingly, the enhanced version was even messier. From an external point of view, it was missing a certain slickness and some its features were hard to use, even for someone knowing the internals. Now it's a huge set of poorly designed code. It's kept together just by a set of tests that verify some of its obscure runtime behavior characteristics and also by the fact that nobody wants to touch it for fear of destabilizing it.

There have been at least three attempts to create a replacement for this API. The replacement would use more modern design principles, more modern coding methodologies, better documentation, and so on. All these approaches would provide a nicer API. They would easily coexist with the old API in the basic scenario where the user of the API creates the whole wizard with all its content, displays it, and at the end takes some action. It's easy to support coexistence on this level, as the API user either uses the old API or the new one, but never both together.

However, all the attempts to create a replacement failed to solve another necessary level of cooperation needed by the NetBeans IDE: the central part of the IDE interface is built around templates and their instantiation into various types of files. We have templates for Java, C++, Ruby, HTML, XML, and so on. In addition, users can create their own templates too. A similar set of templates is available for project types. Whenever users need to create something new, they open the New wizard and select the appropriate template. The template then provides additional panels that are embedded into the already open wizard and that guide the user through the process of creating the actual object. Of all the wizards in the NetBeans IDE, this particular wizard is used roughly 90 percent of the time. However, this wizard presents a challenge in terms of cooperation. It's currently written with the use of the old Wizards API. It would not be complex to rewrite it to a new version. However, this wizard allows every module built by anyone around the globe to register their own templates into it. These registrations have, so far, all been written using the old API. Of course, it's possible to tell people to use the new API for this purpose. On the other hand, it's unlikely that all the existing templates would be rewritten to the new API at once. Simultaneous rewriting is highly unlikely in the world of distributed development. Actually, even for us, working on the NetBeans IDE and in effect having control over the in-house development of all our modules, this was so massive a task that we realized we would not be able to complete it within one release cycle. This immediately implied the need for bridges. Some of the templates would still be written using the old Wizards API, while some would be written using the new version. The dialog needed to understand both versions and it needed to provide them the necessary environment guaranteed by their API.

For some reason, this additional requirement sufficiently repelled everyone who attempted to do the rewrite. I am not sure why, because I know the bridge is possible. However, creating the bridge requires adequate knowledge of both APIs. It would also require changes to the old version to allow mutual cooperation. Moreover, it would mean that developers would not be building something new from scratch, which is usually what they like to do, but they would need to work with the old code as well. As a result, we are still using the old API. At least we managed to make the API use more acceptable by creating a tool to generate the initial skeleton for a wizard. Yes, we have a wizard to generate a wizard—a wizard wizard. That said, some of the rewrite attempts came close to workable solutions, though nobody had enough will to push the solutions to the end of the journey and make them ready for production.

When two APIs need to communicate because a resource needs to be shared between them, one of them needs to know about the other. Alternatively, someone else needs to know about both and coordinate their access to the shared resource. Obviously, if you have two APIs, one new and one old, your ultimate goal is to send the old version into a black hole and make it vanish. This means that the new API needs to be independent of the old API. Otherwise they would need to vanish together, which would defeat the purpose of creating a new API in the first place. However, it's acceptable if the old API depends on the new API, as shown in Figure 15-3. If it ceases to be used, the dependency doesn't prevent it from vanishing independently.

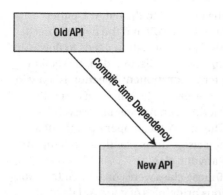

Figure 15-3. *Old API depends on new API*

The other option is to make both APIs unaware of each other and create a *bridge module*. As shown in Figure 15-4, a bridge module knows about both APIs and does exactly what its name suggests: it bridges calls from one API to the other, so that they can share and coordinate their access to their common resource.

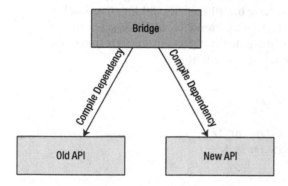

Figure 15-4. *Old and new APIs independent of each other*

"RECOMMENDS" IN NETBEANS

When you are working on a bridge module, you need to make sure that you include the bridge module wherever your code mentions your old API or your new API. In NetBeans, a possible way to do this is to make sure that the APIs "recommend" the bridge module. Recommendation is not a strong dependency, so nothing happens if the module cannot be enabled. However, the advice tells the module system that a module should be enabled if it's possible to turn it on.

Compile-time dependencies can never point from the new API to the old API, either directly or indirectly. At runtime, the situation is different. The old API and the new API need to be aware of each other to share their resources properly. The information needs to flow between them. The way to do this is to use component injection, as discussed in the section "Intercomponent Lookup and Communication" in Chapter 7. Component injection is done in NetBeans via the `Lookup` class, and in the JDK via the `ServiceLoader` class. In both cases, the new API provides a slot where the old API or the bridge module can register and receive callbacks. If nobody registers in the slot, nothing happens. The new API can operate without a problem because it doesn't share its resources with anyone else. This is exactly what happens when the old API disappears and is no longer needed by anyone else.

Imagine, for example, if the `java.security.MessageDigest` class were considered to be too complicated. Or consider if it were seen as violating various principles of good API design. Take this just as an example: the API in question is not bad, although it doesn't follow everything advised in this book. For example, it doesn't clearly separate client API from provider API. The client class extends the `MessageDigestSpi` provider, which is a minor issue. The more important drawback is that the registration is unique, based on rich system property APIs, and it doesn't use the standard Java extension mechanism; that is, `java.util.ServiceLoader`. As a result, you cannot configure the system simply by properly setting the classpath and including the new provider JARs on it. Instead, you need to execute code to set things up or pass the JVM parameters when launching it. This is a bigger flaw, but still not something that should motivate you to completely revamp the API. However, let's pretend the API is seen as unfixable and you've started looking for a replacement. Let's imagine the biggest problem is that the API class extends the service provider and that you want to fix that:

```java
public final class Digest {
    private final DigestImplementation<?> impl;

    /** Factory method is better than constructor */
    private Digest(DigestImplementation<?> impl) {
        this.impl = impl;
    }

    /** Factory method to create digest for an algorithm.
     */
    public static Digest getInstance(String algorithm) {
        for (Digestor<?> digestor : ServiceLoader.load(Digestor.class)) {
            DigestImplementation<?> impl = DigestImplementation.create(
                digestor, algorithm
            );
            if (impl != null) {
                return new Digest(impl);
            }
        }
        throw new IllegalArgumentException(algorithm);
    }

    //
    // these methods are kept the same as in the original MessageDigest,
```

```
    // but for simplicity choose just some from the original API
    //

    public byte[] digest(ByteBuffer bb) {
        return impl.digest(bb);
    }
}
```

Our new API shields its users from the details needed only for the service provider. More-over, it does immediately show that it's an API class because it's made final. Obviously, this is not a huge improvement over the original version, but remember that this is just an example. The new API is a modular library that allows extensions. It can define its own public way for extensibility, but doesn't need to. It can rely completely on the old providers. This might be useful in situations where only the client part of the old API is wrong. In this case, let's also define a way for people who want to write providers. Only in this way can you create a real rewrite that can completely replace the old API and send it to the black hole where you want it to be. Let's now define a new API for providers using an approach called, among NetBeans engineers, *singletonizer*:

```
public abstract class Digestor<Data> {
    protected abstract byte[] digest(Data data);
    protected abstract Data create(String algorithm);
    protected abstract void update(Data data, ByteBuffer input);
}
```

This approach has the benefit of simplifying the life cycle for implementors. All they need to do is implement and register a single interface and define a private object that holds their data. As a result, there needs to be only one interface in the service provider API, while a simi-lar pattern with a factory class would require two classes. Also, the implementor has more freedom in choosing the actual type that will be used to represent its own data structures. For example, to implement a digest by counting the number of processed bytes, you might decide to use **int**[1] as its own data structure:

```
public final class CountingDigestor extends Digestor<int[]> {
    @Override
    protected byte[] digest(int[] data) {
        int i = data[0];
        byte[] arr = {
            (byte) (i & 255),
            (byte) ((i >> 8) & 255),
            (byte) ((i >> 16) & 255),
            (byte) ((i >> 24) & 255)
        };
        return arr;
    }

    @Override
    protected int[] create(String algorithm) {
```

```
        return "cnt".equals(algorithm) ? new int[1] : null;
    }

    @Override
    protected void update(int[] data, ByteBuffer input) {
        data[0] += input.remaining();
        input.position(input.position() + input.remaining());
    }
}
```

NetBeans uses this approach often, especially when mapping deep hierarchies, such as trees, into an interface that can handle operations on them. It leaves correct memory management in the hands of the infrastructure and guarantees correctness. Anyway, all that is a bit off-topic.

The main problem to solve now is to ensure that providers registered via the old API and the new message digestors will be available to the clients of the old API, as well as clients of the new API. As Figure 15-5 shows, this is already beginning to become complicated.

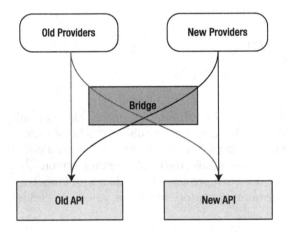

Figure 15-5. *The flow of information from the registered providers toward the users of the APIs*

The bridge needs to be aware of all registered providers and do "double bridging." It needs to convert the old ones to new ones so that the new API can see them. It also needs to convert the new ones to the old ones, so that they are visible to clients of the old API. In the case of our new message digest API, this requires two classes. One registers itself as the new API provider and delegates to the original API:

```
# registration in bridge's META-INF/services/
org.apidesign.impl.security.extension.BridgeToNew
```

```
public class BridgeToNew extends Digestor<MessageDigest> {
    /** initializes the other bridge, and allows us to eliminate stack
     * overflow */
    private static final BridgeToOld oldBridge = new BridgeToOld();
```

```java
@Override
protected MessageDigest create(String algorithm) {
    if (oldBridge.isSearching()) {
        // if the call is initiated from the other bridge, do not do
        // any delegation
        return null;
    }

    try {
        return MessageDigest.getInstance(algorithm);
    } catch (NoSuchAlgorithmException ex) {
        Logger.getLogger(BridgeToNew.class.getName()).log(
            Level.FINE, "Cannot find " + algorithm, ex
        );
        return null;
    }
}

@Override
protected byte[] digest(MessageDigest data) {
    return data.digest();
}

@Override
protected void update(MessageDigest data, ByteBuffer input) {
    data.update(input);
}

static {
    new BridgeToOld();
}
}
```

This ensures that, whenever you request an implementation of the algorithm provided via the old providers, they are consulted and their MessageDigest object is converted into an appropriate object that the new API can consume. You are done with this part. However, you also need to delegate in the opposite direction:

```java
public final class BridgeToOld extends Provider {

    public BridgeToOld() {
        super("spi.Digestor", 1.0, "");
        Security.addProvider(this);
    }

    private ThreadLocal<Boolean> searching = new ThreadLocal<Boolean>();
    final boolean isSearching() {
```

```
        return Boolean.TRUE.equals(searching.get());
    }

    @Override
    public synchronized Service getService(String type, String algorithm) {
        Boolean prev = searching.get();
        try {
            searching.set(Boolean.TRUE);
            if ("MessageDigest".equals(type)) {
                Digest dig = Digest.getInstance(algorithm);
                if (dig != null) {
                    return new ServiceImpl(
                        dig, this, type, algorithm, "",
                        Collections.<String>emptyList(),
                        Collections.<String,String>emptyMap());
                }
            }
            return null;
        } finally {
            searching.set(prev);
        }
    }

    private static class ServiceImpl<Data> extends Service {
        Digest dig;

        public ServiceImpl(Digest dig, Provider provider,
            String type, String algorithm, String className,
            List<String> aliases, Map<String, String> attributes
        ) {
            super(
                provider, type, algorithm, className, aliases, attributes
            );
            this.dig = dig;
        }

        @Override
        public Object newInstance(Object constructorParameter)
        throws NoSuchAlgorithmException {
            return new MessageDigest(getAlgorithm()) {
                private byte[] res;

                @Override
                protected void engineUpdate(byte input) {
                    ByteBuffer bb = ByteBuffer.wrap(new byte[] { input });
                    res = dig.digest(bb);
                }
```

```
        @Override
        protected void engineUpdate(
            byte[] input, int offset, int len
        ) {
            ByteBuffer bb = ByteBuffer.wrap(input);
            bb.position(offset);
            bb.limit(offset + len);
            res = dig.digest(bb);
        }

        @Override
        protected byte[] engineDigest() {
            return res;
        }

        @Override
        protected void engineReset() {
            dig = Digest.getInstance(getAlgorithm());
        }
    };
}


}
```

This is a bit more verbose, as the old API uses the classic factory class design instead of the singletonizer. As a result, you need to implement multiple classes instead of just one. The biggest problem is the registration. Somehow the BridgeToOld class needs to be registered. Putting it into META-INF/services/java.security.Provider doesn't work. Another proprietary and more complicated declarative registration mechanism is available, or you can just make sure that the static bridge registers itself when loaded into memory. This is done in the test by a dummy call to the following:

```
// The java.security.Providers cannot be registered in META-INF/services.
// That is why we need to either configure various properties or
// make some dummy call that will initialize our bridge class.
// Then the bridge class registers itself as a MessageDigest provider
// in its constructor.
//
// This is the call:
Digest initialize = Digest.getInstance("MD5");
```

It's not pretty, but at least your code doesn't need to depend on the bridge classes directly. Hopefully one day the registration of the security providers will be standardized to also use the Java Extension Mechanism. Then it will be enough to include the bridge JAR on the classpath

to make the providers registered with the new API available to the clients of the old
`java.security.MessageDigest` class.

Another aspect to pay attention to is the merging vicious circle that can result in
`StackOverFlowErrors`. The reasons are simple: one bridge registers itself as a provider in the
old API and delegates to the new providers, while another provider is included among the new
ones and delegates to the old providers. As demonstrated in Figure 15-6, this can easily create
an endless loop that the code will walk until it exhausts the available stack space.

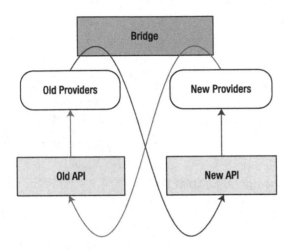

Figure 15-6. *Vicious flows of calls during runtime when double bridging*

This can be fixed in many ways. However, the most clueless fix is to use a thread local
variable. Set it inside one bridge to indicate that one direction of bridging is in progress:

```
private ThreadLocal<Boolean> searching = new ThreadLocal<Boolean>();
final boolean isSearching() {
    return Boolean.TRUE.equals(searching.get());
}
```

```
@Override
public synchronized Service getService(String type, String algorithm) {
    Boolean prev = searching.get();
    try {
        searching.set(Boolean.TRUE);
        if ("MessageDigest".equals(type)) {
            Digest dig = Digest.getInstance(algorithm);
            if (dig != null) {
                return new ServiceImpl(
                    dig, this, type, algorithm, "",
                    Collections.<String>emptyList(),
                    Collections.<String,String>emptyMap());
            }
        }
        return null;
```

```
    } finally {
        searching.set(prev);
    }
}
```

In the other bridge, check for that situation and then skip any attempts to delegate:

```
if (oldBridge.isSearching()) {
    // if the call is initiated from the other bridge, do not do
    // any delegation
    return null;
}
```

Most parts of this book view beauty as being unnecessary. Most parts advocate preferring backward compatibility over beauty because the need for compatibility can be easily justified. However, the example given in this chapter shows that an API doesn't need to get increasingly ugly. It's possible to repair it and create something nice. By creating an alternative API, you can create a new API star that can shine beautifully to all its observers. Those who decide to pay attention to this part of the API universe can simply look at it, completely ignoring any old, dying stars that are burning out somewhere else. By properly creating a bridge module that reflects the light between the old and the new star, you also preserve the investments made by people who once observed and still want to observe the old star. Even though it's dying now, it shines its light and the speed of its extinguishing is completely customer-driven. If customers observe it, it's still alive and delivering the light it promised at the time of its creation. However, as soon as the last observers decide to switch their attention away from it, attracted by the light of its new replacement, the old API star can immediately vanish. It might still lie around somewhere, but it's definitely behind the horizon of the users of that part of the API universe. It's gradually moving into the darkness. One day it might disappear completely, as if falling into a black hole.

This coordinated death of an API, completely driven by its observers, is a way to marry the need for compatibility with the need for beauty. The good news for all of us is that even in the API world there is a way to see a simultaneous prism of truth, beauty, and elegance.

CHAPTER 16

■ ■ ■

Teamwork

Successful projects start small and are developed by a small, coherent group of people. They emerge as large projects where nobody controls everything. People no longer know each other, nor do they understand the area of code someone else is working on. Architects no longer touch the code. They rise a few levels above the keyboard to discuss the necessary changes in the next version of their product while playing golf with existing or future customers. In this setup, it's easy to completely lose track of what is going on. In fact, that is almost necessary. Nobody can understand the whole system. Cluelessness gradually increases. Despite that, it's necessary to produce a new release even in a loosely organized system. There is only one way to do so effectively: selectively choose the aspects of the project that are important and concentrate on those. To that end, this chapter outlines a few recipes that work reasonably well in the NetBeans project.

Organizing Reviews Before Committing Code

As soon as you start to develop as a group consisting not only of people sitting next to each other in the same room but also external contributors, you need procedures to follow when making API changes. Any set of steps is better than nothing at all. However, these steps should include a peer review. Moreover, our experience tells us that the most important thing is to ensure proper review of changes before they are integrated. Only then can the will of the integrator to listen to requested changes be high enough to apply them.

Of course, this is not the only reason why there should be a sequence of steps to follow when performing an API change. Especially if you are working on an open source project, it's in your interest to "live in a fishbowl" and to have answers for external contributors who want to make some kind of change. Properly documenting steps of what needs to be done to integrate an API change is a perfect and simple answer to everyone requesting an API change.

The other reason you probably don't want API changes to "just happen" is that you need to distinguish the intended from the unwanted API changes. You don't want your team to mistakenly integrate incompatible changes, as that hurts users of your library immediately. However, you also don't want your team to make unconscious compatible API changes as that might hurt you in the future. After a few releases, you might find a few new classes or methods that were added some years ago and that compromise the evolution of your API. Now you are not able to change the code in a way you thought would be possible.

DESIGNED BY A TEAM

As I've mentioned many times, in the early days I designed all the NetBeans classes that were meant to be part of the public API. In that situation, you need no formal processes and no rules at all. All these things can simply be in your head. You know the purpose of each element and whether a particular change is aligned with the strategy given to each API. It's easy to maintain consistency. However, this only works when you are the only designer on the project.

Then one day a NetBeans engineer was supposed to change an API for manipulating the toolbars in the main window of the NetBeans IDE. I didn't consider it an important enough problem to work on, so I let him do it. That immediately broke the working style I was used to when designing an API. I could have sat with him and watched every change he performed on his computer, but as I had other things to do, he worked alone and simply delivered the result.

The first problem was that I didn't even notice the API change. There was no "big brother" to watch over and notify others of such changes. When I noticed, I didn't like the change. However, I couldn't formulate the reasons for my dislike—the change had happened a long time before I started to write this book. Moreover, I noticed the change after a release. Given our strong adherence to backward compatibility, we couldn't remove it. We simply had to live with it.

I can't remember the exact problem in this case. Maybe a class in the API exposed implementation details by implementing `MouseListener`. Maybe too many internal fields were needed to be hidden later with a few hacks. The point is that as soon as you allow a team, instead of a single person, to change your APIs, you need to organize and observe the work that is being done on them.

Of course, not every API change deserves the same attention. Sometimes it's necessary to simply supervise the API and ensure that changes are "harmless." The most important aspects to watch for include the ability to allow future evolution, the proper versioning of the change, some kind of consistency with the rest of the library, and a reasonable amount of documentation and test coverage. This is usually enough for small and compatible changes such as adding new methods or classes into an already existing framework. Also, it's usually enough just to prepare the changes, and just before the commit, ask for a review by providing the patch that you want to integrate. Usually the change is so small that the patch is self-descriptive. As open source developers like to say, "Show me the code." That is the only thing that counts anyway.

STANDARD VS. FAST TRACK

NetBeans reviews are open to submitters as well as reviewers. Everyone can participate in them. The review process is described at `http://openide.netbeans.org/tutorial/reviews/` and happens mostly inside our bug-tracking system. Each review request is tracked as one issue, and progress and results of its review are tracked as its changes.

For small changes we have a *fast track* review that is based on an optimistic locking strategy. Submitters prepare the diff of the API change. They put the diff into the issue and wait a week. If there are no objections, the change is applied. We've found this to be a nice compromise between the right to review and the need to integrate the changes. A week is long enough for anyone interested in the problem to find a free moment for review. However, a week is not so long that the submitter's work is blocked in a significant way.

A nice additional aspect is that often the proposed change is slightly different from the one integrated: during the week the submitter does a self-review, rethinks the proposal some more, and fine-tunes it himself. This means that the final integration is better than it would have been without the review, and that is often the case even if no reviewer adds comments at all.

The other review type is called *standard*, and it consists of two rounds. The first takes place before any coding is done, the second before integration. In each of these rounds, there is a discussion in our bug tracking system or in a dedicated wiki page. The discussion is then followed with a conference call with at least four selected reviewers who need to "vote," meaning create a list of their objections. Then either the project is killed or it is allowed to continue under the condition that the objections are resolved.

However, there can be far larger changes. For these, this kind of review might not be sufficient at all. If you want to create a whole new API and still be consistent with the rest of the framework, it doesn't make sense to do the review method by method. Reviewing at a time when methods are already written is much too late. You need to start the review at a time when the concept of the library is being created, as only at that time do you have a real chance to influence the direction of the whole effort. Once code is written, nobody is happy with suggestions such as "base your API on JavaCC," "use ANTLR," and so on. It's important to convince developers to ask for reviews as early as possible. This is hard, especially if the developers consider you to be someone who wants to block or slow their progress. This is common for those who have never participated in the review before, as they have an inaccurate expectation of what an architecture review can do for them.

MY FIRST ARCHITECTURE REVIEW

A team is expected to ask a global Sun architecture review committee's opinion before a project is released to customers. I don't know the exact history of this process. I expect it was started a long time ago to supervise changes in the Solaris operating system and SPARC processors. At least, that is the impression that I got when learning its methodologies, and especially by reading its "20 questions" document. It's a living document that, at the time I first came across it, contained a few hundred Unix-oriented questions. It didn't even mention Java at that time. As you might have guessed, it's continually evolving and now probably contains a set of Java-related questions.

After Sun acquired NetBeans, we produced a few releases before someone realized that we hadn't passed through this review process yet. I was asked to prepare and pass the architecture review. You can imagine how upset I was! Someone who probably doesn't even know how to spell Java is going to tell me, the one who designed NetBeans, something about architecture! How dare they! What kind of advice could I expect from people who knew nothing about NetBeans?

The guidelines were not oriented toward Java. People leading the reviews didn't know much about Java. However, as I slowly crawled through the "20 questions" document and answered their questions, I began to see the light. Before that, I belonged to the camp that believed that architecture and API ends on the level of classes and their methods. I realized the error of my thinking. Based on that experience, I wrote Chapter 3. I realized that, to do architecture and API reviews, you don't need to be an expert in the API domain at all. Many general aspects can be reviewed without needing to understand the actual tasks that the API is supposed to do. For these aspects, there is no real need to understand the actual tasks that the API is supposed to do. Does that sound familiar? Yes, indeed; I've argued this in Part 1 of this book as well. In fact,

I can say that without being asked to pass through the architecture review, I would not have been able to write this book. I hadn't expected that there would be many new technical skills I would learn while working for Sun. However, the architecture review committee is more valuable than anything else I've yet come across at Sun. Therefore, I am thankful to Sun for teaching me how to perform effective architecture reviews.

One thing that scared me when writing documentation for architecture reviews was the fact that I would write them and then lose them after the review. I hate to perform useless work, which is exactly what this task seemed to be. I decided to change the way we do API reviews in NetBeans to make our documentation directly reusable for architecture reviews. We are able not only to pass the review, but also to provide much more detailed documentation to developers using the NetBeans Platform. I open sourced the architecture review process. I changed its name, changed various technical terms, and I rewrote the "20 questions" document to be more NetBeans and Java specific (see the questions at `http://openide.netbeans.org/tutorial/questions.html`). However, I kept the structure untouched. I kept this an open secret for a few years. However, now that all of Sun seems to be quickly moving toward an open source style of development, I am no longer afraid to disclose the whole history behind the creation of the NetBeans Open Source Review Process.

Feel free to learn more about this kind of review by reading the NetBeans API Review instructions. I can only recommend them, as in short, I've found architecture reviews the best thing under the Sun!

Whatever style of work you decide on for your own project, it should include some form of review before committing, at least for architectural changes. My experience suggests that this is the only effective tool you have when coordinating API contributions. Moreover, having the process open to external contributors can decrease your cost of ownership, as discussed in the section "Minimizing Maintenance Cost" in Chapter 14.

Convincing Developers to Document Their API

Anyone who has ever been a developer knows how boring it is to write documentation. Everyone who ever tried to convince a developer to write documentation knows how hard that is. As a result, the general feeling is that developers don't like and are not able to provide documentation for their own code. However, good documentation is the facade that can shield API users from the internal details, and thus integrate cluelessness further into their programming. Also, the API is the main tool for communication between the author of the API and its users. The better the documentation, the less effort is needed to understand and use a library. That is why having good documentation is a must for any successful framework.

However, a developer's attitude usually goes along the following lines: "The code is there, it works, so use it!" They, or at least I, feel that writing documentation duplicates the work that has already been done. As anyone can guess, doing the same or similar work a second time around is boring. That is probably the reason why developers are negative when it comes to writing documentation for their code. Also, when they are forced to write documentation, the documentation is not of good quality. Even if they really try, they cannot write a good introduction, as they see their own API with completely unique eyes and cannot pretend to be newcomers anymore. Even if they try to write a good overview, the low-level details often stick out. They are able to say, "The purpose of this library is to draw an image," which is a good overview sentence. However, engineers are immediately tempted to add a description of how to do it; that is, immediately just show the code, to the deepest level of detail that is unlikely to be useful for newcomers reading the overview with the hope of getting a feel for the functionality of the library.

This is all true, yet I believe it's possible to help developers write good documentation. It just needs a well-thought-out methodology. One of the most promising methodologies is called *working backwards*. I saw a note about that on a friend's blog. As soon as I read it I thought of it as something that could actually work. However, as there is often a long road between thought and action, it took more than a year before I was able to try it out myself. When I did, I was surprised at the result.

The basic idea is simple. Instead of starting with code or a technical proposal, let's start with the last thing that is needed, such as a press release. Write the goals of the project, pretend you are proud of your achievements, and describe what they are. Then follow with a frequently asked questions (FAQ) document. Here you can go into deeper details and explain some details of the technology that are too low-level for the press release. After that, follow with the advice given in the section "The Importance of Being Use Case Oriented" in Chapter 4: use the FAQ to describe the use cases, then include the actual code and its Javadoc.

There are several reasons why this "inversion of workflow" can prove successful. At the time of writing the initial press release, you don't yet have enough technical knowledge to stuff the release with technical details. This requires a bit of self-discipline because every developer wants to code as soon as possible. So you need to defer that joy and write down your own thoughts before jumping to the keyboard to code. Though this needs a bit of self-control, it's not at all unnatural because you must have the overall picture of the project in mind before starting to type the code.

THE FEAR IS MUTUAL

Not only the developers are afraid to write documentation: the technical writers, in turn, seem to be afraid to change the Javadoc! Here I am going to pick on Geertjan Wielenga, one of this book's beloved editors. Without him this book would never have seen the light of day, as my lab journal was not written in colloquial English and desperately needed many additional edits. (I am looking forward to seeing how much, if any, will be left of this sidebar after his language fixes, which in the case of this sidebar is just a euphemism for censorship!)

Geertjan loves to write documentation about the NetBeans Platform. He is a famous blogger, maintains the NetBeans Platform web site, and feeds it with content consisting of tutorials, interviews, stories, and so on. Clearly he is an essential part of the whole documentation effort. With just a little exaggeration, I can say that without him few people would be using the NetBeans Platform today.

On the other hand, his work is just a part of the documentation our project offers. It's the initial part, used by newcomers. However, in addition to that, we have the documentation written by our API writers; that is, the developers. This includes the Javadoc, use cases, and so on. Although these kinds of documentation are of different complexities, they address the same issue: documenting the NetBeans Platform usage. In spite of that, there is little to no connection between these types of documentation. That is a shame, because they are all targeted at our users, and our users want to have as much information as possible. They want to have this information constantly at the ready. When coding in the IDE and using code completion, wouldn't it be useful to jump from there straight to a tutorial related to the usage of the current method? Indeed it would be, and the only required task is to enhance the Javadoc method with a pointer to a related tutorial.

However, we are facing a typical us-versus-them problem. Developers don't know about tutorials, so they cannot add a link to them when writing the Javadoc. Moreover, the tutorials are usually written later than the Javadoc. From another perspective, Geertjan seems to be afraid of changing the Javadoc himself. In various discussions, I've tried to convince him that this is needed, but so far I've failed. So, while developers are afraid of writing documentation, documenters are afraid of changing anything written by developers. As a result, we have two sets of documentation, written more or less independently.

I am sure this situation is not good. I am unsure what to do about it. Maybe we should apply a "working from roots" methodology and not let anyone write a tutorial unless there is a link to it from the Javadoc. That might fix the situation and remove Geertjan's fear to edit it. However, I still need to find out if that would work.

Moreover, one of the reasons why developers don't like to write documentation is that it's forgotten as soon as they finish the code. That is not always true, but often enough to instill the concern of writing documentation. With the "working backwards" style of work, this is prevented. The press release will be needed when the project is finished, if not directly, then at least as a source of information for the marketing department. The FAQs are something to be loved by end users or at least technical writers working on tutorials. The need for use cases and the Javadoc is clear. That is why the likelihood of convincing engineers to write good docs is increased, as they are not doing anything useless or duplicating something that has already been done before.

However, the order of things is important. Start with the press release and move step by step to the code. Without this order, the methodology doesn't work. Recently I wanted to write a "press release" for a finished project and it was painful. The result was not good at all. I started with the overview. However, in the third paragraph I suddenly included a shell command line as an example of how to use the project. This was not a press release at all! However, this is what happens to engineers: they want to share as much useful information as possible, which prevents them from writing press releases after the product is finished. The only point at which they will succeed in this is before they start coding.

I have to admit that I've enjoyed this style of work every time I've tried it. In the end, writing press releases and FAQs was a lot of fun. However, I still have to see if this can be applied to everybody. I hope this can be seen an as entertaining opportunity that can simultaneously be generally applicable in many situations.

Big Brother Never Sleeps

Mistakes happen. However good you are, however good your team is, it's certain that from time to time someone will make a mistake, accidentally modifying an API. If your team is not perfect, or if it incorporates new members occasionally, you need to watch over them. You need to verify that they are not making any overwhelmingly strong promises to your API users. If they do make promises, they must mean them and be able to deliver on them. Of course, the last thing you want to do is to sit beside them and watch every step they take. Instead, you want an automatic system that will notify you of changes in the important characteristics of your API.

The goal for a "big brother" system is clear. Now the question is: what are the important characteristics to check and how often should you check them? Obviously, everything that you check on any regular project needs to be checked when working with APIs and libraries. It's valuable to have an automated build that runs after each commit, or at least a daily build. It's important to verify that your code can still be compiled. It's desirable to run automated tests with it as well. It might be interesting to know the test coverage of your library, as that might identify places that are not tested at all. It might also be interesting to be notified of commits that integrate changes to the library that decrease the test coverage and thus might destabilize the library in the future.

WHEN THERE ARE ENOUGH TESTS

While writing tests, developers often ask how many of them should be written. The simple answer is to write tests whenever they are useful. The more precise and less definitive answer follows:

Various tools out there help to measure test coverage. We've selected EMMA (http://emma. sourceforge.net) for measuring the coverage of our application code by our tests. For example, when invoked from the pop-up menu of a project from NetBeans.org, it instruments the application code and invokes automated tests on it. While running, it collects information about all the called methods, visited classes, and lines, and then it shows a summary in a web browser.

Counting coverage by visited methods is not a very demanding criterion. However, it can be surprisingly difficult to get close to 100 percent coverage. Even if you succeed, there is no guarantee that the resulting application code will work correctly. Every method has a few input parameters. Knowing that coverage testing succeeded with one subset of them doesn't say anything about the other cases.

It's much better to count the coverage by branches or lines. When there is an `if (...) { x(); }` `else { y(); }` statement in a method's code, you want to be sure that both methods, x and y, will be called. The EMMA tool supports this need. By helping us to be sure that every line is visited, it gives us confidence that our application code doesn't contain useless lines.

Still, the fact that a line is visited once doesn't mean that our application code is not buggy.

```java
private int sum = 10;

public int add(int x) {
    sum += x;
    return sum;
}

public int percentageFrom(int howMuch) {
    return 100 * howMuch / sum;
}
```

It's good if both methods get executed and fine if we test them with various parameters. Still, we can get an error if we call add (-10); percentage(5), because the sum will be zero and division by zero is forbidden. To be sure that our application is not vulnerable to problems like this, we would have to test each method in each possible state of memory it depends on, meaning each value of the sum variable. That would give us the ultimate proof that our application code works correctly in a single-threaded environment.

But there is another problem: Java is not single-threaded. Many applications start new threads by themselves. Even if they don't do so, there is also the AWT event dispatch thread, the finalizer thread, and so on. You need to count on some amount of nondeterminism. Sometimes the garbage collector simply kicks in and removes "unneeded" objects from memory, which can change the application's behavior. We used to have a never-ending loop, which could be simulated only if two Mozilla browsers and an Evolution client were running, because then the memory was small enough to invoke the garbage collector. This kind of coverage is immeasurable.

That is why we suggest that people use code coverage tools as a sanity check that something is not under-tested. However, you need to remind yourself that there might still be bugs in an application, no matter how high the code coverage is. To help fight the strange shifts of an application's amoeba shape, we suggest writing a test whenever something breaks. When there is a bug report, write a test to verify it and prevent regressions. That way, coverage will be focused on the code that matters: the parts that were actually broken.

In addition to these regular tests, your library needs a lot of special care. It's likely that you want to publish a Javadoc with each build and make sure it doesn't contain broken links. Moreover, you might be influenced by this book's opinion that the Javadoc is not enough. In such cases, you probably want to find a way to describe other APIs and annotate them in a way that will be easily recognizable to your API's users. Potentially, you also want to assign your API stability categories, as discussed in the section "Life Cycle of an API" in Chapter 4. Last but not least, you want to notify users of your API about the latest changes that have been made. For all these reasons, you might want to employ the NetBeans Javadoc extensions.

NETBEANS JAVADOC EXTENSIONS

To follow the principles of this book, we needed to enhance the standard Javadoc generation tool. We needed it to provide support for proper versioning and for an easier and standard way of drilling down from top-level use cases to individual APIs. I believe that everyone building a library or framework following advice described in this document needs a tool like this. So, feel free to use this set of Ant build scripts and XSL transformations, as they are not NetBeans-specific and can be used independently.

The Javadoc is built around the modified "20 questions" document that contains various intrinsic questions that should guide every module writer to realize the various APIs exposed by the library. For example, there are questions about reading system properties, using reflection to access nonpublic classes, reading files, and opening sockets. The goal is not to force the developer to write "Not applicable," but to document it if it's true. Best of all, the goal is to document it in a categorizable way, in a way that can be processed later.

In the NetBeans project, the name of the file containing the answers is arch.xml. The text of arch.xml is mostly in HTML format. However, there are two important extensions. Either you can use the <api> element, which marks an API, or you can use the <usecase> element to describe an introductory use case. If you use these tags, then their content is taken and inserted into the overview page of the Javadoc. As a result, the main entry point page of an API, such as the Task List API ,[1] contains the overview use cases that can navigate the user to the appropriate classes in the standard Javadoc, as well as a table listing all properties, reflection, and files that form an important API. This is enough to get a first feel of what an API is supposed to do. However, if there is a need to know more, the API user can always read the whole "20 questions" document.

This is by no means all that is interesting to users of an API. They are also interested in knowing what new features are available in the API. This is especially important in the case of libraries with a rapidly evolving design where a few new additions appear several times a month. To deliver this overview, we have another XML file called apidesign.xml. It contains *API change sets*. Whenever we add a new method or class into an existing API, we increase the specification version of its module and also add a change set. The change set contains a human-readable description of what is going on, links to the changed elements in the

---

1. http://bits.netbeans.org/6.0/javadoc/org-netbeans-spi-tasklist/overview-summary.html

original Javadoc, the specification version the change happened in, and a reference to our bug tracking system for those who want to search the absolute history of the API's introduction. This is usually more detail than is needed. The link usually refers to the details of the API review with all comments, replies, and considerations, but sometimes all this is needed, as it forms the ultimate document, potentially explaining the motivations behind the final look and feel of the API.

Our build scripts take the five latest changes and put them into the overview page. The rest is then available on a separate page, where the whole history of the evolution of the API is kept.

The API change sets can be annotated as being source compatible, binary compatible, semantically compatible, or none. This helps us point out changes that deserve API user attention when migrating to a new version. However, it's sometimes not easy to decide whether a change is compatible or not. We still haven't decided whether to aim for 100 percent compatibility or simply 99 percent. The fields allow us only to specify "yes" or "no," which is probably correct, but what should we say when the change classifies as 99 percent compatibility, instead of 100 percent? This varies. As far as I know, we usually annotate it as compatible but add a note describing under which cases compatibility might not be fully accurate.

If you want to learn more about our Javadoc enhancements, feel free to point your browser to http://javadoc.apidesign.org.

Documenting changes is a nice thing. However, on its own it's not enough. You need to track the API itself. First and foremost, this means watching for changes in the signature of public and protected members of public classes. You want to watch for two types of changes. The most important, from the standpoint of clueless assembly of libraries, is to watch for backward-incompatible changes. As soon as you release a new version of your library, you should take a snapshot of its API and then, with every new build, compare the actual state of the API with that snapshot. Nothing should be missing and there should be no incompatible changes.

The other aspect to check is that there are no accidental changes. As pointed out in the section "Organizing Reviews Before Committing Code," the last thing you want is to find that random accidental API changes have sneaked into your API. If they do sneak in at the wrong moment, you need to sustain them in future releases in a compatible way. That is why you need to generate changes on a daily basis, against those from the previous day, and make sure that the differences are sensible.

NETBEANS API SIGNATURE TEST TOOL

The NetBeans tool is based on the one provided as part of the Java Community Process. With a few additions to it, to fit into our Ant build scripts and understand module versioning, we are able to take the snapshots that report both incompatible changes against the snapshot as well as any change against it. If you want to know more about the tool, please visit http://sigtest.apidesign.org.

Signatures are not the only exposed API. You need to check other important aspects. Generally, the layout of various files is of great interest. In the case of modular systems such as NetBeans, it's reasonable to watch over dependencies between individual components because newly added dependencies can restrict the ability of that component to be picked up and separately assembled into some kind of application.

VERIFICATION FRAMEWORK

NetBeans has a special framework for testing these additional APIs as part of the build. The general idea is to have a special Ant task that is configurable using its setters and that can generate plain text output. This output can then be compared using regular text tools to determine whether there are differences. The input of the task is a set of module JAR files, from where the task reads its dependency information. Remember that all the dependencies are stored inside JAR manifests in NetBeans.

The task is configurable to produce various output formats and to write them into a given output file. The possible outputs include a list of all public packages, which can then be passed to the signature processing tool; a list of all modules and their versions, to notify us that a new module is added; and a list of all modules, along with their dependencies.

We used to have a mode when, to allow each developer to test their own changes, the "golden" results were stored in version control, along with the source files. The build failed when they didn't match. This completely shielded us from unintentional changes. However, we discovered that in many cases the changes to golden files weren't of great interest. That is why right now, we run these checks only on the build machine. The golden files generated by previous builds are compared to the new ones. If there is a difference, an e-mail is sent to all the developers. This way everyone interested is notified about the changes made during the day and can check that no unwanted dependency has been added.

I am not sure which of the modes is better. The one that caused the build to fail required too much attention from the developers. The current mode just lets them integrate changes without any kind of self-control. The optimal solution probably lies somewhere in the middle. If we could specify unwanted dependencies, such as "text editor should not depend on compiler" or "HTML support should not require Java support," these would likely be good candidates for breaking the build. We'll see if we find that useful in the future.

It's not important whether you find inspiration in the tools that the NetBeans project uses or whether you choose to develop your own. However, it's important to create some kind of "big brother" system that watches over your developers. Only then can you successfully design an API in a group and not be surprised by the final result.

An alternative is to have a human "gatekeeper" who receives proposed patches and either accepts or rejects them. That might indeed work too. However, it's unlikely to scale well enough. Also, it's not in the spirit of this book to suggest a solution that requires a person who "knows everything." The nirvana we seek is to build our solution around maximum cluelessness, where human knowledge is minimized. This is more likely to be achieved when you have good tools and tests to control the general aspects of an API, rather than a single gatekeeper.

Accepting API Patches

The section "Minimizing Maintenance Cost" in Chapter 14 claimed that maintaining a well-written API is no more difficult than maintaining regular code—sometimes even simpler. However, this depends on the quality of the contributions received from your API's users. If they simply complain, or request changes in your library API that don't make much sense or are not well-justified, you won't simplify your life much. If you accept bad suggestions or contributions, future maintenance can become a nightmare. The way to prevent that outcome is only to accept good suggestions and good patches.

GO MULTITHREADED!

Separating good from bad suggestions can sometimes be difficult. For example, the MPlayer project, which provides an open source movie player and encoder written in C, was advised to take advantage of multicore processors and rewrite its code to be multithreaded. This looks like a reasonable piece of advice. With two cores, the compression speed could be doubled. Also, these days almost everyone has a multicore processor; if not today, almost everyone will have one in the future. Still, the project refused to follow that advice. No wonder, because even the single-threaded version of MPlayer had a hard time avoiding crashing. With multi-threaded code, this would have been even more difficult. In my opinion, the team was right in refusing to start exploiting multicores, even though they risked a potential fork of their project. That's exactly what happened: fans of multithreading created their own project, forking the MPlayer code base. As far as I can tell, after a few years, the original MPlayer is still alive, while I cannot find any information on the fork.

As usual, a good decision is one that reduces time to market and lowers cost of ownership. Nevertheless, if you have an API and someone asks you to make a change, you are usually not motivated by time to market. Your API is already on the market. Unless the requested feature is something that everybody wants, you don't need to hurry. The only concern is the total cost of ownership. If you accept the patch, you'll become its owner. Potentially that will mean that you'll spend too much time or energy maintaining it.

What could be the reason for this risk? You might accept a buggy patch, one that doesn't live up to its promise. This risk cannot be fully eliminated. However, if you ask for reasonable coverage of code lines changed by the patch, you might be confident that at least the basic functionality is acceptable. The next problem is that the fix can cause regressions. Assuming the rest of your library is properly tested as well, this risk can be reasonably eliminated. However, if the patch submitter is the first person who writes a test for your library, then the risk of its integration breaking some of the already existing assumptions might be big. This is yet another reason for having reasonable code coverage. On the other hand, regressions are not the only danger that you need to eliminate. The patch might prevent future evolution. Therefore, you need to review it before integration and measure it according to the suggestions found in this book, as well as by any other suggestions that help guarantee a simple evolution path into the future. Another bad thing might be an underdocumented patch. Again, it's simple to request further documentation or to ask the submitter to provide more high-level use cases. On the other hand, this requirement could be partially replaced by good test coverage, because automated tests are often the best form of documentation. The last aspect that you should pay attention to is proper versioning. In modular systems with version numbers, you should increase the specification version with every API change and document the new behavior available since that version.

The best approach to accepting patches is to do a review before committing them. This is easy to do when you get a patch from an external contributor. However, "review before commit" is the best way to ensure a proper response from the provider of the patch even if it's your closest teammate. Until the change is integrated, the motivation to solve your issues is magnified by the need to have the patch accepted. Usually, after integration the contributor's will to fix additional problems is lowered relative to the time passed since the patch's acceptance. This means that the only suitable time for minimizing the maintenance cost is before integrating a patch. All the problems found later are likely to end up on the plate of the maintainer of the library, rather than the submitter of the patch.

IT'S SO NICE TO ACCEPT PATCHES!

As a maintainer of parts of an open source framework, I can say that I am always pleased to receive good patches from others. Sometimes I feel that the requirements I impose on them are too high and that it's not easy to fulfill all of them. Sometimes I am even in doubt as to whether to accept something that is not properly tested or that is underdocumented. However, I am aware of the potential problems of maintaining buggy patches into the future. Usually I request an improved patch. Either I then receive the improvement or I don't. If not, that probably means I was right, as the submitter probably wouldn't do a good job providing support for the API change later.

From the point of view of the user of a library, you might ask whether it makes sense to contribute patches, especially if the barrier for acceptance is high. It might be better to fork the library or to work around the problem on your own side. Of course, this depends on the overall situation. However, the problems of forking or working around a problem are clear: you increase the cost of your ownership. Despite the fact that you needed to find the problem, identify it, and understand its fix in the library that you are using, all of which are costly processes, you are willing to endure these hassles, rather than donating the fix to the project providing the library. You want to keep the code change to yourself and you then need to remember it in the future. That's because, with every new version of the library, you'll need to apply the patch again. You'll then need to verify that your workaround still works, which is not easy, as the provider of the library doesn't even know that you've forked their library. This is increasingly costly in the long run—certainly more costly than spending a bit of time fulfilling the project's requirements for a proper patch. Fulfilling these requirements is something that you need to do once only, after which you can let the project itself handle all future maintenance problems related to your donated API patch.

Each open source project has different requirements for accepting API patches. However, generally, all these are about balance. Patches that are of poor quality need to be rejected because they have hidden maintenance problems. On the other hand, you want to make it easy for users of an API to donate patches. It should be easier to donate patches than it is to invest in inventing custom workarounds and forks. The final decision on the approach to take is on the side of the user of the API. However, the more widespread an open source project with a good API becomes, the more likely it is that users will understand the strategic long-term advantage of contributing patches. For everyone concerned, taking this approach is the best way to minimize overall costs of ownership.

■■■

CHAPTER 17

Using Games to Improve API Design Skills

The head of my department used to say, "Good judgment comes from experience; experience comes from poor judgment." If you make enough mistakes and you learn from them, you can become a good API designer. I believe that my many bad design decisions have been the biggest source of my current understanding. However, the learning curve is initially painful. It also takes a lot of time, and the knowledge gained isn't easy to transfer.

One of the biggest API design problems is the lack of terminology. People can argue for a long time about whether something is or isn't an API. I've already grown tired of repeating Part 1 to all those I believe need to hear it. Also, people often confuse incompatible changes with any change; again, I am too busy to spend time discussing these issues with every person individually. That is how I came up with the idea of an API Design Fest. An API Design Fest is a design game that is taken slightly to the extreme to prove a point. We played it among the engineers working on the core NetBeans APIs. Since then, arguments about something being an API or not, and arguments about something being an incompatible change or not, take no more than a few seconds. It's enough if I say, "With a change like that you could not win an API Design Fest." At that point, everything becomes crystal clear, all at once. People imagine the rules of the game and with a blink of an eye they see that their change is in fact an API change and that it's not 100 percent compatible. If for no other reason than the clarity that this game gives to all its participants, I recommend it to everyone.

Overview

The API Design Fest takes the form of a contest. Its aim is to teach participants about the evolution problems related to writing an API. People are given a simple task: to write an API. Their work is evaluated, after which they receive a modified task to improve the API. This sequence can be repeated multiple times. After that, their results are evaluated again. However, instead of having a jury select the "nicest" solution, the participants do the evaluation themselves. Everyone gets access to all the solutions and the goal is to find evolution problems in the solutions provided by others. To do this, they write a test that works for the previous version of an API. If the test works for the original version, but not for a subsequent version, points are assigned accordingly. Points are assigned for holes found in solutions provided by others, as well as for writing an API that proves to be bulletproof.

The world premiere of the API Design Fest occurred in the middle of July 2006. It was played by the members of the NetBeans core team. The goal was to practice API design skills and also to check the viability of holding this kind of contest again in the future. I wanted to repeat this contest with OOPSLA 2006 participants, but I needed to put the concept of the contest through its paces. That is why I am still waiting for some future OOPSLA to play it in a conference workshop session. The best practices were likely to be established by means of trying the contest out on professionals who spend most of their working day designing APIs. It was excellent that the members of the NetBeans core team agreed to participate in the pilot version of the API Design Fest.

The contest started on Wednesday, July 12. Participants met in a meeting room and were given access to a skeleton NetBeans project. They were also given a document outlining the use cases of the API they were supposed to design. They worked for an hour and gave the diff of their changes to me for evaluation.

The next day, the participants met again. They received a set of new, additional use cases. They worked for another hour to implement them again. As before, they gave me the results.

Then, the following day, I sent an e-mail describing how to access the sources provided by all the participants. The aim at that stage was to break the APIs written by other participants. Participants were supposed to write a test showing evolution problems in other APIs. The set of tests with their results was sent to me by the end of that weekend.

The results were announced on Monday, July 17. Everyone who found a hole in an API written by another contest participant got one point. Those who had created a bulletproof API—that is, their API had not been hacked by anyone else—got five points. The goal of this competition was to practice API design skills and learn to identify mistakes in designed APIs. Those who mastered this skill became winners. However, the goal was not to show that someone doesn't have enough skills to design APIs. As such, there were no losers in this competition, especially as all the submissions were kept anonymous, having artificial names that I invented randomly. Only those participants who achieved good and interesting results were celebrated as winners.

API DESIGN FEST SOURCES ARE AVAILABLE

The sources of all the participants are available and can be studied, executed, modified, tried, and so on. Just visit `http://source.apidesign.org`.

That's the overview of the first API Design Fest. I'll now provide a detailed description of exactly what occurred over the course of the contest.

Day 1

The world's first API Design Fest started on Wednesday July 13, 2006 with a simple task: *Write an API that allows the construction and evaluation of boolean circuits*. The participants received a project template that contained an empty `Circuit.java` as the suggested source file for their API definition. They also received a test file containing the three tasks that the API was supposed to fulfill:

```
/** The initial quest for this API Fest is to create an API for boolean
 * circuits. Such an API shall be able to compose a boolean circuit from
 * basic elements and evaluate the result given initial values for
 * input variables.
 * <p>
 * The basic elements include:
 * <ul>
 * <li>negation - has one input and one output and changes 0 on input to
 * on output 1 and 1 to 0
 * <li>and - has two inputs and one output. The output is 1 only if both
 * inputs are 1, otherwise it is 0
 * <li>or - has two inputs and one output. The output is always 1,
 * except in the case when both inputs are 0
 * </ul>
 *
 * <p>
 * The boolean circuit can be used to represent boolean formulas and
 * compute the results for certain values of its inputs. The individual
 * tasks are described as tests below.
 *
 * <p>
 * Links of interest:
 * <ul>
 * <li>
 * <a href="http://en.wikipedia.org/wiki/Truth_table">
 * Truth table</a>
 * <li>
 * <a href="http://en.wikipedia.org/wiki/Tautology_(logic)">
 * Tautology</a>
 * </ul>
 */
public class CircuitTest extends TestCase {
    static {
        // your code shall run without any permissions
    }

    public CircuitTest(String testName) {
        super(testName);
    }

    protected void setUp() throws Exception {
    }

    protected void tearDown() throws Exception {
    }


    /**
```

```
 * Create a circuit to evaluate x1 and x2 and then
 * verify that its result is false for input (false, true) and
 * it is true for input (true, true).
 */
public void testX1andX2() {
    fail("task1");
}


/**
 * Create a circuit to evaluate (x1 and x2) or x3 and then
 * verify that its result is false for input (false, true, false) and
 * it is true for input (false, false, true).
 */
public void testX1andX2orX3() {
    fail("task2");
}
/**
 * Create a circuit to evaluate (x1 or not(x1)) and then
 * verify that its result is true for all values of x1.
 */
public void testAlwaysTrue() {
    fail("task3");
}


}
```

The goal was to create the API and then write an implementation for the three empty test cases. The three test cases were supposed to be run successfully against the API.

The reason the initial task of the API Design Fest was to create an API for boolean circuits is because the whole circuit is simply a net of connected circuit elements for NOT, AND, and OR operations, together with some input elements:

- NOT: Has one input and one output, and changes false on input to true on output and true to false.

- AND: Has two inputs and one output. The output is true only if both inputs are true, otherwise it is false.

- OR: Has two inputs and one output. The output is always true, except when both inputs are false.

As a result, the API is relatively small. It can be written in an hour or so. However, it's non-trivial, as most versions of the API allowed products of the API to be consumed by the API again, which created an interesting self reference. Evolving the reference could then lead to not-so-nice problems with backward compatibility. However, that was all in the future at that point. Even more interesting was the description of the initial tasks given in CircuitTest.java:

1. Create a circuit to evaluate x1 and x2 and then verify that its result is false for input (false, true) and that it's true for input (true, true).

2. Create a circuit to evaluate (x1 and x2) or x3 and then verify that its result is false for input (false, true, false) and that it's true for input (false, false, true).

3. Create a circuit to evaluate (x1 or not(x1)) and then verify that its result is true for all values of x1.

The API Design Fest participants did a really good job. Most of them managed to create their APIs after an hour of work. Most of the solutions were pretty inspiring and overall of a high quality.

Some of the solutions revealed problems in the organization of the API Design Fest. I want to mention them here so that others playing the same game can learn from them and make their own fests run more smoothly.

Problem of Nonpublic API Classes

At least two solutions forgot to make an important API class public (for example, the one in the day1/inputandoperation project). This mistake was not noticed at this stage of the API Design Fest. However, in later stages of the competition, this caused a lot of problems. This came about because the boolcircuit.CircuitTest test class and the suggested API's boolcircuit.Circuit class were in the same package. As a result, they could use package private and protected methods for calling each other, and nobody noticed until it was too late.

The lesson to learn is that when you run your own API Design Fest, the API class and test class should be in different packages. If you take this approach, the compiler will discover the usage of the non-API methods and fields.

The Immutability Problem

Developers working on the NetBeans Platform are pretty well trained in not exposing more than is needed, as advised in Chapter 5. As a result, many solutions were written minimalistically. Though they satisfied the given goals, they did nothing more than that. As a result, some of the solutions were not boolean circuits at all! These solutions satisfied all the explicitly given tasks. You could do the computations with AND, OR, and NOT elements. However, to run the same computation with different input values, you had to create a new boolean circuit each time! For example, this applies to day1/inputandoperation. See how the given use cases were dealt with in its API:

```
/**
 * Create a circuit to evaluate x1 and x2 and then
 * verify that its result is false for input (false, true) and
```

```
 * it is true for input (true, true).
 */
public void testX1andX2() {
    inTrue = Factory.createSimpleBooleanInput(true);
    inFalse = Factory.createSimpleBooleanInput(false);
    Operation op1 = Factory.createAndOperation(inFalse, inTrue);
    assertFalse(Circuit.evaluateBooleanOperation(op1));
    Operation op2 = Factory.createAndOperation(inTrue, inTrue);
    assertTrue(Circuit.evaluateBooleanOperation(op2));
}


/**
 * Create a circuit to evaluate (x1 and x2) or x3 and then
 * verify that its result is false for input (false, true, false) and
 * it is true for input (false, false, true).
 */
public void testX1andX2orX3() {
    inTrue = Factory.createSimpleBooleanInput(true);
    inFalse = Factory.createSimpleBooleanInput(false);
    Operation op1 = Factory.createAndOperation(inFalse, inTrue);
    Operation op2 = Factory.createOrOperation(
        Factory.createOperationBasedBooleanInput(op1), inFalse
    );
    assertFalse(Circuit.evaluateBooleanOperation(op2));

    op1 = Factory.createAndOperation(inFalse, inFalse);
    op2 = Factory.createOrOperation(
        Factory.createOperationBasedBooleanInput(op1), inTrue
    );
    assertTrue(Circuit.evaluateBooleanOperation(op2));
}
/**
 * Create a circuit to evaluate (x1 or not(x1)) and then
 * verify that its result is true for all values of x1.
 */
public void testAlwaysTrue() {
    inTrue = Factory.createSimpleBooleanInput(true);
    inFalse = Factory.createSimpleBooleanInput(false);
    Operation not = Factory.createNotOperation(inTrue);
    Operation or = Factory.createOrOperation(
        Factory.createOperationBasedBooleanInput(not), inTrue
    );
    assertTrue(Circuit.evaluateBooleanOperation(or));
    not = Factory.createNotOperation(inFalse);
    or = Factory.createOrOperation(
        Factory.createOperationBasedBooleanInput(not), inFalse
    );
```

```
    assertTrue(Circuit.evaluateBooleanOperation(or));
}
```

A similar situation came about in the day1/alwayscreatenewcircuit solution. As with the previous solution, it had a factory method that created a circuit element from an immutable boolean instead of having a slot that can change its value from true to false:

```
/**
 * Create a circuit to evaluate x1 and x2 and then
 * verify that its result is false for input (false, true) and
 * it is true for input (true, true).
 */
public void testX1andX2() {
    boolean x1 = true;
    boolean x2 = true;

    Circuit outputCircuit = Circuit.and(x1, x2);
    assertTrue(outputCircuit.output());

    x1 = false;
    x2 = true;
    outputCircuit = Circuit.and(x1, x2);
    assertFalse(outputCircuit.output());
}


/**
 * Create a circuit to evaluate (x1 and x2) or x3 and then
 * verify that its result is false for input (false, true, false) and
 * it is true for input (false, false, true).
 */
public void testX1andX2orX3() {
    boolean x1 = false;
    boolean x2 = true;
    boolean x3 = false;
    Circuit outputCircuit = Circuit.or(Circuit.and(x1,x2),x3);
    assertFalse(outputCircuit.output());

    x1 = false;
    x2 = false;
    x3 = true;
    outputCircuit = Circuit.or(Circuit.and(x1,x2),x3);
    assertTrue(outputCircuit.output());
}
/**
 * Create a circuit to evaluate (x1 or not(x1)) and then
 * verify that its result is true for all values of x1.
 */
public void testAlwaysTrue() {
```

```
    boolean x1 = true;
    Circuit outputCircuit = Circuit.or(x1,Circuit.negate(x1));
    assertTrue(outputCircuit.output());

    x1 = false;
    outputCircuit = Circuit.or(x1,Circuit.negate(x1));
    assertTrue(outputCircuit.output());
}
```

The root of this problem lies in the conflicting understandings of the problem that participants in the API Design Fest were supposed to tackle. I hadn't anticipated someone writing a "circuit" without allowing multiple evaluations with different input values. Some participants interpreted the task how I had intended them to, such as in the pin-based solution:

```
/**
 * Create a circuit to evaluate x1 and x2 and then
 * verify that its result is false for input (false, true) and
 * it is true for input (true, true).
 */
public void testX1andX2() throws Exception {
    Circuit c = Circuit.construct(
        Element.createAnd(
            Element.createInput(0),
            Element.createInput(1)
        )
    );

    assertFalse ("false AND true is false", c.evaluate(false, true));
    assertTrue ("true AND true is true", c.evaluate(true, true));
}


/**
 * Create a circuit to evaluate (x1 and x2) or x3 and then
 * verify that its result is false for input (false, true, false) and
 * it is true for input (false, false, true).
 */
public void testX1andX2orX3() throws Exception {
    Circuit c = Circuit.construct(
        Element.createOr(
            Element.createAnd(
                Element.createInput(0),
                Element.createInput(1)
            ),
            Element.createInput(2)
        )
    );

    assertFalse (
```

```
        "(false AND true) OR false is false",
        c.evaluate(false, true, false)
    );
    assertTrue (
        "(false AND false) OR true is true",
        c.evaluate(false, false, true)
    );
}

/**
 * Create a circuit to evaluate (x1 or not(x1)) and then
 * verify that its result is true for all values of x1.
 */
public void testAlwaysTrue() throws Exception {
    Circuit c = Circuit.construct(
        Element.createOr(
            Element.createInput(0),
            Element.createNot(Element.createInput(0))
        )
    );

    assertTrue ("tautology is true", c.evaluate(false));
    assertTrue ("tautology is true", c.evaluate(true));
}
```

However, other participants understood the problem area differently. As a result, their API solved slightly different tasks. That can happen. Some people, having faced the circuit problem before, understood its complexity. To others the problem was new and they did exactly what was required, but nothing more than that.

There is a simple piece of advice to offer here: always make sure you explain the problem domain clearly, so that every participant understands it and so that everyone tries to solve the same problem. However, this advice is not very useful. Experience shows that regardless of how much you try, there will always be problems like this. They can be minimized, but not prevented.

That is why the appropriate "structural" solution to this problem is to prepare for the need to insert a new round into the competition. In the new round, you should clearly specify the additional requirements that the API needs to fulfill. For example, specify that the solution needs to be able to run multiple computations on the same circuit. Then, give participants enough time to extend their existing solution. Of course, this means that those who "got it right" during the first round have nothing to do. However, aligning the solutions is of paramount importance here. For the subsequent tasks to succeed, it's important that every API is at a similar starting position.

The Problem of the Missing Implementation

There was one creative and interesting solution to solving the boolean circuit problem. It was based on parsing. See the sources in day1/parsingsolution:

```java
/**
 * Usage:
 * The first method, parse, must be called with a valid logical expression on
 * input.
 * If it returns zero then it is possible to call the evaluate method with
 * array of input values as a parameter. The evaluate method can be invoked
 * many times with different input values.
 * The parse method can be called anytime to change logical expression.
 */
public class Circuit {

    /** Parses logical expression
     * @param string representation of logical expression
     * Valid tokens:
     * Input values are represented by x and number starting from 1 e.g.: x1
     * AND, NOT, OR, and brackets '(',')' can be used.
     * Example of valid expression: x1 AND x2
     * @return 0 when input expression is validated and parsed.
     * Return nonzero value otherwise.
     */
    public int parse(String expression) {
        return 0;
    }


    /** Evaluate logical expression
     * @param array of boolean input values. Size of array must
     * correspond to number of variables used in expression
     * If size of array is bigger then only first N values are used
     * to evaluate expression. Remaining values are ignored.
     * If size of array is smaller then IllegalArgumentException is thrown.
     * If no expression is set by the parse method then
     * IllegalStateException is thrown.
     */
    public boolean evaluate(boolean [] x) {
        return true;
    }

}
```

The solution focused on specifying the logical formula as a string in the form of x1 AND NOT(x1), parsing it into a representation of the circuit, and then allowing repetitive evaluations with different variables.

This was a nice and flexible solution. It was well documented, unlike some of the other solutions. However, it had one problem: it didn't provide an implementation. That was no surprise, because writing an expression parser in an hour isn't a simple task. Even Googling for an existing implementation and then implementing it might not be achievable within an hour. As a result, this solution could not advance to the next round.

It's important to explain to the participants explicitly that the API Design Fest is heavily focused on the problem of API evolution and on the related problem of functional backward compatibility. It's also important to repeat that the "API includes everything on which the user will need to depend," which includes an implementation! The point of the API Design Fest is to write a *functional* API. Its versions will be compared to each other. That is why the correct implementation of the API is necessary, while the Javadoc is pretty much useless.

The Problem of Possibly Incorrect Results

The last observed problem after Day 1 was that some implementations were incorrect or at least allowed misuse of the API. For example, the day1/stackbasedsolution sources follow:

```
/**
 * Create a circuit to evaluate x1 and x2 and then
 * verify that its result is false for input (false, true) and
 * it is true for input (true, true).
 */
public void testX1andX2() {
    Stack<Character> s = new Stack<Character> ();
    s.addAll(Arrays.asList('1', '1'));
    assertEquals("'1' for '11' input.", '1',
        CircuitFactory.getBasicCircuit(Operation.AND).evaluate(s));
    s.addAll(Arrays.asList('1', '0'));
    assertEquals("'0' for '10' input.", '0',
        CircuitFactory.getBasicCircuit(Operation.AND).evaluate(s));
}


/**
 * Create a circuit to evaluate (x1 and x2) or x3 and then
 * verify that its result is false for input (false, true, false) and
 * it is true for input (false, false, true).
 */
public void testX1andX2orX3() {
    Stack<Character> s = new Stack<Character> ();
    s.addAll(Arrays.asList('0', '1', '0'));
    assertEquals("'0' for '010' input.", '0',
        CircuitFactory.join(CircuitFactory.getTrivialCircuit(),
        CircuitFactory.getBasicCircuit(Operation.OR),
        Operation.AND).evaluate(s)
    );
    s.addAll(Arrays.asList('0', '0', '1'));
    assertEquals("'1' for '001' input.", '1',
        CircuitFactory.join(CircuitFactory.getTrivialCircuit(),
        CircuitFactory.getBasicCircuit(Operation.OR),
        Operation.AND).evaluate(s)
    );
}
/**
```

```
 * Create a circuit to evaluate (x1 or not(x1)) and then
 * verify that its result is true for all values of x1.
 */
public void testAlwaysTrue() {
    Circuit alwaysTrue = CircuitFactory.join(
        CircuitFactory.getTrivialCircuit(),
        CircuitFactory.getBasicCircuit(Operation.NEG),
        Operation.OR
    );
    Stack<Character> s = new Stack<Character> ();
    s.addAll(Arrays.asList('0', '0'));
    assertEquals ("'1' for '00'", '1', alwaysTrue.evaluate(s));
    s.addAll(Arrays.asList('1', '1'));
    assertEquals ("'1' for '11'", '1', alwaysTrue.evaluate(s));
}
```

This solution required a value of each variable to be specified on input as many times as it was used. As a result, the evaluation of x1 OR NOT(x1) is a tautology, because it's a logical expression that is always true. However, some of the APIs sometimes allowed it to yield false, in case the input of the API was not consistent.

Again, this solution satisfied all the tasks for the API Design Fest and was therefore accepted into the next round. However, it's different from the others. Because the starting line for the next round should be the same point for the whole solution, the appropriate action should have been to insert a "Day 1 and a half" round, during which time the APIs should have been fixed so that they reached a similar level.

Solutions for Day 1

The APIs for the representation of boolean circuits created during the first day of the API Design Fest were divided into various groups. The most common group represents a classic example of the defensive programming approach: "Never expose more than you need to expose." Although there were small differences, these solutions included day1/alwayscreatenewcircuit, day1/inputandoperation, day1/pinbasedsolution, day1/elementbasedsolution, and partially also day1/stackbasedsolution. These don't expose constructors. They use factory methods. They provide classes that should not be subclassed. They use package private methods for mutual communication. In other words, these solutions are examples of the "less is more" design approach. Here is the sample code of day1/elementbasedsolution, which has not yet been discussed:

```
public final class Circuit {
    private Circuit() {
    }

    public static Element and(final Element e1, final Element e2) {
        return new Element() {
            public boolean result() {
                return e1.result() && e2.result();
            }
        }
```

```
        };
    }
    public static Element or(final Element e1, final Element e2) {
        return new Element() {
            public boolean result() {
                return e1.result() || e2.result();
            }
        };
    }

    public static Element not(final Element e1) {
        return new Element() {
            public boolean result() {
                return !e1.result();
            }
        };
    }

    public static Variable var() {
        return new Variable();
    }

    public static abstract class Element {
        private Element() {
        }

        public abstract boolean result();
    }

    public static final class Variable extends Element {
        private boolean value;

        public void assignValue(boolean b) {
            value = b;
        }

        public boolean result() {
            return value;
        }
    }
}
```

Exceptional in its implementation was the day1/parsingsolution. It didn't contain the implementation, as it would have been difficult to write an expression parser as well as its implementation during the hour assigned to the first day's task. The slight mistake here lies in the fact that the Circuit class isn't final, which would likely cause problems in the next round of the API Design Fest.

Special attention should be paid to the day1/subclassingsolution. Here is the code of its API:

```java
/** Useful class for building your own circuits.
 *
 */
public abstract class Circuit extends Object {

    /** For your convenience */
    public static Circuit AND = new Circuit() {

        @Override
        public boolean evaluate(boolean[] in) {
            if ( in.length != 2) {
                throw new IllegalArgumentException(
                    "Should have two parameters"
                );
            }
            return in[0] && in[1];
        }

    };

    public static Circuit OR = new Circuit() {

        @Override
        public boolean evaluate(boolean[] in) {
            if ( in.length != 2) {
                throw new IllegalArgumentException(
                    "Should have two parameters"
                );
            }
            return in[0] || in[1];
        }

    };

    public static Circuit NOT = new Circuit() {

        @Override
        public boolean evaluate(boolean[] in) {
            if ( in.length != 1) {
                throw new IllegalArgumentException(
                    "Should have one parameter"
                );
            }
            return !in[0];
        }
    }
```

```
};


/** Feel free to implement and don't hesitate to throw
 * IllegalArgumentEception
 */
public abstract boolean evaluate(boolean... in);


}
```

This solution takes a unique approach to the API problem. It doesn't solve the problem on the level of data structures as the other solutions did. Instead, it operates on the level of meta-data structures; that is, models of data structures. While the other solutions have instances that represent the actual elements in the circuit, the instances in this solution represent *types of elements*. In fact, only three types are predefined: AND, OR, and NOT. Indeed, this is a small trick as it requires subclassing and doesn't allow composition. However, it's an example of a slightly unexpected "meta" approach to solving the problem. It's not surprising that this solution was written by the NetBeans metamodeling framework (MOF, UML, MDR) expert . . .

Day 2

The requirements imposed on every API *change over its lifetime*. The API Design Fest's boolean circuit is no exception. Quite the opposite, in fact: it boosts the frequency of changes to the limit. That is why the main goal of the second day was to absorb a set of significant changes to the requirements. The changes needed to be implemented in a compatible way so that all usages of the API from the first day continued to work. To simulate that, all the participants received a new test class RealTest.java containing new tasks. The participants had to modify their APIs so that they worked for the old implementations as well as for their new ones.

```
/** This file contains the API Fest quest for day 2. Simply turn the
 * boolean circuit into a circuit that can compute with double
 * values from 0 to 1.
 * <p>
 * This means that wherever a boolean was used to represent input or
 * output values, one can now use any double number from >= 0 and <= 1.
 * Still, to support backward compatibility, the operations with booleans
 * have to be kept available and have to work. In fact False shall be
 * treated as 0 and True as 1.
 * <p>
 * The basic elements have to be modified to work on doubles
 * in the following way:
 * <ul>
 * <li>negation - neg(x) = 1 - x, this is a correct extension as
 * neg(false)=neg(0)=1-0=1=true
 * <li>and - and(x,y) = x * y, again this is fine as
 * and(true,true)=1*1=true and also
 * and(false,true)=0*1=0=false
```

```
 * <li>or - or(x,y) = 1 - (1 - x) * (1 - y) and this is also okay as
 * or(false,false) = 1 - (1 - 0) * (1 - 0) = 1 - 1 = 0 = false
 * or(true,false) = 1 - (1 - 1)*(1 - 0) = 1 - 0 * 1 = 1 = true
 * </ul>
 * <p>
 * However, as the circuits with doubles are more rich than plain boolean
 * circuits, there is an additional requirement to allow any user of your API
 * to write its own "element" type. This is all going to be an exercise in
 * the tests below that you are supposed to implement.
 */
public class RealTest extends TestCase {
    static {
        // your code shall run without any permissions
    }

    public RealTest(String testName) {
        super(testName);
    }



    /** First of all create a circuit that will evaluate
     * expression (X1 and X2) or not(x1). Hold the circuit
     * in some variable.
     *
     * Feed this circuit with x1=true, x2=false, assert result is false
     *
     * Feed the same circuit with x1=false, x2=true, assert result is
     * true
     *
     * Feed the same circuit with x1=0.0, x2=1.0, assert result is 1.0
     *
     * Feed the same circuit with x1=0.5, x2=0.5, assert result is 0.625
     *
     * Feed the same circuit with x1=0.0, x2=2.0, make sure it
     * throws an exception
     */
    public void testX1andX2orNotX1() {
        fail("testX1andX2orNotX1");
    }

    /** Ensure that one variable cannot be filled with two different
     * values. Create a circuit for x1 and x1. Make sure that for any
     * usage of your API that would not lead to an x1 * x1 result, an
     * exception is thrown. For example, if there was a way to feed the
     * circuit with two different values 0.3 and 0.5, an exception is
     * thrown indicating that this is an improper use of the circuit.
     */
```

```java
public void testImproperUseOfTheCircuit() {
    fail("testImproperUseOfTheCircuit");
}

/** Write your own element type called "gte" that has two
 * inputs and one output.
 * The output value is 1 if x1 >= x2 and 0 otherwise.
 *
 * Create a
 * circuit for the following expression: (x1 and not(x1)) gte x1
 *
 * Feed the circuit with 0.5 and verify the result is 0
 *
 * Feed the same circuit with 1 and verify the result is 0
 *
 * Feed the same circuit with 0 and verify the result is 1
 */
public void testGreaterThanEqualElement() {
    fail("testGreaterThanEqualElement");
}
}
```

However, because the styles of the solutions from the first day had turned out to be so different from one another, participants first had to get their APIs to a similar level. In some cases, the boolean circuit could not be reused multiple times, which undermined the purpose of creating a circuit. Those solutions that suffered from this problem needed to be fixed during the second day's tasks. Another problem was that some APIs allowed improper usage of the circuit. They allowed a circuit representing a tautology to evaluate to `false`. This also needed to be fixed and in a backward-compatible way, which was quite challenging.

In an ideal world, these two tasks, serving no other purpose than the alignment of the competitors, would have been done in isolation, without the participants knowing the major task of Day 2. However, as we had only had two days for the coding part of the API Design Fest, this work had to be done at the same time. This had several drawbacks, such as that some participants had a difficult time fixing their design while simultaneously implementing the new features for Day 2. On top of that, the new feature was complex and difficult to implement. Mainly, it involved turning the boolean circuit into a "probability" circuit, meaning something that is computed on real values ranging from `0.0` to `1.0` and represented by `doubles`.

Wherever a boolean was used to represent input or output values, participants now had to use a double number x, where x `>=` 0 and x `<=` 1. To support backward compatibility, the operations with the booleans had to be kept available and had to continue to work. Therefore, `false` had to be treated as 0 and `true` as 1.

The basic elements had to be modified to work on doubles in the following way:

- *Negation:* $neg(x) = 1 - x$. This is a correct extension, as `neg(false)=neg(0)=1-0=1=true`.

- and: $and(x,y) = x * y$. Again, this is fine, as and(`true,true`)=1*1=`true` and also and(`false,true`)=0*1=0=`false`.

- or: $or(x,y) = 1 - (1 - x) * (1 - y)$. This is also okay, as $or(false,false) = 1 - (1 - 0) * (1 - 0) = 1 - 1 = 0 = false$. And, for example, $or(true,false) = 1 - (1 - 1) * (1 - 0) = 1 - 0 * 1 = 1 = true$.

To prevent "cheating," whereby a completely new API would be created without any connection to the previous one, the new API had to support the single creation of a circuit that could later be fed with double inputs and subsequently with boolean inputs. Moreover, regardless of how the circuit was constructed, it was also supposed to create the same instance of the object that existed during Day 1. It should operate in the same way and be evaluated using the APIs existing on the first day. This prevents completely independent APIs from being written for Day 2!

Additionally, another task would have been better left for API Design Fest Day 3 or 4. Due to lack of time, we had to focus on this task on Day 2 as well. As the circuits with doubles are richer than plain boolean circuits, there is the additional requirement of allowing any users of the API to write their own "element" type. The task instructed that now the API should not allow just composition of elements, but also allow others to write their own plug-ins for the circuit elements. The individual tasks were as follows:

1. First of all, create a circuit that evaluates expression (x1 and x2) or *not*(x1). Hold the circuit in some variable.

   a. Feed this circuit with x1=true, x2=false, assert result is false.

   b. Feed the same circuit with x1=false, x2=true, assert result is true.

   c. Feed the same circuit with x1=0.0, x2=1.0, assert result is 1.0.

   d. Feed the same circuit with x1=0.5, x2=0.5, assert result is 0.625.

   e. Feed the same circuit with x1=0.0, x2=2.0, make sure it throws an exception.

2. Ensure that one variable cannot be filled with two different values. Create a circuit for x1 and x1. Make sure that an exception is thrown for any usage of your API that would not lead to an x1 * x1 result. For example, if there is a way to feed the circuit with the two different values 0.3 and 0.5, an exception should be thrown indicating that this is an improper use of the circuit.

3. Write your own element type called gte that has two inputs and one output. The output value will be 1 if x1 >= x2 and 0 otherwise. Create a circuit for the expression (x1 and not(x1)) gte x1:

   a. Feed the circuit with 0.5 and verify the result is 0.

   b. Feed the same circuit with 1 and verify the result is 0.

   c. Feed the same circuit with 0 and verify the result is 1.

Now is the right time to try the quest yourself! Get RealTest.java, put it into your project from Day 1, and rewrite your API to satisfy the individual tasks. Do it now or it will be too late, because the best approach to solve the problem is about to be revealed in the following paragraphs!

There are two ways to solve the problem. The first approach is to enhance the existing interfaces and classes in the API to accommodate operations on "probability" circuits. The second approach is to write the API from scratch and to provide a bridge that allows conversion of the boolean circuit and the "probability" circuit from one to the other. You can construct the circuit once and then evaluate it with booleans and doubles later. As all the solutions from Day 1 correctly expected some kind of evolution, all the participants chose to enhance their interfaces. Nobody decided to write a bridge. This was probably a good choice, as creating a proper bridge is significantly more work.

I Want to Fix My Mistakes Problem

In contrast to Day 1, there were no misunderstandings about the description of the tasks on Day 2. However, a feeling amounting to "this isn't nice and needs to be fixed" was noticeable in some cases. Some participants realized that their solution from the previous day was not optimal. They wanted to fix it. However, when fixing a part of an API, you run the risk of creating an incompatible change. It became necessary to explain to some of the participants that the API Design Fest is nothing more than a contest about compatibility. It has nothing to do with beauty. Fixing something that a participant deems ugly isn't necessarily an optimal way of spending time. The goal is simply to enable the API to evolve while maintaining backward compatibility.

Solutions for Day 2

Those who didn't allow multiple execution on the same circuit experienced slight problems with their implementations. Similarly, those who allowed inconsistent evaluations faced significant problems too. They had a lot of tweaking and catching up to do throughout the day. The solutions alwayscreatenewcircuit, inputandoperation, and stackbasedsolution had to begin by fixing problems and only later were able to proceed with the new tasks.

Sooner or later, participants began with the day's real task: the extension of their circuit's capabilities to cover double values ranging from 0.0 to 1.0. Participants used one of two approaches to make their extensions. Some anticipated during Day 1 that extensions would later be needed. They made the class responsible for the computation nonsubclassable during the first day. As a result, they could add a new method to it to perform the operations on doubles. This was the case for alwayscreatenewcircuit, elementbasedsolution, inputandoperation, pinbasedsolution, and welltestedsolution. All these APIs could make use of the benefits of having a nonsubclassable class that could easily be enhanced with new methods during the API's evolution without breaking existing clients.

The other solutions, namely subclassingsolution and stackbasedsolution, represented the circuit element as a subclassable class. As a result, they could not compatibly enhance their classes. They needed to add new classes to represent the circuit with enhanced capabilities. As a result, subclassingsolution introduced FuzzyCircuit. Similarly, stackbasedsolution introduced Circuit2. The idea was the same in each case: give the API users a new method without breaking code that might have implemented their own subclass. See the following:

```java
public interface Circuit2 extends Circuit {
    public double evaluate (double ... input)
    throws IllegalArgumentException;
}
```

Both these approaches are possible, yet both can be dangerous. The danger of adding new interfaces is that the user might find the interface difficult to use. It's particularly difficult to decide when to use the simple interface and when to use the enhanced version. Users can confuse the return types of methods and the types of fields. Enhancing an existing nonsubclassable class with a new method is nicer for clients, but it can be dangerous because of uncertain cooperation between the new and old methods. The participant needs to be careful to do this right.

All the participants on Day 2 of the API Design Fest were able to satisfy the requirements and fulfilled all the given tasks. All the solutions qualified for the final round. You can look for various implementations of RealTest.java in the day2/alwayscreatenewcircuit, day2/inputandoperation, day2/elementbasedsolution, day2/subclassingsolution, day2/pinbasedsolution, day2/stackbasedsolution, and day2/welltestedsolution projects for the actual code. For purposes of this book, I've chosen just one. This is the code provided by day2/welltestedsolution:

```java
public class RealTest extends TestCase {
    static {
        // your code shall run without any permissions
    }

    public RealTest(String testName) {
        super(testName);
    }

    protected void setUp() throws Exception {
    }

    protected void tearDown() throws Exception {
    }


    /** First of all create a circuit that will evaluate
     * expression (X1 and X2) or not(x1). Hold the circuit
     * in some variable.
     *
     * Feed this circuit with x1=true, x2=false, assert result is false
     *
     * Feed the same circuit with x1=false, x2=true, assert result is
     * true
     *
     * Feed the same circuit with x1=0.0, x2=1.0, assert result is 1.0
     *
     * Feed the same circuit with x1=0.5, x2=0.5, assert result is 0.625
     *
     * Feed the same circuit with x1=0.0, x2=2.0
     * , make sure it throws an exception
     */
```

```
public void testX1andX2orNotX1() {
    Circuit c = Circuit.createOrCircuit(
        Circuit.createAndCircuit(Circuit.input(0),
        Circuit.input(1)),
        Circuit.createNotCircuit(Circuit.input(0))
    );
    assertFalse("true, false", c.evaluate(true, false));
    assertTrue("false, true", c.evaluate(false, true));
    assertEquals("0.0, 1.0", 1.0, c.evaluateFuzzy(0.0, 1.0), 0.0);
}

/** Ensure that one variable cannot be filled with two different
 * values. Create a circuit for x1 and x1. Make sure that for any
 * usage of your API that would not lead to an x1 * x1 result, an
 * exception is thrown. For example, if there was a way to feed the
 * circuit with two different values 0.3 and 0.5, an exception is
 * thrown indicating that this is an improper use of the circuit.
 */
public void testImproperUseOfTheCircuit() {
    // does not apply

    Circuit x1 = Circuit.input(0);
    Circuit c = Circuit.createOrCircuit(x1, x1);
    assertTrue("x1 or x1", c.evaluate(true));
    assertFalse("x1 or x1", c.evaluate(false));
    try {
        c.evaluate();
        fail("x1 or x1 with wrong params");
    } catch (IllegalArgumentException iea) {
        //expected
    }
    // the same with two instances of pin
    c = Circuit.createOrCircuit(Circuit.input(0), Circuit.input(0));
    assertTrue("x1 or x1", c.evaluate(true));
    assertTrue("x1 or x1", c.evaluate(true, false));
    assertTrue("x1 or x1", c.evaluate(true, true));
    assertFalse("x1 or x1", c.evaluate(false));
    try {
        c.evaluate();
        fail("x1 or x1 with wrong params");
    } catch (IllegalArgumentException iea) {
        //expected
    }
}
```

```
/** Write your own element type called "gte" that
 * will have two inputs and one output.
 * The output value will be 1 if x1 >= x2 and 0 otherwise.
 *
 * Create a
 * circuit for the following expression: (x1 and not(x1)) gte x1
 *
 * Feed the circuit with 0.5 and verify the result is 0
 *
 * Feed the same circuit with 1 and verify the result is 0
 *
 * Feed the same circuit with 0 and verify the result is 1
 */
public void testGreaterThanEqualElement() {
    Circuit gte = new Gte(Circuit.createAndCircuit(
        Circuit.input(0),
        Circuit.createNotCircuit(Circuit.input(0))),
        Circuit.input(0)
    );
    assertEquals("0.5", 0.0, gte.evaluateFuzzy(0.5), 0.0);
    assertEquals("1.0", 0.0, gte.evaluateFuzzy(1.0), 0.0);
    assertEquals("0.0", 1.0, gte.evaluateFuzzy(0.0), 0.0);

}


public void testSilly() {
    // (x1 and not x2) or x3
    Circuit c = Circuit.createOrCircuit(
        Circuit.createAndCircuit(
        null,
        Circuit.createNotCircuit(null)),
        null
    );
    assertEquals("1 1 1", 1.0, c.evaluateFuzzy(1.0, 1.0, 1.0), 0.0);
    assertEquals("1 1 0", 0.0, c.evaluateFuzzy(1.0, 1.0, 0.0), 0.0);
    assertEquals("1 0 1", 1.0, c.evaluateFuzzy(1.0, 0.0, 1.0), 0.0);
    assertEquals("1 0 0", 1.0, c.evaluateFuzzy(1.0, 0.0, 0.0), 0.0);
    assertEquals("0 1 1", 1.0, c.evaluateFuzzy(0.0, 1.0, 1.0), 0.0);
    assertEquals("0 1 0", 0.0, c.evaluateFuzzy(0.0, 1.0, 0.0), 0.0);
    assertEquals("0 0 1", 1.0, c.evaluateFuzzy(0.0, 0.0, 1.0), 0.0);
    assertEquals("0 0 0", 0.0, c.evaluateFuzzy(0.0, 0.0, 0.0), 0.0);
}
}
```

Day 3: Judgment Day

Up to this point, all the participants had only played on their own field. Honestly, they had played pretty well! But now the time had come to evaluate the work done by others.

In some ways, the API Design Fest was a competition. However, by no means was it a beauty contest! The verbs "to like," "to love," and "to hate" have no meaning in this context. No jury decides which API is the best. Instead, it was each participant's turn to identify holes in the evolutionary plans in the APIs written by the others. For every broken API identified, they received one point, and five points if their own API remained unbroken. The destiny of each API was in the hands of each of the participants.

How do you write a test proving there is an incompatibility problem? You can copy the sample infrastructure project from apifest1/day3-intermezzo/jtulach/against-pinbasedsolution/. Play with it and try to look for incompatibilities, either in the source or in the binary. The advice given to the participants was to put the sources in a folder named yourname/against-nameofapi. Each of these folders had to have a build.xml Ant file that would demonstrate the evolution problems. The more problems found, the more points scored.

A prepared project.properties file needs to be modified. Change the name of the API that you want to work against and change the relative location (if wrong). Then you should have code completion, and also be able to compile, run, and test from inside the NetBeans IDE. As usual in the NetBeans IDE, the sample infrastructure is fully based on Ant, so you can also use the script directly from a command line. Just execute the right build.xml.

The build.xml compiles your test file against an API from Day 1 and makes sure that your test succeeds against the implementation from day1. Then it runs the same test against the implementation from Day 2. If the test run fails, the script succeeds, as you've found an incompatibility. This should identify binary and functional incompatibilities. Additionally, the API also compiles against the Day 2 API and if the compilation fails, the test also succeeds, as you've probably found a source incompatibility.

Now I'll spend some time discussing the rules for finding incompatibilities. First of all, rules are difficult to define because some developers are good hackers who can invent many ways of working around rules. The general principle is: the fewer tricks you use to show an incompatibility, the better! If two solutions show an incompatibility in the same API, the one that uses fewer tricks wins. Now what do I mean by "trick" in this context? At runtime, a trick includes java.security.Permission. The fewer permissions you need to run your code, the better. For example, don't try to use ReflectionPermission, which would indeed show an incompatibility in every solution. Don't use Class.forName(...). That would be too easy, as probably every API added a new class in Day 2. Class.getName() is also a pretty crazy trick, but it might be allowed in some situations. Also, notice that you may use new threads, but starting a new thread requires permission. If two solutions show an incompatibility and one uses more threads, guess which one will be preferred? Also, don't use wildcard imports in the sources. import something.* is a language construct that can break compilation against any API that adds a new class, so import fully qualified names. As you can see, the range of tricks is probably unlimited, so remember the general principle: the fewer tricks, the better.

WANNA HACK?

Wanna try hacking yourself? Few things are simpler: just download the solutions and the sample testing project template and try to find an incompatibility between the two versions of an API!

Conclusions

Day 3 started on Friday afternoon and ended on Sunday. Maybe this was one of the reasons why few people decided to participate in this round. Another reason might have included problems in understanding how to use the testing infrastructure, as well as the fact that looking at code created by others might be considered to be slightly tedious.

Thank goodness we had Petr Nejedlý! He not only wrote a solution that turned out to be unbreakable, but he also managed to break all the other APIs. Sometimes he used unfair methods, such as $getClass().getSuperclass()$ and $getClass().getName()$. Still, being able to find an evolution problem in each API deserves a round of applause. No surprise that Petr won API Design Fest One.

What Was Wrong with subclassingsolution and stackbasedsolution?

The author of the subclassingsolution identified his biggest problem as having made the AND, OR, and NOT constants nonfinal. However, he was wrong. The API's biggest problem was that one class, Circuit, was used as two types of API: the API that people call, as well as the API that people subclass and implement. This, indeed, is a basic design dilemma. Evolution using FuzzyCircuit was in fact the correct approach. Still, you need to remember that changing the type of a field, parameter, or return type breaks binary compatibility in Java. The class file format includes not only the name of the field, but also its type. If the type changes, the application classes compiled independently might not link together. As a result, the following test compiles against both versions. But if it's compiled against a version from Day 1 and then run against a version from Day 2, it produces a NoFieldFoundError and fails:

```
public class CircuitTest extends TestCase {
    public CircuitTest(String n) {
        super(n);
    }

    public void testClass() throws Exception {
        Circuit c = Circuit.AND;
    }
}
```

A similar problem confronted the author of stackbasedsolution. The solution changed the return type of one method. Again, this isn't a binary compatible change and causes NoMethodFoundError to be thrown:

```
public class CircuitTest extends TestCase {
    public CircuitTest(String n) {
        super(n);
```

```
    }

    public void testClass() throws Exception {
        Circuit c = CircuitFactory.getBasicCircuit(null);
    }
}
```

What Was Wrong with inputandoperation?

day1/inputandoperation was a well-designed solution. It was nearly unbreakable. However, there was a problem: its Circuit.java was not final. Also, a new method was added to it during Day 2:

```
public static double evaluateRealOperation(Operation op) {
    return op.performRealOperation();
}
```

Although the method was static, it was easy to write a test that defines the same method of the same name in a subclass of that class. Such code compiles fine against the Day 1 version, but fails to compile against the Day 2 library:

```
public class CircuitTest extends TestCase {
    public CircuitTest(String n) {
        super(n);
    }

    public void testSourceCompatibility() throws Exception {
    }

    // One forgotten final and disaster is here.
    class MyCircuit extends Circuit {
        public double evaluateRealOperation(Operation op) {
            return 0;
        }
    }
}
```

The lesson to take from this is never to forget to add a private constructor, a final keyword, or both to most of the classes exposed in the APIs. Otherwise, the API clients can do unexpected things while using it, such as subclassing classes not intended to be treated that way.

What Was Wrong with alwayscreatenewcircuit and welltestedsolution?

In short, nothing was wrong with these solutions. Petr managed to break both APIs, but only by using unfair tricks! In one case, he exploited a rename of the implementation class, as in the following test:

```
public class CircuitTest extends TestCase {
```

```
    public CircuitTest(String n) {
        super(n);
    }

    public void testClass() throws Exception {
        // Okay, this is not fair as well.
        assertEquals("Created AND circuit", "AndCircuit",
            getName(Circuit.createAndCircuit(null, null))
        );
        assertEquals("Created OR circuit", "OrCircuit",
            getName(Circuit.createOrCircuit(null, null))
        );
    }

    private String getName(Object obj) {
        String base = obj.getClass().getName();
        int lastDot = base.lastIndexOf('.');
        int last = base.lastIndexOf('$');
        if (lastDot > last) last = lastDot;
        return base.substring(last+1);
    }
}
```

He was also able to spot a change in the hierarchy of superclasses in the alwayscreatenewcircuit solution:

```
public class CircuitTest extends TestCase {
    public CircuitTest(String n) {
        super(n);
    }

    public void testReallyUnrealistic() throws Exception {
        // Okay, this is not fair, right?
        assertEquals(null, Circuit.or(false, false).getClass().
                getSuperclass().getSuperclass().getSuperclass());
    }
}
```

None of these tricks deal with aspects that are typically considered to be part of an API contract. Most would agree that these are implementation details. However, it's still good to bear in mind that even changes such as this can be observed from outside the code, even without using any special permissions, and therefore this kind of code can be broken.

Because both authors were in a hurry, as they needed to do additional rewrites at the start of Day 2, they solved the problem of allowing clients to write their own circuit elements by making the Circuit class subclassable. As a result, the class began playing two roles: being part of the APIs that clients call as well as part of those that clients implement. These two solutions would have a difficult time evolving coherently in future iterations of the API. For example, a request to add a unique ID to each circuit element could lead to possible evolution problems,

similar to what happened in the case of inputandoperation. A much better approach is to add an
additional interface and factory method as done by the pinbasedsolution's createGate:

```
/**
 * An abstract transfer function of a gate.
 */
public abstract class Function {
    public abstract double evaluate(double input1, double input2);
}
/**
 * Creates an Element with user-defined transfer function.
 */
public static Element createGate(
    final Element source1, final Element source2, final Function function
) {
    return new Element() {
        double evaluate(double[] inputs) {
            double x = source1.evaluate(inputs);
            double y = source2.evaluate(inputs);
            double result = function.evaluate(x, y);
            if (result < 0.0 || result > 1.0) {
                throw new InternalError("Illegal gate function");
            }
            return result;
        }

        int maxInput() {
            return Math.max(source1.maxInput(), source2.maxInput());
        }
    };
}
```

This approach fulfills the same functionality, but clearly separates the contract for callers
to the API from the contract for the implementors of the API.

What Was Wrong with elementbasedsolution?

The changes made to elementbasedsolution seemed unbreakable at first sight:

```
public final class Circuit {
    private Circuit() {
    }

    public static Element and(final Element e1, final Element e2) {
        return new Element() {
            public boolean result() {
                return e1.result() && e2.result();
            }
        }
```

```java
        public double doubleResult() {
            return e1.doubleResult() * e2.doubleResult();
        }
    };
}
public static Element or(final Element e1, final Element e2) {
    return new Element() {
        public boolean result() {
            return e1.result() || e2.result();
        }
        public double doubleResult() {
            return 1.0 -
                (1.0 - e1.doubleResult()) * (1.0 - e2.doubleResult());
        }
    };
}

public static Element not(final Element e1) {
    return new Element() {
        public boolean result() {
            return !e1.result();
        }
        public double doubleResult() {
            return 1 - e1.doubleResult();
        }
    };
}

public static Element operation(
    final Operation op, final Element... elements
) {
    return new Element() {
        public boolean result() {
            return doubleResult() >= 1.0;
        }
        public double doubleResult() {
            double[] arr = new double[elements.length];
            for (int i = 0; i < arr.length; i++) {
                arr[i] = elements[i].doubleResult();
            }
            return op.computeResult(arr);
        }
    };

}

public static Variable var() {
```

```java
        return new Variable();
    }

    public static abstract class Element {
        private Element() {
        }

        public abstract boolean result();
        public abstract double doubleResult();
    }

    public static final class Variable extends Element {
        private Boolean booleanValue;
        private Double doubleValue;

        public void assignValue(boolean b) {
            booleanValue = b;
        }
        public void assignValue(double d) {
            if (d < 0 || d > 1) {
                throw new IllegalArgumentException();
            }
            doubleValue = d;
        }

        public boolean result() {
            return booleanValue != null ?
                booleanValue : doubleValue >= 1.0;
        }
        public double doubleResult() {
            return doubleValue != null ?
                doubleValue : (booleanValue ? 1.0 : 0.0);
        }

    }

    public static interface Operation {
        public double computeResult(double... values);
    }
}
```

Still, Petr managed to find a sequence of calls and put them in a test that threw a NullPointerException when run in the Day 2 solution, even though it worked correctly in the Day 1 version:

```java
public class CircuitTest extends TestCase {
    public CircuitTest(String n) {
```

```
        super(n);
    }
    /**
     * Okay, elementbasedsolution looked bulletproof. Every code path
     * was exactly the same as in the initial version. Except one.
     */
    public void testEvaluateWithoutAssign() throws Exception {
        Circuit.Variable var = Circuit.var();
        Circuit.Element circuit = Circuit.not(var);

        assertTrue (circuit.result());
    }
}
```

Despite the fact that the API was able to evolve in a source- and binary-compatible way, it had not retained its *functional* compatibility. There was one sequence of calls that could produce different results in different versions. The lesson here is that any change to an API can introduce unwanted side effects. Regardless of how carefully you review changes, there can always be a corner case that remains unnoticed but that can exhibit incompatibilities between different versions of the API.

Play Too!

Running the API Design Fest with the NetBeans core team was fun and entertaining. Two days plus one judgment round were enough to select the winner. Nevertheless, it would have been more pleasant if there had been more rounds and if more time could have been spent on each round.

The main objective of the API Design Fest was to study the evolution of APIs. Backward compatibility was the primary focus, though this isn't the only property of a well-written and well-maintained API. The ability to design an API correctly, make it easy to understand, and document it clearly is crucial as well, though these aspects were not practiced during the API Design Fest.

API Design Fest One turned into a pretty successful event. It would be a shame if this was both the first and last such event, though. The number of APIs to practice evolution on is unlimited. There are many other evolution paths to enrich the game, even when only focusing on a boolean circuit. Imagine new tasks, such as support for multiple outputs, cyclic circuits, and ways of analyzing the structures of unknown circuits.

The API Design Fest is clearly a promising learning and training tool for those who design APIs, for students who need to learn about backward compatibility, and for anyone who likes the mental challenge of interesting puzzles of this kind.

CHAPTER 18

■■■

Extensible Visitor Pattern Case Study

Playing games is one possible road that leads to the learning of API design skills. Another is performing a different kind of mental exercise: finding an interesting problem, analyzing it, finding potential solutions, and deciding which is better and why. While doing this kind of exercise, you can often find yourself discovering surprising results that deepen your insight into the problem.

Let's go through one interesting example here. It started when I first heard about the JDK 1.6 proposal for a new API to model Java sources. An initial version of the API was included in JDK 1.5 in the apt tool, which could do postprocessing of annotations attached to classes, methods, and fields. It had to provide the model of the sources, which was more or less a reflection-like API, but focusing on sources. The apt tool used to have its packages in the com.sun.mirror package, which is not fully official. However, for JDK 1.6, the compiler team started a Java Specification Request (JSR) to define the official API placed in the javax.lang.model package. At that time, I found out about it and about its peer API that was about to define the model for the internals of method bodies.

What raised my interest in this topic was my awareness that the proposal for the evolution of the API claimed to be binary compatible, but source incompatible. Indeed, keeping source compatibility in Java is almost impossible: nearly any change in the API can break compilation of existing sources, as discussed in the section "Source Compatibility" in Chapter 4. However, this was a much bigger threat to compatibility: the plan was to add new methods into interfaces. This is binary compatible according to the virtual machine specification. However, for practical purposes it's not compatible at all. The system will link after you add a method to an interface, but it will throw runtime errors when someone calls a method on an interface that is not implemented. Needless to say, I don't like this kind of compatibility at all.

That is when I started my mental exercise to find a better solution. The compiler developers showed me a paper proposing a solution that would keep all kinds of compatibility based on generics; see "The Expression Problem Revisited."[1] However, they didn't want to use it, and looking at it, I understood why. The solution is heavily based on generics and difficult for normal developers to understand. You would need to study type theory at university for several years to understand what it's all about. This is an example of having a too-correct API: one that

---

1. Mads Torgersen, "The Expression Problem Revisited" in *ECOOP 2004 – Object Oriented Programming: 18th European Conference Oslo, Norway, June 14–18 2004, Proceedings*, ed. Martin Odersky, 123–146 (Berlin: Springer-Verlag, 2004).

you don't want to use because it might scare your users. No wonder the compiler team pre-ferred the solution involving adding methods into interfaces. For practical reasons it's easier, but as a mental exercise it's insufficient. So, let's look at other ways of solving the problem.

Although the javax.lang.model package initiated the problem, it's not restricted to that domain. In fact, it appears whenever you use a visitor in an API. Evolving a visitor is difficult. The methods in the visitor interface are defined once. However, the data structures it operates on might need to evolve. The question is what to do in this situation. Adding methods to the visitor interface is kind of a solution. However, it's a bit "bulldozer-like": not something a rational mind would be proud of. Meanwhile, mental exercises exist to tease the mind and stimulate it to search for beautiful, truthful, and elegant solutions!

The visitor pattern is well known. It separates operations, which are usually on hierarchical data structures, from the representation of data. It allows one team to provide the definition of data structures and a way to traverse them, while other teams can construct the data. Still other teams write the operations to be executed on them. The pattern is simple and easy to use. On the other hand, it contains hidden issues related to the evolution of the data interfaces, as well as the traversal interfaces.

First let's start with a simple example, slowly dig into its evolution problems, and change the solution to address them. In the end, a simple and elegant solution will address all the issues. However, the destination is not our only target, because the journey will be interesting as well. It will illustrate our chain of reasoning. It will also show valuable ideas that can be suf-ficient if you are not very strict and don't need a "truly" extensible visitor, but just something that is good enough.

The first step in thinking about the problem is to create an example case that motivates you to solve the problem. Visitors can be used in many situations, but the most useful situa-tions relate to traversing hierarchies of heterogeneous data structures. One of the most profound hierarchies is the one representing a tree of expressions, such as (1 + 2) * 3 - 8. Let's imagine that you want to represent a model for this simple expression language:

```java
public abstract class Expression {
    Expression() {}
    public abstract void visit(Visitor v);
}
public final class Plus extends Expression {
    private final Expression first;
    private final Expression second;

    public Plus(Expression first, Expression second) {
        this.first = first;
        this.second = second;
    }
    public Expression getFirst() { return first; }
    public Expression getSecond() { return second; }
    @Override
    public void visit(Visitor v) { v.visitPlus(this); }
}
public final class Number extends Expression {
    private final int value;
    public Number(int value) { this.value = value; }
```

```
    public int getValue() { return value; }
    @Override
    public void visit(Visitor v) { v.visitNumber(this); }
}

public interface Visitor {
    public void visitPlus(Plus s);
    public void visitNumber(Number n);
}
```

This gives you a model that can only represent numbers and the "plus" operation. However, it's powerful enough to create a structure for expressions such as 1 + 1 or 1 + 2 + 3. It also lets you easily create write operations on such models. For example, you can print any expression by writing the following:

```
public class PrintVisitor implements Visitor {
    StringBuffer sb = new StringBuffer();

    public void visitPlus(Plus s) {
        s.getFirst().visit(this);
        sb.append(" + ");
        s.getSecond().visit(this);
    }

    public void visitNumber(Number n) {
        sb.append (n.getValue());
    }
}

@Test public void printOnePlusOne() {
    Number one = new Number(1);
    Expression plus = new Plus(one, one);

    PrintVisitor print = new PrintVisitor();
    plus.visit(print);

    assertEquals("1 + 1", print.sb.toString());
}
```

These are all well-known basics from any programming book. However, let's simulate some problems now. Let's evolve the language by improving it to support yet another construct. Imagine you want to add -. It's natural to then introduce a new class:

```
/** @since 2.0 */
public final class Minus extends Expression {
    private final Expression first;
    private final Expression second;

    public Minus(Expression first, Expression second) {
```

```
        this.first = first;
        this.second = second;
    }
    public Expression getFirst() { return first; }
    public Expression getSecond() { return second; }
    public void visit(Visitor v) {
        /* now what? add new method to an interface!? */
        v.visitMinus(this);
    }
}
```

However, simply adding the data class is not enough. You also need to enhance the Visitor with a new visitMinus method. However, this is easier said than done because adding the method into an interface is not compatible evolution. It might not fail during linkage, although the old code is no longer compilable against the new version of the Visitor interface. The new version adds a new unimplemented method. Also, execution will fail with java.lang. AbstractMethodError as soon as someone tries to feed the old visitor with new data structures:

```
Number one = new Number(1);
Number two = new Number(2);
Expression plus = new Minus(one, two);

PrintVisitor print = new PrintVisitor();
plus.visit(print); // fails with AbstractMethodError

assertEquals("1 - 2", print.sb.toString());
```

It appears that an inevitable evolution problem is hidden in this popular design pattern. It might work fine for the design of in-house systems, but as soon as it appears in a publicly available API, it almost immediately renders itself nonextensible. That is why this pattern is not suitable for designing a universe, at least not in its current form. You need to find a clever reincarnation of a visitor that will be appropriate for the API design pattern constraints. The reincarnation will be discussed as part of the mental exercise that you'll perform in the following sections.

Abstract Class

First, a simple and more or less workable solution is to turn the Visitor into an abstract class. Indeed, abstract classes are said to be useless in the section "Are Abstract Classes Useful?" in Chapter 6. However, if you need a trivial form of evolution, you cannot stop thinking about them. They are the most instantly available solutions in Java if you need subclassability and yet a relatively low risk of having new methods added. Instead of using an interface in the first version of the API, if you decide to use an abstract class with all methods abstract, you have the following opportunity to enhance the visitor in version 2.0, after introducing the Minus class:

```
/** @since 2.0 */
public final class Minus extends Expression {
```

```java
    private final Expression first;
    private final Expression second;

    public Minus(Expression first, Expression second) {
        this.first = first;
        this.second = second;
    }
    public Expression getFirst() { return first; }
    public Expression getSecond() { return second; }
    public void visit(Visitor v) {
        v.visitMinus(this);
    }
}


public abstract class Visitor {
    public abstract void visitPlus(Plus s);
    public abstract void visitNumber(Number n);
    /** @since 2.0 */
    public void visitMinus(Minus s) {
        throw new IllegalStateException(
            "Old visitor used on new exceptions"
        );
    }
}
```

The `Minus.visit(Visitor)` calls the `visitMinus` method. The exception thrown in its default body is useful for developers who have written their own visitor in version 1.0 and want to use it with 2.0 data structures. As they have not overridden the method because they didn't know it was about to be added, it's relatively natural to get an exception, as this is an unexpected situation for the visitor. It's better to terminate the execution than to silently continue without any warning. Otherwise it would be hard to find potential behavior problems.

You might argue that adding a method into a class is not fully compatible. Existing subclasses might already have the method defined. The method might not be public—or even if it is, it can do something completely different from what it's supposed to do from version 2.0 onwards. However, with visitors, this is not the case. Along with adding a new method, you also add a new class. Because the bytecode of the virtual machine encodes the parameter types into the method identification, the method that would match the newly defined method could not exist, even if it had the same name.

This new "abstract class"–based version of the visitor only minimally differs from the classical visitor pattern with an interface. It promises to solve most of the evolution problems. It guarantees enough source compatibility. It's binary compatible. Of course, it throws exceptions when mixing old visitors with new language elements. However, that is just a small drawback. We've made significant progress; the visitor pattern is again in the game for helping us design our API universe.

Preparing for Evolution

There might be cases when throwing an exception is not appropriate default behavior. For example, when you want to verify whether the tree is valid for language version 1.0, you have to do the following:

```
private class Valid10Language extends Visitor/*version1.0*/ {
    public void visitPlus(Plus s) {
        s.getFirst().visit(this);
        s.getSecond().visit(this);
    }
    public void visitNumber(Number n) {
    }
}


public static boolean isValid10Language(Expression expression) {
    Valid10Language valid = new Valid10Language();
    try {
        expression.visit(valid);
        return true; // yes, no unknown elements
    } catch (IllegalStateException ex) {
        return false; // no, probably from visitMinus of Visitor/*2.0*/
    }
}
```

Writing this code is possible, but unusual. First of all, it uses exceptions for regular execution control and not for exceptional states. The second problem is that you have to know, at the time of writing, when only Visitor version 1.0 is available, all future methods are going to throw an exception. This can indeed be mentioned in documentation, but only if the author of the Visitor API is aware of its evolution problems. However, when the author is aware of them, there is a better approach. Moreover, there is also a third problem. You need to recognize that this exception is the right one, signaling a missing handler for the new element in the language. This might be difficult, as similar exceptions can also be thrown from other places. In short, this API is ugly, at least for this task.

Because you already know that the first version of an API is never perfect, it's better to prepare for evolution right from the start. You should look for a solution that will allow developers to handle unknown elements themselves. They can choose to throw an exception or they can do something more appropriate, as in the case of language validation. That is why it's much better if the first version of a Visitor immediately defines a fallback method:

```
public abstract class Visitor/*1.0*/ {
    public void visitUnknown(Expression exp) {
        throw new IllegalStateException("Unknown element faced: " + exp);
    }
    public abstract void visitPlus(Plus s);
    public abstract void visitNumber(Number n);
}
```

The `visitUnknown` method isn't called in the first version of the interface. However, it's there as an easily discoverable warning that there will be evolution. Then it will be the default fallback for all newly added expression constructs:

```
public abstract class Visitor/*2.0*/ {
    public void visitUnknown(Expression exp) {
        throw new IllegalStateException("Unknown element faced: " + exp);
    }
    public abstract void visitPlus(Plus s);
    public abstract void visitNumber(Number n);
    /** @since 2.0 */
    public void visitMinus(Minus s) {
        visitUnknown(s);
    }
}
```

Although the change is minimal and the default behavior remains the same—when an unknown element is faced, `IllegalStateException` is raised—this version is more polite to the API users who want to validate the expression tree. In this version you need no exception acrobatics:

```
private class Valid10Language extends Visitor/*version1.0*/ {
    boolean invalid;

    @Override
    public void visitUnknown(Expression exp) {
        invalid = true;
    }
    public void visitPlus(Plus s) {
        s.getFirst().visit(this);
        s.getSecond().visit(this);
    }
    public void visitNumber(Number n) {
    }
}

public static boolean isValid10Language(Expression expression) {
    Valid10Language valid = new Valid10Language();
    expression.visit(valid);
    return !valid.invalid;
}
```

By thinking in advance about evolution, you've allowed writers of the visitors to use the API in a much cleaner way, as the handling of all the unknown elements has been redirected into the `visitUnknown` method. This is where common handling can now be provided. This has greatly increased the capabilities of the API in this particular use case, while it has not negatively influenced any other existing usages. Only two abstract methods still need to be implemented, as before, and code that worked in the previous section continues to work without modifications.

Default Traversal

Remember that API users are always trying to stretch the design of your API to its limit, and that they always want to do more than you thought. It's fine to tell them that these are not valid use cases and that the API was not intended for their corner cases at all. However, the more use cases you support without overcomplicating the API, the more users of your API will be satisfied. The more satisfied users are, the more useful your API will be. That is why it makes sense to ask what is beyond the horizon of the current API and to determine what is genuinely impossible. A simple problem that the visitUnknown method doesn't support is the traversal of the whole structure of an expression while paying attention to selected nodes only. Indeed this is not a pure visitor pattern, it's more of a scanner; however, this little terminology issue won't prevent you from trying to find an optimal API to solve such problem. Such a scanner can easily be written for a static language. However, if the language evolves as the set of element grows, you'll have a problem. The obvious solution via visitors looks like the following:

```
private class CountNumbers extends Visitor/*version1.0*/ {
    int cnt;

    @Override
    public void visitUnknown(Expression exp) {
        // not a number
    }
    public void visitPlus(Plus s) {
        s.getFirst().visit(this);
        s.getSecond().visit(this);
    }
    public void visitNumber(Number n) {
        cnt++;
    }
}

public static int countNumbers(Expression expression) {
    CountNumbers counter = new CountNumbers();
    expression.visit(counter);
    return counter.cnt;
}
```

That solution might work well with language version 1.0, but as soon as you get language constructs containing Minus, everything goes wrong. You could override the visitUnknown method, but the question would be what to do in it? Probably nothing, but that is wrong, as the subtrees under Minus would be completely ignored and an expression such as 1 + (3 - 4) would be said to contain just one number:

```
Number one = new Number(1);
Number three = new Number(3);
Number four = new Number(4);
Expression minus = new Plus(one, new Minus(three, four));

assertEquals(
```

```
        "Should have three numbers, but visitor does not " +
        "know how to go through minus",
        3, CountNumbersTest.countNumbers(minus)
);
```

It's fine to know that you've reached an unknown element, but for a visitor searching for specific elements (as CountNumbers does), you would like to have the ability to do a "default visit." That would, in the case of Minus, only invoke *getFirst().visit(this)* and *getSecond(). visit(this)*. If you could use this "default visit" in visitUnknown, the amount of numbers in 1 + (3 - 4) would be correctly counted as 3, even if you used the old visitor written for the expression language version 1.0. The only question is how to invoke the "default visitor."

A naive idea would be to put this as the default implementation of every Visitor method. You can do that as Visitor is now a class. This won't work, because you cannot write Valid10 as I've discussed previously. There would be no place or situation where the visitUnknown method would be called. All the methods would have the default behavior, which is not what you want. You want to give users of the API a proper tool for various situations. They should be notified that there is an unexpected element in the expression tree. Only then should they decide what to do with it: whether to report it as an error, use it as an indication that their code should return false, or crawl through it and see what's underneath it. All these possibilities are valid use cases and should be supported, preferably in a way that allows the users of the API to make conscious decisions at the time of writing their code and that remain valid even if the API is enhanced with new elements and functionality. A possible enhancement is to allow the visitor implementation to decide whether unknown elements should be traversed or not by a return value of the visitUnknown method:

```
public abstract class Visitor/*1.0*/ {
    public boolean visitUnknown(Expression e) {
        throw new IllegalStateException("Unknown element faced: " + e);
    }
    public void visitPlus(Plus s) {
        if (visitUnknown(s)) {
            s.getFirst().visit(this);
            s.getSecond().visit(this);
        }
    }
    public void visitNumber(Number n) {
        visitUnknown(n);
    }
}
```

This way you get the default behavior for unknown elements, but can also decide to do nothing or even perform a "deep" default visit. With an API like this, you can perform every task I've asked for so far, even counting the amount of numbers in the expression tree:

```
private class CountNumbers extends Visitor/*version1.0*/ {
    int cnt;

    @Override
    public boolean visitUnknown(Expression exp) {
```

```
        return true;
    }
    @Override
    public void visitNumber(Number n) {
        cnt++;
    }
}

public static int countNumbers(Expression expression) {
    CountNumbers counter = new CountNumbers();
    expression.visit(counter);
    return counter.cnt;
}
```

This code not only works with one version of the API, but is ready to work forever. If the tree grows with new elements, the **return** true provided from the default method guarantees that all the elements will be processed. The actual traversal is left up to the provider of the API. The provider is also in control of all the API elements, which guarantees the consistency and proper behavior of this task.

Clean Definition of a Version

So far I've discussed what can happen when the Visitor is turned into an abstract class. Though everything has worked, notice that our original simple abstract class changed from having just a few abstract methods into a complicated combination of methods providing relatively complicated default behavior. The set of methods will grow with each new language version. Each new method will contain an @since description. It will be increasingly difficult to accept only language 7.0 and ignore expression elements from any other version of the language. Yet this seems like a reasonable API requirement. If I were to write a tool to process elements of a language, I would want to have a view of the structure of the elements as created for that particular version. Instead of subclassing one large class with visit methods accumulated over multiple releases and searching its Javadoc to identify which methods have been added for a particular version, I would want a clean interface that has only the methods I am interested in. This way, the compiler would give me confidence that I've implemented all the methods that are necessary during compilation. This is a much easier, and in fact, a more clueless approach than subclassing some methods and running the program, only to discover that some other method needs to be implemented as well, overriding it, and so on indefinitely. From this point of view, it would be much better if you had a separate interface for each version of the language. So you would have the following:

```
public interface Visitor {
    public void visitUnknown(Expression e);
}
public interface Visitor10 extends Visitor {
    public void visitPlus(Plus s);
    public void visitNumber(Number n);
}
/** @since 2.0 */
```

```java
public interface Visitor20 extends Visitor10 {
    public void visitMinus(Minus s);
}
```

The first version of the API includes one visitor only, while the second version needs to add a new element, as well as a new type of visitor. The subsequent changes to the API would increasingly add more. As a result, there would be many other interfaces, each for the traversal over expressions supported by the actual version of the language. However, this has a clear advantage: when you decide to implement visiting for version 7.0, you only implement Visitor70. That's just like when you want to print elements of language version 2.0: you can implement the right interface and it's guaranteed that all necessary visit methods for version 2.0 are provided:

```java
class PrintVisitor20 implements Visitor20 {
    StringBuffer sb = new StringBuffer();

    public void visitUnknown(Expression exp) {
        sb.append("unknown");
    }

    public void visitPlus(Plus s) {
        s.getFirst().visit(this);
        sb.append(" + ");
        s.getSecond().visit(this);
    }

    public void visitNumber(Number n) {
        sb.append (n.getValue());
    }
    public void visitMinus(Minus m) {
        m.getFirst().visit(this);
        sb.append(" - ");
        m.getSecond().visit(this);
    }
}
```

```java
Number one = new Number(1);
Number two = new Number(2);
Expression plus = new Minus(one, two);

PrintVisitor20 print = new PrintVisitor20();
plus.visit(print);

assertEquals("1 - 2", print.sb.toString());
```

The API is clearer, which is good. However, you are forced to complicate the implementation slightly. Now each expression element needs to contain the logic for correct dispatch to the correct visit method:

```
public void visit(Visitor v) {
    if (v instanceof Visitor20) {
        ((Visitor20)v).visitMinus(this);
    } else {
        v.visitUnknown(this);
    }
}
```

You've had to use runtime inspection to determine what you need to call. Again, you are giving up on compiler checks. You won't determine whether you've made a mistake until the appropriate code is run. Of course, this code is part of the implementation of the language structure, which in this example is written only once, by you. That is why it's possible to selectively pay enough attention to it to make it correct. Still, these ugly and dangerous pieces of code will be spread throughout many classes in their visit methods. As a result, it becomes difficult to keep track of where you are in your code. Yet another problem is that the length of the code can grow with each new language version, especially if you allow nonmonotonic evolution.

Nonmonotonic Evolution

Usually the evolution goes in just one direction: it's monotonic. However, imagine a situation where you create a new version of your expression language that considers integers useless and treats all numbers as **double**. Of course, you could still support integers, but let's suppose that your code assumes no visitor needs to use integers anymore. As a result, the Number class has no place in the data structures representing a model of version 3.0:

```
/** @since 3.0 */
public final class Real extends Expression {
    private final double value;
    public Real(double value) {
        this.value = value;
    }
    public double getValue() {
        return value;
    }
    public void visit(Visitor v)
}
```

```
/** @since 3.0 */
public interface Visitor30 extends Visitor {
    public void visitPlus(Plus s);
    public void visitMinus(Minus s);
    public void visitReal(Real r);
}
```

Note that not only have you defined a new element in the model, but you've also introduced a new visitor. The visitor is special: it doesn't extend any of the previous visitors defined for versions 1.0 and 2.0 of the language. Subclassing doesn't make sense: Visitor30 doesn't define visitNumber, because there are no integer numbers in version 3.0 of the expression language. Only real numbers are supported.

This works fine and satisfies our previous requirement to clearly define the language. As soon as you decide to accept the 3.0 version, you have to implement Visitor30. However, by doing this you've complicated the implementation of the visit methods even more. Now all the data elements need to perform runtime checks for yet another visitor type. For example, the already complicated implementation in Minus would get even more complicated:

```
/** @since 2.0 */
public final class Minus/*3.0*/ extends Expression {
    private final Expression first;
    private final Expression second;

    public Minus(Expression first, Expression second) {
        this.first = first;
        this.second = second;
    }
    public Expression getFirst() { return first; }
    public Expression getSecond() { return second; }

    public void visit(Visitor v) {
        if (v instanceof Visitor20) {
            ((Visitor20)v).visitMinus(this);
        } else if (v instanceof Visitor30) {
            ((Visitor30)v).visitMinus(this);
        } else {
            v.visitUnknown(this);
        }
    }
}
```

The internal implementation of version 3.0 is certainly uglier than version 2.0. With every new nonmonotonic version, this is going to become even worse.

Data Structure Using Interfaces

Throughout the discussion of visitors, it has been assumed that the data structure is represented using classes that were, as far as possible, final. As a result, there would always be only one implementation of each element and the usage of runtime instanceof checks would be limited to one library.

However, sometimes it's better not to use classes at all. The main reason for this is related to performance. Imagine that you create thousands or even millions of instances. Every byte counts and having one object instead of two can make a significant difference. For example, compilers and other language processors usually need to do more than create instances of model classes such as Number. They also need to keep additional associated information, such as the offset of the element in the text. To let the existing types be enhanced with new data without the overhead of delegation, you need to allow subclassing. This can also be useful if the implementor wants to provide an implementation of additional interfaces using multiple inheritance. If you need to optimize memory consumption and prevent the creation of additional model object instances, using interfaces for the model definition makes sense.

However, as the model represents a client API, turning classes into something that developers can implement might seem to be against all the recommendations put forward in this chapter. Yes, if you use interfaces for the model, you must get them right the first time. After that, there is no way of adding additional methods without breaking all the existing implementations. Surprisingly, this doesn't mean that there is no way to evolve the APIs. The visitor pattern makes this possible nicely.

First, you can create new model elements in new releases of the API, like you created Minus in version 2.0. Adding new classes into the API is fully binary compatible, and almost source compatible, so this is an absolutely correct evolution strategy. If the new classes extend the Expression base class, you can always pass them into at least visitUnknown(Expression). Then it's simply a question of adding a new visit method into the visitor interface. You've already seen this is possible in both scenarios. With abstract classes, you can add new methods, while with interfaces you can define a new visitor interface for the new language version. Moreover, there is always the option of using nonmonotonic evolution. This approach can be useful when you need to recover from a wrong model interface containing elements that are no longer needed, exactly as you did with Real and Visitor30, which don't mention Number at all.

It's always better to get the interface right when releasing the first version. However, with visitors there seems to be a way to recover from possible design mistakes. Even using interfaces for representing the expression nodes seems to be an acceptable style. As evolution is allowed, this can be classified as a proper API design pattern.

Client and Provider Visitors

There is one rather ugly problem associated with the use of interfaces: you've seen how ugly the visit method can become after a few language revisions. This was said to be acceptable, as there is only one implementation and you can get it right. However, with interfaces, when there is no default implementation, the ugly code needs to be present in every implementation of each interface. Also, these implementations need to be kept in sync. With every new version of the API that defines a new visitor, all the implementations need to be updated to have proper checks for v **instanceof** VisitorXY. This is bad, as the likelihood that things will get out of sync is significant.

To solve this inconvenient situation you need an API improvement trick. This trick is essential for this chapter and is based on separating the client and provider APIs as outlined in Chapter 8. All the previous examples used the VisitorXY types for two different purposes. Some developers implement it to walk through the model data classes or interfaces. In other cases, one or more implementations of the model classes use it to correctly dispatch from inside their implementations of the visit methods. This is the root cause of the evolution problems you've seen with the visitor pattern so far. Luckily the solution is simple: split the class in two. Here is the improved version of the expression language 1.0:

```
public interface Expression {
    public abstract void visit(Visitor v);
}
```

```java
public interface Plus extends Expression {
    public Expression getFirst();
    public Expression getSecond();
}
public interface Number extends Expression {
    public int getValue();
}

public abstract class Visitor {
    Visitor() {}

    public static Visitor create(Version10 v) {
        return create10(v);
    }

    public interface Version10 {
        public boolean visitUnknown(Expression e);
        public void visitPlus(Plus s);
        public void visitNumber(Number n);
    }

    public abstract void dispatchPlus(Plus p);
    public abstract void dispatchNumber(Number n);
}
```

In this example, the model classes are represented by interfaces, but final classes would work as well if there is no need for performance optimizations. Expression defines the visit method that takes the "client visitor," which maybe should be called "dispatcher" instead. This is the visitor that no external module implements but on which the correct dispatch methods can be called. Wanting to write a visitor, the users of the API implement the Visitor.Version10 "provider visitor" interface, converting it using Visitor.create. They can then use it for expression.visit(v) calls. As a result, it's easy to accommodate evolution requirements. The evolution to language version 2.0 that adds the Minus expression would make the following additions:

```java
/** @since 2.0 */
public interface Minus extends Expression {
    public Expression getFirst();
    public Expression getSecond();
}

public abstract class Visitor {
    Visitor() {}
    /** @since 2.0 */
    public static Visitor create(Version20 v) {
        return create20(v);
    }
```

```java
/** @since 2.0 */
public interface Version20 extends Version10 {
    public void visitMinus(Minus m);
}


/** @since 2.0 */
public abstract void dispatchNumber(Number n);
}
```

All the other methods and classes would remain. A new "provider visitor" interface would extend the old one. A factory method would also convert the visitor to a "client visitor" with a new method that implementations of Minus.visit(Visitor) might call to do its dispatching.

Similar changes would happen to the 3.0 version that replaces integers with reals. However, the Version30 interface would not extend anything that exists, because 3.0 is a nonmonotonic change in the model and you don't need all the previous methods, just a few of them. See the following:

```java
/** @since 3.0 */
public interface Real extends Expression {
    public double getValue();
}
public abstract class Visitor {
    Visitor() {}


    /** @since 3.0 */
    public static Visitor create(Version30 v) {
        return create30(v);
    }

    /** @since 3.0 */
    public interface Version30 {
        public boolean visitUnknown(Expression e);
        public void visitPlus(Plus s);
        public void visitMinus(Minus s);
        public void visitReal(Real r);
    }

    /** @since 3.0 */
    public abstract void dispatchReal(Real r);


}
```

Triple Dispatch

The visitor pattern is often called "double dispatch" because the actual method in the visitor that is called when expression.*visit*(visitor) is invoked depends on the dispatch of the call to the actual expression subtype, as well as the dispatch to the visitor. The "client and provider visitor" pattern described here could also be called "triple dispatch" because the actual method that gets called in the provider visitor is a function of the expression, the language version, and the implementation of the visitor. Let's look at how the Visitor.create methods are implemented for version 3.0. Here is the method for visitors written against version 1.0:

```
static Visitor create10(final Visitor.Version10 v) {
    return new Visitor() {
        @Override
        public void dispatchPlus(Plus p) {
            v.visitPlus(p);
        }

        @Override
        public void dispatchNumber(Number n) {
            v.visitNumber(n);
        }

        @Override
        public void dispatchMinus(Minus m) {
            if (v.visitUnknown(m)) {
                m.getFirst().visit(this);
                m.getSecond().visit(this);
            }
        }

        @Override
        public void dispatchReal(Real r) {
            v.visitUnknown(r);
        }
    };
}
```

Only Plus and Number elements were present in language 1.0, so only these are dispatched, while all other elements call the visitUnknown method. Moreover, the handling of the Minus element checks the returned value, and if true, performs a "deep" visit to support the CountNumbers visitor that I discussed earlier. The handling of visitors written for the 2.0 language model is a bit simpler, because there is no need to provide a fallback for the Minus handling code:

```
static Visitor create20(final Visitor.Version20 v) {
    return new Visitor() {
        @Override
        public void dispatchPlus(Plus p) {
            v.visitPlus(p);
        }
```

```
        @Override
        public void dispatchNumber(Number n) {
            v.visitNumber(n);
        }

        @Override
        public void dispatchMinus(Minus m) {
            v.visitMinus(m);
        }

        @Override
        public void dispatchReal(Real r) {
            v.visitUnknown(r);
        }
    };
}
```

The support for visitors of the 3.0 language model is more complicated, but still possible. The reason for this is that it's reasonable to convert integers in old models to reals, which requires a bit of additional work:

```
static Visitor create30(final Visitor.Version30 v) {
    return new Visitor() {
        @Override
        public void dispatchReal(Real r) {
            v.visitReal(r);
        }

        @Override
        public void dispatchNumber(final Number n) {
            class RealWrapper implements Real {
                public double getValue() {
                    return n.getValue();
                }
                public void visit(Visitor v) {
                    n.visit(v);
                }
            }
            v.visitReal(new RealWrapper());
        }

        @Override
        public void dispatchPlus(Plus p) {
            v.visitPlus(p);
        }
```

```
        @Override
        public void dispatchMinus(Minus m) {
            v.visitMinus(m);
        }
    };
}
```

The new element in this solution is the RealWrapper class that decorates an object representing an integer and allows it to be seen as a real. In this way, the Version30 can traverse older versions of models that provide integers.

A Happy End for Visitors

The "client and provider visitor" pattern is a good answer to any questions or problems faced so far. It's also the real "extensible visitor":

- It's possible to add new elements into the model.

- It supports the visitUnknown method.

- It supports default deep traversal over unknown elements.

- Language model versions are clearly separated as each has its own visitor interface, while it's possible to freely mix models and visitor versions and iterate with any visitor over any model.

- There is support for nonmonotonic evolution.

- The solution is type safe. It doesn't need to use any reflection or introspection.

- Usage of interfaces for model classes is possible and doesn't prevent type-safe evolution.

You couldn't ask for much more! You've reached a happy end. All this came about just because you followed one important rule: *You separated the client and provider interface into two parts* as advised by Chapter 8. Old wisdom claims that "any problem in computer science can be solved with another layer of indirection." This looks like it is true also in the API design world.

Syntactic Sugar

In spite of our happy end, more needs to be discussed. When rewriting the Print visitor example to the new style, you find that traditional code doesn't compile in the visitPlus method:

```
public class PrintVisitor implements Visitor.Version10 {
    StringBuffer sb = new StringBuffer();

    final Visitor dispatch = Visitor.create(this);

    public void visitPlus(Plus s) {
        // s.getFirst().visit(this); // does not compile, we need:
```

```
        s.getFirst().visit(dispatch);
        sb.append(" + ");
        s.getSecond().visit(dispatch);
    }

    public void visitNumber(Number n) {
        sb.append (n.getValue());
    }

    public boolean visitUnknown(Expression e) {
        sb.append("unknown");
        return true;
    }
}
```

The Expression.visit method expects Visitor and the PrintVisitor class only implements the Version10 interface. To type correctly, you need to always create new "dispatchers,"
or keep a reference to one such dispatcher, exactly as you did with the **final** Visitor dispatch
variable. This variable is needed anyway to start the dispatch, so this change simply moves it
into the visitor implementation, so that it can be accessible from the visit methods. However,
this requires a double reference to get the Visitor object, as it's an instance variable of the
Print class. Also, finding this trick might be difficult. On the other hand, a note in the Javadoc
and a snippet of sample usage should solve these problems. However, this is a traditional fix
without any syntactic sugar, without any new improvements to the visitor pattern.

The other solution enhances the interfaces so that the correct way of writing a visitor is
easy to find. Each method in the VersionXY interface gets a new parameter, Visitor self:

```
public abstract class Visitor {
    Visitor() {}

    public static Visitor create(Version10 v) {
        return create10(v);
    }

    public interface Version10 {
        public boolean visitUnknown(Expression e, Visitor self);
        public void visitPlus(Plus s, Visitor self);
        public void visitNumber(Number n, Visitor self);
    }

    public abstract void dispatchPlus(Plus p);
    public abstract void dispatchNumber(Number n);
}
```

self is always the Visitor that was passed to the Expression.visit(Visitor) method and
can be used instead of this in the old Print visitor example:

```java
public class PrintVisitor implements Visitor.Version10 {
    StringBuffer sb = new StringBuffer();

    public void visitPlus(Plus s, Visitor self) {
        s.getFirst().visit(self);
        sb.append(" + ");
        s.getSecond().visit(self);
    }

    public void visitNumber(Number n, Visitor self) {
        sb.append (n.getValue());
    }

    public boolean visitUnknown(Expression e, Visitor self) {
        sb.append("unknown");
        return true;
    }
}

@Test public void printOnePlusOne() {
    Number one = newNumber(1);
    Expression plus = newPlus(one, one);

    PrintVisitor print = new PrintVisitor();
    plus.visit(Visitor.create(print));

    assertEquals("1 + 1", print.sb.toString());
}
```

Which of these styles to use is the decision of the pattern user. The first is harder to discover but otherwise simple. The second is more complex. However, the second is needed by anyone trying to use the visitor recursively. Anyway, regardless of the actually chosen style, it's clear that a properly implemented visitor is a good API design pattern that can serve as a building block in our API universe.

CHAPTER 19

■ ■ ■

End-of-Life Procedures

Most of the suggestions in this book tell you to keep things compatible, always to design libraries and APIs compatibly, and never to do anything that could break the code of any of your API's clients. This means that you shouldn't remove a method, field, class, or package from an API, because doing so is likely to create an incompatibility for some potential client. As a result, you can either leave a library unmodified or you can add new items to it. An interesting question to ask is what would happen if developers started behaving like this. Wouldn't the amount of code grow without any limitation whatsoever? Wouldn't developers spend most of their time maintaining existing libraries? Would developers have the time to write any new code at all?

Our experience tells us that this is unlikely. On the one hand, a library might need maintenance because it's full of bugs, so it's unlikely that people will use it in that state anyway. On the other hand, the library might be working as expected, so it's better not to touch it at all. There might be pressure to add new features or to adapt the API to new requirements. This could be part of a "marketing attack," where changes are used to convince developers that the library is useful to them. However, this probably means that the number of users is significant. These investments would then really pay off. However, sometimes there are cases where the whole library is still acceptable and useful, while certain parts need to be removed. Is there a way to remove just part of an API?

As has been mentioned several times before, even a slight incompatibility might lead to the perception that the whole library is evolving in an incompatible way. As "incompatibility" is mostly the wrong message to send to the external world, it's desirable to avoid it as far as possible. An extreme example can be found in the root of the Java framework, in its core libraries. As of the 1.5 release, the core classes are packaged in `rt.jar`. All its content is a superset of all the previous releases from 1.0 onwards; that is, from 1996. All the API classes are still there, even ten years after they were *deprecated*, meaning marked as unusable and subject to deletion. They are still there because the promise of compatibility is more important than cleaning up the libraries. This includes not only single methods and classes, but also whole packages, such as `java.beans.beancontext`. These are there without any other reason than compatibility. They are maintained simply to fulfill the promise once made to Java developers.

Indeed, delivering long-term compatibility is a huge achievement. Time and money have to be invested in keeping promises of this kind. Sustaining solutions is costly, and sustaining those that are known to be wrong, or that have been superseded by newer versions, is boring, especially over several years. There has to be a significant vision motivating that level of compatibility. The motivation has to be so significant that people coming from this background need to believe that this is the only way of working. They need to believe that either they maintain compatibility or they renege on their promises and break compatibility completely. This kind of view results in claims such as "APIs are like stars: once you have them they are not going to go away," which is true from a certain point of view. However, when approached with a more dynamic mindset, it can easily be seen to have been in vain.

The point here is that with a little help from good runtime support, and with careful treatment of your APIs, it's possible to get rid of classes that are no longer needed. The NetBeans project provides examples of that. A long time ago we started with a base set of APIs called OpenAPIs, packaged in the monolithic openide.jar. After a few years of maintenance, most of our APIs became polluted with deprecations. Certain classes turned out to have been the worst possible choice, which prevented future evolution of the whole API. Our project got rid of these classes by using modularity. Also, we had a little bit of help from the NetBeans Runtime Container, which enabled us to extract unwanted classes into their own JAR file. We were able to slowly deprecate these classes, removing them from the product while retaining backward compatibility for the users of these APIs.

The Importance of a Specification Version

The primary precondition that allowed NetBeans to approach an understanding of "compatible removals" was the fact that we realized that it's not enough to express a dependency on a specific API, but that it's necessary to specify the version of the API as well. It's not enough to say the following:

```
import java.awt.*;
```

You not only have to specify the package, but you have to say that the dependency is on a certain package revision. For example, you have to specify that the java.awt package is from JDK 1.2. This type of information has to be included in each application using that package. If it's there, it can instruct the runtime system to arrange the environment in a way that the environment of java.awt revision 1.2 will be reproduced.

The Importance of Module Dependencies

Another necessary condition that has also applied to NetBeans is that you should not specify application libraries via paths to actual JAR files, but via dependencies. Such dependencies need some kind of interpretation, but this interpretation can add additional logic that hides potential inconsistencies and incompatibilities between revisions of the library.

With the classic Java -classpath approach, you could only say, "I need rt.jar because that is the JAR file that contains the java.awt package." However, this exposes far too many implementation details. After all, the actual requirement is to specify the following: my application was compiled against JDK 1.2 and it requires the java.awt package in the state it was in revision 1.2.

This might not seem like a big improvement, but it actually opens the door to "compatible removals." The runtime system can understand the history of certain components: in this example, packages such as java.awt. It can therefore inject the expected set of classes into the actual runtime path. That is why it could be possible that a newer revision, such as 1.3, of that package doesn't contain the java.awt.Canvas class. Indeed, nobody compiling against version 1.3 can use the class, but what about developers who had compiled against 1.2 and want to run against version 1.3? Do they have to get `ClassNotFoundErrors`? No, not at all. Because their application states that they want version 1.2, the runtime system "gets it" and injects the classes to mimic the old revision. They might be deprecated, hanged, or absent by now, in the newer revisions. However, if their old versions are still kept around, the system can make them transparently available. The `java.awt.Canvas` class can look exactly like the one from version 1.2. As a result, the application links and runs fine. This is an example of how you can enable compatible development, even when your API shrinks.

AUTOMATIC DEPENDENCY ADJUSTMENTS

The NetBeans Module System allows every module to provide a set of hints that may be used to adjust the dependencies. The dependencies serve to reproduce the environment in which certain modules were created.

For example, the NetBeans project decided to get rid of the `SystemOption` class, an old and superfluous class for managing the persistence of user settings. It was replaced by the use of `java.util.Preferences`. Deprecating this class was easy, as it was part of its own module, `org.openide.options`, which contained almost nothing else and may have been fully deprecated as well. However, the problem was that various other modules exposed an API based on `SystemOption` from their own API. For example, our support for editors used to provide **public class** `PrintSettings` **extends** `SystemOption`. We could not get rid of `SystemOption` and keep `PrintSettings`. Therefore, we decided to deprecate `PrintSettings` as well. The original situation is sketched in Figure 19-1. Version 6.7 of the `org.openide.options` module contains the `SystemOption` class. The `PrintSettings` class is in the `org.openide.text` module together with other classes such as `CloneableEditorSupport`. The version of the `org.openide.text` module is 6.15 and the module has a dependency on `org.openide.options` version at least 6.7, as it needs its classes on the classpath.

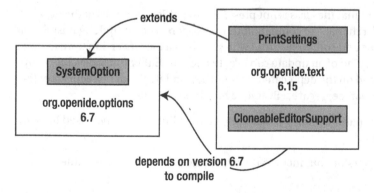

Figure 19-1. *PrintSettings and SystemOption before deprecation*

We moved the `PrintSettings` class from the `org.openide.text` module to the `org.openide.options` module and increased its specification version to 6.8, as can be seen in Figure 19-2. The version of the `org.openide.text` module has been increased to 6.16; it no longer needs a dependency on `org.openide.options`. The module contains just `CloneableEditorSupport` and similar, still useful classes. The other, to be deprecated classes are now in their own module, which is no longer needed by any other part of the system. This supports the evolution plan to deprecate the module completely as soon as its API users switch away from their use of `SystemOption` and `PrintSettings`.

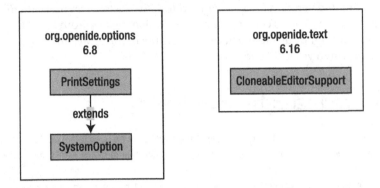

Figure 19-2. *PrintSettings and SystemOption after deprecation*

However, we intended to maintain backward compatibility. Removing `PrintSettings` from a module was clearly not compatible at all. But the class is still around, just in a different module. It's enough to specify an automatic module dependency trigger saying that if someone wants to use `org.openide.text` in a version older than 6.16, please also change the module's dependencies to also request `org.openide.options` > 6.8. This means that every old user of `org.openide.text` still continues to see all its classes as they were at the time of compilation. Those who need only the `CloneableEditorSupport` class can increase their dependency to `org.openide.text` > 6.16 and contribute to the deprecation of the `org.openide.options` module by no longer needing it.

It should be pointed out that the class is not present in the official libraries of the new version. It's just kept around for the sake of compatibility. Developers who compile against the old version successfully compile and run, while those who switch to a newer version have to update their code. In NetBeans this kind of an update can take two forms. Either those developers update their code not to depend on the deprecated class or they update the dependencies of their application to rely on `java.awt-deprecated`. Everyone has three choices:

1. Remain in fully compatible mode and compile against libraries as they used to be in the previous version.

2. Update to a newer version, but include the deprecated library in the module dependencies.

3. Update to a newer version and update the code not to refer to the old and removed class.

The experience of the NetBeans project shows that developers are often concerned about easy upgradeability to a new version. In this case, they prefer solution number 1. That means they don't want to do anything and their application has to continue to run. Fine, we have an answer for them: simply remain in the compatible mode for the previous version and everything will work as expected.

However, our experience also shows that there are people who want to keep their development up to date. They want to use the latest features of the new release and they don't mind if changes to the code have to be made. Those people are likely to select solution number 3. They'll update their code and make it compilable and usable with the latest version of the library.

The point is that the number of people who want to touch and modify their code, but still use deprecated libraries, and who would therefore select solution number 2, is minimal. You might be searching for an easy solution, in which case running in a fully compatible environment is your choice, as in the previous version. Alternatively, you are willing to update your sources, meaning it's much more reasonable to upgrade fully to all the new features, without the use of any "end-of-lifed" classes.

Please note that this is different from simple deprecations. Deprecations are just compile-time warnings. In this case the decisions are visible at runtime. The runtime emits warnings alerting developers to switch to newer versions, as a result of old and not updated dependencies. This makes developers aware that their code is getting old and that they have time to update. NetBeans' experience shows that they do go through with updates in these circumstances.

Over time, fewer and fewer projects will rely on the old APIs. Of course, new projects don't see the old API at all, but even the older ones eventually get updated to a newer version. The good thing about "compatible removals" is that the update doesn't need to happen for all projects at once. Either developers decide to switch or they don't, but for each and every one of them a familiar runtime environment is ready for use.

Should Removed Pieces Lie Around Forever?

You might think that instead of using deprecated annotations on classes that shouldn't be used at all, I am simply suggesting to move them to separate JAR files. However, they still need to be kept around to keep backward compatibility. This is more or less true, but not completely.

It's true that the NetBeans team keeps deprecated APIs around for some time. However, as soon as all our NetBeans IDE modules stop relying on them, they simply lie on disk without being used. They are neither loaded into memory during execution, nor are they used during compilation, unless someone really needs them because of compatibility problems. This indeed saves computer resources. However, the larger benefit comes when a compatible bridge is no longer needed. This happens when the number of known users of the old version of the API drops below a certain limit. Then the "default" download of the framework, such as the NetBeans IDE, can stop including the API. That doesn't mean that the API is deleted completely: it can still be available for download, though the default distribution doesn't need to include it anymore. This is another sign to those who might not have migrated to the new version yet that it's the right time to do so. Despite that, they are not forced to do so: they have the option of downloading the compatibility bridge. A reasonable runtime container should be able to do the download automatically as needed, completely shielding the application from the incompatibilities the framework might provide.

By using technologies such as this, you can achieve complete compatibility and still guarantee a lot of freedom in the evolution of the APIs, including the ability to remove an API's pieces. The NetBeans project uses this approach and it has proven itself successful. We are able to treat our APIs like diamonds, while throwing the parts that turn out to be fakes into the trash.

Splitting Monolithic APIs

As written in the section "Modularizing Applications" in Chapter 2, this book advocates modular design and a component-based architecture. An ideal application is composed of modular building blocks that are assembled and glued together. However, for this to work, you need reasonably sized components. Here "size" doesn't mean the amount of kilobytes in the library download. That is no longer an issue these days, at least not on a desktop computer with a functioning Internet connection. Nor does "size" refer to the amount of visible classes. You don't need to use them all. "Size" is measured by the number of external dependencies. It's highly unreasonable to depend on one single library because it contains some small but useful functionality, while being forced to depend on dozens or thousands of additional libraries simply because they are needed to fulfill all the library's dependencies. When this happens, there is no better cure than splitting the monolithic library into smaller pieces.

OLD NETBEANS OPENIDE AND JAVA RT.JAR

Monolithic libraries happen, although they shouldn't, at least not if you follow the spirit of this book. However, because they happen from time to time, you need to prepare for this reality. Often projects start small, then grow and can develop to the size of Java's `rt.jar` or the old NetBeans `openide.jar`.

The reason for such bloated libraries lies somewhere in the deep hidden expectation that this API is the most important in the world. Therefore, the API is seen to need to belong to the API's "core." This way, more and more code is shifted onto the pile of dirt that constitutes the core library APIs, while the size increases to such an extent that nobody wants to or is able to stay outside of it. `rt.jar` is an example of a library that should be split, but who knows when the Java team will find enough courage to do so.

`openide.jar` was a JAR file that originally contained all the public NetBeans APIs. These APIs were the ones needed by all the NetBeans IDE modules. As these modules need many services, a huge set of APIs was in this JAR file. The APIs provided functionality ranging from managing windows, viewers, and editors, to services for compilation, execution, and debugging. All these were in one JAR; all these were packaged and deployed together. Even if you wanted to create an application without execution support, you had to include the JAR anyway.

It took us a long time to fix all these issues. After many phases, performed over many releases starting with NetBeans IDE 5.0, we don't have this monolithic API library anymore. Instead, we now have about 15 to 20 smaller APIs, which can individually be turned on or off depending on where they are used.

What are the possible ways of cutting a large monolithic JAR into smaller pieces? You can either cut the packages or the classes. Nothing else makes sense. Smaller units than classes exist, but it's difficult to feed the JVM anything smaller than a class without some kind of bytecode patching. So, let's investigate the cases of splitting a JAR's classes and packages.

BYTECODE PATCHING

For most people, bytecode is beyond the horizon of our understanding. It's neither impossible to understand, nor the case that I wouldn't perform some manipulations if I wanted to do so. I did it a few times in the past. However, It's clearly beyond my cluelessness level. I don't want to need to remember anything about it. If necessary, I can undertake a journey beyond my knowledge horizon to explore, meet, and alter some byte-code. However, I am always glad to arrive safely back home and try to forget that experience as quickly as I can. I expect a similar attitude among most other Java developers.

On the other hand, times are changing and bytecode weaving is no longer something that is considered unsound and dangerous. Especially due to wider and wider acceptance of aspect-oriented technologies, developers have started seeing bytecode manipulation as an acceptable alternative. An important reason for this is that there is now a higher-level language that allows these manipulations. You no longer need to deep dive into the array of bytes directly or with a low-level library. Instead, it's enough to write an *aspect*. Aspects are not as powerful as plain bytecode manipulation, but this is what assembly programmers used to say about C as well: too high-level, too slow, and so on.

However, the benefits of extending our horizon by giving us higher-level primitives for certain bytecode manipulations, as provided by aspects, outweighs any drawbacks associated with them not being absolutely general. They helped to change common attitudes among Java developers. These days at least some byte-code changes are no longer taboo. However, I don't have enough experience with such higher-level tools, so I'll leave this topic for other authors.

The only difference between splitting individual classes and splitting packages relates to whether the packages are "sealed." If they are sealed, you'll have a hard time convincing the classloaders and the virtual machine to accept one class being in two different JAR files. When moving whole packages into their own JARs, you are unlikely to face problems of this kind.

Now, the problem is what to do with classes that depend on too many of the newly created JARs. What if they depend on so many that they don't fit into any of them? For example, in NetBeans we had the following:

```
public abstract class TopManager {
    public abstract ExecutionEngine getExecutionEngine();
    public abstract CompilationEngine getCompilationEngine();
}
```

To get rid of the class, we created yet another JAR file, called it openide-compat.jar, and added to it any class that didn't fit anywhere else. For example, that's how the TopManager class ended up there. The final problem to solve was finding an API to which to move the getters. The natural place was to introduce **static** ExecutionEngine.*getDefault*() and similar instance methods for the compilation engine, while making the TopManager delegate to these new methods. We deprecated the manager class and replaced all references to it. That way, we were able to let the openide-compat.jar remain in existence, especially for external users of the API. For those users requesting the old environment that contained TopManager, we also included automatic dependencies as detailed in the section "The Importance of Module Dependencies."

SMALL VS. LARGE APIS

One of my colleagues recently complained that the NetBeans editor support is too modular. He complained that we have one module providing bookmarks, another handling indentation, and yet others for code folding, code completion, and settings. In his view, this makes the life of the user of the editor APIs difficult, as every-thing is spread in many places, to the point where individual parts are almost impossible to find.

The colleague proposed—and also tried to create—a single, unified API for using the editor functionality. Instead of dozens of small APIs, he wanted users to be able to see and learn just one single API that would contain all that is necessary to create an editor.

I believe that this combination provides a perfect balance between the technical details of an API and the API's usability. The small modules provide low-level, assembler-like APIs that enable everything to be controlled, while the encapsulation wrapper can approach everything from a high-level perspective. The user can start with the wrapper and be productive almost immediately. When the need to use the assembler-like APIs arises, there could be an easy migration path, or better, the possibility to mix them with the high-level APIs. This is a pretty good position from a user's point of view.

Moreover, the stability categories and the life cycle of individual modules can vary. For example, a high-level module might become obsolete sooner, while the low-level, technical modules might need to stay compatible for a longer period of time. In such situations, you can simply abandon the old high-level module, while creating new abstractions from scratch. The low-level "assembly language" of the detailed APIs would stay the same, providing the basis for cooperation between old and new high-level abstractions, while the abstractions can be created quickly and efficiently. For example, something like the Servlet API would stay, while various web frameworks could appear and disappear weekly.

I consider this a good solution for overcoming the potential proliferation of many small, low-level API modules.

This kind of abstracting functionality into a newly created supertype is useful in the process of splitting and end-of-lifing old APIs. It's a bridge delegating the old method calls into a new, smaller API. With surgery such as this, you can keep the library's important functionality, while providing it in a slim and efficient form.

With a proper evolution plan and sound end-of-life procedures, there is a way to balance the backward compatibility, correctness, preservation of investments, and other evolution and technical aspects of an API with the need for its simplicity, understandability, as much clueless use as possible, elegance, and beauty. We've reached the end of our API journey and it seems that when you understand the API world, its needs, and its laws of evolution, you can shape it into a form containing all that the creators of the oldest and most perfect science always searched for—beauty, truth, and elegance. A properly designed API universe ain't a bad place to be.

■ ■ ■

The Future

It's time to wrap up the notes that I've gathered over the last ten years. For now, I've also finished with my advice and tips explaining experiences that I gained when designing the NetBeans APIs. That doesn't mean this topic is fully explored and there is nothing more to say. This is no definitive guide—I could continue to write for the next few months or years. However, that would just prevent this book from getting into the hands of its readers. Everyone I've talked to tells me a book such as this is needed, so I want to get it out now. But before I conclude, let me say a few last words about the future of API design and software engineering as a whole.

Part 1 presents all of API design as a scientific discipline with a strong rational background, not as the art that it sometimes pretends to be. It defines terminology and initial prerequisites that can objectively help us measure if an API design is good. These rules try to be language neutral and applicable to any programming language, not just Java. The theory is unlikely to be complete. Other principles of API design exist elsewhere or are still waiting to be discovered. However, that should not scare us, as Chapter 1 gives us a tool to evaluate the quality of various principles—to find out whether a certain piece of advice helps us design better shared libraries and their APIs or not. It gives us the grand meta-principle: selective cluelessness. This cluelessness is a tool that can measure whether various goals really help. That's because if they allow people to know less while achieving more and building better software systems more easily, then this advice is good. There is a need for this advice, especially in the future, when software systems will outsize the intellectual capacity of any of their designers.

The biggest part of this book is dedicated to projections of such theory into Java. Sometimes these projections are widely applicable and sometimes they apply only to object-oriented languages. Sometimes they are trivial, sometimes they are complex, and sometimes they are controversial. Again, it's unlikely they cover everything, but they provide a good starting set of API design patterns for Java. We've seen that it's possible to design APIs in Java. It's just necessary to know the meaning of various language constructs from the standpoints of evolution and the API user.

Part 3 provides tips, tricks, and descriptions of daily procedures that should be fulfilled when designing and especially maintaining APIs. This is where I expect the biggest evolution. As the tools improve, so will the practices. In any event, the future goal is clear: software assembly skills, and API design, which is software assembly's essential part, need to be simplified and made available to the public. Let's look in more detail at how to do so.

Principia Informatica

When Isaac Newton published his *Philosophiae Naturalis Principia Mathematica* in 1687, it was a tremendous moment for the history of science. This three-part book, seen by some as the best single scientific write-up ever made, contained important results and principles such as the initial definition of forces, their mutual interactions, definitions of laws of movement, and also a new mathematical tool making all that possible (differential calculus). It was an amazing achievement for a single person.

However, the most important aspect of that book was not what it contained, but how it treated things that it missed. Isaac Newton was well aware of the fact that though he managed to provide explanations for things previously unexplainable, his mechanical world likely didn't fully reflect the real world. Today we all know that indeed it doesn't. Still, because his work was ready for that from the beginning, it's still useful and important. For a certain set of applications it gives good enough results, and even more importantly, can be used as a teaching tool. The theory is reasonably approachable and understandable to beginners, to whom it provides a perfect introductory step toward modern physics.

Newton was not the first person to create such a theory. Many great minds before him tried that as well, most importantly Descartes. However, humility is the difference. While Descartes believed he could explain the whole world himself, and tried that in his work, Newton notably admitted that his work wasn't definitive at all. This not only left the doors open to successors, but let him concentrate on proper explanations of the phenomena he knew how to explain, whereas Descartes needed to explain everything. Obviously that is a massive task, and in some situations, such as when explaining interactions of two moving bodies, he could not go deep enough and his conclusions were sometimes not valid. As far as I know, this is not true for *Principia Mathematica*. What it contains is valid to this day.

Moreover, *Principia Mathematica* leaves the exploration of the whole complexity of the world for others. As such, it managed to stimulate an enormous activity among European scientists. They adopted and extended Newton's theories and techniques in ways that their author could not predict in his wildest dreams. Because of this scientific cooperation, physics became the driving force behind the industrial revolution that pushed Europe forward in the 18th and 19th centuries.

The usefulness of *Principia Mathematica* extends beyond giving everyone a solid tool for describing, or at least approximating, the behavior of the real world. It's also useful for providing strict and solid background theory that stays valid even if the world starts to differ or is known to differ from the theory. You can always verify the preconditions. If the real ones match the ones in the theory, you can apply the theory's conclusions to real objects and get reasonable results applicable to the real world. The match is common for almost all cases we face in the world around us. Because most of the world we deal with does not rely on high velocities or microscopic objects, Newton's theory is a universal tool for understanding our everyday real-world problems. That is an enormous success for a book written more than 300 years ago.

After reading this book you can likely see that I have deep respect for the work that Newton did and particularly for the style in which he did it, especially for its humility. I wanted to follow the same path and structure, and approach the topic of API design in the same style that Newton approached his mechanical world. I wanted to establish a forum in which others could express their ideas, and I wanted to present and explore some of them. However, I was always ready to admit that my knowledge and my advice are not finite. There is much more work to be done, and this book is just a first step. Indeed, somewhere in the shadow of my soul, I would like it to be as important of a step as *Principia Mathematica*. However, I do indeed realize why this book cannot be like *Principia Mathematica*. This book is just a journal—a collection of notes that I've recorded in the NetBeans laboratory over the last ten years. This is far away from the situation of Newton's *Principia Mathematica*, which was result of many more years of scientific work, publications, and letter exchanges. Nevertheless, I decided to follow a similar structure. Part 1 tries to form the everlasting skeleton behind API design. It's as objective as possible. It's not tied to any programming language and as such it's supposed to be generally applicable. Just like Newton took Euclid's geometric space with the additional abstraction of forces and inserted it into the real world, the structure described in the theory should be applicable and insertable in any programming language that already exists or that will appear in the foreseeable future.

Based on this skeleton I wrote down a lot of recommendations for proper API design in Java. This advice is unlikely to last as long as the theory. As soon as Java dies or morphs significantly, it could be rendered invalid. However, at the time of creation and writing of this book, it's important. A whole set of developers are writing their libraries and APIs in Java and they might find this advice useful. Moreover, I've indeed not formulated the theory out of nothing. I mostly extracted it from my real Java experience (a good example of empiricism, isn't it?), and these Java adventures are captured in Part 2 of this book. They can be seen as guides that lead to the creation of the theory principles, or you can see them as the results of that theory. Indeed, the best scenario would be if they were both at once. However, that is unlikely, as this book is not as strict as Newton's *Principia Mathematica*. There are no real proofs, and even where I attempt to make some, they're more scratch proofs than real proofs.

Anyway, I intentionally leave the doors open for those who want to build upon this book. Use the design tips in your project, expand on them, and publish them. Use this book as the starting material for your lessons about API design, prove me wrong, and build upon that. I was not able to cover a lot of topics due to lack of time, lack of intellect, and lack of patience. You are more than welcome to explore them and to provide some hints. Following is a list of topics that I think deserve further investigation.

Cluelessness Is Here to Stay

Predicting the future is always hard, and every prediction is associated with a bit of risk and uncertainty. If I had to bet on something happening, then I'd bet on cluelessness. I'd say it is bound to conquer the software engineering world. I've discussed the reasons in detail in Chapter 1, but let's pick a few and look how they can evolve in the future.

The need for more and more programmers is likely to last for a while, if not forever. The languages or tools these developers use might change. However, as long as society continues to need information, there will always be a demand for people who can help organize it. It's unlikely that those people will be more clever or better educated than us. Still, they'll be asked to work on bigger systems, provide more sophisticated results, and render them in more colorful ways or in more dimensions. In short, they'll be asked to achieve more than we do today. With their skills remaining at approximately the same level as ours, it's clear what will happen: the portion of the systems that individuals will understand will get smaller and smaller. This is a perfect environment for cluelessness, especially because we don't want the big systems to be unreliable. Even if we can understand just a portion of them, we still want them to work properly and not get out of control. Selective cluelessness gives an answer to that problem: choose what the key aspects of these systems are and make sure they are checked and verified to work as expected. Cluelessness is here to stay.

The other reason for that is that assembling applications from big chunks is so convenient. I can see that on various Linux forums. The majority of their traffic includes tips and tricks on installing some package and tweaking configuration files, as well as samples of shell scripts that you can execute to achieve some highly desirable effect, such as having an X Window system come up after a resume. The amount of this kind of information greatly outweighs the number of tips suggesting how to patch some C source of a program, how to debug it, and so on. Again, this is an indisputable sign of cluelessness. Most Linux users don't have a clue how their application is written. The only things they care about are its command-line options, the output that it emits, and voilà! Execute the binary, and use `pipe` and `grep` to find the important information. Then process it and the system is done and working. Cluelessness par excellence. Moreover, this also shows the importance of APIs. The command-line options and the text printed by the Unix utilities is their most important API, used by all those power Unix users, isolating them completely from the internal details of the utilities' implementations. I know it from my own experience. Whenever I need to fix a problem on my computer, I look for a solution based on existing binaries. I even spend a day writing shell scripts, or massaging configuration files to find a solution, before opening the debugger and library source code and hunting down bugs in the C code. The barrier between these two worlds is so big, and crossing it is so painful, that most us would rather stay on the side of scripting and command-line arguments. For example, I've made dozens of attempts to work around some bug in X server. However, only once in the last five years have I needed to download the source code and fix some segmentation fault. Because it's so easy to invoke and combine Unix applications and so easy to assemble them into bigger chunks of functionality, the number of users greatly exceeds the number of hackers digging inside the library's C sources. The ratio between these two groups is so big that it's clear proof of why simple, consistent, and easy-to-use APIs are important. This observation is indeed not limited just to the world of Unix, but is general. The more good APIs we have, the bigger the systems we'll be able to build without understanding all their details. Cluelessness is here to stay.

The task for the future is to look for more situations where selective cluelessness can be used and find ways to apply it properly. I've discussed the importance of good APIs and automated testing in this effort deeply in this book. However, numerous other tools and practices will help us design more reliable systems with the current amount of knowledge we have—or even a lower or more targeted level of knowledge than we have right now. At the end, whenever I design a system, I don't want to keep the details of why it works in my brain. That would occupy valuable space that I want to fill with memories about my friends, hobbies, family, and life. Of course I need the system to work properly, if for no other reason than not having to fix bugs in it. From time to time I'll need to come back to it and modify it to do something. At that moment I want to recall all the important knowledge about it, apply it, and forget it immediately. Cluelessness is my friend. Anyone who discovers a technique to intensify such an approach is my hero, and certainly not just mine. Cluelessness is a friend for all of us.

API Design Methodology

When my friend Tim Boudreau still seriously considered helping me with this book, he always said, "We need to create a methodology."

I listened with my jaw dropped and objected, "But we don't have a methodology. We have just a set of advice. It's not a checklist to follow."

"Never mind," Tim replied, "Make it a checklist, make it a methodology. Without it nobody will really listen to you!"

Well, I never felt comfortable with his point of view, but there has to be something to it, because I still keep it somewhere in the back in my mind. Now, when presenting the API design future, I'd like to talk a bit about it.

This book contains much advice, mostly just in the form of notes. It's based on my own adventures with designing a Java framework, and as such, it's more of a checklist of things you should not do: things that might limit your ability to successfully maintain the API of your library or framework in subsequent releases. At the beginning of my architect days, I knew nothing about proper methodology. The design decisions were mostly driven by instinct. Over time, as mistakes started to accumulate and hurt me, I started to learn and some sort of methodology started to crystallize.

I am still reluctant to formulate a methodology. I'd rather leave it for others, but I am not afraid to predict how it should look. This book contains Part 1, and any methodology should have a theoretical background. However, just like Newton's laws don't define how to design a bridge that won't fall, it's not the goal of the theory to provide a handbook for those who want to apply it to real situations. The design part of this book is mostly a projection of the theory to a particular programming language, and the daily advice part also concentrates more on tools and processes than methodology. Still, I guess that the last part can be a good initial point for exploration of an API design methodology.

Before we start our search for an API design methodology, we need to find a proper name for it. Names are the most important attributes of things and events. If we have a good name, then after hearing it the right bells in our mind start to ring, and the right bells create the right attitude, which influences the acceptance of the methodology. So, let's look at possible good names we could use for such a methodology. The name could include "high." High is good—definitely better than "low." It can even be an adjective, as in "highly effective." Yes, "effective"; let's include effective. Costs are always too high, so let's lower them by using a highly effective methodology. Also, let's add some form of "structure" to the naming. Structure is always good—better than chaos—and if used in a rational way, oh yes, let's call it "rational" as well. Then it can produce enhanced results. By the way, "enhanced" is also a strong name for a methodology that can provide consistent results. "Consistent" is not bad. I feel a kind of threat there, like a slight attack of disorder. Better to replace it with "unified." Yes, unity is good; unity is what all our developers need! So I guess we've found proper strong words to call our methodology, and now we can also try to find some content for it. No; I'm just kidding, let's start once again.

The theory, as well its applications and then the process advice given in this book, always works with the assumption that things are never perfect, that things evolve. In a perfect, static world, we could use reason to explore every possible solution and then choose the best one. It might take time, but at some point we might obtain the best possible result. This is the style of thinking you can apply to reasoning about the geometry of static objects. However, our world is not like that: our world is changing. It would be useless to search years and years for a perfect solution, when at the time of discovery, the solution might no longer be applicable to the state of our world at that time. Of course, admitting that we are not searching for the perfect solution somehow concedes most of the slickness and beauty. However, it's at least honest, and it might simplify the search for truth.

Software engineering always oscillates between rationalism and empiricism. Sometimes it's closer to math, where it searches for absolute and perfect solutions. Sometimes it gets closer to empiricism, where it can accept even imperfect solutions that satisfy our requirements and senses. Perception defines what is acceptable. The first school of thought has resulted in methodologies that advocate perfect planning and perfect documentation that is created before the start of coding. With a good planning phase, the coding is just a piece of cake. This is a perfect tool for a world that is static or perfectly known. However, both our world and our knowledge of it are changing. That is why there is another movement that resulted in a set of methodologies pioneered by Extreme Programming (XP). These methodologies inherently admit that our knowledge is never perfect, and advise how to deliver successful systems even with such a disadvantage. My impression is that this stream of thought has grown and became strong in the last decade.

When thinking about various approaches to API design, I can see that the range of methodologies also spans and oscillates between rationalism and empiricism. I have deep respect for both these approaches, and like it when truth is also beautiful, as that makes me feel it's more elegant. However, as you know after reading this book, beauty is not a necessary condition of truth. We can achieve good API design without fully understanding everything, using only partial knowledge about the world just as methodologies such as XP do. Now, I believe our search for a proper name for a future methodology based on the style of API design advocated in this book is over. XP belongs to a group of software methodologies called *agile*. Let's call our methodology *Agile API Design*.

Agile API Design is a pretty slick name built from strong words. It rings the right bells in the mind and it's not an empty name—the name is backed by content. I swear that I didn't think about the name before I started to write this last futuristic part of the book. However, when I look back on all the advice given in prior chapters, I find it absolutely perfect. All those refrains such as "the first version is never perfect," "know your users," "get ready for future evolution," and so on are parallel to the advice given by agile software methodologies. I am still reluctant to provide the actual methodology here, but if you use advice from this book when developing your library or framework, feel free to tell everyone that you are following Agile API Design principles.

Languages Ready for Evolution

The advice provided in the book intentionally tries to stay within the boundaries of Java. It would indeed be possible to think about various language extensions that could make the burden of API design a more pleasant experience. However, that would be just like creating a new programming language. Such a language might be easier to use and program in, but it would be harder to adopt. That's because the software industry is usually conservative in the selection of the programming languages that are used for coding of its software projects. This is not surprising. A new language requires new skills, and it takes time to train developers to have them. That is why it seemed important for me to demonstrate that even in plain Java, you can practice Agile API Design. However, getting your API ready for evolution sometimes requires a bit of insight into the internals of the compiler and the virtual machine in order to do the right tricks to make things work correctly. Sometimes these tricks are ridiculously complex (such as the accessor in the section "Allow Access Only from Friend Code" in Chapter 5 or the access modifier in the section "Delegation and Composition" in Chapter 10). That is why it makes sense to ask how some future language or software build system such as Maven could turn these tricks into natural coding constructs.

I've intentionally used the word "future," as I am not aware of any language or system that can provide that functionality right now. The most that you can find now are homemade systems that help with various aspects of the API design, but there doesn't seem to be any other general solution.

Some parts of the solution should be in the compiler, or at least reflected in the sources, and processed by some annotation processor later. For example, it should be possible to tell the compiler that when you compile with JDK target milestone 1.5 no methods and classes introduced in subsequent Java releases should be available. This should work for any library, not just `rt.jar`. The solution is easy, if we can identify the state of an API in a particular version. For example, our libraries and their APIs could annotate each class, method, and field with some `@Version(1.4)` attribute. If the compiler paid attention to this attribute and ignored everything newer than the version of library you want to compile against, this should generate a "not found error." Of course, this would require that each element visible in the API be annotated with the `@Version` attribute. This means that the packaging and versioning becomes part of the language. That is a significant mental shift that no compiler guy I've spoken with has been ready to make. I know language designers have thought about modularity. However, that is a modularity created for the Modula programming language back in the '70s. That kind of modularity solves how you can compile the program part by part, module by module, but it doesn't prescribe what should happen if one part changes. It's a kind of static form of modularity, not dynamic assembly from independent parts. It might have been a step forward 30 years ago, but since then the world has become more agile and we should adjust our languages to that.

Better compiler support would be nice, but not everything can be done in a compiler. The system has to be more complex. It needs to be aware of its own history. For example, it should yield an error when you try to remove a method or class from an API and it has already been published in a previous version. For that it's necessary to have a snapshot of all important previous versions and let the compiler or other part of the system check that no violation of binary backward compatibility has occurred. Again, this needs to work in orchestration with proper version numbering. There needs to be a policy that enables you to express that the new version of a library is completely incompatible with the previous one, in which case the binary compatibility check would be suppressed completely. As in many cases, there have been attempts to provide tools for such kinds of functionality. However, they are not general enough, and they need a lot of manual configuration and intervention to set them up properly. The language or system of the future should make this instantly ready whenever you start to develop a new library.

Yet another thing to consider is whether the access modifiers such as public, protected, and final are not obsolete. Given all the discussion in the section "Delegation and Composition" in Chapter 10, I consider this likely. For the purposes of designing an API, I would much rather see a way to specify whether a class or interface is supposed to be subclassed, and potentially restrict who can do so. Then for each method you could either specify if it's supposed to be callable or if it's a slot where developers can or have to inject their own code. No method should have dual meaning. Where there is a dual meaning, describing the second meaning should be more complicated than describing the more likely case. For example, the way to express a callable method—for example, public final—should not be more complicated than public, which has a dual meaning. I am not advocating removal of access modifiers. However, I want them to be more aligned with the tasks people do when designing an API. If the access modifiers were primarily designed to express people's intention with an API element, then the infamous and dangerous "reuse by accident" coding style, so common in current mainstream object-oriented languages, would be prevented. I don't want to prescribe how the access modifiers should look, but I know that the current situation requires so much attention when designing an API that we desperately need something more clueless: something people will use without so much time needed to think about it; something that will make it hard to misinterpret the author's intentions.

Although I was not polite when talking about compilers in this section, I don't mean it as a rant. Moreover, I'll be glad to be found wrong. If there already is a system and language suitable for Agile API Design, I'll be glad for that. If not, I'd like to ask the language designers to think about their solutions from this new, agile angle. In the meantime, I am looking at what can be done from the outside, if you own the runtime and build system, like we do in the case of the NetBeans Runtime Container.

The Role of Education

Cluelessness is all around us. Are we ready for that? Do we teach people about it? Do we tell them how to build gigantic applications from tons of libraries picked up from all over the world? I am afraid that the answer to all these questions is "No," and I'd like this to change in the near future.

From time to time I visit various universities and present to their students. I still live under the impression that the schools would rather teach basic coding skills than advocate and explain how to do code reuse. Unsurprisingly, the universities seem to prefer the rationalistic approach, offering a learning journey that is enlightened by beauty and elegance. Of course, it's perfect if programmers know how to write quicksort or understand a bunch of graph-related algorithms. However, that is not everything they should know.

TEACHING SKIING

By chance, I once attended a ski instructor course. I didn't have time to do the exams, so I am not certified to teach new skiers and I have to earn my living being a software architect, but I do know the methodology well enough to build this thought on it.

A ski instructor always starts with teaching basics to ensure people are able to stay on their skis and at least generally understand the technique for making a turn. After a few practice hours, the instructor usually has to divide the students into two categories: one style optimized for "survival" and the other for "racing." With both styles, you greatly enjoy skiing and can get down any hill, However, only with the latter group can you feel the centrifugal force that is one of the biggest reasons why people love riding motorbikes, skiing, and snowboarding.

I believe a similar teaching style should be used for programmers as well. We need everyone to understand the basics, which in my opinion should include the principles of selective cluelessness. Only that way can we guarantee that regardless of how good programmers are, the systems that they produce are reliable. After a while there should be a fork in the road. One path should lead to the mastering of practical skills such as reusing foreign components and orientation in legacy code. The other should be a more "academic" path oriented toward discovering new ways of applying cluelessness, producing more sharable libraries, and so on.

I'd like to end this skiing parable with a slightly unrelated, but interesting observation: good tools help. When I was young, it was not easy to practice the "racing skiing style," as the skis were not optimized for turning. When I tried snowboarding for the first time in 1996, I almost immediately switched and gave up on skis for years. However, ski makers caught on with the trend, and these days, with carving skis, turns are easy. The tool improved, and as a result the ratio of the "racing skiers" improved as well. These days, the number of skiers exploiting the centrifugal force is much higher than ten years ago. Good tools help to make higher standards more easily accessible to the masses, and that is the reason why we need good tools for API design as well.

We need to teach both camps. We need people to do the "science": to discover new principles and algorithms, and to find methodologies, rules, and important points of doing clueless development. However, we also desperately need people who will be able to do a good and reliable job—those who will live the life of selective cluelessness. However, this all needs to be taught. Otherwise, as soon as students leave the university, they'll find that the software engineer's life is different from what they expect. Not everyone is able to finish school and then create and work for ten years on their own framework. Most students start a job and are handed the task of maintaining code written by someone else. This is something for which the university doesn't prepare them at all.

BEING AFRAID OF FOREIGN CODE

I'll go so far as to claim that these days students are afraid of code they didn't write. Last year I taught a course about the NetBeans Platform at the Johannes Kepler University at Linz. Part of that course was to finish a small project. I gave the students three options: build a new module to add some functionality on top of the NetBeans Platform, find an existing module that is missing some kind of functionality and modify it or patch it to do something new, or fix three bugs. In my opinion, the simplest of these tasks is the last one. NetBeans has a few thousand open bugs and many of them are easy to fix, just not important enough to justify the developers' time to fix them. Often that might be just a single line fix. Then, the second simplest task is to enhance an existing module. The already existing code can serve as a sample. It's just necessary to plug into it, but you don't need much knowledge—in most cases you're led by example. It's much easier than writing something from scratch. However, guess which task the students took? Nobody fixed any other bugs, one person donated a patch to some module, and the rest wrote their own code. Simply put, students are afraid of foreign code. That is not good news for them, because as soon as they leave the university, they'll spend most of their work time digging out bugs in legacy code they inherit from someone else.

The other thing to nitpick regarding the current state of computer science education is the way that it measures the quality of student code. At the time I attended my university, we just wrote a program, showed it to the teacher, and either got approval or not. However, at that time access to the Internet was rare and the open source movement was not as strong as it is today. That is why I would expect some progress since my university days, especially given the power of the Internet and the number of existing open source projects seeking contributions. However, there doesn't seem to be any progress. Students still create their own projects from scratch, show them to the professor, and that's it. The project is then forgotten. It would be much more valuable to show students how to work with existing code. For example, they could be evaluated on the integration of their solution into some existing open source project. The best grade would be for someone who manages to get the code into the project's code base, as that is not just about coding skills, but about communication and the ability to work with the rest of the community. Average grades would be for those who make the project work, but whose work is refused for integration as not being good enough. This could be beneficial for teachers, as most of the evaluation is done by the members of the community. Still, I have not found any signs of this.

The role of education is important for developing new engineers who will take over our projects. We need them to be ready for the task, to be able to maintain existing code, to be able to operate in selective cluelessness style, and to be able to assemble their solutions from massive building blocks. Everyone should have the skill to consciously work in cluelessness mode. Everyone should be able to evaluate whether massive building blocks such as libraries or frameworks are ready for reuse or not. Also, they should have the "selective" part of cluelessness; for example, they should understand that nobody works on a project forever and that the knowledge of the project is hidden in its automated verification tools and tests. Although taught to be clueless, these engineers should be able to make their knowledge "buildable." For example, they should not be afraid to deep dive into the Linux kernel, debug the NetBeans Platform sources, and so on.

Share!

The era of Agile API Design has just started. This book is just a beginning. Knowledge related to proper API design will evolve, and I hope that I've given it a good initial boost by writing and publishing this book. However, it's necessary for others to build on this base and share their findings. Just as ten generations of physicists enriched, improved, and extended the work done by Newton, many more people will need to come and share their work to make Agile API Design the design choice for the future. As sharing is important, and as today cooperation can happen more easily than in the times of Isaac and company, I've registered a domain that can be used for discussions, corrections, and add-ons to the ground formed by this book. Please visit http://agile.apidesign.org and join us with your comments and thoughts. I've rented the domain for the next 3 years, but in case this book receives any attention, I am ready to prolong it for the next 300 years. Enjoy cluelessness and API design.

Bibliography

Bloch, Joshua. *Effective Java*. Upper Saddle River, NJ: Prentice Hall, 2001.

Dijkstra, Edsger. "On the fact that the Atlantic Ocean has two sides." http://www.cs.utexas.edu/~EWD/transcriptions/EWD06xx/EWD611.html, 1976.

Dijkstra, Edsger. *Selected Writings on Computing: A Personal Perspective*. New York: Springer-Verlag, 1982.

Drepper, Ulrich. "How to Write Shared Libraries." http://people.redhat.com/drepper/dsohowto.pdf, 2006.

Gamma, Erich, Richard Helm, Ralph Johnson, and John Vlissides. *Design Patterns: Elements of Reusable Object-Oriented Software*. Upper Saddle River, NJ: Addison-Wesley, 1995.

Hansen, Per Brinch. "Java's Insecure Parallelism." http://brinch-hansen.net/papers/1999b.pdf, 1999.

Hunt, Andy, and Dave Thomas. *Pragmatic Unit Testing in Java with JUnit*. Raleigh, NC and Dallas, TX: Pragmatic Bookshelf, 2003.

Orwell, George. *Nineteen Eighty-Four*. London: Secker & Warburg, 1949.

Rooney, Garrett. "Preserving Backward Compatibility." http://www.onlamp.com/pub/a/onlamp/2005/02/17/backwardscompatibility.html, 2005.

Torgersen, Mads. "The Expression Problem Revisited." In *ECOOP 2004 – Object Oriented Programming: 18th European Conference Oslo, Norway, June 14–18 2004, Proceedings*, edited by Martin Odersky, 123–146. Berlin: Springer-Verlag, 2004.

Vopěnka, Petr. *Úhelný kámen evropské vzdělanosti a moci*. Prague: Práh, 1999.

Index